MULTICULTURAL ISSUES IN COUNSELING:
New Approaches to Diversity

Second Edition

Edited By Courtland C. Lee, PhD

MULTICULTURAL ISSUES IN COUNSELING
2nd Edition

10 9 8 7 6 5 4 3

American Counseling Association
5999 Stevenson Avenue
Alexandria, VA 22304

Director of Acquisitions
Carolyn Baker

Director of Publishing Systems
Michael Comlish

Copyeditor
Lucy Blanton

Cover design by Jennifer Sterling, Spot Color

Library of Congress Cataloging-in-Publication Data

Multicultural issues in counseling : new approaches to diversity /
   edited by Courtland C. Lee — 2nd ed.
     p. cm.
   Includes bibliographical references and index.
   ISBN 1-55620-156-7 (pbk. : alk. paper)
    1. Cross-cultural counseling—United States.   I. Lee, Courtland
C.
   BF637.C6M84   1996   96-48042
   158'.3—dc21   CIP

To the Next Generation of
Professional Counselors

TABLE OF CONTENTS

PREFACE

$\int$ ince its publication in 1991, *Multicultural Issues in Counseling: New Approaches to Diversity* has become an important book in the counseling profession. It is one of the first, and still one of only a few, books to provide actual direction for culturally responsive counseling practice. It has provided professional counselors with strategies for optimal mental health intervention with culturally diverse client groups. In addition, the book has been widely adopted as a textbook in counselor training programs. Although it was written for the North American mental health community, it has sparked interest in multicultural counseling issues in other parts of the world as well.

Developments in both multicultural counseling theory and practice in the past few years have made it necessary to consider the recency and relevancy of many ideas in the book, however. Because of the dynamic nature of scholarship in this discipline, the editor and many of the contributing authors felt compelled to reexamine the ideas on cross-cultural counseling practice that were presented. In order to stay on the cutting edge of such practice, it was decided that the time had come to revisit the content of the book. Out of that decision came this second edition. It is an attempt to synthesize the most recent ideas on counseling across cultures. This edition provides many of the original contributing authors with an opportunity to update their thinking on culturally responsive counseling. The book also introduces several new contributing authors who offer different interpretations of the content of some of the original chapters. In addition, this edition features several new chapters that broaden the scope of multicultural counseling theory and practice.

Like its predecessor, the purpose of this book is to present culturally responsive intervention strategies and techniques for counselors and selected human development professionals working with, or preparing to work with, diverse client groups in a variety of settings. It provides practicing counselors and those preparing to enter the profession with direction for optimal mental health intervention with clients from a number of cultural backgrounds.

Focus of the Book

This book deals with multicultural counseling, defined as a relationship between a counselor and a client that takes both the personal *and* cultural experiences of each individual into consideration in the helping process. The focus of the book is on cultural experiences related to racial and ethnic factors in counseling. It addresses the counseling and human development needs of selected groups of people, commonly referred to as racial or ethnic minorities in American society. The book is devoted to multicultural counseling practice with selected client groups. The ideas presented have been developed out of both the professional and personal experiences of the chapter authors, who are scholars from the specific cultural group in question or have intimate knowledge of a particular group. Like the first edition, this book offers guidance for multicultural counseling practice but is not intended to be a "cookbook" or a "how-to" manual. It is designed to help counselors apply their awareness of and knowledge about cultural diversity to appropriate skills development with specific client groups.

Overview of Contents

This book is divided into three parts: Introduction, Direction for Culturally Responsive Counseling, and Conclusion. The two chapters in Part I serve as an introduction and lay a conceptual foundation for the rest of the book. They incorporate new thinking about multicultural counseling theory and practice that has emerged since the publication of the first edition of the book. In chapter 1, Courtland C. Lee discusses how the evolution of multicultural theory and practice has generated much promise for the counseling profession. He also considers the potential pitfalls that must be considered, and hopefully avoided, when engaging in cross-cultural mental health intervention. In chapter 2, Lee provides a conceptual framework for understanding the context of culture in multicultural counseling and examines important dynamics that should be considered in culturally responsive counseling practice.

Part II offers direction for culturally responsive counseling interventions for minority groups. The 16 chapters are divided into five sections that focus on Native Americans, African Americans, Asian Americans, Latino Americans, and Arab Americans. Each section reviews cultural dynamics and their role in shaping mental health, examines social challenges that may impact development, and introduces strategies for addressing these challenges. The specific counseling practices described evolve from understanding and appreciation for the unique history and cultural experience of each group. Case studies underscore and illustrate the authors' discussions on culturally responsive counseling.

The first section focuses on the Native American experience. In chapter 3, Grace Powless Sage examines how the unique relationship that American Indians have had with the United States government affects adult development in—and thus counseling of—American Indian adults. She also examines the therapeutic aspects of an Indian women's group that incorporates traditional and contemporary practices.

In chapter 4, Roger Herring provides direction for culturally responsive counseling interventions with indigenous—Native American—youth in the United States. He offers recommendations for synergetic counseling that may help to create a culturally responsive counseling environment for these youth.

The second section deals with the African American experience. Three of its chapters—5, 6, and 8—are new for this edition. In chapter 5, C. Emmanuel Ahia provides a conceptual framework for counseling with African Americans. He examines a number of African assumptions and cultural traditions inherent in the philosophy known as *Afrocentrism*, considered by many scholars as the basis of an African American worldview, and discusses its relationship to the mental health of African Americans.

In chapter 6, Donna Y. Ford focuses on middle-class African Americans, a population that has received little attention in the social science literature. She contends that middle-class status does not inoculate African Americans from the harsh realities of race in American society, addresses a dozen variables affecting the socioemotional and psychological well-being of middle-class African Americans, and offers recommendations for counseling with this group.

In chapter 7, Janice M. Jordan addresses the counseling of African American women using the cultural sensitivity of the counselor as a core requirement. A counselor with cultural sensitivity is one who is aware of her or his own culture, knowledgeable and accepting of the interaction of cultural and individual factors in the development of the client, and works with her or his client from a cultural content orientation. Jordan uses case studies to explore factors affecting the lives of African American women and their experience in counseling.

Similarly, in chapter 8 Courtland C. Lee and Deryl F. Bailey explore the issues and challenges in counseling with African American male youth and men. These authors offer historical and cultural perspectives on the psychosocial development of African American males and offer two case studies that provide strategies for counseling with this client group.

In chapter 9, the role of the African American church in promoting mental health is explored by Bernard L. Richardson and Lee N. June. They present intervention strategies and tools that employ the resources of this important institution and provide counseling professionals with specific guidelines for working within a church context.

The third section explores the Asian American experience. In chapter 10, David Sue examines some important Chinese cultural values and their impact on Chinese American development. He includes a case study illustrating the importance of these values and their influence on the counseling process and describes an assertiveness training group for Chinese Americans.

In chapter 11, Satsuki Ina discusses the internment experience of many Japanese Americans during World War II and the resulting psychological ramifications for both internees and members of their families. The social, political, and cultural issues affecting the development of Japanese Americans are highlighted in her description of an intensive group counseling experience for former internees.

In chapter 12, Rita Chi-Ying Chung, Fred Bemak, and Sumie Okazaki examine the refugee experience of many Americans from Southeast Asia and discuss how that experience presents mental health challenges to these people. The authors present the Multi-Level Model (MLM), a comprehensive approach to counseling refugees. MLM not only takes into account the intricacy of the refugee's historical background, past and present stressors, the acculturation process, and the psychosocial ramifications of adapting to a new culture but also provides a psychoeducational approach that includes cognitive, affective and behavioral interventions.

In chapter 13, the Korean American experience is examined by Dosheen Toarmino and Chi-Ah Chun. These authors provide information on the culture, sociodemographics, and immigration history of Korean Americans and discuss the mental health status of Korean Americans in terms of both inter- and intraethnic differences. Lastly, through case studies, Toarmino and Chun consider counseling issues unique to Korean Americans.

The fourth section considers the Latino American experience. In chapter 14, Sandra I. Lopez-Baez examines important issues to consider when counseling with women from this cultural group and discusses aspects of Latino culture that relate to the socialization of women. A series of case studies highlight counseling issues important for Latinas.

In chapter 15, Silvia Echevarria Rafuls and Martha Gonzalez Marquez use a Framework for Cultural Awareness and a case study of La Familia Fernandez to present a family-oriented systems perspective that places Cuban American clients within the multidimensional context of family, community, and therapeutic systems. The counseling approach is culturally based and resource-oriented; the framework is based upon the belief that practitioners need continually to address their own individual issues toward diversity as part of their work with clients in order to be culturally sensitive.

In chapter 16, Madonna G. Constantine and Augustine Barón explore issues in assessing and counseling Mexican American college students. The authors discuss core psychosocial/cultural concepts useful in client conceptualization and treatment planning, explore appropriate assessment methods, and provide a case example.

In chapter 17, Jesse M. Vazquez presents a historical and political overview of the Puerto Rican experience and discusses the impact of socioeconomic status on Puerto Rican development in the United States. Through a case study, he explores the challenges of racial/ethnic identity and the problems of racism that confront Puerto Ricans as well as implications for counselors.

The fifth and final section examines the Arab American experience, which has not yet received much attention in the counseling literature. In chapter 18, Morris L. Jackson provides a comprehensive examination of Arab culture, particularly religion and family dynamics and their influence on Arab American mental health. Through a case study, Jackson offers specific intervention strategies that counselors can use to increase their effectiveness with Arab American clients.

Part III concludes the book with chapter 19, in which Courtland C. Lee examines the issues related to the training of culturally responsive professional counselors. Lee also considers a research agenda in the emerging discipline of multicultural counseling.

Acknowledgments

Like its predecessor, this book owes its development to a number of people. As editor I want to acknowledge their contributions to the project. Again, I must start by thanking the contributors for the time and creative energy they put into preparing their chapters for this edition of the book. Their scholarly efforts are greatly appreciated.

A special note of appreciation goes to Carolyn Baker, ACA Acquisitions and Development Editor, for her support and patience. Her quiet oversight and encouragement were most welcome. Her belief in this project helped to keep me motivated and focused through the challenging editorial process.

I am also deeply indebted to Elisabeth "Libby" Parker and Nora Brookfield, who served as my editorial assistants in the development of this book. I am grateful to them for dealing effectively with all of the "administrivia" associated with preparing the manuscript for this edition of the book.

Finally, I must acknowledge my wife, Antoinette, who endured some neglect while the book was being developed. Thank you for your love, support, and understanding.

ABOUT THE AUTHORS

Courtland C. Lee received his PhD from Michigan State University. He is professor of counselor education at the University of Virginia. He has published numerous articles and book chapters on counseling across cultures. He is also the author of two books on counseling African American males. Dr. Lee is the former editor of both the *Journal of African American Men* and the *Journal of Multicultural Counseling and Development*. In addition, he is a past president of the Association for Multicultural Counselling and Development and has served on the executive council of the International Round Table for the Advancement of Counseling. Dr. Lee is a consultant on multicultural issues both in the United States and abroad.

C. Emmanuel Ahia received his BA and MA from Wheaton College and his PhD from Southern Illinois University, Carbondale. He also received a JD degree from the University of Arkansas School of Law. He is associate professor of counseling and school psychology at Rider University Graduate School, Lawrenceville, New Jersey. He is a National Certified Counselor and is licensed to practice law in Pennsylvania. He has published in the areas of mental health law, family legal issues, conflict resolution, and sociopolitical aspects of multicultural identity development. He is a past president of the New Jersey Association for Multicultural

Counseling and serves on the Pennsylvania Bar Association's committee on elderly persons' legal affairs.

Deryl F. Bailey received his BS and MEd from Campbell University. He served as a school counselor and founded Project: Gentlemen on the Move, a program for African American male high school students. He is a doctoral student and Holmes scholar at the University of Virginia.

Augustine Barón received his BA in psychology, magna cum laude, from Loyola University, New Orleans, and his MA and PsyD degrees in clinical psychology from the University of Illinois at Urbana-Champaign, where he was a Ford Foundation fellow. He presently serves as associate director of the Counseling and Mental Health Center at the University of Texas in Austin. Dr. Barón is a diplomate in clinical psychology of the American Board of Professional Psychology, and a fellow of the American Psychological Association. His interests include the management of workforce diversity, the administration of university psychological services, and gay/lesbian mental health issues. He is cofounder and national coordinator of the Research Consortium of Counseling and Psychological Services in Higher Education and editor of *Explorations in Chicano Psychology* (Praeger, 1981).

Fred Bemak is an associate professor and chair in the department of Counseling and Human Services at the Johns Hopkins University. He has given seminars and lectures, and conducted research in Latin America, Asia, and the Caribbean on cross-cultural counseling and at-risk youth and families. Dr. Bemak is a former Fulbright scholar, Kellog Foundation international fellow, and recipient of the International Exchange of Experts Fellowship through the World Rehabilitation Fund. He has been working nationally with refugees for the past 13 years as a researcher, clinician, and program and clinical consultant and is currently working on a book with Rita Chi-Ying Chung, Thomas Bornemann, and Paul Pedersen entitled *Multicultural Counseling of Refugees: A Case Study Approach to Innovative Interventions.*

Rita Chi-Ying Chung received her PhD in psychology in New Zealand and was awarded the Medical Research Council Fellowship for postdoctoral work in the United States. She is the former project director for the National Research Center on Asian American Mental Health at the University of California at Los Angeles and a consultant for the World Bank. Dr. Chung was recently a visiting professor holding a joint appointment with the departments of psychology and psychiatry at the Federal University of Rio Grande do Sul in Brazil. She has written extensively on Asian and refugee mental health and has worked in the Pacific Rim, Asia, and Latin America. Currently she is an adjunct associate professor at the George Washington University and also holds an adjunct appointment at the Johns Hopkins University.

Chi-Ah Chun received her BA from the University of California, Berkeley, and her MAs from Korea University and the University of California, Los Angeles (UCLA). She is currently a graduate student in the doctoral program for clinical psychology at UCLA and the project director of the Chinese American Psychiatric Epidemiological Study at the National Research Center on Asian American Mental Health.

Madonna G. Constantine received her BS and MA degrees from Xavier University of Louisiana, New Orleans, and her PhD in counseling psychology from the University of Memphis. She is currently an assistant professor in the counseling psychology program at Temple University in Philadelphia. Dr. Constantine is formerly a staff psychologist and director of practicum training at the University of Texas at Austin's Counseling and Mental Health Center. She is a licensed psychologist and has served as a consultant to numerous universities, organizations, and corporations across the United States in the area of multicultural diversity. Her professional interests include multicultural counseling and education, women's health issues, and college student development.

Donna Y. Ford is an associate professor of educational psychology at the University of Virginia. She earned her master's degree in education (counseling emphasis) and her PhD in education from Cleveland State University. Her primary research areas are gifted education, underachievement, counseling, and socioemotional development among African American students. She is author of a forthcoming book entitled *Reversing Underachievement Among Gifted Black Students: Promising Practices and Programs.*

Roger D. Herring received his BA from Pembroke State University, his MA (history) and MA (psychology) from Appalachian State University, his EdS (counseling) from Appalachian State University, and his EdD (counselor education) from North Carolina State University. He is currently an associate professor of counseling at the University of Arkansas-Little Rock. He has written extensively on issues of Native American mental health.

Satsuki Ina received her BA from the University of California, Berkeley, and her EdM and PhD from Oregon State University. She is an associate professor in the counselor education department at California State University, Sacramento, and is in private practice as a licensed marriage, family, and child counselor. As a founding member of the Consortium for Change in Sacramento, she has provided consultation on cross-cultural issues in Europe and Japan, and throughout the United States.

Morris L. Jackson received his BS and MEd from the University of Hartford and his EdD from the George Washington University. He has contributed insights to multicultural counseling for the last two decades. He has been adjunct professor at the Virginia Polytechnic and State University, American University, Bowie State University, George Washington University, Trinity College, and Johns Hopkins University. He studied Arabic language and culture at the King Saud University in Saudi Arabia. He worked as an academic adviser at the Royal Embassy of Saudi Arabia Cultural Mission in Washington, D.C. Currently, he is director, Return to School Programs, Enrollment Services, at the American University.

Janice M. Jordan received her BA from Antioch College, her MEd from the University of Delaware, and her PhD from the University of Maryland. She is the associate director of the Center for Counseling and Student Development and assistant professor of education at the University of Delaware. She is a past president of the Association for Multicultural Counseling and Development.

Lee N. June is currently an assistant provost for adademic student services and multicultural issues, vice president for student affairs and services, and professor of counseling psychology at Michigan State University. He is a former director of the counseling center at Michigan State. He is editor of two books, *The Black Family: Past, Present, and Future* (1991) and *Men to Men* (1996). He earned a bachelor of science in biology from Tuskegee University, a master of education in counseling, and a master of arts and doctorate of philosophy in clinical psychology from the University of Illinois at Urbana-Champaign. He also did further studies at Haverford College in psychology and at Duke University's Divinity School.

Sandra I. Lopez-Baez received her BA from the University of Puerto Rico, her MA from Marshall University, and her PhD from Kent State University. She is a professor and director of the graduate program in counseling and human development at Walsh University in Canton, Ohio. She also serves as coordinator of the clinical track in counseling. Her professional interest in cross-cultural and multicultural issues has led to work as a consultant, lecturer, and private practitioner in delivering mental health services.

Martha Gonzalez Marquez received her PhD from Purdue University in marriage and family therapy. She is a clinical member and approved supervisor for the American Association for Marriage and Family Therapy (AAMFT). She is also an active member of the American Family Therapy Academy (AFTA). She currently pursues her qualitative research and clinical interests in cultural awareness and diversity as an associate and faculty member of the Gainesville Family Institute, a postgraduate institute accredited by the Commission on Accreditation of Marriage and Family Therapy Education of the AAMFT.

Sumie Okazaki received her BS from the University of Michigan and her MA and PhD from the University of California, Los Angeles. She is currently an assistant professor of psychology and Asian American studies at the University of Wisconsin-Madison and a visiting assistant researcher at the University of California, Los Angeles.

Silvia Echevarria Rafuls received her PhD from Purdue University in marriage and family therapy, her MSW from Barry University, and her BA in psychology from Florida International University. She is currently an assistant professor in the counselor education department at the University of Florida and is a licensed clinical social worker in the State of Florida. She is on the executive board of the Association of Hispanic Faculty, sits as a member of the Minority Mentor Council, and is faculty adviser for the Cuban American Student Association at the University of Florida. She is a clinical member of the Association for Marriage and Family Therapy and an active member in the American Family Therapy Academy. She has conducted qualitative research with Latino families.

Bernard L. Richardson received a BA in sociology from Howard University, a MA and PhD in counseling from Michigan State University, and a master's of divinity from Yale University. He is currently the dean of the chapel at Howard University and associate professor of pastoral counseling in its Divinity School. He is a former associate professor at Southern Connecticut State University and former pastor of the Archer Memorial African Methodist Episcopal Zion Church in Windsor, Connecticut. He is coeditor of the first edition of *Multicultural Issues in Counseling: New Approaches to Diversity.*

Grace Powless Sage received her PhD from the University of Montana. She is the director of psychogical services at Dull Knife Memorial College in Lame Deer, Montana. She is an expert panel member for the National Center for the Advancement of Prevention in Washington, D.C. She has interests in cross-cultural training, with a special emphasis on American Indian issues. She has worked as a staff psychologist and a consultant at both the University of Colorado-Boulder and at Cornell University.

David Sue received his PhD from Washington State University. He is professor and director of the mental health counseling program at Western Washington University. He is a licensed psychologist and an associate of the center for Cross-Cultural Research at Western Washington University.

Dosheen Toarmino came to the United States from Korea in 1985 and received her BA in psychology from the University of Nevada, Reno (UNR). She is currently a graduate student in the doctoral program for clinical psychology at UNR and finishing her externship at West Hills Hospital in Nevada. Her research interests involve ethnic minority health issues and verbal behavior, particularly second language learning.

Jesse M. Vazquez received his PhD from New York University. He is professor of counselor education in the School of Education, Queens College of the City University of New York. Since 1975, he has served as director of the college's Puerto Rican Studies Program. He has worked as a counselor and consultant in a variety of social service agencies and educational settings. He is currently president of the National Association for Ethnic Studies and was a founding board member of the Puerto Rican Studies Association.

PART I
INTRODUCTION

THE PROMISE AND PITFALLS OF MULTICULTURAL COUNSELING

Courtland C. Lee

American society has experienced tremendous change over the past four decades. The turmoil of the civil rights movement of the 1950s and 1960s, for example, contributed to a wider recognition that the United States is truly a pluralistic nation. The concept of pluralism has received its impetus not only from the great economic, legislative, and social gains made during the struggles for civil rights but, more recently, also from the dynamics of changing population demographics. Projections of the United States population into the 21st century indicate that ethnic minority groups will experience a substantial rate of growth, due to higher birth rates and an increase in non-European immigration, while the White population of European origin will decline significantly (Spencer, 1989). This projection has led to forecasts that by the year 2000, 75% of those entering the nation's workforce will be women and ethnic minorities (Johnston & Packer, 1987; Okocha, 1994; O'Neil, 1992). Similarly, estimates are that by the year 2020 the majority of school-age children in the United States will be from ethnic minority groups (Lee, 1995).

The realities of cultural pluralism have had an important impact on the profession of counseling. Social progress and major changes in population demographics have been the impetus for the evolution of multicultural counseling as an important discipline within the helping professions. This discipline has been referred to as "the hottest topic" in the counseling profession (Lee, 1989a). Broadly conceptualized, multicultural counseling considers not only the personality dynamics but also the cultural backgrounds of both counselor and client in creating a therapeutic environment in which these two individuals can purposefully interact. Multicul-

3

tural counseling, therefore, takes into consideration the cultural background and individual experiences of diverse clients and how their psychosocial needs might be identified and met through counseling (Axelson, 1993; Pedersen, 1991). Within this context, professional counselors must consider differences in areas such as language, social class, gender, sexual orientation, and ethnicity between themselves and their clients. These factors may be potential impediments to effective intervention, and counselors need to work to overcome the barriers such variables might produce in the helping process (Sue & Sue, 1990).

Significantly, the concept of multicultural counseling has become the impetus for the development of a generic theory of multiculturalism that is becoming recognized as the fourth theoretical force in the profession (Pedersen, 1991). As such, multicultural theory joins the other three major traditions—psychodynamic theory, cognitive-behavioral theory, and existential-humanistic theory—as primary explanations of human development. Basic to the theory of multiculturalism is the notion that both client and counselor bring to the therapeutic dyad a variety of cultural variables related to age, gender, education, religion, and ethnic background. In essence, cultural diversity is a characteristic of all counseling relationships, and all counseling is multicultural in nature (Pedersen, 1991, Ponterotto & Casas, 1991; Sue & Sue, 1990; Sue, Ivey, & Pedersen, 1996). A generic theory of multiculturalism, therefore, provides a broad conceptual framework for counseling practice.

This evolution of multicultural counseling into a theoretical force with a broad framework for practice has generated much promise for the mental health professions. However, such counseling practice can also be fraught with potential pitfalls.

The Promise of Multicultural Counseling

The promise of multicultural counseling as a professional discipline can be considered in several significant ways. One example of the promise is that traditional counseling theory has been enriched by the diverse notions of optimal mental health and normal development inherent in multicultural thought. The ideas on counseling theory and practice put forth by scholars from diverse cultural backgrounds that have emerged in the counseling literature, particularly in the past two decades, have generated an important new knowledge base. This base includes the fundamental concept that cultural differences are real and must be actively considered in mental health interventions. The awareness emerging from this relatively young area of thought has generated a realization that counseling as a profession must be inclusive of a variety of ways of thinking, feeling, and behaving as well as responsive to diverse worldviews (Sue, Ivey, & Pedersen, 1996).

Another example of the promise of multicultural counseling as a professional discipline is that the theory and practice associated with multicultural mental health intervention have fostered the emergence of an international perspective on counseling as a potential force in human development. As the world prepares to enter the 21st century, there is a growing awareness of a new global interconnectedness. With old ideological barriers falling and new alliances replacing long-standing animosities, there is great anticipation about a new era of mutual respect and cooperation among nations. This has been heightened by universal improvements in communication and travel that have made the world, in many respects, a global village (Lee & Sirch, 1994).

As this concept of interconnectedness continues to gain acceptance, it has prompted efforts in many parts of the world to reconfigure social, economic, and cultural institutions to make them more responsive to interactions across national boundaries. The counseling profession in North America has taken a series of significant steps to adopt a global perspective to address more effectively mental health challenges that increasingly transcend political borders. The American Counseling Association, for example, has held several successful bilateral professional conferences in recent years with counseling associations in England, Mexico, and Scotland. These conferences have proven to be fertile ground for exploring differences and commonalities in the issues that confront professional counseling organizations as they attempt to address both the professional development of their members and the mental health issues of citizens in their respective countries.

In many parts of the world, both individually and organizationally, counseling and related professionals are moving beyond provincial conceptions of theory, research, and practice to join in collaborative efforts to foster notions of mental health and human development that stretch across geopolitical and cultural boundaries. There has been greater understanding among helping professionals, due in large measure to the stimulation provided by the concept of multiculturalism, that *multicultural* implies *international*.

Yet another example of the promise of multicultural counseling as a professional discipline is the fact that multicultural notions of counseling have fostered a new sense of social responsibility and activism within the profession. Working with culturally diverse clients, counselors have often been forced to consider the negative effects of phenomena such as racism, sexism, homophobia, and other forms of oppression on the development of culturally diverse client groups (Cook, 1993; Priest, 1991; Schreier, 1995; Solomon, 1992). This has led to an awareness that the etiology of problems often lies not in clients but, rather, in intolerant or restrictive environments. The only way that many client groups will be able to maximize abilities and interests is to eradicate these systemic impediments to their development.

Counselors who work with culturally diverse client groups, therefore, have been called on to become agents of systemic change, channeling energy and skill into helping clients from diverse backgrounds break down institutional and social barriers to optimal development (De La Cancela & Sotomayor, 1993; Evans & Wall, 1991; Ponterotto & Pedersen, 1993). When necessary, mental health professionals must be willing to act on behalf of disenfranchised clients in an advocacy role, actively challenging long-standing traditions and preconceived notions that may stand in the way of optimal mental health and development (Lee, 1989b). With the evolution of multicultural counseling, counselors are realizing, perhaps as never before, that if they are not a part of the solution, then they are a part of the problem.

A final example of the promise of multicultural counseling as a professional discipline is evident in the gradual emergence of a new type of helping professional: the culturally responsive counselor. Such an individual is one who has the awareness, knowledge, and skills to intervene successfully in the lives of clients from culturally diverse backgrounds. A culturally responsive counselor uses strategies and techniques that are consistent with the life experiences and cultural values of clients. In order to implement these strategies and techniques, such a professional must have awareness and knowledge related to issues of cultural diversity (Sue, Arredondo, & McDavis, 1992).

A culturally responsive counseling professional is able to view each client as a unique individual while taking into consideration not only the client's common experiences as a human being (i.e., the developmental challenges that face all people) but also the specific experiences that come from the client's cultural background. And a culturally responsive counseling professional does this while constantly in touch with his or her own personal and cultural experiences as a unique human being who happens to be a helping professional.

The growing demand for this type of helper has brought about a renaissance in the professional development of counselors (Brown & Landrum-Brown, 1995; McRae & Johnson, 1991; Midgette & Meggert, 1991; Sue, D. W., 1991). The need to be culturally responsive has put the responsibility on counselors to examine their own cultural heritage, values, and biases and how these might impact upon clients from diverse backgrounds. In addition, counselors have been required to gain knowledge about the history, experiences, and cultural values of diverse client groups. The acquisition of such cultural knowledge has been found to be important in developing empathy toward culturally diverse clients. It also forms the basis for employing counseling skills that are consistent with clients' cultural backgrounds and individual experiences.

The Potential Pitfalls of Multicultural Counseling

Although multicultural counseling holds much promise as an emerging specialty within the profession, there are some potential pitfalls to its practice that must be considered. The first is that in considering the concept of cultural diversity in counseling, there is the danger of assuming that all people from a specific cultural group are the same and that one methodological approach is universally applicable in any counseling intervention with them. Indeed, a review of much of the psychological or counseling literature related to multicultural issues could leave the impression that there is an all-encompassing reality for any particular cultural group and that all people from that group act, feel, and think in a homogenous fashion. Such an impression invariably leads to a monolithic perspective on the experiences of a specific group of people as well as to stereotypic thinking, in which individuals are considered indistinguishable in terms of attitudes, behaviors, and values. Counseling professionals with such a perspective run the risk of approaching clients not as distinctive human beings with individual experiences but, rather, merely as cultural stereotypes.

A second potential pitfall is that the focus on cultural dissimilarities in multicultural counseling theory and practice may serve to accentuate human differences and may have the potential for fostering renewed forms of intolerance (Margolis & Rungta, 1986; Pedersen, 1983). This is certainly a distinct possibility if counselors reduce cultural realities to a stereotypic level.

The third potential pitfall of the discipline has to do with perceived and actual counselor competence. As multicultural counseling theory continues to question the validity of traditional counseling practice with diverse groups of people, there is a danger that helping professionals will become self-conscious about their level of competence to work with diverse clients. A question often asked by counselors in a frustrated tone is "How can I really be effective with a client whose cultural background is different from mine?" Groping for an answer to this crucial question has the potential of driving many talented professionals away from cross-cultural counseling encounters.

A fourth potential pitfall is that those counseling professionals who are not aware of cultural dynamics and their impact on the psychosocial development of clients from diverse backgrounds may run the risk of engaging in unethical conduct in their interventions (Lee & Kurilla, 1993). However, ethical standards related to guiding counseling practice with culturally diverse client groups are lacking (Casas, Ponterotto, & Gutierrez, 1986; Casas & Thompson, 1991; Ibrahim & Arredondo, 1986; Pedersen, 1995). Therefore, because of limited guidance ethical conduct could be a constant challenge when counseling across cultures.

The fifth potential pitfall is that although much promise is inherent in therapeutic modalities that are culturally responsive, it must be understood that counseling, as a formal profession, is not highly valued or seen as a valid helping resource among many groups of people (Leung, Wagner, & Tata, 1995). Traditional counseling theory and practice often runs counter to important developmental aspects of indigenous helping models found among diverse cultural groups (Lee & Armstrong, 1995; Lee, Oh, & Mountcastle, 1992; Vontress, 1991). In addition, traditional counseling practice has often failed to meet the needs of people from diverse cultural backgrounds. The multicultural counseling literature, for example, has long suggested that people of color are inappropriately served by mental health services (Casas, Ponterotto, & Gutierrez, 1986; Ibrahim & Arredondo, 1986; Ponterotto & Casas, 1987)) and are likely to underutilize professional counselors (Ivey & Authier, 1978; Leung, Wagner, & Tata, 1995; Sue, S., 1977; Sue, McKinney, Allen, & Hall, 1974).

Further, when traditional counseling is considered in a multicultural context, it often becomes a sociopolitical process (Katz, 1985; Sue & Sue, 1990). Specifically, for many people from culturally diverse backgrounds, counseling has been perceived as a tool of oppression and social control (Katz, 1985). This is due, to a large extent, to the fact that the only counseling many culturally diverse people have often received has been a forced, rather than voluntary, experience with a culturally insensitive or unresponsive agent of some aspect of the broad social welfare system. Additionally, in many instances, counseling has come after they have committed an offense against the social order. Generally, in both situations, the goal of counseling is not development but rather remediation or punishment. Counseling in the perception of many people from diverse cultural backgrounds, therefore, becomes a process that the dominant society employs forcibly to control their lives and well-being.

The final potential pitfall of multicultural counseling involves the challenge of moving beyond awareness and knowledge into actual practice. Although the renaissance in the professional development of counselors has advanced the notion of culturally responsive helpers, the concept of *multicultural counseling skills* is still rather tenuous. In many instances, pre- and in-service training experiences provide opportunities for counselors to develop a new level of awareness and an updated knowledge base to address the concerns of culturally diverse clients. However, such training tends to stop short of actual comprehensive skill acquisition. There is generally little exposure to counseling modalities that incorporate cultural dynamics or indigenous aspects of helping. Counselors on the frontlines of multicultural service delivery often express the need for less theory and more practical direction for addressing client concerns in a culturally responsive manner.

Probably no cookbooks or how-to manuals can be realistically developed for working with culturally diverse clients. However, if multicultural counseling is to continue evolving as a discipline, comprehensive approaches to service delivery must be developed, implemented, and evaluated. Personal awareness and cultural knowledge must be translated into culturally responsive practice.

Conclusion

The approach of the 21st century is portending an American culture in which diversity and pluralism will be hallmarks of the society. People who represent diverse cultural backgrounds characteristic of this pluralism will be attempting to develop their abilities and interests within this new social order. Multiculturalism as a generic approach, therefore, represents a significant challenge to the counseling profession, bringing both great promise and potential pitfalls. If counselors are to have an impact on the development of increasingly diverse client groups, counseling practice must be grounded in responsiveness to cultural diversity. Developing such responsiveness should be an integral part of the personal growth process of all counselors. This process involves acquiring not only the awareness and knowledge but also the skills for effective multicultural intervention. This book attempts to capitalize on the promise of multicultural counseling by providing mental health professionals with direction to enhance those skills.

References

Axelson, J. A. (1993). *Counseling and development in a multicultural society* (2nd ed.). Pacific Grove, CA: Brooks/Cole.

Brown, M. T., & Landrum-Brown, J. (1995). Counselor supervision: Cross-cultural perspectives. In J. G. Ponterotto, J. M. Casas, L. A. Suzuki, & C. M. Alexander (Eds.), *Handbook of multicultural counseling* (pp. 263–286). Thousand Oaks, CA: Sage.

Casas, J. M., Ponterotto, J. G., & Gutierrez, J. M. (1986). An ethical indictment of counseling research and training: The cross-cultural perspective. *Journal of Counseling and Development, 64,* 347–349.

Casas, J. M., & Thompson, C. (1991). Ethical principles and standards: A racial-ethnic minority research perspective. *Counseling and Values, 35,* 186–195.

Cook, E. P. (Ed.). (1993). *Women, relationships, and power: Implications for power.* Alexandria, VA: American Counseling Association.

De La Cancela, V., & Sotomayor, G. M. (1993). Rainbow warriors: Reducing institutional racism in mental health. *Journal of Mental Health Counseling, 15,* 55–71.

Evans, N. J., & Wall, V. A. (Eds.). (1991). *Beyond tolerance: Gays, lesbians, and bisexuals on campus.* Alexandria, VA: American College Personnel Association.

Ibrahim, F. A., & Arredondo, P. M. (1986). Ethical standards for cross-cultural counseling: Counselor preparation, practice, assessment, and research. *Journal of Counseling and Development, 64,* 349–352.

Ivey, A., & Authier, J. (1978). *Microcounseling: Innovations in interview training.* Springfield, IL: Charles C Thomas.

Johnston & Packer. (1987). *Workforce 2000: Work and workers for the 21st century.* Indianapolis, IN: Hudson Institute.

Katz, J. H. (1985). The sociopolitical nature of counseling. *Counseling Psychologist, 13,* 615–624.

Lee, C. C. (1989a). Who speaks for multicultural counseling? [Editorial]. *Journal of Multicultural Counseling and Development, 17,* 1–3.

Lee, C. C. (1989b). Needed: A career development advocate. *Career Development Quarterly, 37,* 218–220.

Lee, C. C. (Ed.). (1995). *Counseling for diversity: A guide for school counselors and related professionals.* Boston: Allyn & Bacon.

Lee, C. C., & Armstrong, K. L. (1995). Indigenous models of mental health intervention: Lessons from traditional healers. In J. G. Ponterotto, J. M. Casas, L. A. Suzuki, & C. M. Alexander (Eds.), *Handbook of multicultural counseling* (pp. 441–456). Thousand Oaks, CA: Sage.

Lee, C. C., & Kurilla, V. (1993). Ethics and multiculturalism: The challenge of diversity. In D. E. Cermele (Ed.), *Ethical issues in professional counseling.* New York: Hatherleigh.

Lee, C. C., Oh, M. Y., & Mountcastle, A. R. (1992). Indigenous models of helping in non-Western countries: Implications for multicultural counseling. *Journal of Multicultural Counseling and Development, 20,* 3–10.

Lee, C. C., & Sirch, M. L. (1994). Counseling in an enlightened society: Values for a new millennium. *Counseling and Values, 38,* 90–97.

Leung, F.T.L., Wagner, N. S., & Tata, S. P. (1995). Racial and ethnic variations in help-seeking attitudes. In J. G. Ponterotto, J. M. Casas,

L. A. Suzuki, & C. M. Alexander (Eds.), *Handbook of multicultural counseling* (pp. 415–438). Thousand Oaks, CA: Sage.

McRae, M. B., & Johnson, S. D. (1991). Toward training for competence in multicultural counselor education. *Journal of Counseling and Development, 70,* 131–135.

Margolis, R. L., & Rungta, S. A. (1986). Training counselors for work with special populations: A second look. *Journal of Counseling and Development, 64,* 642–644.

Midgette, T. E., & Meggert, S. S. (1991). Multicultural counseling instruction: A challenge for faculties in the 21st century. *Journal of Multicultural Counseling and Development, 70,* 136–141.

Okocha, A. (1994). Preparing racial ethnic minorities for the workforce 2000. *Journal of Multicultural Counseling and Development, 22,* 106–114.

O'Neil, J. (1992). Preparing for the changing workplace. *Education Leadership, 49,* 6–14.

Pedersen, P. B. (1983). The cultural complexity of counseling. *International Journal for the Advancement of Counseling, 6,* 177–192.

Pedersen, P. B. (1991). Multiculturalism as a generic approach to counseling. *Journal of Counseling and Development, 70,* 6–12.

Pedersen, P. B. (1995). Culture-centered ethical guidelines for counselors. In J. G. Ponterotto, J. M. Casas, L. A. Suzuki, & C. M. Alexander (Eds.), *Handbook of multicultural counseling* (pp. 34–49). Thousand Oaks, CA: Sage.

Ponterotto, J. G., & Casas, J. M. (1987). In search of multicultural competence within counselor education programs. *Journal of Counseling and Development, 65,* 430–434.

Ponterotto, J. G., & Casas, J. M. (1991). *Handbook of racial/ethnic minority counseling research.* Springfield, IL: Charles C Thomas.

Ponterotto, J. G., & Pedersen, P. B. (1993). *Preventing prejudice: A guide for counselors and educators.* Newbury Park, CA: Sage.

Priest, R. C. (1991). Racism and prejudice as negative impacts on African American clients in therapy. *Journal of Counseling and Development, 70,* 213–215.

Schreier, B. A. (1995). Moving beyond tolerance: A new paradigm for programming about homophobia/biphobia and heterosexism. *Journal of College Student Development, 36,* 19–26.

Solomon, A. C. (1992). Clinical diagnosis among diverse populations: A multicultural perspective. *Families in Society, 73,* 371–77.

Spencer, G. (1989). *Projections of the population of the United States by age, sex, and race: 1988 to 2080* (U.S. Bureau of the Census Current Population Reports, Series P-25, No. 1018). Washington, DC: U.S. Government Printing Office.

Sue, D. W. (1991). A model for cultural diversity training. *Journal of Counseling and Development, 70,* 99–105.

Sue, D. W., & Sue, D. (1990). *Counseling the culturally different: Theory and practice* (2nd ed.). New York: Wiley.

Sue, D. W., Arredondo, P., & McDavis, R. J. (1992). Multicultural counseling competencies and standards: A call to the profession. *Journal of Counseling and Development, 70,* 477–486

Sue, D. W., Ivey, A. E., & Pedersen, P.D. (Eds.). (1996). *A theory of multicultural counseling.* Pacific Grove, CA: Brooks/Cole.

Sue, S. (1977). Community mental health services to minority groups: Some optimism, some pessimism. *American Psychologist, 32,* 616–624.

Sue, S., McKinney, H., Allen, D., & Hall, J. (1974). Delivery of community mental health services to Black and White clients. *Journal of Consulting and Clinical Psychology, 42,* 594–601.

Vontress, C. E. (1991). Traditional healing in Africa: Implications for cross-cultural counseling. *Journal of Counseling and Development, 70,* 242–249.

2

CULTURAL DYNAMICS:
Their Importance in Culturally Responsive Counseling

Courtland C. Lee

U nderstanding the complex role of culture is a major challenge in counseling practice. Knowledge of cultural realities has become a professional imperative as counselors encounter increasingly diverse client groups. However, when culture is considered as a variable in the counseling process, it has the potential of becoming a source of conflict and misunderstanding and may create barriers between helper and client who differ in terms of cultural background.

This book considers culture as ethnicity and places multicultural counseling into a context that focuses on the importance of ethnicity in the relationship between helper and helpee. The book also focuses on individual development within a cultural context that emphasizes the dynamics of ethnic minority group membership. The purpose of this chapter is first to provide a conceptual framework for understanding culture in context and then to overview the important cultural dynamics that shape psychosocial development among ethnic minority groups. The chapter thus provides a conceptual basis for the ideas on culturally responsive counseling practice in Part II.

Culture in Context

In Merriam-Webster's dictionary (1995) a definition of *culture* is "the customary beliefs, social forms, and material traits of a racial, religious, or social group" (p. 282). This broad definition implies that culture is a multidimensional concept that encompasses the collective reality of a group of people. It is from this collective reality that attitudes, behaviors, and values are formed.

As indicated in chapter 1, all counseling interventions are, to some extent, multicultural or cross-cultural in nature (Pedersen, 1991). Both counselor and client bring to the counseling relationship a set of attitudes, behaviors, and values that have been reinforced through long-term association with a specific group. Although counselor and client can be members of the same group, their individual differences imply the presence of subtle cultural differences.

The dictionary's definition lends credence to the notion that all counseling is a multicultural process, but this broad conceptualization tends to cloud some important issues that must be considered when obvious cultural differences exist between client and counselor. Such differences make a broad definition of the concept of culture somewhat tenuous in actual multicultural counseling practice (Brislin, 1990; Locke, 1990; Triandis, Bontempo, Leung, & Hui, 1990).

If the multicultural counseling discipline is to have any relevance in addressing differences between helper and helpee, then culture is best considered within a specific context. Scholars in the field of multicultural counseling have suggested a need for clarification of the concept of culture within the context of the discipline (Johnson, 1990; Ponterotto & Benesch, 1988; Sue & Zane, 1987). Implied in many of these suggestions is the idea that *culture* as a construct be clarified in terms of *race* and/or *ethnicity*.

These contextual suggestions appear logical for two important reasons. First, as the United States enters the 21st century, issues related to race/ethnicity are assuming new dimensions. Groups that have traditionally held minority status are beginning to outnumber that portion of the population that traces its cultural origins to Europe (Spencer, 1989). Second, it must be understood that counseling has traditionally been a professional discipline that represents European and European American culture. Counseling practice has generally been most effective with people whose cultural traditions and social background have mirrored that culture (Ponterotto, Casas, Suzuki, & Alexander, 1995; Sue & Sue, 1990).

The definition of *culture* that concerns the beliefs, forms, and traits of a racial group provides a primary context for understanding the concept of culture within counseling practice. In Merriam-Webster's dictionary (1995), a definition of *race* is "a family, tribe, people, or nation belonging to the same stock" (p. 961). The commonality inherent in this definition addresses the concept of ethnic group, which has gained much credibility as a multicultural counseling construct. Again, according to Merriam-Webster (1995), *ethnic* relates "to large groups of people classed according to common racial, national, tribal, religious, linguistic, or cultural origin or background" (p. 398).

The terms *racial* and *ethnic group* are generally used interchangeably. Both are often used to refer to groups of people that share similar physiological traits and/or personality characteristics. These traits and characteristics are either genetically transferred or have become reinforced through group association over long periods of time.

But these terms are not synonymous. *Race* is an archaic anthropological/biological classification of human differences that historically carries negative political implications. What is important from a mental health perspective, however, are not genetically transferred physiological traits but, rather, personality characteristics among people that become reinforced through association over time. It is these long-standing dynamics of thinking, feeling, and behaving that form the cultural basis of an ethnic group. This makes implicit the importance of the concept of ethnicity, or ethnic group, as a multicultural counseling construct.

Given the changing population demographics of the United States, the concept of culture in counseling may be best understood within the context of the mental health issues and developmental dynamics of those ethnic groups that do not trace their cultural origins to Europe. This includes Native American groups and those with African or Asian cultural backgrounds. Likewise, it also includes ethnic groups from the Caribbean Basin, Central and South America, or Mexico whose culture represents an amalgam of Spanish, Indian, and African influences. Increasingly, it also includes people with Arab or Middle Eastern ancestry. The needs of people with these cultural backgrounds have generally been misunderstood and inadequately addressed within the European and European American cultural context that forms the framework of the counseling profession (McFadden, 1993; Ponterotto et al., 1995; Sue & Sue, 1990).

The Dynamics of Culture as Ethnicity: Themes for Culturally Responsive Counseling

Any discipline that seeks to impact upon the psychosocial development of a group of people must take into account the dynamics shaping that development. Culturally responsive counseling practice must be predicated on an understanding of cultural dynamics and their pivotal role in fostering optimal mental health.

When culture is considered in terms of ethnicity, there are a number of dynamics that may need to be considered in counseling interactions with clients from non-European cultural backgrounds. Implicit in these dynamics are the beliefs, social forms, and material traits that constitute distinct cultural realities. Dynamics that may need to be considered in culturally responsive counseling include the relationship between ethnic identity and degree of acculturation, language, kinship influences, sex role socialization, religious/spiritual influences, immigration experience, and historical hostility.

This list of dynamics is by no means exhaustive, given the demographic realities of American society, but even a cursory review of ethnic groups with non-European cultural backgrounds suggests that these are some of the more salient influences on psychosocial development. Although the influence of these dynamics may vary across clients, a working knowledge of them and how they may shape personality development should frame the therapeutic context of culturally responsive mental health intervention.

The Relationship Between Ethnic Identity and Degree of Acculturation

Counseling effectiveness with members of ethnic groups that have non-European cultural origins may ultimately hinge upon an understanding of the concepts of ethnic identity and acculturation and the relationship between them. An appreciation of this relationship, and its influence on psychosocial development, is fundamental to culturally responsive counseling.

Ethnic identity refers to an individual's sense of belonging to an ethnic group and the part of an individual's personality that is attributable to ethnic group membership (Rotheram & Phinney,

1987). Ethnic identity may considered as the inner vision that a person possesses of himself or herself as a member of an ethnic group. It forms the core of the beliefs, social forms, and personality dimensions that characterize distinct cultural realities for an individual.

The development of ethnic identity has traditionally been conceptualized as an evolutionary linear stage process (Atkinson, Morten, & Sue, 1993; Cross, 1971, 1995) or, more recently, as a dynamic personality status process in which racial information is simultaneously interpreted and internalized at a variety of levels (Helms, 1995). It is important to point out that most models of ethnic identity development in the United States have been developed in a context in which people of European origin have been in a position of social and cultural dominance with respect to other groups. In this country European Americans have generally enjoyed cultural privilege in their relationship with other ethnic groups (McIntosh, 1989). This cultural privilege has profoundly influenced the attitudes of European Americans toward members of ethnic minority groups (Helms, 1990, 1995). Likewise, the perceptions of this cultural privilege held by people from ethnic minority groups has profoundly influenced attitudes they hold of themselves and European Americans as racial beings (Atkinson et al., 1993; Helms, 1990, 1995). Ethnic identity development, therefore, occurs in a milieu characterized by complex social interaction among individuals from ethnic minority groups and the European American majority in the United States. The essence of this interaction for ethnic minority individuals is found in the concept of acculturation.

Acculturation, within the context of contemporary American society, refers to the degree to which an individual identifies with or conforms to the attitudes, lifestyles, and values of the European-American-based macroculture. For individuals from ethnic minority groups, it is generally a process of willing or unwilling attitudinal and behavioral changes brought about by overt and covert pressure from social, educational, or economic institutions within the macroculture (Marin, 1992).

Psychosocial development is greatly influenced by a sense of ethnic identity and the degree of acculturation among groups of people with non-European cultural origins. The relationship between these two concepts shapes attitudes, behaviors, and values.

Figure 2-1 presents a matrix that illustrates the important relationship between ethnic identity and acculturation in the psychosocial development of individuals from ethnic minority cultural groups.

As the four quadrants of the figure demonstrate, the relationship between ethnic identity development and acculturation may be conceptualized in the following manner:

- **Strong sense of ethnic identity/high degree of acculturation.** This quadrant characterizes the relationship between ethnic identity and acculturation for those individuals considered to be *bicultural*. In other words, these individuals have a strong sense of belonging to their particular ethnic group while also possessing a high degree of identification with or conformity to the macroculture. Bicultural individuals can move comfortably, both physically and psychologically, between their ethnic culture and the macroculture.

    A concrete example of such movement is language competency. Bicultural individuals tend to be bilingual. They have generally mastered the standard English characteristic of the macroculture but still maintain fluency in their ethnic language or linguistic traditions. People classified in this quadrant find value and validity in both forms of communication. They are

ACCULTURATION

		HIGH	LOW
	STRONG	Bicultural individuals	Individuals marginal to macroculture—high ethnic group identification
ETHNIC IDENTITY			
	WEAK	Individuals marginal to ethnic group— high macroculture identification	Individuals marginal to both ethnic group and macroculture

Figure 2-1 *Relationship Between Sense of Ethnic Identity and Degree of Acculturation*

usually capable of moving from the English of the macroculture to the language of their ethnic group with relative ease.

- **Weak sense of ethnic identity/high degree of acculturation.** People whose experiences represent this quadrant have a limited sense of belonging to their ethnic group, and little in the dynamics of their personality is reflective of ethnic group membership. These individuals, however, have a high degree of identification with the macroculture. People with these experiences tend to be marginal to the culture of their ethnic group. This marginalization may result from a conscious choice to adopt exclusively the attitudes, behaviors, and values of the macroculture. Often such a choice is motivated by overt or subtle macroculture messages about the unacceptability or undesirability of significant aspects of ethnic minority cultural practices. Many individuals represented in this quadrant internalize the idea that the key to social, educational, or economic advancement in American society is predicated on a complete rejection of an ethnic minority worldview and total conformity to macroculture values.

  Such marginalization may, however, also be the result of a lack of contact with the individual's ethnic group culture. This is often the case, for example, when children are raised with little sense of their ethnic heritage due to cross-cultural adoption or other factors that may remove them from contact with the experiences of their ethnic group. In such cases the marginalization from ethnic group experiences is not by choice but rather from lack of exposure.

- **Strong sense of ethnic identity/low degree of acculturation.** This quadrant represents the experience of those people who have strong ethnic identity and who have little identification with or are marginal to the macroculture. Excellent examples of the experiences representative of this quadrant are found among those people who are recent immigrants. Although many learn the language and adopt the practices of the macroculture, many others continue to nurture the cultural customs of the "old country."

  Likewise, members of ethnic minority groups who are born in the United States but have had limited social or economic opportunities due to systemic barriers such as racism are also represented in the quadrant. Effectively barred from all but superficial participation in the macroculture, many of these individuals find cultural validation exclusively within their ethnic group.

- **Weak sense of ethnic identity/low degree of acculturation.** People with experiences representative of this quadrant are marginal to both their ethnic group and the macroculture. They have a limited sense of belonging to any group, and very little of their personality is attributable to specified group membership. Such a person will be considered physically, mentally, and spiritually ill in any culture. This person will be highly dysfunctional.

Importantly, the relationship between a sense of ethnic identity and the degree of acculturation for any person may be influenced by a number of variables such as age, gender, ethnic group, length of residence in the United States, level of education, extent of experience with racism, and socioeconomic status. It is also necessary to consider that the dynamic nature of human development and behavior make it impossible to categorize individuals neatly into any one of the four quadrants. Both ethnic identity development and acculturation are dynamic processes, and an individual may experience ongoing movement across the matrix. Such shifts might be due to a combination of intrapersonal and environmental factors at any given point in an individual's life.

The dynamics of ethnic identity and acculturation and the important relationship between them need to be factored into culturally responsive counseling. Psychosocial development is greatly influenced by an individual's sense of ethnic identity and degree of acculturation. Similarly, the relationship between these two concepts is a crucial aspect of mental health. Assessing ethnic identity and acculturation processes, therefore, can serve as an important vehicle for understanding the reality and issues confronting ethnic minority clients. Counseling professionals need to be sensitive to issues of ethnic identity and carefully explore the degree of cultural similarity or dissimilarity between themselves and clients. Analysis of ethnic identity or acculturation levels should provide the focus of any counseling intervention with ethnic minority clients.

Language

Counseling is an activity that relies on communication between counselor and client. Language, therefore, is an important variable in all counseling interactions, but it assumes complex dimensions in cross-cultural helping interactions. The practice of counseling is predicated on an understanding of standard English, but many clients from ethnic minority backgrounds do not necessarily value this language tradition as a primary means of communication.

Language is culture. It is the cornerstone of ethnic identity. Language structures meaning, determines perception, and transmits culture. It communicates thought and subjective cultural experiences at deep and subtle levels (Sue & Sue, 1990; Westwood & Ishiyama, 1990). Acquisition and use of language is a primary aspect of psychosocial development and socialization in all cultures. Mastery of language generally implies mastery of culture.

Verbal and nonverbal communication is a cultural phenomenon involving the use of symbols of meaning that are culturally defined. The same words or gestures can have different meanings depending on the cultural context in which they are used (Gudykunst & Kim, 1984; Hall, 1976; Wallen, 1972; Westwood & Borgen, 1988).

Culturally responsive counseling, therefore, must be based on an appreciation of and sensitivity to possible language differences between counselor and client. These include differences in language fluency, accent, dialect, and the use of nonverbal communication (e.g., eye contact, body language, facial expressions, emotional expressions). Failure to respect language differences in a counseling relationship invariably leads to misunderstanding and the possible alienation of clients.

An appreciation for language dynamics must be a central theme in culturally responsive counseling. Clients from ethnic minority cultural backgrounds must be able to tell their story in a manner that is most comfortable and appropriate for them (Sue, Arredondo, & McDavis, 1992; Westwood & Ishiyama, 1990).

Kinship Influences

Immediate and extended kinship networks must be considered as primary sources for promoting mental health and normal development among most ethnic minority groups. Such networks may include immediate and extended family, friends, or community cultural resources. Within these networks can be found hierarchical structures and carefully defined age and/or gender roles that promote a collective unity among people. This collective unity provides the basis for a worldview that emphasizes communalism rather than individualism (Attneave, 1969; Nobles, 1991).

Kinship support networks are crucial in providing resolution to both situational and developmental problems related to educational, career, or personal-social matters. In many instances, the supportive dynamics of these indigenous networks may keep an individual from needing to seek outside decision-making or problem-resolution assistance. Culturally responsive counseling practice, therefore, must include an understanding of and appreciation for the role of kinship dynamics in mental health and well-being.

Sex Role Socialization

Sex role socialization may need to be an important dynamic to consider when counseling across cultures. Many ethnic groups with non-European cultural origins have developed different perceptions of the roles of men and women. These differential gender perceptions can influence the expectations considered normal for psychosocial development. Such expectations, therefore, can account for fundamental differences in personality development for men and women (Arredondo, Psalti, & Cella, 1993; Davenport & Yurich, 1991; Fouad & Post-Kammer, 1989).

When necessary, sex role socialization and its effects on development should be considered in culturally responsive counseling. Counselors may need to be aware of how gender-based differences in developmental expectations are manifested in decision making and problem resolution among the men and women of a particular ethnic group.

Religious/Spiritual Influences

Although religion and spirituality are universally accepted as major influences on human development, they have only recently been considered as important or appropriate issues in the counseling process (Georgia, 1994; Kelly, 1995; Pate & Bondi, 1992). However, culturally responsive counseling may be enhanced if the influence of religion and spirituality is considered a crucial dynamic in the helping process. The philosophical tenets inherent in religious or spiritual beliefs influence all aspects of human development and interaction, and for many ethnic minority groups, there is often little distinction made between religious and secular life.

Within the cultural traditions of many groups, religious institutions or spiritual centers are important sources of psychological support. Likewise, religious or spiritual leaders have been expected not only to provide for spiritual needs but also to offer guidance for physical and emotional concerns. These institutions and their leaders have been an important indigenous source of help for decision making and problem resolution in many cultures for generations (Lee & Armstrong, 1995; Lee, Oh, & Mountcastle, 1992; Vontress, 1991).

Immigration Experience

Many individuals from ethnic minority groups are relatively recent arrivals to the United States. For these people, the immigration experience may be an important dynamic of culture that merits consideration in the counseling process.

Immigration in some cases has been prompted by political upheaval in other parts of the world. Many recent immigrants arrive here as refugees from repressive governments. In addition to cultural beliefs and practices, these people bring with them the trauma associated with forced separation from family and homeland. In other cases, individuals are lured here by the age-old promise of economic and social opportunity. Because many of these immigrants enter the country without proper documentation (i.e., illegally), they must face the two major challenges that often confront so-called *undocumented aliens*. The first is living with knowledge that at any time immigration officials might send them back to their country of origin. The second, which is common to all recent immigrants, is reconciling the desire to maintain cultural customs from back home with the pressure to adopt major aspects of the American macroculture.

Whatever the reason for immigration, the experience of suddenly finding oneself a stranger in a new land can effect human development in ways that need to be considered in culturally responsive counseling. Counseling professionals, therefore, should be aware of the possible influence immigration experiences have on the attitudinal orientations, behavioral repertoires, and value systems of clients from ethnic minority groups.

Historical Hostility

Counseling ethnic minority clients in the United States requires sensitivity to a dynamic that can be labeled *historical hostility* (Grier & Cobbs, 1968; Vontress, 1995; Vontress & Naiker, 1995; Willie, Kramer, & Brown, 1973). The essence of this dynamic can be observed anywhere in the world where there has been a long-term pattern of exploitation or oppression between one group of people favored and another group devalued on, for example, the basis of ethnicity, religion, or politics.

Sadly, the history of the United States is replete with examples of negative social encounters between European Americans and people from other cultural backgrounds—from the enslavement of Africans, to the systematic destruction of Native American culture, and to the internment of Japanese Americans citizens during World War II. The motivating force defining these encounters has generally been racism or other forms of social and economic oppression. Over time, the social and political process associated with racism and oppression in the United States has taken a collective physical and psychological toll on ethnic minority groups. This toll is seen in intense negative feelings that members of ethnic minority groups often possess, either overtly or covertly, toward members of the majority group in the United States (Grier & Cobbs, 1968). Whether these feelings are justified or warranted at any given point in time is generally rendered moot by the nature of the often exploitative and destructive relationship between European Americans and people from non-European backgrounds in the United States.

With respect to counseling, historical hostility can manifest itself in resistance to the helper and the helping process. As discussed in chapter 1, counseling has often been a sociopolitical process for many members of ethnic minority groups (Katz, 1985; Sue & Sue, 1990). Mental health services have been perceived as a tool of oppression and social control in many ethnic minority communities (Katz, 1985). Often counseling is a forced, as opposed to a voluntary, experience with a culturally insensitive or unresponsive agent of some aspect of the broad social welfare system.

Historical hostility is a cultural dynamic that must be factored into the counseling equation with many clients from ethnic minority backgrounds. This is particularly the case for those clients whose counseling issues relate to the stresses of racism, prejudice, discrimination, or socioeconomic disadvantage. Resistance to counseling might include denial of problems, viewing counseling as something that is done to an individual rather than with him or her, distrust of the counselor and the process, silence, passive aggressive behavior, or premature termination. These phenomena may be symptomatic of generalized negative feelings about the dominant group fostered by generations of negative intergroup relations.

Conclusion

Although all counseling contains an element of cultural diversity, the demographic realities of American society clearly suggest that a primary focus in multicultural counseling should be on ethnicity and its potential influence on the helping process. Culturally responsive counseling, therefore, should be based on an understanding of culture in an ethnic group context. In addition, the cultural dynamics that shape personality among people of ethnic minority backgrounds must be considered as important themes in counseling practice.

Part II of this book expands on these cultural themes and their role in both the psychosocial development of and effective counseling with ethnic minority client groups. Each of its 16 chapters examines methods to address the mental health issues of a unique individual within his or her cultural context.

References

Arredondo, P., Psalti, A., & Cella, K. (1993). The woman factor in multicultural counseling. *Counseling and Human Development, 25,* 1–8.

Atkinson, D. R., Morten, G., & Sue, D. W. (1993). *Counseling American minorities: A cross-cultural perspective* (4th ed.). Madison, WI: Brown and Benchmark.

Attneave, C. (1969). Therapy in tribal settings and urban network interventions. *Family Process, 8,* 192–210.

Brislin, R. W. (1990). *Applied cross-cultural psychology.* Newbury Park, CA: Sage.

Cross, W. E. (1971). The Negro-to-Black conversion experience. *Black World, 20,* 12–27.

Cross, W. E. (1995). The psychology of Nigrescence: Revising the Cross model. In J. G. Ponterotto, J. M. Casas, L. A. Suzuki, & C. M. Alexander (Eds.), *Handbook of multicultural counseling* (pp. 93–122). Thousand Oaks, CA: Sage.

Davenport, D. S., & Yurich, J. M. (1991). Multicultural gender issues. *Journal of Counseling and Development, 70,* 64–71.

Fouad, N. A., & Post-Kammer, P. (1989). Work values of women with differing sex role orientations. *Journal of Career Development, 15,* 188–198.

Georgia, R. T. (1994). Preparing to counsel clients of different religious backgrounds: A phenomenological approach. *Counseling and Values, 38,* 43–51.

Grier, W. H., & Cobbs, P. M. (1968). *Black rage.* New York: Bantam.

Gudykunst, K. B., & Kim, K. Y. (1984). *Communicating with strangers: An approach to intercultural communication.* Reading, MA: Addison-Wesley.

Hall, E. T. (1976). *Beyond culture.* Garden City, NY: Anchor Press.

Helms, J. E. (1990). *Black and White racial identity: Theory, research, and practice.* Westport, CT: Greenwood.

Helms, J. E. (1995). An update of Helms's White and People of Color racial identity models. In J. G. Ponterotto, J. M. Casas, L. A. Suzuki, & C. M. Alexander (Eds.), *Handbook of multicultural counseling* (pp. 181–198). Thousand Oaks, CA: Sage.

Johnson, S. D. (1990). Toward clarifying culture, race, and ethnicity in the context of multicultural counseling. *Journal of Multicultural Counseling and Development, 18,* 41–50.

Katz, J. H. (1985). The sociopolitical nature of counseling. *Counseling Psychologist, 13,* 615–624.

Kelly, E. W. (1995). *Spirituality and religion in counseling and psychotherapy: Diversity in theory and practice.* Alexandria, VA: American Counseling Association.

Lee, C. C., & Armstrong, K. L. (1995). Indigenous models of mental health intervention: Lessons from traditional healers. In J. G. Ponterotto, J. M. Casas, L. A. Suzuki, & C. M. Alexander (Eds.), *Handbook of multicultural counseling* (pp. 441–456). Thousand Oaks, CA: Sage.

Lee, C. C., Oh, M. Y., & Mountcastle, A. R. (1992). Indigenous models of helping in non-Western countries: Implications for multicultural counseling. *Journal of Multicultural Counseling and Development, 20,* 3–10.

Locke, D. C. (1990). A not-so-provincial view of multicultural counseling. *Counselor Education and Supervision, 30,* 18–25.

McFadden, J. (Ed.). (1993). *Transcultural counseling: Bilateral and international perspectives.* Alexandria, VA: American Counseling Association.

McIntosh, P. (1989). White privilege: Unpacking the invisible knapsack. *Peace and Freedom, 2,* 10–12.

Marin, G. (1992). Issues in the measurement of acculturation among Hispanics. In K. F. Geisinger (Ed.), *Psychological testing of Hispanics* (pp. 235–251). Washington, DC: American Psychological Association.

Merriam-Webster's Collegiate Dictionary (10th ed.). (1995). Springfield, MA: Merriam-Webster.

Nobles, W. W. (1991). African philosophy: Foundations of Black psychology. In R. L. Jones (Ed.), *Black psychology* (3rd ed., pp. 47–63). Berkeley, CA: Cobb & Henry.

Pate, R. H., & Bondi, A. M. (1992). Religious beliefs and practice: An integral aspect of multicultural awareness. *Counselor Education and Supervision, 32,* 108–115.

Pedersen, P. B. (1991). Multiculturalism as a generic approach to counseling. *Journal of Counseling and Development, 70,* 6–12.

Ponterotto, J. G., & Benesch, K. F. (1988). An organizational framework for understanding the role of culture in counseling. *Journal of Counseling and Development, 66,* 237–241.

Ponterotto, J. G., Casas, J. M., Suzuki, L. A., & Alexander, C. M. (Eds.). (1995). *Handbook of multicultural counseling.* Thousand Oaks, CA: Sage.

Rotheram, M. J., & Phinney, J. S. (1987). Introduction: Definitions and perspectives in the study of children's ethnic socialization. In J. S. Phinney & M. J. Rotheram (Eds.), *Children's ethnic socialization.* Beverly Hills, CA: Sage.

Spencer, G. (1989). *Projections of the population of the United States by age, sex, and race: 1988 to 2080* (U.S. Bureau of the Census Current Population Reports, Series P-25, No. 1018). Washington, DC: U.S. Government Printing Office.

Sue, D. W., & Sue, D. (1990). *Counseling the culturally different: Theory and practice* (2nd ed.). New York: Wiley.

Sue, D. W., Arredondo, P., & McDavis, R. J. (1992). Multicultural counseling competencies and standards: A call to the profession. *Journal of Counseling and Development, 70,* 477–486.

Sue, S., & Zane, N. (1987). The role of culture and cultural techniques in psychotherapy. *American Psychologist, 42*, 37–45.

Triandis, H. C., Bontempo, R., Leung, K., & Hui, C. H. (1990). A method for determining cultural, demographic, and person constructs. *Journal of Cross-Cultural Psychology, 21*, 302–318.

Vontress, C. E. (1991). Traditional healing in Africa: Implications for cross-cultural counseling. *Journal of Counseling and Development, 70*, 242–249.

Vontress, C. E. (1995). The breakdown of authority: Implications for counseling young African American males. In J. G. Ponterotto, J. M. Casas, L. A. Suzuki, & C. M. Alexander (Eds.), *Handbook of multicultural counseling* (pp. 457–473). Thousand Oaks, CA: Sage.

Vontress, C. E., & Naiker, K. S. (1995). Counseling in South Africa: Yesterday, today, and tomorrow. *Journal of Multicultural Counseling and Development, 23*, 149–157.

Wallen, J. L. (1972). *The interpersonal gap*. Portland, OR: Northwest Regional Educational Laboratory.

Westwood, M. J., & Borgen, W. A. (1988). A culturally embedded model for effective intercultural communication. *International Journal for the Advancement of Counseling, 11*, 115–125.

Westwood, M. J., & Ishiyama, F. I. (1990). The communication process as a critical intervention for client change in cross-cultural counseling. *Journal of Multicultural Counseling, 18*, 163–171.

Willie, C. V., Kramer, B. M., & Brown, B. S. (Eds.). (1973). *Racism and mental health*. Pittsburgh, PA: University of Pittsburgh Press.

PART II
DIRECTION FOR CULTURALLY RESPONSIVE COUNSELING

The Native American Experience

Contemporary Native Americans (a term that encompasses American Indians as well as Eskimos and Aleuts) are the descendents of the indigenous inhabitants of the North American continent. As a cultural group they have had a long and troubled history. The basis of their trouble has been their relationship with the United States government—a relationship often marked by conflict and oppression. There is a great deal of diversity among this cultural group, but culturally responsive counselors need to be aware of some common elements that contribute to Native mental health and psychosocial development. These include spirituality, a strong reverence for nature, and a deep respect for one's people.

3

COUNSELING AMERICAN INDIAN ADULTS

Grace Powless Sage

Culturally responsive counseling for American Indian adults requires an under-standing of the impact of their history as well as their identity issues and world-views. It also requires understanding their patterns of sociocultural development, including the differences between urban and rural-reservation American Indians and intergenerational differences. This chapter overviews these areas, presents general strategies to facilitate effective counseling for this broad cultural group, and provides a case study to illustrate the effectiveness of combining traditional and contemporary practices.

The Impact of History

Much has been written on the history of American Indians and their unique relationship with the United States, but it cannot be overstated that tribal relationships with the United States government have impacted each tribal group immeasurably (Deloria, 1969, 1970). Three important issues must be highlighted in order to understand the dynamics of the tribal relationships with the federal government. One is the need for awareness and sensitivity to the impact of the government on tribes and on the consequent relationship to mental health and mental health services. A second issue is the role of traditional healers and traditional health care and the circumstances that prevail that lead to choosing one system over another (Guilmet & Whited, 1988). The third issue is how the historical relationship between the American Indian tribes and the United States government has created a dependency perspective that invariably results in tribal problems being perceived as the responsibility of federal agencies (Trimble, Manson, Dinges, & Medicine, 1984).

The most obvious way in which the federal government impacted, and continues to impact, American Indians is the need and demand for land. Few tribal groups have not been the victims of relocation on one or more occasions. Furthermore, no tribe has escaped the severe loss of population through starvation, disease, and warfare, often at the hands of the federal government.

The government has demonstrated ambivalence toward American Indians by promoting (sometimes simultaneously) both love and hate, reservation and romanticization, colonialization and extermination, self-determination and subjugation, treatment and neglect. On one hand, the United States government signed treaties with tribes it recognized as sovereign nations. On the other hand, the United States government exterminated the same tribes or forced them into dependent relationships and on to reservations (Deloria, 1983; Trimble, 1988). The predominant view of the United States government was that the only way to manage the Indian situation was for Indians to give up their distinctive and unique way of life completely and adopt the dominant culture (Deloria, 1983; Trimble, 1988; Witt, 1980); and the government "guardians and stewards" of American Indians provided services to help engage and increase Indian adaptiveness and acculturation into the dominant society (Trimble, 1988). These opposing sentiments and policies continued to contribute to difficulties in making Indians understand what was "good for them" (Deloria, 1983). American Indians have had to try to identify who they were and what their needs were while under the direct influence of their roller-coaster relationship with the United States government. It is little wonder that many American Indians believe the only way to independence is through continued dependence on the government.

The long history of confusing messages from the federal government has created a double bind from which there seems to be no escape. For example, it is a government agency—the Indian Health Service—that provides contemporary mental health services; and although the government has given the American Indian people no reason for trust, American Indians must trust the agency in order to utilize these services.

Identity Issues and Worldviews

Identity Issues

American Indian identity as discussed, defined, argued, and developed across individual, family, tribe, group, and nation is complex. Even the designations—American Indian, Native American, Indian—cause this diverse population difficulty in terms of generic identity and context within the United States.

Basic questions for many American Indians around identity issues include:

- Who is an Indian? (What blood quantum is required?)
- What tribe are you? (Are you enrolled?) Most American Indians agree that the most respectful identification is an individual's tribe or nation—which requires an answer to this question.
- What is your "Indianess" based on? (What are your values?)

Answers to these questions and the way the individual responds reflect a cultural commitment to tribe and family or to an idea and attitude fostered by the majority United States culture. Often the commitment and balance for an individual can be found in seeking knowledge and skills related to the Indian culture and applying them in the contemporary lives of the tribal communities.

Related to the issue of American Indian identity is cultural identity—which is connected to the complex issue of language. Leonard Crow Dog, a Lakota medicine man explained (Crow Dog & Erdoes, 1990):

Our modern Sioux language has been White-man-ized. There's no power in it. I get my knowledge of the old tales of my people out of a drum . . . but above all out of the ancient words from way back, the words of the grandfathers, the language that was there at the beginning of time. . . . If that language, these words, should ever die, then our legends will die too.

Language is the most accommodating and common way in which cultural understanding, social and family relationships, beliefs and values, and biases and prejudices are learned and practiced. A cultural change must take place when language from another and different culture is adopted, for whatever reason. Practically speaking, this does not always indicate a change in the individual's sociocultural environment, and the subsequent adaptation of the new language often helps to create a "new" culture. The new culture that is born is intergenerational, bilingual, and a mediation between the old and the new. Thus American Indians can have a close identification with a culture because of language, and they can do so without necessarily decreasing identification with their own culture (Oetting & Beauvais, 1990).

Worldviews

Understanding tribal worldviews, belief systems, and values of American Indians enables culturally responsive counseling. Although all have been influenced by intertribal contacts as well as contacts with non-Indians, there is consistency in values across tribes despite tribal diversity, and there has been a persistence of values and resistance to obliteration despite United States policies of assimilation, acculturation, termination, and genocide.

Core values illustrative of worldviews that most tribes seem to have in common include

- sharing—by which many tribes gain honor and respect;
- cooperation—which for the family and tribal group is of paramount importance and takes precedence over the individual;
- interrelationships with extended family—which are highly valued; and
- respect for elders—because of their wisdom and knowledge and because they are the connection between all that has gone before and all that is yet to come. (One American Indian put it this way: "When an American Indian elder dies, it is like a rare book that is lost forever.")

Other worldview concepts held in common are more cosmological:

- All things in the world—humans, animals, rocks, plants—have spirits, and there is a creator.
- All elements of the environment (such as the past, present, and future, and the body, mind, and spirit) are interconnected and related.

The interconnectedness worldview is captured in the concept of seven generations, the concept that there is an obligation and responsibility to the seven generations who have gone before (the past) and an equal accountability to the seven generations yet to come (the present and future). Full discussions of this important concept are contained in Arnold Krupat's *Native American Autobiography: An Anthology* (1994); W. C. Vanderwerth's *Indian Oratory* (1971) and John G. Neihardt's *Black Elk Speaks* (1961).

Sociocultural Development Patterns

In providing mental health services to American Indians, culturally responsive counselors should consider not only the impact of history but also the effects of sociocultural development patterns. However, because there is an enormous amount of cultural difference and heterogeneity with American Indians as a group (Deloria, 1983), important considerations include not only differences between American Indians who live in urban settings and those who live on rural reservations, regional differences, and intergenerational differences but also differences in understandings of and explanations for diseases of the mind and body. These differences affect the rates of mental and physical well-being as well as of alcoholism, substance abuse, and suicide (Beiser, 1981; Beiser & Attneave, 1982).

Urban and Rural Differences

Urban American Indians are more than likely to be extremely migratory. They may migrate from urban setting to urban setting, or from reservation to urban setting and back. Some are searching for the American dream, some are looking for economic opportunity and adequate housing, and others are seeking educational opportunity (Witt, 1980). Many are mixed-bloods and have limited, if any, relationship to the reservation of their parent or parents. The Indian and non-Indian relationships they experience are quite different from those of their parents.

Close identification with the non-Indian world increases migratory American Indians' sense of invisibility, which decreases their sense of identity and self-esteem (Ablon, 1964, 1971). This results in individuals rarely identifying themselves as American Indians when they access or utilize services, or participate in cultural events or ceremonies. Instead they accept any identification that is given to them by service professionals or others, and as a result, they feel isolated and removed from the non-Indian world as well as from the American Indian world (Ablon, 1964, 1971).

Conversely, not identifying with the dominant culture—the non-Indian world—can for migratory American Indians lead to isolation, passivity, increased stress, anxiety, and depression (Trimble, Manson, & Dinges, 1983). The most pervasive and eroding of these is isolation. When they migrate to urban settings, many Indians lose their traditional role models and images, which may exacerbate their feelings of psychological vulnerability. Returning to the reservation can be a booster shot to help regain balance, self-esteem, and self-concept, and to steady a fragile self and tribal identity as American Indians (Guilmet & Whited, 1988).

Those American Indians who have not engaged in migratory behavior, whether born and raised on a reservation or in an urban setting, have different but related problems. The sense of being invisible simply does not exist on a reservation because everyone knows their genealogy. That fact, in and of itself, provides individuals with a strong sense of community and tribal identity. For instance, on a reservation when a person of mixed blood participates in traditional tribal ceremonies or seeks the services of a medicine man or woman, the reservation community perceives this as an assertion of that person's Indianness. However, seeking services from an Indian Health Service counselor might reinforce the reservation community's perception that the person is not really Indian. Alternatively, the test for urban Indians' identification is less strained because their perceptions and understandings of traditional Indian ceremonies are similar to those their dominant culture counterparts hold. Thus they are unlikely to seek services other than those considered appropriate to the majority culture, such as counseling and psychotherapy.

Regional Differences

Understanding regional differences among American Indians may seem unnecessary until there is an occasion to work or live with an Eastern woodlands tribal member, or a Northern Plains tribal member, or, perhaps, a Southern Plains tribal member. Regional differences impact worldviews, traditional ceremonial practices, cultural beliefs, language, eating habits, and clothing habits (Trimble, 1986). Successful functioning (being in balance), as well as underlying pathology, can be highly influenced by regional differences (Neligh, 1988; Trimble et al., 1983). However, these regional variables do not exist in isolation but rather are defined and developed in tandem with tribal, urban, reservation, and intergenerational differences. Discerning the level of impact from each of these differences while keeping in mind the impact of the majority culture and its sociodevelopmental processes is difficult (and thus often neglected) but important to attempt.

Intergenerationl Differences

The extent of intergenerational differences often depends on where the individual was raised. Difficulties and differences among generations are produced by school experiences, by 20th century lifestyles, music, and technology. Alcohol or substance abuse in the family can add to or exacerbate intergenerational differences and difficulties. The pressures, stress, and depression can become devastating, and communication may be neglected because all energy is being expended in meeting basic survival needs.

Differences in Understandings and Explanations for Disease

Illness is traditionally seen by American Indians as an imbalance of various elements. Each tribe has its own understanding of equilibrium and balance within its oral history and religion, but all talk about conditions or behavior in terms of where it lies on a continuum of balance (Trimble et al., 1984). The understandings and explanations for diseases of mind and body (although not all tribes discriminate between the two) are based on the concept that a cure (restored balance) requires interwoven healing. Thus if an individual is, for example, plagued by diabetes, gall bladder problems, or infections, healing benefits can be sought both from contemporary medical treatment and from ceremonies and treatment conducted by medicine men and women. Balance is thus achieved/restored by using the total healing system.

But missionaries from other organized religious groups have influenced American Indians' thinking and definition of what is appropriate behavior—and created yet another dilemma for American Indians from the different tribes. For example, if a person is a good Christian, how could he or she partake of pagan ceremonies? Alternatively, if a person is a good Indian, how could that person disown his or her own culture and tradition and adopt other beliefs? So if an American Indian is feeling out of balance with the world, does he or she choose to see a traditional healer, go to talk with someone about his or her difficulties, or pray? And, after all, would he or she have problems of mental illness, alcoholism, and substance abuse if the U.S. government hadn't treated Indians the way it did? So, therefore, isn't it the government's responsibility to take care of the problem?

In speaking with tribal elders, it becomes clear that an understanding of mental health and appropriate mental health care can be viewed as a system that is given significance and develops only within a sociocultural context. Although many elders do not understand the role or the responsibilities of conventional counselors, and are caught in a maze of misunderstanding where medical technology develops quickly and assumes superiority, they do understand their experience: American Indian people go to the hospital and die, or their "spirit" is transformed into something unrecognizable such as mental illness or a coma.

Historically, the mental health model has followed a medical model because of dominant Eurocentric beliefs, financial power, prejudices, and stereotypical attitudes toward the traditional healers of most American Indian tribes (Guilmet & Whited, 1988). Only recently have different perspectives emerged and the need for holistic health care advocated by many health care professionals (Guilmet & Whited, 1988). But the long neglect or outright obliteration of traditional healers and healing practices has had its own set of consequences. Today elders and American Indian adults, many of whom have a history of isolation from their culture and have experienced the domination of the U.S. government, often lack understanding of the role of traditional healers in their own tribes. Furthermore, they are almost totally uninvolved with the non-Indian alternative healing practices that have been flourishing for some years (Guilmet & Whited, 1988). At this point, for some tribes and many American Indian adults, the isolation seems total and has created a culture of its own.

Strategies and Techniques to Facilitate Counseling

In any counseling system with American Indians, there are often challenges associated with issues of underutilization of services, definitions of health and illness, multicultural issues, and the unequal distribution of resources and power. The psychological effects of oppression, genocide, and termination are well documented. Unfortunately, these effects are often explored, discussed, and researched in terms of pathologies and negative images. Given that "Cross-cultural therapy implies a situation in which the participants are most likely to evidence discrepancies in their shared assumptions, experiences, beliefs, values, expectations, and goals" (Manson & Trimble, 1982), a balanced perspective is necessary for providers of counseling services to the diverse American Indian communities. But what competencies does a counselor need in working with adult Indians? How can a counselor engage and empower American Indians and combine what sometimes are (or appear to be) two contrasting systems of healing?

The first and most important strategy is gaining a knowledge and understanding of the sociocultural history of American Indian people. Counselors must understand what defines a healthy individual according to the individual's community, whether that be on a reservation or in an urban setting. They must understand the practices and activities of their clients. That is, practitioners must understand the meaning and intent of the migratory practices for American Indians and acknowledge the necessity of developing a supporting network to maintain a sense of balance in their world. Thus counselors must also understand that aspects of contemporary counseling techniques conflict with migratory practices in many ways, such as in set appointment times and in using a linear process leading to specific goals. Further, practitioners must recognize the conflict inherent in trying to operate in differing cultural milieus—a recognition that is sometimes more therapeutic and supportive for their clients than any contemporary counseling intervention.

The community (reservation or urban) sees the migratory practices as necessary and supports the pattern through providing money, disseminating information (who is traveling where and when), and exerting considerable pressure on individuals to remain connected with the family. In fact, many American Indians believe that to be poor is not to be without money but to be without family and relatives (Primeaux, 1977). Thus a healthy individual is the American Indian who designs a life that maintains connection to family.

Connectedness to family is also provided through ceremonial practices that give expression to the restoration and preservation of identity. To alleviate the feeling of being caught between two cultures, counselors can provide support for preserving what is strong and enduring from the history, tribe, and family of the individual—while at the same time continuing to adapt to the technology and progress of the dominant culture. Counselors and programs that confront these complicated processes of integration by supporting and incorporating (rather than suppressing) cultural patterns are much more likely to be successful with American Indian clients.

Understanding sociocultural history also involves the identification of value conflicts for both counselor and client. Some of these conflicts relate to the counseling process, such as those between individual versus group accomplishment and goal-oriented therapy versus ceremonies as therapeutic agent. Other value conflicts relate to education because the expectations and values the non-Indian places on members of the American Indian community to conform to the dominant culture's beliefs about achievement and competition often lead to feelings of inadequacy and frustration as well as poor self-image (Jilek-Aall, 1976).

Still other value conflicts involve communication styles as they affect self-worth, self-concept, and understanding. Because the history of American Indian identity is maintained through oral tradition, American Indians are likely to see words as powerful and value laden. Thus some individuals may avoid using words casually (as in making small talk) or frivolously (as in anger) at any cost. The fact that the main entry into a counseling situation is with words increases the potential for a problem situation. Counselors need to remember that American Indians accept periods of silence, especially in unfamiliar circumstances such as counseling, and that speaking and silence should both be natural parts of the process.

Related to value conflicts over communication styles are conflicts over the sense of self-identification. In non-Indian society, those individuals most often valued are more verbal and demonstrative, have an advanced academic degree, are steadily employed, define and promote their individualism and individual identity, and are competitive on an individual level. When American Indians must make their own identity within these dominant culture guidelines, it often means alienating themselves from their own culture. Ironically, even when an American Indian does adopt the dominant culture, he or she almost never finds membership, acceptance, understanding, success, or power in the non-Indian culture—despite the strengths he or she possesses or the contributions he or she makes. However, the criteria of acceptance, success, or power may all be defined, achieved, and seen differently depending on each system (the dominant culture, the American Indian culture, the individual American Indian's own culture).

A second important strategy to facilitate counseling American Indian adults is learning about the stories, religion, and communications that are the vestiges of the remaining intact American Indian culture as well as a sensitive and vital part of tribal communities. As community members recount who they are and how they are related to others, for example during yearly ceremonies, their resiliency and strength become apparent. Traditional healers, indigenous helpers, and community memory keepers are often the vital connection between Western professional mental health providers and the Native American community. To gain authentic worldviews and keys to understanding, counselors can benefit from direct dialogue or from listening, respecting nonverbal cues, and following the example that is being set. The traditions, rituals, and symbolism are part of the behaviors, beliefs, and values that are honored and followed. The relevance and significance often go beyond the individual and lead to a deeper and richer understanding of a different way of being in the universe. Successes in establishing a relationship with the environment, balancing a way of life between the traditional and Western context, and negotiating natural and traditional healing can only come about when those paths are undertaken in sacred ways. The strength and ability to survive deserves study and attention as the depth of the Indian stronghold continues to grow.

A third strategy is being aware that tribal social structures and relationships are ever changing and provide increasing need for understanding and investigation. Indian communities continue to evolve in many ways as they enter the 21st century. Many tribal groups are interested in tribal revitalization in terms of language, customs, rituals, ways of being, and tribal identities. The ways in which Western providers can assist and facilitate this revitalization is through actively investigating and integrating new ways to conceptualize diagnoses; through overhauling the field of psychometrics to include restandardizing objective and projective tests for all groups; through questioning assumptions and stereotypes that continue to drive caregiving policies directed at American Indian communities, both urban, rural, and reservation; and through requiring accountability and assistance in preserving the fundamental right to continue to exist as a people. American Indians have long used their cultural, political, and spiritual resources to accommodate this most basic natural and instinctive value in the universe: to continue to survive and create images and identity, practice worldviews, broaden experiences, and enrich the understanding of Black Elk's vision—the coming together of all the nations in a harmonious manner.

The Case Study of Mary

The case study presented here illustrates many of the issues and challenges related to sociocultural development patterns. It also describes a specific, beneficial, and practical intervention: the Indian Women's Group.

Mary was born on the reservation. She was sent away to school when she was 12 and did not return to the reservation until she was 20. By the time she returned, her mother had died from pneumonia. She didn't remember her father, who was the medicine man of the tribe, very well. Shortly after she returned, she became pregnant by a non-Indian man she met in a bar. When her son John became old enough, he went to the mission school on the reservation. Because he was a bright child, the priest encouraged Mary to move to an urban area about 1,000 miles from the reservation. When John was 8, she moved. After that, Mary and her son made occasional visits to the reservation when she could afford to.

Mary's father was born and raised on the reservation, although his parents had lived and been born on original tribal lands. Because his own sons—Mary's brothers—had been killed or had died, he looked forward to teaching and leaving to his grandson John the ways of the medicine man. On one of Mary and John's visits from the city to the reservation, he told John that one day he, too, would be able to heal the people of the tribe and be held in great respect and esteem. John felt his grandfather was out of step with the 20th century. He argued with his grandfather about the practical usefulness of his medicine and looked with disdain at the people who sought his grandfather's help, advice, and healing. John also felt disgusted and angry with his mother for making him visit his grandfather.

Mary, who had herself gone away to school when she was young and now lived in the city, could not validate the grandfather's way of life. Even though she had not completed school she had learned enough to know that some things—like her father being a medicine man—were simply not discussed. And she remembered having difficulty fitting in when she returned to the reservation. Now, even though it pained her greatly to see the widening gap between her father and her son, she felt powerless to do anything about it. She did not understand her father's ways, and she could not really understand her son's either. In response to the growing distance between the two men, she became more and more depressed and began to drink heavily. She blamed herself for not understanding her father's beliefs, for sending her son to a missionary school, and then for moving away so her son could get a "better" education in the city. She felt totally disenfranchised by her family and her community, and she wrestled constantly with trying to discover her own identity.

Mary's drinking and depression continued and became quite disabling. Then one day at the Indian Center she heard about an Indian Women's Group that was forming. A woman who was currently a member of the group encouraged her to join. Mary was initially hesitant about the group, was not quite sure what it meant, but decided to join. It could give her a chance to get away from the tension in her home and a chance to enjoy beadwork, her favorite pastime.

The Indian Women's Group that Mary joined illuminates the therapeutic aspects of combining traditional and contemporary practices to create successful interventions. The purpose of gathering the women together was simple and achievable: to encourage support for each other and to serve as an alternative to their drinking (although the women did not have to be drinking to be involved). The group, which also provided time for socializing and reestablishing relationships within the community, was started by two women. One, the leader, was a woman who had left the reservation to complete a degree in postsecondary education. Like Mary, she had feelings of disenfranchisement, but she felt that through a group she could assist in her own healing at the same time that she assisted in healing other women. The other was an elderly medicine woman who strongly influenced the leader and was willing to serve as the leader's mentor in the group process.

Women in the community were solicited to join the group. Despite initial hesitation and numerous questions, the group was established. More women wanted to join, others left, but eventually the group stabilized, with a stable group of "old" members and a small number of "new" members so that a steady number of women always participated.

The group's blend and integration of traditional and contemporary therapeutic practices was unique. Beadwork and sewing ribbon shirts were commonplace, as was—sometimes—making favorite foods. Tanning hides and cutting dancing outfits were also tasks performed to help in the healing process. As the women worked, they exchanged ideas and worldviews. No one was diagnosed or labeled. Although everyone in the group knew who was having drinking problems or facing relationship issues, the group somehow focused on a story or "recipe" for how a similar situation had been handled in their lives, most often without direct confrontation. Occasionally the leader would make a comment or an interpretation, but always in the context of what the other group members had said. The older medicine woman always ended the group with a prayer to tie together the learning and relationship building that had been part of the group members' experience that night. Everyone remarked on the enjoyable experience and, almost always, suggested someone else in the community who might benefit from the Indian Women's Group.

When Mary attended the Indian Women's Group, she met other women who like herself were busy working on crafts they enjoyed while talking about how things were going in their lives. Mary began to feel that there wasn't anything terribly wrong with her and that many other women had questions and concerns about their families just like hers. Many were experiencing ambivalence and feelings of disenfranchisement just the way she was. They felt dislocated when they returned to the reservation after attending boarding school just as she had. Many felt sad and depressed just the way she did. She also discovered that the reasons for their depression were basically the same as hers. She was amazed that other women in her tribe were experiencing the same kind of family difficulties. She knew that many of them drank, and now she connected their drinking with their depression—as she connected her own drinking with her own depression.

By giving her feelings a name—depression—Mary was able to deal more effectively with them and gain a sense of control over her own life. By identifying the circumstances for her drinking, she felt empowered. She saw participating in the group of women as healing and as helping her reconnect with her tribal history. Mary was not stigmatized or labeled because of her membership in the group, but was instead sought out by other women in the tribe as someone they could turn to for support. Mary was also able to identify what caused the conflict between her father and son as well as what caused her own conflict with her American Indian identity and beliefs. By identifying what she could and could not control, she achieved balance. From the integration of both her worlds, she began to feel power within herself.

If intervention or treatment is to be effective, all family members need to be included, and each family member must be recognized as unique and different—even though all have contributed to the problem. In Mary's case, her son sought treatment, initially from the Indian Health Service on the reservtion. Later he sought the assistance of a young medicine man on the reservation—for whom his grandfather was the spiritual and medicine leader. Mary's father continued to use and offer his medicinal and spiritual leadership to those who requested it, but he no longer pressured his grandson to join in.

Generally speaking, the competencies and lessons necessary for counselors to treat American Indians successfully result from a mixture of different elements. Some can be gleaned from an advanced academic background, but the success of the Indian Women's Group is attributable in large part to the combination of worldviews. The theoretical underpinnings for the group process may have come from the profession, but the relationships, bonding, reinforcement, and sense of community came from the sharing of values and the cultural understanding group members had for one another. There is no quick or easy way to achieve either the competencies, the lessons, or the abilities to combine different healing systems. Suggestions for practitioners include gathering information about different cultures and cultural views; learning about cross-cultural counseling techniques, diagnostic issues, and pathology; and beginning to explore the racism that exists in mental health systems. Additionally, practitioners should have some experiential training that includes an exploration of their own biases and prejudices.

Conclusion

It is important to recall the risk of generalizations, especially when applied to American Indian or Native American populations. However, a few recommendations merit summarizing. First, it is important to have cross-cultural curriculum for training potential counselors. Second, practitioners will contribute to the sense of invisibility if they are not aware of and sensitive to the diversity between and within the group of people called American Indians or Native Americans. The warning 20 years ago from Vine Deloria, Jr., in *We Talk, You Listen* is still appropriate today:

> . . . Further generalizations about how we are all alike—all people—are useless today. Definite points of view, new logic, and different goals define us. All we can do is try to communicate what we feel our group means to itself and how we relate to other groups. Understanding each other as distinct peoples is the most important thing. (1970, pp. 15–16)

Third, practitioners must have a thorough understanding of American Indians' history, their relationship to the U.S. government, and their unique sociodevelopmental experiences. Finally, practitioners must understand and be able to integrate the variety of, and acknowledge the viability of, traditional and contemporary treatment practices.

References

Ablon, J. (1964). Relocated American Indians in the San Francisco Bay area: Social interactions and Indian identity. *Human Organization, 23,* 296–304.

Ablon, J. (1971). Cultural conflict in urban Indians. *Mental Hygiene, 55,* 199–205.

Beiser, M. (1981). Mental health of American Indian and Alaska Native children: Some epidemiological perspectives. *White Cloud Journal, 2* (2), 37–47.

Beiser, M., & Attneave, C. L. (1982). Mental disorders among Native American children: Rates and risk periods for entering treatment. *American Journal of Psychiatry, 139,* 193–198.

Crow Dog, M., & Erdoes, R. (1990). *Lakota Woman.* New York: Grove Weidenfeld.

Deloria, Jr., V. (1969). *Custer died for your sins.* New York: Avon.

Deloria, Jr., V. (1970). *We talk, you listen.* New York: Dell.

Deloria, Jr., V. (1983). Indians today, the real and the unreal. In D. R. Atkinson, G. Morten, & D. W. Sue (Eds.), *Counseling American minorities: A cross-cultural prospective* (2nd ed.). Dubuque, IA: Wm. C. Brown.

Guilmet, G., & Whited, D. (1988). Mental health care in a general health care system: The experience of the Puyallup. In S. M. Manson & N. Dinges (Eds.), *Behavioral health issues among American Indians and Alaska Natives: Explorations on the frontiers of the biobehavioral sciences* (Journal of the National Center Monograph Series, Monograph 1, pp. 290–324). Denver, CO: National Center, University of Colorado Health Sciences Center.

Jilek-Aall, L. (1976). The western psychiatrist and his non-Western clientele. *Canadian Psychiatric Association Journal, 21* (6), 353–359.

Krupat, A. (Ed.). (1994). *Native American autobiography: An anthology.* Madison: University of Wisconsin Press.

Manson, S. M., & Trimble, J. E. (1982). American Indian and Alaska Native communities: Past efforts, future inquiries. In L. R. Snowden (Ed.), *Reaching the underserved: Mental health needs of neglected populations* (Vol. 3, pp. 143–163). Beverly Hills, CA: Sage Annual Reviews of Community Mental Health.

Neihardt, J. G. (1961). *Black Elk speaks: Being the life of a holy man of the Oglala Sioux.* Lincoln, NE: University of Nebraska Press.

Neligh, G. (1988). Major mental disorders and behavior among American Indians and Alaska Natives. In S. M. Manson & N. Dinges (Eds.), *Behavioral health issues among American Indians and Alaska Natives: Explorations on the frontiers of the biobehavioral sciences* (Journal of National Center Monograph Series, Monograph 1, pp. 116–159). Denver, CO: National Center, University of Colorado Health Sciences Center.

Oetting, E.R., & Beauvais, F. (1990). Orthogonal cultural identification theory: The cultural identification of minority adolescents. *International Journal of the Addictions, 25,* 655–685.

Primeaux, M. (1977). Caring for the American Indian patient. *American Journal of Nursing, 77,* 91–94.

Trimble, J. E. (1986). American Indians and interethnic conflict: A theoretical and historical overview. In J. Boucher, D. Landis, & K. Arnold

(Eds.), *Interethnic conflict: Myth and reality* (pp. 127–144). Beverly Hills, CA: Sage.

Trimble, J. E. (1988). Stereotypical images, American Indians, and prejudice. In P. Katz & D. Taylor (Eds.), *Eliminating racism: Profiles in controversy* (pp. 210–236). New York: Plenum Press.

Trimble, J. E., Manson, S. M., & Dinges, N. (1983). Toward an understanding of American Indian concepts of mental health: Some reflections and directions. In A. Marsella & P. Pedersen (Eds.), *Intercultural applications of counseling therapies*. Beverly Hills, CA: Sage.

Trimble, J. E., Manson, S. M., Dinges, N., & Medicine, B. (1984). American Indian concepts of mental health. In P. Pedersen, N. Sartorius, & A. Marsella (Eds.), *Mental health services: The cross-cultural context* (pp. 199–220). Beverly Hills, CA: Sage.

Vanderwerth, W. C. (1971). *Indian oratory: Famous speeches by noted Indian chieftains*. Norman: University of Oklahoma Press.

Witt, S. H. (1980, Spring). Pressure points in growing up Indian. *Perspectives*, pp. 24–31.

4

COUNSELING INDIGENOUS AMERICAN YOUTH

Roger Herring

The "correctness" of behavior can only be evaluated in terms of the particular sociocultural context in which it occurs.

(LITTLE SOLDIER, 1985, P. 191)

This chapter provides direction for culturally responsive counseling interventions with indigenous youth in the United States. Indigenous people are those whose ancestors were the first to inhabit a specific area. Indigenous—or Native American—people in the United States are found in the lower 48 states (American Indian), and Alaska (Eskimo, American Indian, Aleut). Approximately 2 million Native people live in the United States. Nearly 39% of these people are under 20 years old (U.S. Bureau of the Census, 1990). Recent projections suggest that Native Americans are likely to double within the next 15 years, proportionally the fastest growing ethnic group in the United States (Herring, 1992).

Sixty-three per cent of Native Americans live off reservations (U.S. Bureau of the Census, 1990). A major result of this shift is reflected in the increase of intertribal and interethnic marriages. Over 60% of Native Americans are of mixed ancestry (Herring, 1994a). Diversity is also noted by the 517 federally recognized Native entities (196 in Alaska, 321 in the lower states), 365 state-recognized tribes, and 52 tribes without official recognition—not to mention over 150 different languages spoken (Herring, 1994a; Thomason, 1991).

Significant Issues

Before examining counseling practice with indigenous youth, three significant issues deserve attention: Native cultural perspectives, barriers to effective counseling with this population, and the importance of adopting a proactive approach to counseling Native young people.

Native Cultural Perspectives

Counselors must possess and demonstrate knowledge of the dynamics of Native culture if they are to intervene effectively in the lives of youth from this background. Although variations exist across indigenous groups, Native values reflect a harmony of the individual with the tribe, the tribe with the land, and the land with the Great Spirit (Garrett & Garrett, 1994). Central to this harmony is constancy—the timelessness and predictability of nature as the basis of existence.

An extensive discussion of Native cultural practices is not practical here (consult the resources and references at the end of this chapter for a broader analysis). However, a review of the most important value dynamics related to the Native worldview and optimal mental health for indigenous people—cooperation and sharing; modesty; being versus doing; present-time orientation; importance of tribe, elders, and family; spirituality; and harmony, balance, and holism—is warranted.

Note that Native youth may experience conflict when attempting to internalize the values of the macroculture while seeking to maintain traditional roles necessary for the preservation of these and other cultural values and practices. The gap between macroculture expectations and Native cultural values may be labeled *cultural discontinuity* and can leave many Native youth confused about who they are (Garrett, 1995).

Cooperation and sharing. Views concerning property accentuate the Native belief that whatever belongs to the individual belongs to the group, and vice versa. Native youth are socialized to cooperate and share possessions. Competition for the sake of "beating" others or "showing others up" is highly frowned upon.

Modesty. Individual praise is welcomed if it has been earned, but praise must come from someone else, usually in the presence of a group. Boasting, bragging, and loud behavior that attracts attention to oneself are discouraged in Native group-oriented cultures. Self-absorption of this nature brings disharmony to oneself and family. A Native who is "singled out" or "put on the spot" will usually drop his or her head and eyes as a sign of respect for elders or honored persons.

Being versus doing. The traditional Native way of life emphasizes "being over doing" (Garrett & Garrett, 1993). *Being* implies "It's enough just to be; our purpose in life is to develop the inner self." Conversely, *doing* advocates "Be active; work hard, apply yourself fully, and your efforts will be rewarded."

Present-time orientation. Traditional Native youth are generally not socialized to think of long-term goals and the future. They are present-oriented and "live in the now." *Indian time* means that "things begin when everyone has arrived and they are ready, and things end when they are finished" (Garrett & Garrett, 1993).

Importance of the tribe, elders, and family. Traditional Natives experience a unique relationship between themselves and their tribe: they are extensions of their tribal group (Garrett & Garrett, 1994). Personal identity is rooted in tribal membership and heritage. The extended family (at least three generations) and tribe take precedence over all else. Natives judge themselves and their actions according to whether or not they are benefiting the tribe and its continued harmony. For Natives, "who you are is where you come from" and "if you know my family, clan, tribe, then you know me" (Iron Eye Dudley, 1992). If Native Americans are asked to talk about themselves, most describe some aspect of their family or tribal heritage.

Elders are highly respected persons and play important roles by functioning as parents, teachers, community leaders, and spiritual guides. Traditionally, the primary responsibility of grandparents is to rear children, and that of parents is to provide economic support. Native families reflect a multigenerational support system of interdependence that provides cultural continuity.

Survival of the individual is synonymous with that of the family in traditional Native cultures. Family relationships include more than the biological connections of the nuclear family. For example, the claiming of nonblood relatives (i.e., fictive kin) as family members is commonly practiced (Iron Eye Dudley, 1992). The extended Native American family often assumes a primary responsibility for child care and supervision (e.g., the Lakota concept of *tiospaye*, or communal responsibility).

Spirituality.   Native people view all things as having spiritual energy and importance. Spirituality emphasizes the harmony derived from a person's connection with the universe. Everything has purpose and value of personhood, including plants (e.g., tree people), animals (our four-legged brothers and sisters), rocks and minerals (rock people), the land (Mother Earth), the winds (the Four powers), Father Sky, Grandfather Sun, and Grandmother Moon (Garrett & Garrett, 1993). Spiritual being essentially demands that if individuals seek their place in the universe, all else will follow naturally.

Harmony, balance, and holism.   At the very heart of a Native worldview is the Circle of Life, represented by the Medicine Wheel (Garrett & Garrett, 1994). The circle, as a sacred symbol, reflects growth in nature. Nature progresses only as long as the ongoing and contingent cycles that permit the process of life continue in an intricately balanced fashion. The components of the Circle of Life represent the four directions—spirit (East), nature (South), body (West), and mind (North)—and symbolize the individual's sacred relationship to life.

Native people have their personal "medicine" wherein they choose one of the four directions to focus their energy, and to seek their balance. In seeking his or her medicine, the person is seeking to balance these four directions, that is, to balance self and the universe. Being in harmony implies being "in step with the universe"; being in disharmony indicates being "out of step with the universe" (Garrett & Garrett, 1993, 1994).

Holism, as represented by the circle, or hoop of life, is a key concept of Native American philosophy (Heinrich, Corbine, & Thomas, 1990). Mind, body, spirit, and nature are perceived as one process, and little separation exists between religion, medicine, and the activities of daily life (Garret & Garrett, 1993, 1994). Illness is identified as a disruption of the essential harmony of life, or as an imbalance of various elements, or as a break in the hoop of life.

Barriers to Effective Counseling With Native Youth

A number of potential barriers may prevent effective counseling with Native youth. One is that many live as both Natives and as U.S. citizens. This dualism places significant stress on many young people as they attempt to retain their traditional values while seeking as well to gain acceptance as citizens. By adolescence, sociocultural, economic, and political influences may produce a high degree of alienation among Native youth. They not only experience the personal identity challenges of adolescence, but many also have the additional burden of ethnic identity issues to contend with (Herring, 1994a). As an example, many mixed-blood American Indians now accept the label of *second-class Indianness* or *other Indian* status. They say they are one-quarter Indian or half Indian, accepting the idea that blood quantum somehow determines their degree of Indianness (Wilson, 1992). Others, however, insist on being recognized as American Indian, and still others cease worrying about the issue altogether. The potential psychological helplessness and increasing sense of hopelessness created by such challenges to ethnic identity may serve to alienate Native youth from professional counselors.

Another barrier to effective counseling with Native youth, reflected in the underutilization of mainstream counseling resources by indigenous people (LaFromboise, 1988), is that many Natives recognize the need for professional help only when community-based helping networks are unavailable or undesirable (Wienbach & Kuehner, 1985). This reluctance to use mainstream European American mental health resources among many Native people often emerges from the collective historical memory of the treatment received from non-Natives. Further, many Native people believe mental illness to be a justifiable outcome of human weakness or the result of avoiding the discipline necessary for the maintenance of cultural values and community respect.

Yet another barrier to effective counseling with Native youth may be perceived incompatibility between conventional counseling approaches and indigenous approaches. Native American Indians who enter counseling, for example, often express concern about how conventional Western psychology superimposes biases onto their problems and shapes their behavior in a direction that conflicts with their cultural lifestyle (LaFromboise, 1988).

A Proactive Approach to Counseling With Native Youth

Culturally responsive counseling with Native youth is predicated on adopting a proactive, developmental perspective (Herring, 1994a, 1997a, 1997b). Counselors need a positive view of the integrity and dignity of an Indian identity (Ortiz, 1993). Such a perspective requires that counselors recognize that Native cultural values reflect both commonalities and differences across groups of people. This perspective is characterized by the concept of cultural commitment.

The degree of separation from indigenous culture may result in varied levels of commitment to Native customs and traditional values among Native youth. Zitzow and Estes (1981) suggested a continuum to assess cultural commitment in Native youth. The ends of this continuum are *Heritage-Consistent Native American (HCNA)* and *Heritage-Inconsistent Native American (HINA)*. The HCNA's predominant commitment is to traditional culture. Indicators of heritage-consistency may include (a) growing up near a reservation, (b) having an extended family orientation, (c) being involved in tribal religious and cultural activities, (d) being educated on or near a reservation, (e) socializing primarily with other Natives, (f) being knowledgeable about or willing to learn about tribal culture, (g) placing a low priority on materialistic goals, and (h) using silence as a sign of respect. Conversely, the HINA's commitment reflects behaviors and lifestyles adapted from mainstream culture. Zitzow and Estes (1981) emphasized that these orientations are not mutually exclusive and overlaps may occur.

Within this context, the continuum of acculturation found among Native families can be generally described as comprising four types (Garrett & Garrett, 1994; Herring, 1997a, 1997b; LaFromboise, Trimble, & Mohatt, 1990):

- **Traditional.** A traditional family adheres to culturally defined styles of living. Family members generally communicate in their Native language and practice only traditional beliefs and values. This family strives to return to an ancestral way of life and isolation from non-Native peoples.
- **Transitional.** A transitional family retains only rudimentary elements of a traditional way of life, preferring instead to live within the majority culture. However, this family does not fully

accept its cultural heritage nor identify with mainstream culture and values. The members generally speak both the Native language and English.

- **Bicultural.** A bicultural family generally accepts and practices both mainstream values and the traditional values and beliefs of its cultural heritage simultaneously.
- **Assimilated.** An assimilated family has fully adopted the values and belief structures of the dominant society. Such a family no longer accepts or recognizes any affiliation with its ethnic heritage or culture.

Counselors must be open to what Native youth convey about themselves and their family background. Counselors should understand that cultural commitment and Native family patterns are affected by gender, generation, residence, education, socioeconomic status, and migration experiences.

Synergetic Counseling With Native Youth

Synergetic counseling offers a viable modality for non-Native counselors in their work with Native youth (Herring, 1997a, 1997b). Synergetic counseling is based on the premise of employing the most appropriate strategy for a client by considering variables such as ethnicity, culture, gender, and environment. Implicit in this is the recognition of cultural and environmental influences on the client. In order to engage effectively in synergetic counseling, a counselor needs to develop an open-mindedness toward a client's worldview (Herring & Walker, 1993).

Synergetic Recommendations

Practical synergetic recommendations that may help to create a culturally responsive counseling environment for Native youth include the following:

Address openly the issue of ethnic dissimilarity in the counseling relationship. The Native client will be more likely to perceive a counselor as sensitive and open if ethnic dissimilarity is dealt with in a forthright manner. Counselors should openly admit that they may say culturally uninformed things during the helping process and encourage the client to correct errors or clarify misperceptions.

Consider the sense of ethnic identity and degree of acculturation of the client.   Zitzow and Estes (1981) suggested the use of cues from dress, daily activities, family involvement, body language, participation in tribal functions, friendship patterns, and eye contact in assessing the relationship of ethnic identity and acculturation for Native youth.

Allow for schedule flexibility.   Traditional Native clients often prefer open-ended sessions that are free from time constraints to insure appropriate closure to issues. Therefore, counseling sessions with Native youth may need to be scheduled in a flexible fashion.

Be open to the participation of family members and tribal elders in the counseling process.   Counseling sessions with Native youth may be conducted more effectively in the home environment. Also, tribal elders may be included if desired by the client.

Incorporate the creative arts.   Counselors with training and expertise in creative practices such as art, dance, or music therapy may want to incorporate such aspects of Native cultural life into counseling interventions (Dufrene & Coleman, 1992). A Native counselor familiar with the various values and beliefs related to art and healing is preferred for implementing such interventions. However, if such personnel are unavailable, non-Native counselors should acquire sensitivity and respect for Native culture in order to use these creative practices with credibility.

Integrate natural healing practices.   Consideration should be given to integrating natural healing practices into individual treatment strategies or implementing them within ongoing treatment programs (Heinrich et al., 1990). Such healing practices currently being incorporated into approaches to mental health treatment with traditional Native Americans include:

(a) *four circles*—concentric circles of relationships between client and Creator and extended family as a culturally based structural concept of self-understanding;

(b) *talking circle*—a forum for expressing thoughts and feelings in an environment of total acceptance without time constraints, using sacred objects (e.g., feathers or stones), the pipe, and prayer; and

(c) *sweat lodge*—a physical and spiritual self-purification ritual emphasizing the relationship of the human to all of creation.

Traditional healing systems incorporate cultural metaphors to represent the illness and then symbolically manipulate them to effect healing. Counselors must be able to identify what these metaphors are within the client's reality. Consider the following case (adapted from Heinrich et al., 1990, pp. 130–131):

A Native American Indian lad of 14 or 15 is led into a sweat lodge. Here he will begin the most significant episode of his life, one that will have a far-reaching impact on his future. In this small cubicle made of saplings, birch bark, and hides, he will prepare himself for the purifying vision quest that will immediately follow.

He enters the door that faces East, just as the sun does each day. The solemnity and sacredness is confirmed by the cedar and sage that cover the entrance and floor except for a center pit. Hot rocks are placed into this pit and sprinkled with medicinal herbal water. The intense steam produced symbolizes his people's ascending prayers to the Great Spirit.

The sweat is created by four separate placings of hot stones, representing the four directions of the universe. The stones are added over a period of time to allow the prayers to the deities of each of these directions to continue for hours. The medicine man inside the lodge with the boy assists. The intent of these sublimations is to provide spiritual guidance and to make the boy receptive for the yet-to-come real test.

Upon emerging from the sweat lodge, the young man makes another prayer and offers tobacco to the four directions. He is now ready for that important experience—his vision quest, his search for a sign that will lead him for the rest of his life.

The youth is taken next to an isolated area. He will be left alone and will have no human contact for 4 days and nights (although family members will probably check on his well-being from time to time without his knowledge). He might be placed on a platform above the ground for security, but he will bring nothing with him. There he will sit without food and water in reflection and prayer. He will ponder what his family and tribal elders have told him. He will remember the teachings and his experiences. He will examine his goals and plans. He will search for a vision.

His fasting will allow his mental capacities to be more attentive to nature around him, to be directed toward and focused on his relationship with the universe and his role in it. He will marshal all his abilities, skills, fears, experiences, goals, and hopes to further the quest. Whether it be in a dream state or in full consciousness, a real element of his future will be revealed. He will have sought after and received some vision of his role, his life's work.

Although non-Native counselors are not advised to direct traditional ceremonies, rituals, and healing arts, a client's participation may be beneficial (Dufrene, 1991; Dufrene & Coleman, 1992, 1994). It may be important, therefore, for counselors to form consultative relationships with members of Native communities who conduct such healing practices.

Allow time for trust to develop before focusing immediately on deeper feelings. The counselor should allow a warm-up time by talking about common interests, or other neutral topics, before focusing on counseling issues (Eldredge, 1991).

Use appropriate eye contact. Even if a Native youth avoids eye contact, which is a culturally appropriate behavior and sign of respect for authority figures, the counselor should maintain eye contact (without staring) sufficient for appropriate conversation.

Respect the uses of silence. A Native client's verbal and nonverbal language should not be misinterpreted. Silence, for example, should be viewed in positive terms. Native clients may exhibit silence, a seeming lack of attentiveness, and passive noncompliance in counseling sessions (LaFromboise et al., 1990). Traditional Native youth are unlikely to ask a question and often will refuse to answer a question because that represents putting self above others (Wieder & Pratt, 1990).

The techniques of silence, restatement, and general lead tend to be most effective with Native clients because they are the least intrusive and allow plenty of room for clarification (Herring, 1990). Silence may be the beginning of a disclosure or may signify deep thought (Plank, 1994). Therefore, it should be respected and considered an important therapeutic tool with many Native clients.

Incorporate spirituality and humor into counseling. Counselors must respect the spiritual and humorous dimensions of Native culture. Spirituality in Native culture is prominently acknowledged; and although specific practices are determined by individual tribal values, beliefs, and customs (Peregoy, 1993), counseling sessions could, for example, begin and end with a prayer. Prayers indicate acknowledgement of higher powers that direct one's physical and mental well-being (Dufrene & Coleman, 1992, 1994). Further, traditional Native youth believe that healers can only be successful if they seek the aid of spiritual forces.

Contrary to many stereotypes, Native people love to laugh. From the use of the clown motif in ceremonies and rituals to the use of practical jokes, humor is a prominent feature of Native culture (Herring, 1994b), and contemporary Native artists and authors continue to use irony, highlighted contradiction, and other manifestations of Indian humor. Native humor is unique, especially in its observation of the obvious and use of exaggeration. Native humor also reaffirms and enhances the connectedness experienced in being part of the group (Garrett & Garrett, 1993, 1994; Herring & Meggert, 1994). The non-Native counselor is cautioned to use humor very discreetly and appropriately in counseling interactions.

The Case Study of Michael Redhorse

The case study presented here illustrates many of the concepts and strategies of synergetic counseling. It is adapted from Herring (1997b) and Sodowsky & Johnson (1994).

Michael Redhorse is a Native student in an urban junior high school. His school has a small number of Native students who moved from reservations to the city so that their parents could find employment opportunities. Michael is an academically and artistically talented sophomore who informs his counselor that he is returning to the reservation to live with his grandparents. Michael believes that his return to the reservation will, for all practical purposes, end his formal education. However, he feels an intense need to become immersed in his tribal cultural and art work.

Presenting issue. It is evident that Michael is experiencing an identity conflict characteristic of cultural discontinuity. He appears to be trying to validate his ethnic identity as a Native American Indian, and he is finding this increasingly difficult to do in his present environment. He feels that his identity will be affirmed and his artistic talents enriched through a total immersion in a Native cultural context. This appears to be so strong an urge for Michael that he is willing to sacrifice his formal macroculture education.

Synergetic intervention. Aspects of synergetic counseling provide a framework for addressing Michael's issue. Ever mindful of the cultural context, and ever mindful of the fact that Michael is an adolescent and that most teenagers experience identity conflicts, the counselor should create an atmosphere for honest interaction with Michael by maintaining an open mind and not prejudging his disclosures. Any personal values expressed by the counselor concerning the value of formal education may be a hindrance in developing a working alliance with Michael. The counselor should allow Michael to tell his story in his own way and in his own time. It is important to acknowledge and support Michael's desire to affirm his tribal identity and increase his skill as a tribal artist.

The goal of counseling should be to reinforce Michael's desire for cultural validation while helping him to maximize his educational opportunities. Important questions to explore with Michael include How are his parents and grandparents responding to his wish to return to the reservation? What type of support does he have in his family, school, and local Native community? How have his parents adapted to life in the city? What will he miss if he leaves the city for the reservation? What expectations does he have about his life with his grandparents and his tribe on the reservation?

With Michael's permission, it might be helpful to invite the participation of his parents, grandparents, and tribal elders in the counseling process. It might be important to discern how his parents and grandparents are responding to his wish to return to the reservation and how they perceive the importance of his education. The counselor might consider ways of helping family members assist Michael in finding a balance between his ethnic identity and acculturation.

In addition, reaching out to Michael's Native community may faciltate his decsion making. Consulting with tribal elders about getting Michael involved with traditional cultural practices (e.g., sweat lodge, vision quest), might be useful. This could prove a valuable way to help Michael validate his ethnic identity and provide his creative talents with new outlets. The counslor might also want to have tribal elders consult with school officials about ways to alleviate the cultural discontinuity students like Michael experience in the school setting.

Conclusion

We all want to "walk the path of Good Medicine," and we can always use a little help in doing so. If counselors consider the ideas offered in this chapter, then potential cultural gaps existing between them and their Native youth clients can be bridged in the helping process. However, counselors may need to come first as students of culture, and second as professionals to the relationship with Native youth (Garrett & Garrett, 1994).

References

Dufrene, P. (1991). A comparison of the traditional education of Native American healers with the education of American art therapists. *Art Therapy, 8,* 17–24.

Dufrene, P. M., & Coleman, V. D. (1992). Counseling Native Americans: Guidelines for group process. *Journal for Specialists in Group Work, 17,* 229–235.

Dufrene, P. M., & Coleman, V. D. (1994). Art and healing for Native American Indians. *Journal of Multicultural Counseling and Development, 22,* 145–152.

Garrett, M. W. (1995). Between two worlds: Cultural discontinuity in the dropout of Native American youth. *The School Counselor, 42,* 186–195.

Garrett, M. W., & Garrett, J. T. (1993). *Full circle: A path to healing and wellness.* Unpublished manuscript. Greensboro: University of North Carolina-Greensboro.

Garrett, M. W., & Garrett, J. T. (1994). The path of good medicine: Understanding and counseling Native Americans. *Journal of Multicultural Counseling and Development 22,* 134–144.

Heinrich, R. K., Corbine, J. L., & Thomas, K. R. (1990). Counseling Native Americans. *Journal of Counseling and Development, 69*, 128–133.

Herring, R. D. (1990). Understanding Native American values: Process and content concerns for counselors. *Counseling and Values, 34*, 134–137.

Herring, R. D. (1992). Seeking a new paradigm: Counseling Native Americans. *Journal of Multicultural Counseling and Development, 20*, 35–43.

Herring, R. D. (1994a). Native American Indian identity: A people of many peoples. In E. P. Salett & D. R. Koslow (Eds.), *Race, ethnicity, and self: Identity in multicultural perspective* (pp. 170–197). Washington, DC: National Multicultural Institute.

Herring, R. D. (1994b). The clown motif as a counseling tool with Native American Indians. *Journal of Multicultural Counseling and Development, 22*, 153–164.

Herring, R. D. (1997a). *Counseling diverse ethnic youth: Synergetic strategies and intervention for school counselors.* Fort Worth, TX: Harcourt Brace.

Herring, R. D. (1997b). Synergetic counseling and Native American Indian students. *Journal of Counseling and Development, 74*, 542–547.

Herring, R. D., & Meggert, S. (1994). Humor as a counseling intervention with Native American Indian youth. *Elementary School Guidance and Counseling, 29*, 67–76.

Herring, R. D., & Walker, S. S. (1993). Synergetic counseling: Toward a more holistic model with a cross-cultural specific approach. *Texas Counseling Association Journal, 22*, 38–53.

Iron Eye Dudley, J. (1992). *Choteau: A Sioux reminiscence.* Lincoln: University of Nebraska.

LaFromboise, T. D. (1988). American Indian mental health policy. *American Psychologist, 43*, 388–97.

LaFromboise, T. D., Trimble, J. E., & Mohatt, G. V. (1990). Counseling intervention and American Indian tradition: An integrative approach. *The Counseling Psychologist, 18*, 628–654.

Little Soldier, L. (1985). To soar with the eagles: Enculturation and acculturation of Indian children. *Childhood Education, 12*, 185–191.

Ortiz, S. (1993). The language we know. In P. Riley (Ed.), *Growing up Native American: An anthology* (pp. 29–38). New York: William Morrow.

Peregoy, J. J. (1993). Transcultural counseling with American Indians and Alaskan Natives. In J. McFadden (Ed.), *Transcultural counseling* (pp. 163–192). Alexandria, VA: American Counseling Association.

Plank, G. A. (1994). What silence means for educators of American Indian children. *Journal of American Indian Education, 34*(1), 3–19.

Sodowsky, G. R., & Johnson, P. (1994). Worldviews: Culturally learned assumptions and values. In P. Pedersen & J. C. Carey (Eds.), *Multicultural counseling in schools: A practical handbook* (pp. 59–80). Needham Heights, MA: Allyn & Bacon.

Thomason, T. C. (1991). Counseling Native Americans: An introduction for non-Native American counselors. *Journal of Counseling and Development, 69*, 321–327.

U.S. Bureau of the Census. (1990). *The 1990 census of population and housing.* Washington, DC: U. S. Government Printing Office.

Weider, D., & Pratt, C. (1990). On being a recognizable Indian among Indians. In D. Carbaugh (Ed.), *Cultural communication and intercultural contact* (pp. 45–64). Hillsdale, NJ: Lawrence Erlbaum.

Weinbach, R. W., & Kuehner, K. M. (1985). Selecting the provider of continuing education for child welfare agencies. *Child Welfare, 64*, 477–488.

Wilson, T. P. (1992). Blood quantum: Native American mixed bloods. In M. P. Root (Ed.), *Racially mixed people in America* (pp. 108–125). Newbury Park, CA: Sage.

Zitzow, D., & Estes, G. (1981). The heritage consistency continuum in counseling with Native American students. *Proceedings From the Contemporary American Issues, 3*, 133–142. Los Angeles: University of California-Los Angeles Publication Services.

Additional Resources

Literature

Contemporary Native Life

Bruchac, J. (1993). *Dawn land.* Golden, CA: Fulcrum. This saga illuminates the centuries-old value system of the Abenaki.

Ekoomiak, N. (1990). *Artic memories.* New York: Holt Winston & Rinehart. A picture book of an Inuit childhood in Quebec depicts a lifestyle that is almost extinct. Text in Inuktitut and English.

George, J. C. (1987). *Water sky.* San Francisco: Harper. Lincoln goes from Boston to stay with an Eskimo family and learn what happened to his uncle, who tried to stop the whaling there.

Hirschi, R. (1992). *Seya's song.* Vancouver, Canada: Sasquatch Books. A S'Klallam grandmother and grandfather pass on their language and stories to a young girl.

Kendall, R. (1992). *Eskimo boy: Life in an Inupiaq village.* New York: Scholastic Books. Norman is a 7-year-old Inuit who is learning about his heritage and the modern world.

Markle, S. (1992). *The fledglings.* New York: Bantam. Fourteen-year-old Kate and her Cherokee grandfather fight to save eagles from poachers in the mountains of North Carolina.

Ness, T. V. S. (1993). *The gift of Changing Woman.* New York: Holt Winston & Rinehart. An Apache girl experiences a ceremony to teach her the story of creation and her place in the world.

Paulsen, G. (1978). *The night the white deer died.* New York: Delacorte Press. A 15-year-old European American girl learns about prejudice from an old Pueblo Indian.

Thompson, P. (1993). *Song of the wild violets.* Chicago: Book Publishing. Life on a Chippewa reservation is hard in the 1940s, but violets help a young girl rekindle her parents' pride in their heritage.

Wood, T. (with W. N. Afraid of Hawk). (1992). *A boy becomes a man at Wounded Knee.* Photographs convey the story of 8-year-old Wanbi, who joins his family for a 5-day trek commemorating the massacre of the Lakotas 100 years ago. Cheyenne, WY: Walker.

Native Folklore (excellent sources for storytelling)

Begay, S. (1992). *Ma'ii and Cousin Horned Toad.* New York: Scholastic Books. Navajo teaching tale includes text in Navajo. Coyote is hungry but is too lazy to get his own food.

Belting, N. (1992). *Moon was tired of walking on air.* Boston: Houghton Mifflin. Creation myths from Native groups in South America.

Caduto, M., & Bruchac, J. (1992). *Keepers of the animals: Native American stories and wildlife activities for children.* Golden, CA: Orchard Books. A teacher's guide to reading Abenaki stories (also on audiocassette).

Goble, P. (1992). *Crow chief.* Golden, CA: Orchard Books. A combination of several Plains Indian tales explains why crows are black.

Goble, P. (1993). *The girl who loved wild horses.* Golden, CA: Aladdin Books. A girl loves taking care of her tribe's horses so much that she decides to become one herself in order to run free.

Hillerman, T. (1986). *The boy who made dragonfly.* Albuquerque: University of New Mexico Press. Retelling of a Zuni myth about how a young boy and his sister gain the wisdom to become the leaders of their people.

Hinton, L. (Trans.). (1992). *Ishi's tale of lizard.* New York: Farrar Straus Giroux. Translation of a Yahi tale. Ishi, the sole survivor of the Yahi people, emerged from hiding in 1911.

London, J., & Pinola, L. (1993). *Fire race.* New York: Chronicle Books. The tale of what happens when Coyote steals fire from yellow jackets.
McDermott, G. (1993). *A trickster tale from the Pacific Northwest.* Fort Worth, TX: Harcourt Brace Jovanovich. How the raven steals the sun from the Sky Chief so that the people can have light.

Native Poetry

Bruchac, J. (Ed.). (1989). *New voices from the longhouse: An anthology of contemporary Iroquois writing.* New York: Greenfield Review Press.
Bruchac, J., & London, J. (1992). *Thirteen moons on Turtle's back: A Native American year of the moon.* New York: Philomel.
Hirschfelder, A., & Singer, B. (Eds.). (1992). *Rising voices: Writings of young Native Americans.* New York: Scribner.
Jones, H. (1993). *The trees stand shining: Poetry of the North American Indians.* New York: Dial Books.

General

Ballantine, B., & Ballantine, I. (Eds.). (1993). *America's fascinating Indian heritage.* Pleasantville, NY: Reader's Digest Association.
Cahape, P., & Howley, C. B. (1992). *Indian nations at risk: Listening to the people.* Charleston, WV: Appalachia Educational Laboratory. (ERIC Clearinghouse on Rural Education & Small Schools)
Callahan, C. M., & McIntire, J. A. (1994). *Identifying outstanding talent in American Indian and Alaska Native students.* Washington, DC: Office of Educational Research and Improvement.
Journal of American Indian Education. College of Education, Arizona State University, Tempe, AZ 85281.
Stoutenburgh, J., Jr. (1990). *Dictionary of the American Indian: An A-to-Z guide to Indian history, legend, and lore.* New York: Wings Books.
Unlearning "Indian" stereotypes (Stereotypes in U.S. History Books). CIBS Resource Center, 1841 Broadway, Rm. 300, New York, NY 10023.
U.S. Office of Technology Assessment. (1990, January). *Indian adolescent mental health* (OTA-H-446). Washington, DC: U.S. Government Printing Office.
Woodhead, H. (Ed.) (1994). *The American Indians* (Vols. 1–16). Richmond, VA: Time-Life. (Time-Life Education, P.O. Box 85026, Richmond, VA 23285).

Films and Videos

1. The following may be purchased or rented from Insight Media, 2162 Broadway, New York, NY 10024; (212) 721-6316, fax (212) 799-5309, 800-233-9910:

More than Bows and Arrows (1992, 60 min.)
The American Indian collection (1990; Sioux, Apache, Navajo; 5 vols., 60 min. each)
Indians of North America (1993, 5 vols., 30 min. each)
Live and remember (1986) (Dakota Sioux, 29 min.)
Native American cultures (1992, 2 vols., 60 min. each)
The faith keeper (1991, Turtle Clan of Onondaga Nation, 58 min.)
Inughuit (1985, 85 min.)
The eternal drum (1994, 25 min.)
Emergence (1981, Navajo, 14 min.)
Native American history (1993, Columbian & North America, 2 vols., 50 min. each)
Cede, yield, and surrender (1991, 25 min.)
How the West was lost (1993; Navajo, Nez Perce, Apache, Cheyenne, Lakota; 6 segments, 50 min. each)
Columbus didn't discover us (1992, 24 min.)
Surviving Columbus (1990, Pueblo, 60 min).

2. Other media resources include:
Racial and sexual stereotyping (28 min., Films for the Humanities & Sciences, P.O. Box 2053, Princeton, NJ 08543-2053, 800-257-5126, fax 609-275-3767)
An eagle must fly (BYU, 1226 Spring Street, NW, Provo, Utah 84560)
Differences (Windwalker Cinema Associates, Inc)
Sacred ground (P.O. Box 9232, Swank Motion Pictures, Seattle, WA 98109)
Good to be Indian: Proud and free (Robeson County Title IV Indian Education Project, Box 1328, Lumberton, NC 28358)
Land of the eagle (1991, 8 vols., Time-Life Video, 777 Duke St., Alexandria, VA 22314)

Shenandoah Film Productions, 538 G St., Arcata, CA 95521 (Native American owned)
Canyon Records, 4143 N. 16th St., Phoenix, AZ 85016
Indian House, Box 472, Taos, NM 87571.

The African American Experience

Counseling interventions with African Americans should be predicated on an understanding of their culture and its crucial role in fostering optimal mental health and psychosocial development. An examination of this culture reveals that Americans of African descent have developed a worldview that is grounded in African-oriented philosophical assumptions.

Professional counselors need to find ways to incorporate African/African American cultural dimensions into the helping process. Likewise, within African American communities, institutions that provide a network of indigenous social support, such as the Black church, may need to be incorporated into the counseling process.

Within the social sciences literature, the African American experience has traditionally been viewed as a monolithic entity. It is important for counselors to remember that there are many aspects and facets to this cultural experience.

5

A CULTURAL FRAMEWORK FOR COUNSELING AFRICAN AMERICANS

C. Emmanuel Ahia

C ounseling African Americans presents counselors with an opportunity to become more aware of the cultural issues that form a basic worldview for this client group. Although these issues impact upon each African American differently, they underlie African American psychosocial development and are important in establishing a cultural context for counseling interactions. This chapter provides a cultural framework for counseling African American clients through an overview of the concept of Afrocentricity and explorations of its relationship to African American mental health and its implications for counseling African Americans.

Afrocentricity: A Theoretical Overview

Any contemporary discussion of counseling African Americans must begin with an examination of Afrocentricity. Afrocentricity is an existential point of view that puts Africa at the center of one's cosmology (Asante, 1992). The central theme of Afrocentrism is the idea that people of African descent must acknowledge, understand, and love their "Africaness" in order to understand and deal effectively with the past, present, and future. Afrocentricity reframes many psychoeducational concepts, often considered deviant or pathological in a Eurocentric context, into positive developmental notions for people of African descent.

Afrocentric scholars are in general agreement that there exists a composite of African-oriented existential tendencies, philosophies, behaviors, ideas, and artifacts among people worldwide who trace their roots to Black Africa (Asante, 1991, 1992; Asante & Asante, 1993; DuBois, 1969; Muntu, 1961; Williams, 1974). The fact that these African universals are theorized to exist suggests that mental health and psychosocial development among people of African descent is related to the degree and nature of their awareness of and responsiveness to Afrocentricity (Akbar, 1979; Baldwin, 1981; Belgrave et al., 1994; Brookins, 1994; Nobles, 1986; Nobles & Goddard, 1992).

As a psychological resource, Afrocentricity represents—to use Jung's (1958) term—the *collective unconscious* among African peoples. This collective unconscious is made up of African folklore, mythology, and historical, social, and political events.

Afrocentricity is evident in a number African-oriented traditions and customs. These include such concepts as perception of reality, concept of time, spirituality, human relations, family membership, and holism. In traditional African societies, these concepts are significant representations of a collective African cultural ethos. The work of Mbiti (1970) on African religion and philosophical traditions has offered perhaps the best explanation of these concepts.

Perception of reality.   The traditional African-oriented perception of reality can be described as field-dependent or field-sensitive. This pattern of conceptualizing and processing reality tends to take into consideration the interactions between and among objective and subjective realities as well as the consequences or implications of such interactions. Among the Ibos of eastern Nigeria, for example, a common way to test the manner in which a child perceives reality is with the "birds on a tree" quiz. The child is told that 100 birds are on a tree when a hunter shoots one of them. The child is then asked, "How many birds are left on the tree?" In Western thinking, the obvious answer is 99. However, for an Ibo child the correct answer is always zero because the child is expected to factor in all other realities, not just the numerical. In this case, the greater reality of the birds' natural behavior is to fly away when one of them is shot.

Concepts of time. The African concept of time embodies a people-oriented or event-oriented utility. Time is fluid and gets it meaning and importance from the essence of people and events. Social events, as opposed to fixed calendars or mechanical devices, control responses to time.

Most traditional African cultures are concerned with two dimensions of time, the past and the present. The concept of the future is considered *no time*. Individuals can only reflect on what has been and what is. What will be is generally out of the realm of consideration.

Spirituality. In traditional African societies, religion/spirituality permeates human existence. An individual's entire life is a spiritual phenomenon. Spirituality is an integral part of a unity principle in which humans, animals, plants, and natural phenomenon are interrelated in a natural order with God being the driving force.

A strong belief in a spirit world pervades traditional African worldviews. Spirits belong to the ontological realm of existence between human beings and God. Africans generally recognize two categories of spiritual beings: those created as spirits and those who were once human beings. Human fate is controlled by the spirit world.

Human relations. The African-oriented view of human nature is characterized by cooperative interdependence and group centeredness in human relationships. Every human life is deemed to be existentially relevant to the functioning, well-being, and dynamics of a community.

Achieving adult status has considerable social implications because African societies are adult oriented rather than youth oriented. Age and maturity affect leadership selection, social interaction, respect, responsibility, and cultural education. A younger person is expected to respect older persons unconditionally. Advanced age, in and of itself, is deemed respectable and honorable. Young people who show disrespect for their elders encounter different forms and degrees of social sanctions and isolation.

Family membership. The traditional African family is extended in nature. For example, individuals with strong African identity tend to take obligatorily financial responsibility for even distant relatives. Most African languages do not have words for cousin, nephew, second cousin, niece, uncle, aunt. In many cases, these family relations are described simply as *brother* or *sister.* This is done not merely for simplicity but reflects the true African-oriented family structure and close sense of family belongingness.

Holism. Generally traditional Africans make little distinction between body, mind, and spirit. Africans perceive a strong interconnectedness among the cognitive, affective, and behavioral realms of personality. The traditional African personality responds to external stimuli in a holistic fashion. In social gatherings, for example, Africans are more like to participate rather than merely spectate. A traditional African is more likely than not to become cognitively, affectively, and behaviorally expressive to music or other affective stimuli.

It is important to note that given the vast cultural and ethnic group differences among African people, these concepts may be manifested in a variety of ways. There are significant geographic, language, religious, ethnic, and historical variations in the manifestation of these concepts throughout Black Africa.

Afrocentricity and the Mental Health of African Americans

African American scholars have concluded that there are aspects of the African American cultural experience that have evolved out of African realities and that have a significant relationship with psychosocial development and mental health (Cross, 1974; Guthrie, 1980; Nobles, 1991; Pasteur & Toldson, 1982; White & Parham, 1990). These conclusions have led to the development of an Afrocentric conceptual framework for understanding African American psychosocial development.

An examination of traditional African American culture, in which rudimentary Afrocentric ways of life have been preserved in relatively large measure, reveals that Americans of African descent have developed a worldview grounded in many of the African-oriented philosophical concepts just described. These concepts constitute a cultural tradition that places a high premium on harmony among people and their internal and external environments, fosters self- and group development through behavioral expressiveness, and recognizes the need for holistic development (Nobles, 1991).

Nobles (1991) has identified kinship or collective unity as an important foundation for African American psychological and social development. In spite of all the challenges to its integrity, for example, the family is the bedrock of African American psychosocial well-being (Billingsley, 1992; Hill, 1972; McAdoo, 1988).

In addition to the family, the African American cultural experience offers other institutions that provide a network of psychosocial support. The Black church, for example, has been a historical bastion of group solidarity. It is an institution that has traditionally been devoted to nurturing both spirituality and Black consciousness.

Spirituality is a hallmark of African American life and culture and has been identified by Pasteur and Toldson (1982) as *Black expressiveness*—a phenomenon representing a healthy fusion of the cognitive, affective, and behavioral aspects of personality characteristic of Afrocentricity. This expressiveness is generally characterized by a high degree of affective energy exhibited in interpersonal interactions and behavior among African Americans.

Implications of Afrocentricity for Counseling With African Americans

African American scholars have suggested that the counseling profession seek new directions in its efforts to help African American clients empower themselves. These new directions should include modalities that incorporate Afrocentric elements to promote psychosocial development (Belgrave et al., 1994; Lee & Lindsey, 1985; Pasteur & Toldson, 1982), and counselors should consider the African American family and community as major therapeutic resources.

Counseling should be considered within the context of the family unit in promoting African American psychosocial development. Whenever possible, counseling services should be offered in a supportive family group format in which members can draw on each others' strengths for problem resolution or decision making. Further, family intervention must provide for the inclusion of significant others and the inherent strength of kinship social support processes, where appropriate, as an integral part of counseling.

The African American community offers other institutions, in addition to the family, that can provide resources such as a network of social support that can be incorporated into the counseling process. The oldest and perhaps most important of the indigenous community support systems is the Black church. Counseling approaches should incorporate aspects of the multifaceted African American religious/spiritual experience as appropriate and effective.

Within the context of indigenous family and community support systems available to African Americans for help with problem resolution or decision making, counselors should also find ways to promote Black expressiveness. This holistic concept is often the key to optimal mental health and should form the basis of many counseling modalities for African American clients.

Conclusion

As the African American experience moves into the 21st century, a new perspective on counseling with African Americans is needed. Counseling must be conducted with the knowledge that African American culture fosters attitudes, behaviors, and values that are psychologically healthy and that within African American culture are the resources for addressing mental health challenges and problems. Counseling interventions, therefore, should be undertaken from an Afrocentric perspective that focuses on promoting optimal mental health and well-being. Counselors should strive to promote African American development within an Afrocentric context of kinship, behavioral and emotional expressiveness, and holistic development.

There is an old saying, "You can take the Black man out of Africa, but you can not take Africa out of the Black man." To varying degrees African Americans possess attitudes, values, and behaviors that are characteristic of their African heritage. The essence of Afrocentricity suggests that this may provide an important key to culturally responsive counseling with African Americans.

References

Akbar, N. (1979). African roots of Black personality. In W. D. Smith, K. Burlew, M. Mosley, & W. Whitney (Eds.), *Reflections on Black psychology*. Washington, DC: University of America Press.

Asante M. K., & Asante, K. W. (1993). *African culture: The rhythms of unity*. Trenton, NJ: African World Press.

Asante M. K. (1991). Multiculturalism: An exchange. *The American Scholar, 60*, 267–272.

Asante, M. K. (1992). *Kemet, Afrocentricity, and knowledge*. Trenton, NJ: African World Press.

Baldwin, J. A. (1981). Notes on an Afrocentric theory of Black personality testing. *Western Journal of Black Studies, 5*, 172–179.

Belgrave, F. Z., Cherry, V. R., Cunningham, D., Walwyn, S., Letlaka-Rennert, K., & Philips, F. (1994). The influence of Afrocentric values, self-esteem, and Black identity on drug attitudes among African American fifth graders. *Journal of Black Psychology. 20*, 143–156.

Billingsley, A. (1992). *Climbing Jacob's ladder: The enduring legacy of African American families*. New York: Simon & Schuster.

Brookins, C. C. (1994). The relationship between Afrocentric values and racial identity attitudes: Validation of the belief systems analysis scale on African American college students. *Journal of Black Psychology, 2*, 128–142.

Cross, A. (1974). The Black experience: Its importance in the treatment of Black clients. *Child Welfare, 52*, 158–166.

DuBois, W. E. B. (1969). *The suppression of the African slave trade*. New York: Schocken Books.

Guthrie, R. V. (1980). The psychology of Black Americans: A historical perspective. In R. L. Jones (Ed.), *Black psychology* (2nd ed.). New York: Harper & Row.

Hill, R. (1972). *The strengths of Black families*. New York: Emerson-Hall.

Jung, C. (1958). *The archtypes and the collective unconscious*. In G. Adler, M. Fordham, & H. Reed (Eds.), *Collected works* (Vol. 9, Pt. 1, Bollingen Series XX). New York: Pantheon Books.

Lee, C. C., & Lindsey, C. R. (1985). Black consciousness development: A group counseling model for Black elementary school students. *Elementary School Guidance and Counseling, 19*, 228–236.

Mbiti, J. S. (1970). *African religions and philosophy*. Garden City, NY: Doubleday.

McAdoo, H. P. (Ed.). (1988). *Black families*. Newbury Park, CA: Sage.

Muntu, J. J. (1961). *The new African culture*. New York: Grove Press.

Nobles, W. W. (1986). *African psychology: Toward its reclamation, reascension, and revitalization.* Oakland, CA: Black Family Institute.

Nobles, W. W. (1991). African philosophy: Foundations of Black psychology. In R. L. Jones (Ed.), *Black psychology* (3rd ed., pp. 47–63). Berkeley, CA: Cobb & Henry.

Nobles, W. W., & Goddard, L. L. (1992). *An African-centered model of prevention for African-American youth at high risk* (DHHS Publication No. ADM 92-1925:87-92). Washington, DC: U.S. Government Printing Office.

Pasteur, A. B., & Toldson, I. L. (1982). *Roots of soul: The psychology of Black expressiveness.* Garden City, NY: Anchor Press/Doubleday.

White, J. L., & Parham, T. A. (1990). *The psychology of Blacks: An African American perspective.* Englewood Cliffs, NJ: Prentice Hall.

Williams, C. (1974). *The destruction of Black civilization.* Chicago: Third World Press.

6

COUNSELING MIDDLE-CLASS AFRICAN AMERICANS

Donna Y. Ford

National reports highlight a crippling loss of faith and hope among African Americans,[1] most often those in poverty. These reports, supported by research, reveal that some African Americans are losing or have lost faith in the American dream. Excessive poverty, unemployment, underemployment, and poor school achievement have become a reality for far too many people of color.

Much of what we know or presume to know about African Americans is based on groups characterized by poor achievement and low socioeconomic status (SES). That is, seldom are successful or middle-class African Americans the focus of research and practice. Subsequently, counselors and other helping professionals are left with impressionistic data and speculations on the perceptions, values, experiences, and struggles of an important segment of the Black population. This heavy focus on poor achievement or lower SES minorities and the minimal research on middle-class Blacks raise serious questions about the generalizability of the findings and conclusions. It also paints a profile of homogeneity that ignores the unique issues facing African Americans of middle-class status.

Middle-class African Americans, like Blacks on all rungs of the socioeconomic ladder, face problems associated with race. However, the quality and quantity, the nature and extent, of the problems can be markedly different. There is a need to fill the void in our awareness and understanding of the various factors that contribute to socioemotional and psychological concerns among middle-class Black children and adults. An underlying premise of

---

1. The terms *Black* and *African American* are used interchangeably in this chapter.

this chapter is that middle-class status does not inoculate African Americans from the harsh realities of race in American society. The chapter describes the emergence of middle-class status, addresses more than a dozen factors affecting the socioemotional and psychological well-being of middle-class Blacks in particular, discusses potential barriers to counseling middle-class African Americans, provides a case study, and suggests counseling interventions to improve the mental health of successful Black children and adults.

The Emergence of Middle-Class Status Among African Americans

During slavery, approximately 10% of Blacks had free status and were less oppressed and less stigmatized than other Blacks. Historically, opportunities for higher status and opportunity were linked to similarities to Whites in appearance, education, occupation, or lifestyle. In the 18th and 19th centuries, gradual improvements in opportunities for Blacks were accelerated by a series of historical events. For instance, movement from the South to the North, and from rural to urban settings, resulted in increased interactions between Black and White Americans as well as increased opportunities. The emergence of middle-class Blacks is a recent occurrence, owing much to the civil rights movement of the 1950s and 1960s (Pinderhughes, 1988). Traditionally, respectability and religiosity were stronger predictors or indicators of middle-class status than education and occupation. During the latter quarter of the 20th century, a discernible middle-class stratum of Blacks with levels of income and education roughly comparable to that of Whites existed. A wave of Blacks entered educational, occupational, political, and social arenas from which they had been excluded. According to Pinderhughes, doors that opened for previously excluded Blacks became the doors through which all minority groups competitively squeezed. Following the civil rights movement, Black students in colleges and universities increased 30- to 40-fold. The number of Black mayors increased from 2 to more than 200. Black homeowners, professionals, government employees, and others of high income status also increased (Pinderhughes, 1988).

The middle class is that group of propertyless workers occupying the more highly rewarded white-collar or nonmanual positions in the economy, such as professors, teachers, small business owners, and administrators. Education, type of occupation and income as well as neighborhood and family background have been factors used to draw status distinctions within the Black community (Landry, 1980). Income is perhaps the most important economic resource of members of the middle class, primarily because it determines the quantity and quality of goods and services that can be consumed. Several reports have highlighted the closing gap in income between Blacks and Whites. The pictures painted, although often optimistic, are based on incomplete data. Income, an important factor in the middle-class equation, does not translate into wealth. That is, whereas income is by far the most immediate and most important source of an individual family's standard of living, it is not the same as wealth. The term *wealth* is often associated with liquid assets, including savings accounts, shares, government bonds, stocks, and property. It is in these areas that Blacks seem to differ dramatically from Whites. Specifically, Landry (1980) reported that fewer than one in three Blacks, compared to 60% of Whites, report ownership in terms of wealth. Thus home ownership, even among middle-class Blacks, is often a dream rather than a reality. Further, middle-class Blacks tend not to own homes and instead often reside in lower market value homes, often in restricted and/or segregated areas. Thus even though there exists a middle-class Black population with achievements that seem impressive, particularly relative to that of other Blacks, the population is far from being the economic equal of its White counterpart—a condition that should temper considerably our enthusiasm over its emergence (Landry, 1980).

Wilson (1978), in *The Declining Significance of Race*, maintained that the higher the educational achievement, the less race determines economic placement and chances for mobility. Wilson argued that class advantage mitigates racial restrictions and barriers, and that the absence of stresses generated by poverty and poor educational opportunities makes for immunity to mental illnesses in the middle class. However, the social honor and prestige of middle-class status may differ in significant ways between Blacks and Whites, and the attainment of middle-class status may carry a designation of betrayal among those locked into racial oppression. Ransford (1977) denied the existence of an open market of race relations and the suggestions that racial ascription can be offset by socioeconomic achievement and that rewards are based on performance rather than race or skin color. He argued instead that Blacks have difficulty in cashing in on all power and status fronts, and that even with comparable levels of education and training, Blacks and Whites experience power and wealth differentials. The result is that middle-class Blacks may be highly represented among the working poor, or be one generation removed from the poor but metamorphosed by reason of being upwardly mobile.

Much diversity is found among Black middle-class individuals and families: lower middle class, upper middle class, and elite middle class. Each group fosters different lifestyles, employment opportunities, work activities, and types of material acquisition. Notwithstanding these differences, Coner-Edwards and Edwards (1988) have identified core characteristics of all groups:

- **The implicit or explicit embracing of the predominant culture.** Under close or closer scrutiny, middle-class Blacks are not as detached, defiant, or exclusive of the predominant society. They often adopt or embrace values and activities commonly associated with the dominant culture.
- **A belief in the work ethic or achievement ideology.** Middle-class Blacks believe that hard work and effort increase their chances for having the advantages afforded by society; that they must work hard to achieve success, and be willing to work even harder to maintain it; and that they have emerged through the window of opportunity because of their own efforts.
- **A strong sense of self and empowerment.** Having achieved upward mobility and otherwise proved themselves, middle-class Blacks demonstrate increased pride, self-esteem, and empowerment, and they see themselves as having what it takes to make it. Thus their racial minority status takes a relative rather than pervasive position in their lives.
- **A sense of the importance of the fact of their blackness.** Middle-class Blacks embrace their heritage and show a strong sense of pride in themselves, which can be partly attributed to attaining comparable and higher positions than other minority groups.

- **Quality of life pursuits.** Middle-class Blacks are involved in activities that are directed toward self-actualization and improving their quality of life.

Factors Affecting the Mental Health of Middle-Class African Americans

Counselors and other helping professionals must acknowledge the core characteristics and strengths of middle-class Blacks and at the same time understand the factors affecting and issues accompanying success or middle-class status for this population. Success can be a double-edged sword for middle-class Blacks, and there is often a psychological and socioemotional price to be paid for success. For many Blacks, the emergence into the middle class can be both an external struggle against tremendous societal oppression and an internal psychological conflict. However, emergence can also be viewed as a growth process, within which goals need to be set and worked toward (Coner-Edwards & Edwards, 1988, p. 8).

Factors that represent social sources of stress and place a socioemotional and psychological price of success for African American children and adults include limited access and glass ceilings, double standards, exclusion and isolation, powerlessness, voicelessness and invisibility, token status, second guessing, pigeonholing, and guilt by association. Factors indicative of the socioemotional and psychological price of success include identity conflict issues, allegiance issues, survival guilt issues, and achievement ideology issues.

Limited Access and Glass Ceilings

Even with high levels of education and income, many Blacks find that certain doors are still closed to them. Despite laws against housing and employment discrimination, for example, many home owners and businesses still find ways to prevent integration. An African American physician seeking residence in a racially segregated community may find that "the house has just been purchased." A Black professor may find that "the apartment was rented yesterday" or "is no longer available." In educational settings, discrimination takes on a different form. Black students, for example, have less access to academically rigorous programs, such as gifted education, advanced placement, and honors courses, are severely overrepresented in special education classes, low ability groups, and vocational tracks (Ford, 1996; Harris & Ford, 1991).

As adults, Blacks seldom reach their full potential, due in large part to glass ceilings. According to Cose (1993), the number of African Americans earning high incomes has risen in the last decade, but only a handful have climbed near the top of the corporate structure. Compared to their White counterparts, African Americans are less likely to be promoted, be the chief executive officer or administrator, or receive salaries commensurate with training and experience. Thus they are both underemployed and underpaid.

Such glass ceilings in schools and workplaces not only limit the potential of Black children and adults but also contribute to anger, frustration, resentment, and boredom. These glass ceilings limit access and reinforce the reality that many middle-class Blacks are victimized by the "great social injustice of differential reward" (Washington, 1980, p. iii) or discrepancies in mobility.

Double Standards

Successful Blacks may complain of having to expend more time and energy to arrive at the same position as their White counterparts, of working "twice as hard to get half as far." Or, as one academically successful Black male reported, "If you want to be successful, you have to work twice as hard as White people" (Ford, 1995). These double standards relative to energy expenditure place additional pressures upon Blacks, resulting in burnout, apathy, and hopelessness.

Exclusion and Isolation

Blacks who have moved up the socioeconomic ladder often find it lonely at the top. Many African Americans discover that the racial demons that have plagued them all their lives do not recognize business hours (Cose, 1993, p. 55). Thus even if Blacks succeed in cracking or jarring closed doors, they risk rejection and isolation from their White counterparts. For example, Black students in predominantly White schools may have great difficulty finding a close friend or company for lunch, getting a date or an invitation to social events, and they may feel uneasy at such events if invited. These feelings of alienation may leave African American students with the perception that they have few options except to avoid classes and social events where they are the only or one of few minorities. If honors courses, debate teams, and school organizations are, for example, predominantly White, Black students are less likely to seek admission. Because these decisions limit the future potential of Black students, they have unfortunate long-term implications.

Powerlessness

Middle-class Blacks may find that success is more evident in their title than in their actual power. A Black vice president of a company or a Black school administrator may find him- or herself relegated to tasks pertaining to minorities, with only restricted or focused authority. Some African Americans may find that their supervisors are reluctant to release control, and as a result, the breadth of their responsibilities is reduced. Others find that they were never intended to have real decision-making authority but were hired or promoted to serve as window dressing. Further, middle-class Blacks may find that the political pressures are so great that they retard the development of equitable and credible initiatives, and the middle-class Blacks find themselves perpetuating the status quo. The result of such limitations is that their power is only a facade. Feelings of anger, frustration, discouragement, and hurt may result.

Voicelessness and Invisibility

When African Americans are few in numbers, they have a limited voice. Although they may express concerns related to injustices on the job or in school, their concerns may be ignored or given lowered priority. In other instances, the limited presence of African Americans renders them invisible and easy to ignore.

Token Status

Middle-class Blacks, because they are few in number, may be perceived as a "credit" to their race, as "truly exceptional" persons able to make it despite social injustices. Blacks are often expected to be the expert on all issues related to Blacks and other minorities when they are the only or one of few Blacks in a particular setting. This expectation of having to know it all places a heavy burden on the shoulders of African Americans and increases their level of stress or overload. There may also be discomfort when Blacks realize that they actually know little about their racial and cultural heritage. As a student commented, "Every time we talk about Blacks in school, which is rare, I am expected to know everything. This is the only time my classmates and teachers try to learn something from me. I don't have all of the answers. Who could?"

Similarly, Black professors at institutions of higher education may be expected to teach multicultural classes, even if this is not their area of expertise. They are also expected to mentor all or most minority students, and they are asked to serve on numerous committees, which gives the committees an image of diversity. These multiples roles and expectations contribute to burnout and overload among middle-class Black professionals and students.

Second Guessing

An additional stress for middle-class African Americans is the constant scrutiny to which they are subjected, the constant questioning of their competence and their motives underlying decisions, and the minimizing of the quality of their work and efforts. Questions of competence come in many guises, from full-scale attacks to subtle comments. For example, White supervisors, administrators, or colleagues may express surprise when the Black employee or student does well—but not when he or she fails. Second guessing, whether direct or indirect, blatant or subtle, serves to build a superior-inferior hierarchy, with Blacks at the bottom.

Middle-class Blacks may also be distressed by the accusation that their decisions are driven by motives based on racial considerations, such as overidentification with Blacks and a lack of concern for others. Thus Blacks are presumed to be dishonorable, unfair, and self-seeking regardless of their efforts to provide detailed explanations for the basis of their decisions. Anger, resentment, and frustration are only a few possible responses middle-class African Americans may have to these painful tactics.

Pigeonholing

Blacks may be pigeonholed in certain positions. For example, they may be hired as vice presidents, but the position is in minority affairs, a Black community, or a poverty-stricken area. These positions have a narrow focus, have limited power, and are accompanied by issues that are complex and difficult to resolve. Similarly, when designated as gifted, Black students are often identified as gifted in creativity, leadership, and visual and performing arts rather than as gifted intellectually and academically (Ford, 1995). The implicit message is that Blacks can sing and dance, for example, but do not need to—or cannot—succeed in academically rigorous course work. Not surprisingly, students become bored in school, and angry and resentful at the messages that undermine their competence.

Guilty by Association

Middle-class Black students and adults may be stereotyped by White Americans when they are seen as members of a group rather than as individuals. The stereotypes and fears associated with Blacks in general are attributed also to middle-class Blacks. Black males often complain of being stopped by police officers or followed in stores without cause. In essence, middle-class Blacks are presumed to be guilty because they are Black.

Identity Conflict Issues

Smith (1989) maintained that racial identity development is a process of coming to terms with racial group membership as a salient reference group. Rotheram and Phinney (1987) defined *self-identification* as the accurate and consistent use of an ethnic label based on the perception and conception of belonging to an ethnic group.

Race affects socioemotional and psychological health in significant ways because the complexity of identity development increases as a function of color and physical features. The issue of race may be more salient for Blacks than any other group. For instance, White Americans are much less likely to experience the chronic stress and problems associated with racial identity because the color of their skin is not a barrier to success.

In his revised model of racial identity or the psychology of nigrescence, Cross (1995) described more completely how African Americans progress and regress in the process of becoming Afrocentric. According to the model, Blacks in Stage I—Pre-Encounter hold one of at least three attitudes toward race: low salience, social stigma, and anti-Black. Those holding a low-salience attitude do not deny being physically Black, but they consider their blackness as having an insignificant role in their daily lives, their well-being, or how they define themselves. Cross contended that these individuals are unlikely to give much thought to race issues and appear unaware of such problems. Overall, they view themselves as "human beings who just happen to be Black" (p. 98). African Americans who hold social stigma attitudes not only have low-salience attitudes, but they also see their racial orientation as something to be ashamed of and negotiated. By default, race is attributed some significance, but not in the positive sense. Anti-Black attitudes constitute the third and most extreme type of pre-encounter individual. Such persons see their racial status as negative, loathe other Blacks, feel alienated from other Blacks, and do not perceive the Black community as a potential resource or support base.

All three pre-encounter types favor European cultural perspectives on, for example, beauty, art, communication modes, and academic preferences. In essence, many in Stage 1 have been socialized to be bicultural, but they do not necessarily hold pluralistic and multicultural notions. Some, for instance, may consider multicultural education to be unnecessary, wasteful, or inferior (Cross, 1995, p. 103). Relative to SES, Cross contended that pre-encounter attitudes transcend social class boundaries, with low-salience, social stigma, and anti-Black attitudes being expressed at all economic levels.

In Stage 2—Encounter, individuals experience an "identity metamorphosis" (Cross, 1995, p. 104) in which a major event or series of events induces cognitive dissonance. These events, either positive or negative, tear away at pre-encounter attitudes and push individuals toward increased awareness of their status as a racial being. The encounter, therefore, results in great emotionality, guilt, anger, and anxiety for having minimized or denied the significance of race. Similarly, individuals in Stage 2 feel anxious upon realizing that there is another level of blackness to which they should aspire.

Stage 3—Immersion-Emersion represents what Cross (1995) referred to as the "vortex of psychological nigrescence" (p. 106). African Americans in this stage begin to rid themselves of their raceless identities and begin constructing their new frame of reference. Yet this stage is also characterized by anxiety, primarily about becoming the "right kind of Black person" (p. 106). Equally problematic, all that is White is perceived as evil, oppressive, and inhuman while all that is Black is proclaimed superior.

In the immersion phase of Stage 3, African Americans immerse themselves in the world of blackness. For example, they attend political or cultural meetings that focus on Black issues, along with issues of justice and equity. Cross described this stage as being energized by rage, guilt, and a developing sense of pride. Individuals accept themselves as racial beings. Common themes are selflessness, dedication, and commitment to Blacks. Individuals may experience creative, inspirational bursts of energy that communicate the richness of their racial heritage. Taken to the extreme, African Americans in the immersion phase have difficulty controlling the impulse to confront White authority figures, even on a life-or-death basis. That is, the threat of death is not feared.

In the emersion phase of Stage 3, there is a marked decline in the racist and emotional attitudes. This leveling off occurs when African Americans encounter a role model who, for example, displays a more sophisticated and calmer personae. Through role models, Blacks learn to replace romantic and romanticized notions of blackness with a deeper and more serious understanding of Black issues.

Stage 4—Internalization is marked by the integration of a new identity, an identity that is more authentic and naturalistic. This identity includes high salience to blackness, which can take on several manifestations, including biculturalism. An internalized identity serves several functions: defending and protecting the persons from psychological problems associated with living in a society where race matters, providing a sense of belonging and social affiliation, and providing a basis for interacting and communicating with people, cultures, and situations beyond the world of blackness (Cross, 1995).

Finally, Stage 5—Internalization-Commitment is characterized as action oriented. Here African Americans devote much time and energy, perhaps a lifetime, to finding ways to translate their personal sense of blackness into a plan of action, a commitment to Black affairs, and improvements in the circumstances of African Americans.

Cross (1995) acknowledged that individuals can regress or get stuck at one stage. Whether they regress, become stuck, or progress through the stages of racial identity depends, in large part, on the individual's personality, support base, resources, and experiences. For example, middle-class Black children and adults in predominantly White settings may experience more negative encounters based on race than those in predominantly Black settings. They may also experience such encounters at an earlier age than Blacks in predominantly Black settings. Further, the opportunity for middle-class Black children and adults to learn more about their blackness and racial heritage seems to be small given the demographics of their environment (i.e., predominantly White).

Allegiance Issues

Allegiance issues are not uncommon among middle-class Blacks who may experience conflict relative to supporting the beliefs, values, and norms of the dominant culture as opposed to their parent culture. Consequently, they show ambivalence about their abilities and consider them as envied by others—yet personally undesirable. As middle-class Blacks interact with the mainstream society, they also desire acceptance by other Blacks who have not achieved such status. Some Blacks, for example, are not completely comfortable in either world. Others are less involved in activities in the Black community as they move up the SES ladder and become more affiliated with the predominant society. Thus successful or middle-class Blacks must reconcile this issue or be tormented by feelings of abandonment, isolation, guilt, and rejection. This duality of cultures (particularly when conflicting), and concerns over individual (personal) versus group achievement, can contribute to socioemotional and psychological difficulties. More than a century ago, W.E.B. DuBois described this phenomenon when he wrote about two warring souls fighting with each other to be accepted in White America (Weis, 1985). Leanita McClain, the first Black female elected to the board of directors of the *Chicago Tribune*, was subsequently perceived by many as acting White. She described the dilemma of bicultural stress most poignantly in her newspaper column entitled "The Middle-Class Black's Burden":

> I run a gauntlet between two worlds, and I am cursed and blessed by both. I travel, observe, and take part in both; I can also be used by both. I am a rope in a tug of war.
>
> If I am a token in my downtown office, so am I at my cousin's tea. I assuage White guilt. . . . I have a foot in each world, but I cannot fool myself about either. . . . Whites won't believe that I remain culturally different; Blacks won't believe that I remain culturally the same.

McClain (1983) described this identity issue as hellish confusion whereby successful Blacks feel guilty and stressful about their success. Success sometimes leads African Americans to ask themselves, as did McClain, "I have made it, but where?" (Campbell, 1984, p. 74). McClain eventually committed suicide.

Not surprisingly, therefore, many educators and counselors have noted a significant change in the aspirations of Blacks toward academic achievement and social mobility. Although previous generations had defined success for one Black person as success for all Blacks, more recently Blacks are less apt to view the achievements of individual Blacks as progress for all Blacks. The "all for one and one for all" collective sense of success has all but disappeared for some Blacks, replaced by the perception that successful Blacks have "sold out." This change is most apparent in the concepts of brotherhood, sisterhood, peoplehood, and fictive kinship. Staiano (1980) described part of this cultural philosophy of collectivism as a coping mechanism against racism and discrimination.

Maslow (1962) highlighted the significance of peoplehood when he noted that the sense of belonging is essential for mental health. An unhealthy sense of belonging works in opposition to the sense of peoplehood. A sense of peoplehood represents a cultural symbol of collective identity and ethnic consolidation as well as mutual interdependence among Blacks (Barnes, 1980; Green, 1981). It implies a particular mind-set, or worldview, among Blacks, and denotes the moral judgment the group makes on its members (Fordham, 1988).

Smith (1989) argued that race serves to create a common referent of peoplehood such that individuals tend to define themselves in terms of membership in a particular group. Thus this collective identity represents the sense of belonging that is psychologically important for people of color. To reinforce the belief that they are still legitimate members of the Black community, Blacks may sabotage any chance they have of succeeding outside of it. With this anti-achievement ethic, highly capable Blacks may underachieve, drop out, and otherwise fail to reach their academic potential in school and life (Ford & Harris, 1994). This underachievement may be especially evident when middle-class Black students attend predominantly White schools. During this time, they may become confused about which culture to support.

In short, detachment from one's race, whether perceived or real, threatens the survival of the Black community and its culture, and creates suspicion among Blacks about member loyalty. Hence, the Black community may reject successful or middle-class Blacks not because they have achieved but because they appear removed and detached from their indigenous community. The Black community rejects middle-class and successful Blacks who identify with the dominant culture, desire to join it, and accept its behaviors as paradigms worth copying.

Which culture, then, should African Americans emulate when trying to fulfill their potential? Which belief and value system should they incorporate? Again, middle-class Blacks may vacillate between allegiance to their racial group and the dominant group. Some Blacks adopt racelessness as a pragmatic strategy, but for others it represents only a pyrrhic victory (Fordham, 1988). However, no matter how raceless an individual tries to be, color is always present and visible to all.

Survival Conflict and Guilt Issues

The notion of survival conflict can shed light on the many socioemotional and psychological factors affecting the motivation and achievement of African Americans who may feel guilt, anxiety, and ambivalence over having survived when others who seem to be equally, if not more, deserving did not. Survival conflict is a negative reaction to surpassing the accomplishments of family and/ or peers. It manifests itself in one or more emotional responses, including guilt, ambivalence, anxiety, or depression. These feelings become debilitating if not recognized, resulting in a devaluation of self-concept, accomplishments, and ambitions. As with fear of success, individuals suffering from survival conflict fear or anticipate negative consequences from competitive striving.

African Americans who succumb to negative feelings associated with success do so to help maintain loyalty and a sense of belonging to their family and peers. They seek social and cultural continuity. Piorkowski (1983) noted that as individuals move from a lower social class standing to a higher one, they often experience "social class change anxiety." These successful persons find themselves in a quandary because as achievement increases, so too does guilt. To escape survival conflict, Blacks may resort to self-sabotage, procrastination, dropping out, and other behaviors that thwart success. Higher SES Blacks may also overcompensate to allay their feelings. For instance, they may overextend themselves to "prove" to other Blacks, particularly lower SES Blacks (and themselves), that they have not forgotten who they are or where they came from. In an effort to assuage the guilt, many go home for visits with gifts and and money. Coner-Edwards and Edwards (1988) reported that middle-class Blacks may save most of their earnings or dress less well than they can afford out of a fear of appearing hedonistic or overindulgent. Others become absorbed in their work and refrain from involvement in social activities. In essence, they must resolve their guilt at the risk of losing ties or feeling rejected by their community, or they may never be able to enjoy their attainment.

Personality appears to play a major role in how individuals react to success and achievement. For instance, low self-esteem and low assertiveness are related to feelings of survival conflict and guilt. These individuals cannot fend off conflicting messages and statements. Racial identity, described earlier, also plays an important role in survival conflict. That is, Black students with a positive racial identity are more likely to be concerned with racial and cultural affiliations. Further, those individuals who have close relationships with their families and peers seem more likely to experience survival conflict because of concerns over survival of the individual versus the group.

Achievement Ideology Issues

The American dream has been defined in both the popular press and scholarly work in terms of the life chances associated with the middle class—a home, a car or two, a good neighborhood, a college education, the ability to purchase adequate health care. However, Blacks have historically been blocked from the realization of the American dream in these areas. And even when middle-class status was achieved, African Americans found that money still could not buy them a meal at certain restaurants, a home in certain neighborhoods, or a job in certain businesses or professions. Similarly, middle-class Black families could not educate their children at the school of their choice. Although laws have wiped away, at least on paper, the inequities, middle-class Blacks may still find certain doors closed and locked. They may have achieved the American dream relative to the key characteristics just listed, but it is unrealistic to assume that they have truly "arrived." Counselors and other helping professionals thus must examine whether Blacks have invested realistically in the notion of the achievement ideology. To what extent are middle-class Blacks failing to achieve balanced lives because they work all the time? Are they riddled with guilt when they take time off or attempt to enjoy work and leisure? How secure do they feel about their socioeconomic status and other indices of success?

Potential Barriers to Counseling Middle-Class African Americans

In general, Blacks and other racial minorities underutilize counseling services. In their study of the reasons minority students do not seek counseling, Atkinson, Jennings, and Liongson (1990) found the counselor's race to be significant. For those minority students most closely identified with their ethnic culture, findings indicated that the availability of culturally similar or culturally sensitive counselors is an important determinant of counseling service utilization (p. 348). The issue of race may be particularly important for Black children and adults in Stage 3—Immersion-Emersion of identity development.

Another similar explanation for underutilization is that Black students may not believe that White counselors have the skills necessary to meet the needs of those who are racially and culturally diverse. The expectation, therefore, is negative or inappropriate counseling.

Although (as just noted) research has indicated that racial identity affects students' willingness to seek counseling, little attention has yet been given to understanding how an individual's racial identity affects his or her mental health. The consideration of racial identity in the counseling process is essential, however, not only because of the myriad problems associated with racial identity development but also because attitudes that both denigrate an individual as a successful Black person and promote wishes to be White may be psychologically maladaptive as well as non-self-actualizing.

Parham (1989) cogently delineated issues that counselors might need to address when working with Black children and adults: One is *self-differentiation versus preoccupation with assimilation*, in which the individual strives to become comfortable with the recognition that he or she is a worthwhile human being, irrespective of valuation and validation from Whites. A second issue is *ego-transcendence versus self-absorption*, whereby successful African Americans strive to become secure enough with themselves to develop personal ego strength.

Middle-class Black children and adults must achieve congruence between the real self and the ideal/perceived self if they are to become fully functioning individuals with well-integrated identities. A positive racial identity may result when counselors provide the support necessary to free successful Blacks from the racial stereotypes others impose upon them. Therefore, counselors are urged to work with these Black students and adults on problems associated with academic achievement and upward mobility because, as stated by Graves (1977), achieving a measure of success in society is, by and large, a far more difficult task for African Americans than it is for other Americans.

Defense mechanisms—those techniques individuals use to protect themselves from pain or discomfort—can be destructive to the helping process. As Yalom (1985) stated, individuals with neurotic defenses are frozen in a closed position; they are not open for learning, and they are generally searching for safety rather than growth. Through defense mechanisms, individuals can withdraw from, distort, or attack problems. Using these defenses, which include denying problems or projecting problems onto others, can produce a general inability in African-American clients to grow and to overcome the issues for which they had sought counseling.

Denial is the conscious screening out of unpleasant information that might threaten sense of self and peoplehood. When thoughts or feelings are unacceptable, individuals try to disown and/or deny them (Perls, 1976). African Americans who rationalize and deny reality may be unable to progress toward healthier stages of social-emotional and psychological development. Dudley (1988) noted that Blacks may spend an inordinate amount of time and energy maintaining the belief that racial factors have little to do with their current status. (Such individuals may be in racial identity development Stage 1—Pre-Encounter.) This belief may be maintained by a narcissistic psychological defense that consists of denying the devalued status assigned to the Black individual, and of maintaining a more grandiose view of the self. Such a defense enables Blacks to view themselves as special, as a special subgroup of Blacks, or beyond racial categorization. However, by denying external barriers to achievement, African Americans may come to internalize them, or to believe that the attacks are based on substance. Consequently, they may be falsely led to believe that their capabilities and competencies are seriously limited. If attacks are persistent, Black children and adults may have lowered self-perceptions and become devastated. In essence, because of the myriad defense mechanisms that can interfere with counseling, a major task of the counselor will be to help Stage 1—Pre-Encounter, Stage 2—Encounter, and Stage 3—Immersion-Emersion African Americans to explore their defense mechanisms.

The Case Study of Joseph

The case study of Joseph, an African American adolescent from a middle-class family, illustrates many of the factors and barriers explored in this chapter.

Joseph, a 14-year-old Black male, currently attends high school in a middle-class community. Joseph's parents (a professor and an accountant) bought him to counseling because of depression and bouts of anger. During counseling, Joseph often reflects upon his school experiences. Joseph attended a predominantly Black public elementary school. He has happy, positive memories about these school years and often boasts about his school achievement. His mother indicated that Joseph was identified as gifted and placed in the district's gifted education program in the second grade. He had also received numerous awards and other recognition for his academic achievement.

The family moved to a predominantly White suburb when Joseph was in middle school. Shortly thereafter, his parents began to notice a significant decline in Joseph's interest in school and academic performance. Joseph no longer made the honor roll, for example, nor was he interested in doing so. His teachers, all of whom were White females, expressed concern that Joseph was a behavioral problem and that he often disrupted class, was off task, seldom completed assignments, talked out of turn, and thrived on his status as the class clown. Joseph presented a different picture. He described his teachers as mean, unfair, and boring. He reported that many of the teachers ridiculed and embarrassed him. He complained that teachers were insensitive and often seemed to enjoy demeaning Blacks. Joseph also recalled being teased by both Black and White students, many of whom could not understand why Joseph spoke "proper English." Joseph was teased most often when he visited friends in his former neighborhood.

By the end of the first grading period, one teacher requested that Joseph be referred for child services for special education evaluation. Joseph's parents were shocked. How could their son be identified as gifted in one school and referred to special education in another? They refused to have Joseph evaluated. They held numerous meetings with administrators and teachers regarding why Joseph was not placed in the gifted program, as he had been identified earlier. Unable to resolve this issue and their differences with several teachers, Joseph's parents transferred him to another school, which was also predominantly White and middle class. The problems were similar in this school. Teachers complained that Joseph talked too much and asked too many questions, particularly about minority groups and issues of justice. For example, Joseph questioned teachers when they stated that Christopher Columbus discovered America, and he questioned their constant focus on slavery and their inattention to the contribution of Blacks to American history. Joseph also expressed frustration and anger at being what he called a *token* at certain times during the school year. For instance, he recalled having to be the expert on all issues related to African Americans. One student asked Joseph to explain why so many Blacks commit crimes. Another student wanted to know why Black people are so good at sports. Others asked how his parents could afford a nice house and to live in their neighborhood. Joseph also described his experience when trying out for both tennis and basketball. When he failed to make the basketball team but made the tennis team, Joseph was teased unmercifully.

Much of what Joseph discussed in counseling had not been shared with his parents. For the most part, they thought that Joseph was adjusting well to school, although his grades were not at the level they expected. They were also unaware that Joseph attempted to buy friendships and peer acceptance. During one counseling session, Joseph described how he stole money from his parents so that he could always have it to show the White students. He stated, "I did not want them to think that I was just another poor Black kid." When this did not work, that is, the teasing, isolation, and rejection continued. Joseph became more frustrated and angry. When his parents brought Joseph to counseling, he had been suspended for fighting.

Questions to explore in this case include What are Joseph's major concerns? What needs is he trying to meet? What factors have contributed to his difficulties? How could they have been prevented? How can a counselor help Joseph to deal effectively with his concerns? To what extent will peers, teachers, and family members be involved in the counseling process?

Counseling Interventions for Middle-Class African Americans

Counseling Black children and adults requires gathering information from a variety of sources (talking to students, parents, teachers; making several objective measurements) to understand better how successful Blacks feel about themselves, their social relationships, satisfaction with life, and future. An important question to explore is How can racial identity development be enhanced or facilitated? According to Erikson (1968), the process of racial identity development is a major developmental task that occurs during the fifth stage of psychosocial development. His stages of development are mediated by successful resolution of conflicts in earlier stages. Accordingly, if middle-class Blacks do not progress successfully through the first four, healthy racial identity is jeopardized. As so often indicated, threats to the mental health of middle-class Blacks include conflicts with members of their racial group over issues of commitment to their indigenous culture, that is, over their fears of being perceived as acting White or as rejecting the Black culture in any way.

In addition to Erikson's (1968) stages and Cross's (1995) five stages discussed earlier, Banks' (1979) five stages for understanding ethnic identity development can also help ensure effective counseling for successful Blacks. Whatever the framework, counselors must help successful and middle-class Blacks reach higher stages of racial identity so that they can function well within several racial and cultural settings, and appreciate the differences among these cultures as well. To help Black adults and children reach this level of functioning, however, counselors must attend to the affective and cultural dimensions of being not only Black but also successful.

Counselors must thus teach Blacks how to cope effectively with feeling isolated from White Americans or rejected by African Americans. These feelings have been expressed by many successful Blacks, including Leanita McClain who once reported being "uncomfortably middle class" (Campbell, 1984, p. 70). Exploring feelings of isolation may be especially important during Cross's Stage 1—Pre-Encounter, Stage 2—Encounter, and Stage 3—Immersion-Emersion of racial identity development. Just as important, counselors are advised to speak openly with Blacks about racial issues. As Kochman (1981) stated, Blacks often prefer to speak openly about issues of racism and discrimination rather to ignore or avoid such discussions. Thus counselors who are culturally sensitive develop open and trusting relationships with their middle-class Black clients.

Injustices associated with race are a reality in America. "For most Blacks in America, regardless of status, political persuasion, or accomplishments, the moment never arrives when race can be treated as a total irrelevancy. Instead, too often it is the only relevant factor defining our existence" (Cose, 1993, p. 28). Because racially motivated attacks strike at the core of the Black person's identity, a strong emotional response is normal. To survive, Blacks must expect such feelings, recognize that they are normal, learn not to be frightened by them, and learn how to use them to their own best interests. Given the intensity of the racial attacks on Blacks in general and middle-class Blacks in particular, it is especially important that African Americans learn how to manage their emotional responses to racism. A supportive system that provides an avenue for expressing feelings and exploring alternatives for managing these feelings is invaluable.

A trusting counseling relationship, role models and mentors, group counseling, and family counseling are potentially helpful intervention strategies.

A Trusting Relationship

The emphasis placed on the counseling relationship (versus the techniques) as the major counseling strategy is an important issue when counseling Black children and adults. The quality of the counseling relationship, measured by the degree of empathy, unconditional positive regard, congruence, and active listening on the part of counselors, both enhances the relationship and encourages greater disclosure on the part of Black children and adults.

Counselors must use intervention techniques designed for specific cultural groups but avoid being culturally encapsulated and blindly applying the same techniques to all clients and across all situations. That is, when working with middle-class Blacks, counselors must attend to universal needs common among all populations while also attending to cultural needs. The counseling relationship requires that counselors emphasize similarities among diverse groups or individuals and the universality of the human experience. Perhaps most importantly, the counseling relationship is promoted when counselors respect and appreciate not only individual differences but also differences among and within groups.

Role Models and Mentors

Mentoring can facilitate the intellectual or vocational development of persons identified as proteges. Whatever form it takes, mentoring provides emotional support, enhances self-esteem, corrects dysfunctional attitudes and behaviors, and teaches values and ethics (Pasch, Krokow, Johnson, Slocum, & Stapleton, 1990). Counselors must take an active role in facilitating mentor relationships for African Americans, particularly children. Without role models, Black children may have a lower probability of being positive about success and achievement. Thus mentors and role models serve as important and powerful resources in the prevention of academic and socioemotional problems.

Group Counseling

Group counseling can be especially effective with Black children and adults because of their cultural orientation to communal work. Group counseling encourages Black children and adults to view themselves as a central part of the larger social community. Sharing, cooperation, and reciprocity are essential elements of social interaction among Blacks (Harrison, Wilson, Pine, Chan, & Buriel, 1990). Group counseling might also enhance the self-esteem and racial identity of middle-class Black children and adults. When African Americans have the opportunity to speak with others who share their concerns, they may become more comfortable with being "different." In addition, group counseling experiences may also help African Americans increase their sense of hope and optimism, decrease their feelings of alienation, develop more effective coping techniques, and acquire more effective socialization skills.

Family Counseling

The family, as a primary socialization agent, has an integral part in child development, including racial identity. Exum (1983) recommended that counselors consider carefully the family's stage of racial identity development. For example, because families in Stage 1—Encounter of identity development may be too preoccupied with self-discovery to benefit fully from counseling with White counselors, Exum recommended referring such families to multicultural counselors. Exum also cautioned that families in the immersion phase of Stage 3 are the most difficult to work with because of their strong anti-White feelings. Such families may reject counseling or insist upon working only with a Black counselor.

Equally important, fearing that schools will emphasize competitiveness and individualism, which are antithetical to values espoused in the Black culture, some parents resist placing their children in predominantly White schools. Counselors (and, of course, teachers) must help African American parents understand that high-level academic courses and programs (e.g., gifted education, honors) should not be perceived as prerogatives of White students. Increasing the participation of Black students in these programs requires the support and participation of parents and significant others in the students' lives. Other strategies include conducting parent workshops and seminars as well as providing resource materials on issues related to being both Black and successful. Interventions must educate Black parents about the psychological, emotional, and social needs of their children, and include information about what success means to their children.

Black families, particularly extended families, also play an important role in promoting the social and emotional health of its members. Their involvement in counseling, therefore, may be highly facilitative. Family members can increase the sense of cohesion, connectedness, and understanding that may be necessary for some middle-class Blacks to appreciate their achievements. Key issues worth exploring in family counseling are (a) family achievement orientations, (b) support networks within home and community, (c) educational involvement, (d) self-differentiation (individual versus group identity and achievement), and (e) maintaining cultural value and heritage as well as ties to the larger, less economically advantaged Black community.

Summary and Conclusions

Although racial discrimination and economic stratification continue to be major sources of stress for many people of color, some nonetheless have been able to acquire the requisites for upward mobility. Middle-class Blacks have been able to travel through the narrow window of opportunity that exposes them to the "good life," but class analysis remains a neglected approach to understanding the Black experience in America, and few scholarly works have stimulated any real discussion of the Black experience in terms of socioeconomic status. Middle-class African Americans are victims of both racial injustice and social injustice. They represent a group that approached the door of equal opportunity and opened it by the handle of equal opportunity (Washington, 1980, p. iii). They now face both promise and peril, and many have found that classism does not mitigate racism.

There is much diversity among African Americans relative to income, education, occupation, lifestyles, values, and family background. Thus Blacks represent a unique mixture of racial, historical, and cultural heritages. More often than not, however, middle-class Blacks are omitted from discussions of Blacks, the Black community, and inner-city Blacks, despite the reality that middle-class Blacks exist among all three (Pinderhughes, 1988, p. v).

Assuming that middle-class Blacks have "arrived" in America, that this group is free from discrimination faced by less affluent Blacks is naive. Long-standing oppression and deprivation continue to affect the psychology and achievements of many Blacks, including those who achieve middle-class status. The results of social injustices can be deeply embedded and outside of awareness. Negative self-perceptions, serious role conflicts, bicultural stress, and self-defeating behaviors are realities in the lives of Blacks who, by virtue of higher socioeconomic status, should be inoculated from the problems of those trapped in poverty and oppression. Large numbers of middle-class Blacks unknowingly carry around the effects of oppression as an internalized source of stress (Pinderhughes, 1988). Counselors, as an integral part of the helping equation, have both the presence and the power to help successful, middle-class Black children and adults to lead rewarding lives.

References

Atkinson, D. R., Jennings, R. G., & Liongson, L. (1990). Minority students' reasons for not seeking counseling and suggestions for improving services. *Journal of College Student Development, 31,* 342–350.

Banks, J. A. (1979). *Teaching strategies for ethnic studies* (2nd ed.). Boston: Allyn & Bacon.

Barnes, E. J. (1980). The Black community. In R.L. Jones (Ed.), *Black psychology* (2nd ed., pp. 106–130). New York: Harper & Row.

Campbell, B. M. (1984, December). To be Black, gifted, and alone. *Savvy,* pp. 67–74.

Coner-Edwards, A. F., & Edwards, J. (1988). The Black middle class: Definitions and demographics. In A. F. Coner-Edwards & J. Spurlock (Eds.), *Black families in crisis: The middle class* (pp. 1–9). New York: Brunner/Mazel.

Cose, E. (1993). *The rage of a privileged class.* New York: HarperCollins.

Cross Jr., W. E. (1995). The psychology of nigrescence: Revising the Cross model. In J. G. Ponterotto, J. M. Casas, L. A. Suzuki, & C. M.

Alexander (Eds.), *Handbook of multicultural counseling* (pp. 93–122). Thousand Oaks, CA: Sage.

Dudley Jr., R. G. (1988). Blacks in policy-making positions. In A. F. Coner-Edwards & J. Spurlock (Eds.), *Black families in crisis: The middle class* (pp. 15–27). New York: Brunner/Mazel.

Erikson, E. H. (1968). *Identity: Youth and crisis.* New York: Norton.

Exum, H. A. (1983). Key issues in family counseling with gifted and talented Black students. *Roeper Review, 28*–31.

Ford, D. Y. (1995). *Correlates of underachievement among gifted and nongifted Black students.* Storrs, CT: The National Research Center on the Gifted and Talented, University of Connecticut.

Ford, D. Y. (1996). Desegregating gifted education: A need unmet. *Journal of Negro Education 64*(1), 52–62.

Ford, D. Y., & Harris III, J. J. (1994). Promoting achievement among gifted Black students: The efficacy of new definitions and identification practices. *Urban Education, 29*(2), 202–229.

Fordham, S. (1988). Racelessness as a factor in Black students' school success: Pragmatic strategy or pyrrhic victory? *Harvard Educational Review, 58*(1), 54–84.

Graves, E. G. (1977, November). There's room at the top, but the entry price is high. *Black Enterprise, 8,* 5.

Green, V. M. (1981). Blacks in the United States: The creation of an enduring people? In G. P. Castile & G. Kushner (Eds.), *Persistent peoples: Cultural enclaves in perspective.* Tucson: University of Arizona Press.

Harris III, J. J., & Ford, D. Y. (1991). Identifying and nurturing the promise of gifted Black American children. *Journal of Negro Education, 60*(1), 3–18.

Harrison, A. O., Wilson, M. N., Pine, C. J., Chan, S. Q., & Buriel, R. (1990). Family ecologies of ethnic minority children. *Child Development, 61*(2), 347–362.

Kochman, T. (1981). *Black and White styles in conflict.* Chicago: University of Chicago Press.

Landry, L. B. (1980). The social and economic adequacy of the Black middle class. In J. R. Washington, Jr. (Ed.), *The dilemmas of the new Black middle class* (pp. 1–13). State College: University of Pennsylvania, Afro-American Studies Program.

Maslow, A. (1962). *Toward a psychology of well-being.* Princeton, NJ: Van Nostrand.

McClain, L. (1983, July 24). How Chicago taught me to hate Whites. *The Washington Post,* pp. C1, C4.

Parham, T. A. (1989). Cycles of psychological nigrescence. *The Counseling Psychologist, 17*(2), 187–226.

Pasch, M., Krokow, M. C., Johnson, C., Slocum, H., & Stapleton, E. M. (1990). The disappearing minority educator—no illusion. A practical solution. *Urban Education, 25*(1), 207–218.

Perls, F. (1976). *Gestalt therapy verbatim.* New York: Vintage Books.

Pinderhughes, C. A. (1988). Foreword. In A. F. Coner-Edwards & J. Spurlock (Eds.), *Black families in crisis: The middle class* (pp. iii–v). New York: Brunner/Mazel.

Piorkowski, G. K. (1983). Survivor guilt in the university setting. *The Personnel and Guidance Journal, 61*(10), 620–622.

Ransford, H. E. (1977). *Race and class in American society: Black, Chicano, Anglo.* Cambridge, MA: Schenkman.

Rotheram, M. J., & Phinney, J. S. (1987). Introduction: Definitions and perspectives in the study of children's ethnic socialization. In J. S. Phinney & M. J. Rotheram (Eds.), *Children's ethnic socialization* (pp. 10–28). Newbury Park, CA: Sage.

Smith, E. M. J. (1989). Black racial identity development. *The Counseling Psychologist, 17*(2), 277–288.

Staiano, K. V. (1980). Ethnicity as process: The creation of an Afro-American identity. *Ethnicity, A7,* 27–33.

Washington, J. R., Jr. (Ed.). (1980). *The dilemmas of the new Black middle class.* State College: Penn State, Afro-American Studies Program.

Weis, L. (1985). *Between two worlds: Black students in an urban community college.* New York: Routledge & Kegan Paul.

Wilson, W. (1978). *The declining significance of race.* Chicago: University of Chicago Press.

Yalom, I. D. (1985). *The theory and practice of group psychotherapy* (3rd ed.). New York: Basic Books.

7

COUNSELING AFRICAN AMERICAN WOMEN FROM A CULTURAL SENSITIVITY PERSPECTIVE

Janice M. Jordan

African American females who present for counseling are a unique clientele. Like other women, they are burdened with the problems of being women in a male-dominated society that does not fully value the feminine perspective. Unlike other women, they are also faced with issues resulting from long-standing negative, stereotypical images. Their true contribution to the building of this country continues to be ignored and, therefore, devalued. Further, despite the achievements of African American women in the past and in recent years, the negative images are still advanced, albeit through more subliminal means. Counseling African American women, then, demands not only a more feminist perspective but also a more cultural perspective.

In the first edition of this book, counseling African American women was approached from a developmental group perspective (Jordan, 1991). This edition addresses counseling African American women individually using the cultural sensitivity of the counselor as a core requirement. Factors affecting the lives of African American women and their experience in counseling—racial identity, cultural mistrust, and self-esteem and empowerment—are presented, each with an illustrative case study. Contemporary issues are also briefly considered. The terms *African American* and *Black* are used interchangeably throughout.

109

Cultural Sensitivity

Counselors who hope to be successful with African American girls and women must be sensitive to the culture(s) the clients represent. Although numerous authors have called for the need for cultural sensitivity (Atkinson, Morten, & Sue, 1993; Stewart, 1981) in counseling, only recently has anyone attempted to clarify what *cultural sensitivity* means and how it can be operationalized (Ridley, Mendoza, Kanitz, Angermeir, & Zenk, 1994). It is generally agreed that neither knowledge of cultures nor skills alone is enough for a counselor to be considered culturally sensitive. Essential to the formula are an awareness of one's own culture and awareness of the culture of the counseling profession. Moreover, the culturally sensitive counselor must be knowledgeable of the interaction of culture and the individual that produces that unique woman who is seeking help (Ridley et al., 1994).

Counselors may believe that the problem of cultural sensitivity is solved if they are the same race as their clients. However, this is not necessarily the case. The training process required to become a counselor is part of an educational system that is steeped in Western culture. One purpose of this system is to perpetuate the culture by dictating acceptable beliefs and behaviors. Rewards are most often given to those who negotiate the system in the prescribed manner. Therefore, it is possible to complete a training program with a sensitivity only to the culture of the educational system. When this occurs, a Black counselor is no more culturally sensitive than his or her White colleague in the training program.

Recently the Council for the Accreditation of Counseling and Related Educational Programs (CACREP) and the American Psychological Association (APA) have required that training programs include training in multicultural issues in counseling. Often this requirement has been translated into an elective course in multicultural counseling while the remainder of the curriculum is taught in the same manner as before. It has long been the responsibility of the individual counseling trainee to seek resources and training opportunities that allow him or her to develop the requisite sensitivity to work effectively with Black clients.

If a counselor is truly culturally sensitive, her or his approach in working with a Black woman will emanate from a "culture content orientation, rather than a universal orientation" (Thompson, Worthington, & Atkinson, 1994). That is, she or he will consider and address the client's culture as an integral part of her presenting concern(s). Thompson et al. (1994) defined the universal content orientation as the "counselor's exploration of clients' problems as they relate to issues shared universally . . . irrespective of culture" (p. 156). The culture content orientation has been found to be especially beneficial in establishing the therapeutic bond necessary for a successful counseling experience (Thompson, et al., 1994).

Counselors with cultural sensitivity, then, are those who (a) are aware of their own culture, (b) are knowledgeable and accepting of the interaction of cultural and individual factors in the development of their clients, and (c) work with their clients from a cultural content orientation.

The case of Tara illustrates the work of a culturally sensitive counselor:

Tara was a 29-year-old African American single mother of three boys, ages 11, 4, and 2. She was referred to counseling by her case worker because of feelings of depression and suicide ideation. She was employed as a cook in a small restaurant for a little more than minimum wage and no benefits. She received money from Aid to Families With Dependent Children (AFDC) and sporadic minimum child support payments from the father of her two youngest children. The father of the oldest child made no payments. She and her three children shared a house with an older sister and her children. She was a short, petite, woman with very short straightened hair. She arrived for the first session dressed in black jeans and a light colored T-shirt and sneakers.

Counselor: I understand that your case worker suggested that you come to counseling.

Tara: Not really. I called her and told her I felt like if I didn't get no help I was going to do something crazy. Then my kids wouldn't have nobody to take care of them.

Counselor: So, your love and concern for your children made you ask her for help.

Tara: Uh huh.

Counselor: That was a big step for you to take. I imagine it was pretty hard for you as a Black woman to ask a White caseworker for help.

Tara: (brief smile) It did take me a pretty long time. I don't like her knowing my business that much. You know, it's bad enough I got to have welfare in the first place. Then they give you this case worker who thinks she ought to know everything you do. She's all right, but it's just the idea.

During the first session, Tara became more relaxed and disclosed that she had suffered periodic bouts with depression since age 14 at which time she had overdosed on aspirin. She reported feeling unwanted and ugly, then and now. As treatment progressed she also revealed that she was sexually abused by an uncle with whom she lived. She remained in treatment for the full course of treatment, which was 12 sessions. Around the eighth session, the counselor helped her get in touch with a Black woman in the community who was to serve as a mentor. By termination, Tara had contacted her mentor and had participated in two activities with her.

The therapeutic bond between the counselor and Tara began to form when the counselor reflected the difficulty a Black woman might have asking a White for help. This statement demonstrated to the client that the counselor was sensitive to the role race plays in the difficult process of asking for help. Acknowledgements such as these let the Black female client know that the counselor appreciated her whole self.

Racial Identity Development

Cultural sensitivity can also refer to being attuned to the racial identity development of the Black woman. Her stage of racial identity, within the Cross (1995) framework, can determine the degree to which a cultural content orientation is important. Given her racial identity development, it is apparent that because a client can be visibly identified as a Black woman does not mean that she shares the same beliefs, experiences, values, and view of the world as all other Black women. Rather, the extent to which she thinks and behaves from a Black frame of reference determines how appropriate the cultural content orientation will be in the counseling process. For example, unless the goal of the counseling experience is to promote racial identity development, the Black woman who is in Stage 1—Pre-Encounter will probably respond quite favorably to the universal content orientation.

The case of Carol illustrates a Black woman who entered counseling in Stage 1—Pre-Encounter (Cross, 1995).

Carol was a 21-year-old Black woman, a senior in college, referred by her group counselor to individual counseling with a Black female counselor. Carol had been a member of an eating disorders group, but was making little progress in the process group. Her group counselor determined that Carol needed individual counseling to address identity issues and had confronted Carol with her attitudes about Blacks, and thus herself.

Counselor: What do you believe is the reason your group counselor referred you to me?

Carol: She said I need to do something about my attitude about Black people.

Counselor: What attitude is that?

Carol: She said that I'm racist. So did some of the group members.

Counselor: What do you think?

Carol: I don't know if it's racist or not. I have a White boyfriend, and all my friends are White.

Counselor: I guess that there has to be more than that to make them describe you as racist.

Carol: I just don't have much to do with Black people at all. Especially Black men. Ne'er-do-wells. That's what they are. Black people don't have much ambition to do anything with their lives. Even the ones who are here in college.

Counselor: It must be pretty distressing, then, for you to be here with me as your counselor.

Carol: You're different.

Carol's statements about Blacks, as well as her behaviors in her daily life, indicated that she was in Stage 1—Pre-Encounter of racial identity development. The goal of her individual counseling, determined by the individual counselor in consultation with the group counselor, was to help Carol develop her racial identity. She could not be able to tackle her eating disorder adequately until she had a more positive sense of self. Her beliefs about Blacks were first confronted by being in treatment with a Black counselor, a fact with which the counselor confronted her in the first session. Carol remained in individual counseling for eight sessions during which she was continuously confronted with her frame of reference and its effects on how she viewed herself. She received support for exploring the history of Blacks in the United States through readings and talks with her maternal grandparents. As she did, she began experiencing difficulties in her relationship with her boyfriend, who she reported thought she was "going off the deep end." She believed it was because she started making him see that she was Black. Carol was also beginning to view herself as a Black woman. She terminated as graduation approached.

Cultural Mistrust

Mistrust of counselors and the counseling process remains a factor in the counseling of African American women. It is another interference with the development of the therapeutic bond that is essential if the client is to really "show herself" to the counselor. Some researchers have found that African Americans often feel more trusting of similar race counselors, tend to disclose more, have more favorable outcomes, and report more satisfaction with the counseling experience (Ridley, 1984). Others have proposed that the mistrust brought to the counseling process is a byproduct of the cultural mistrust that African Americans have developed for survival in a racist society (Terrell & Terrell, 1981; Watkins, Terrell, Miller, & Terrell, 1989). Thompson et al. (1994) specifically examined the relationship among the cultural mistrust of Black women, self-disclosure, counselor content orientation, and counselor race. They found that low levels of mistrust related to a greater number of self-disclosures to Black counselors, whereas high levels of mistrust were related to less self-disclosure to White counselors.

Not all African American women exhibit the same level of mistrust. Those who are highly mistrustful have been found to have a tendency to perceive a counselor as less credible and less capable of helping with certain problems (anxiety, dating problems, shyness, and feelings of inferiority) when the counselor is White (Watkins et al., 1989). These mistrustful women may also have generalized mistrust of counselors—including Black counselors, who may be viewed as having "made it" and thus as out of touch with the real issues of African Americans (Thompson et al., 1994).

The culturally sensitive counselor, then, will also be aware of the issue of cultural mistrust when working with African American women. In particular, the White counselor working with a highly mistrustful Black woman needs to be especially attuned to the issues of general anxiety, shyness, dating problems, and feelings of inferiority as presenting concerns. Watkins et al. (1989) believed that "sensitivity to mistrust issues in interaction with these identified problem areas can be valuable counseling information of which to be mindful" (p. 449).

Mistrust is manifested in a variety of behaviors. One form is the client who presents herself for help but is only willing to respond to specific questions from the counselor, even when she understands the counseling process entails more. Another form is failure to disclose intimate information about self (Thompson et al., 1994).

The case of Gail illustrates a highly mistrustful Black woman whose mistrust is manifested in her responding behavior:

Gail was a 20-year-old college student when she self-referred to a Black female counselor for individual counseling. During the previous semester she had experienced a prolonged period of isolating herself from everybody and everything. She did not attend class and remembered mostly just sitting in her room. She did, however, manage to pass all her classes. The following is an excerpt from her first session.

Counselor: It would be helpful if you would tell me what brings you to counseling.
Gail: I told the woman I saw during intake. She didn't tell you?
Counselor: I do have some notes from her, but I would like to hear it directly from you. This way, we'll be sure that I have the most accurate picture.
Gail: (after a couple of minutes of silence) I don't talk much. Why don't you ask me questions and then maybe I can answer them, like that.
Counselor: Counseling would probably go a lot better, and you would get more out of it, if we didn't have to depend on me to ask the right questions. Why don't we start with you telling me something about yourself?
Gail: What do you want to know?
Counselor: How does it feel to be here in counseling?
Gail: (after a couple minutes of silence) I don't know. I thought you were going to ask me questions like how many people in my family, like that.

Although Gail had elected to come to counseling on her own, she did not trust the counselor or the process. Therefore, she attempted to control the nature of the counselor's questions. In later counseling sessions, Gail started to disclose, then stopped short of allowing the counselor a closer look at her. Gail attended five sessions, canceled her sixth session, and never returned. Her high mistrust led to premature termination (Terrell & Terrell, 1984).

There seem to be no proven techniques for overcoming the mistrust of the highly mistrusting African American woman. The high level of mistrust of the society, over which counselors have no control, generalizes to the counseling process. Understanding that high levels of mistrust may be encountered can help to mediate the feelings of frustration and ineffectiveness that can result from working with highly mistrustful clients.

Self-Esteem and Empowerment

How clients feel about themselves is often an issue that must be addressed during counseling before any real change can occur. This issue, more than any other, determines whether clients have the power to take the risks required for behavioral and life changes. This is particularly true for African American females whose image has been tainted by myths and stereotypes throughout the history of this country (Jordan, 1991). It continues to be difficult for African American girls and women to counteract the negative pictures with which they are consistently confronted. Counselors working with African American girls and women will undoubtedly encounter some clients who have not been successful at fighting the negative images and who have, therefore, incorporated negative images into their belief systems about themselves. The culturally sensitive counselor will be aware of self-esteem issues and will work to help African American females develop a sense of pride and dignity in their Black womanhood.

The client's initial presentation does not always portray her real feelings about herself. The tradition of being the strong woman can lead to the creation of a facade of high self-esteem and powerfulness. However, the facade, when cracked, can reveal a drastically different portrait. Cracks occur when some event in the woman's life leads to her getting in touch with an internalized belief that is part of her belief system. For Boyd (1993), the event was a divorce, which translated into failure as a strong Black woman. Often, the emotions directly resulting from the event are what brings the woman to counseling. The negative beliefs about herself are yet to be revealed as a true source of disease. It is the role of the counselor to facilitate the revelation and help the woman replace the negative beliefs with more positive beliefs.

Even though negative belief systems can be changed throughout the life span, the ideal situation is to intercept the internalization of the negative messages at an early age. Counselors who work with African American girls can take a more proactive approach than those who work with adults. Awareness of the messages and their media can help counselors to develop interventions for African American girls to learn to counteract the negative messages. Jordan (1991) presented an eight-session developmental group intervention aimed at self-definition and positive self-esteem that can be adapted to younger Black females. Intercepting the negative messages to Black girls can occur in informal ways as well. For example, the culturally sensitive school counselor can identify numerous opportunities for letting African American girls know that they are worthwhile and deserving of love.

The case of Brenda illustrates intercepting a negative message to an African American adolescent:

Brenda was a 16-year-old Black female referred for counseling by her case worker who also drove her to her sessions. Brenda had lived in a foster home for 3 years, ever since her mother was arrested on drug charges. Brenda was referred to counseling for her aggressive, combative behavior in school. She has worked well with her counselor, an African American woman. The following excerpt was extracted from the eighth session. Brenda had been disturbed by a confrontation with a teacher the previous day.

Brenda: So I just tried to tell her that all Black people wasn't like she said. She got all mad and everything and said I needed to read my books before I started arguing with her. But she was wrong. I did my reading. Like, she ain't got to try and treat me like I don't know nothing.

Counselor: Sounds like you got pretty angry with her.

Brenda: Well, wouldn't you if she was saying something that you know was wrong about Black people? I bet you woulda said something, too, if you was there.

Counselor: You're right. I probably would have said something if I didn't agree with it. I would have tried to be respectful doing it.

Brenda: I was, Dr. J. I said, " 'scuse me, Miss Jones, I don't agree with all that because Black people did a lot of work when they didn't even get paid for it, like when they was slaves." And she musta thought I was trying to 'dis her or something. But wasn't what I said respectful?

Counselor: Sounds like it. If you think you used the best tone of voice you could, you weren't trying to 'dis her. And your argument was good. So you can feel good about what you did.

Brenda: But why she gotta act like I'm the dumb one or something?

Counselor: I'm not sure. You haven't said anything to me that makes me believe you're dumb.

Because the relationship between Brenda and the counselor was already firmly established, the counselor used that to counteract the "dumb" message that Brenda believed she was getting from her teacher. Brenda avoided internalizing a negative belief because she received affirmation from an adult that she liked and trusted. Brenda also learned that she could maintain a respectful manner even when she was angry. In the course of her 16 sessions of counseling, many more issues of self-esteem were addressed. Brenda has since graduated from high school.

Contemporary Issues

Cultural sensitivity also means being aware of the problems and issues in the environment that affect the client's sense of security, power, and identity. Issues such as increased violence and HIV/AIDS must be understood in terms of the toll they take, the havoc they wreak, in the African American community. Nowhere are the effects of these two major contemporary issues felt more acutely than in African American women.

As violence in the United States increases, the age of both the perpetrators and victims decreases. Those assaulting and those being assaulted are young men and women, boys and girls. A mother now has to be concerned not only with the safety of her children but also of herself. The pervasiveness of that fear increases as she realizes that so much of the violence is random, that no matter how well she has raised her children, they can be victims by merely waiting for a bus, or walking to school, or playing outside. As great as the fear is of the mothers, it is just as great for the children. Children in the most violent communities have to develop psychological defenses against the violence, often manifested in their seeming insensitivity to the death and violence they witness. Many have lost siblings, friends, and neighbors to the violence.

Until safety needs are satisfied, higher order needs such as self-esteem cannot be addressed. Counselors must be aware that these are real issues for some African American girls and women and that what is considered normal human development may be mutated by environmental factors. The feeling of powerlessness springs from the reality of powerlessness. The counselor attends, then, to affirming the legitimacy of the feelings and of the woman.

The infection and death rates for HIV/AIDS represent another havoc-wrecking contemporary problem. Unfortunately, many members of the African American community continue to bury their heads in the sand even as the disease has become a leading cause of death among African American women ages 18 to 44. AIDS cases in adolescents are disproportionately concentrated among minorities (DiClemente, 1989). Blacks comprise 51% of the adolescent females with AIDS, with most contracting the disease through unprotected heterosexual contacts (Centers for Disease Control, 1992). Despite these alarming numbers and resulting deaths, which have left scores of orphans, the African American community in general still views AIDS as a shameful disease that should not be discussed. It should, by all means, be left out of obituaries!

The shame of the disease makes it all the more difficult to deal with the loss of mothers, sisters, and daughters. The shame prevents open discussion and grieving; the anger that remains turns into bitterness. Culturally sensitive counselors recognize the shame associated with HIV/AIDS and understand that the stress of having an HIV-infected relative or of losing an AIDS-stricken relative is not easily acknowledged in counseling. However, the therapeutic benefits of sharing the shame cannot be stressed enough. Actually verbalizing the name of the infection/disease is a big step for some Black women. Once they can face it by verbalizing it, by acknowledging that it is in their lives, they can learn to let go of the shame.

In addition to these two largest, and perhaps most devastating, contemporary issues are numerous others. Culturally sensitive counselors understand the need to constantly reeducate themselves regarding the important issues affecting the communities and their clients.

Conclusion

Being a culturally sensitive counselor cannot be accomplished by attending only to those things presented in this chapter. Counselors who are truly culturally sensitive instead understand that much of the work involved in achieving this status is done in attaining a true sense of how they are a product of their own culture. Having done this work, counselors are able to maintain boundaries between themselves and Black female clients and between their cultural interpretation and the client's culture. Counselors who continuously seek only skills for counseling African American girls and women will never achieve a satisfying repertoire.

References

Atkinson, D. R., Morten, G., & Sue, D. W. (1993). *Counseling American minorities: A cross-cultural perspective* (4th ed). Madison, WI: Brown and Benchmark.

Boyd, J. A. (1993). *In the company of my sisters: Black women and self-esteem.* New York: Dutton.

Centers for Disease Control. (1992). U.S. AIDS cases reported through March 1992. *HIV/AIDS Surveillance.* Atlanta, GA: Author.

Cross Jr., W. E. (1995). The psychology of nigrescence: Revising the Cross model. In J. G. Ponterotto, J. M. Casas, L. A. Suzuki, & C. M. Alexander (Eds.), *Handbook of multicultural counseling* (pp. 93–122). Thousand Oaks, CA: Sage.

Cross, W. E. (1978). The Thomas and Cross models of psychological nigrescence: A review. *Journal of Black Psychology, 5,* 13–31.

DiClemente, R. J. (1989). Epidemiology of AIDS, HIV prevalence, and HIV incidence among adolescents. *Journal of School Health, 62,* 325–330.

Jordan, J. M. (1991). Counseling African American women: "Sister-friends." In C. C. Lee & B. L. Richardson (Eds.), *Multicultural issues in counseling: New approaches to diversity* (pp. 51–63). Alexandria, VA: American Association for Counseling and Development.

Ridley, C. R. (1984). Clinical treatment of the nondisclosing Black client: A therapeutic paradox. *American Psychologist, 39,* 1234–1244.

Ridley, C. R., Mendoza, D. W., Kanitz, B. E., Angermeir, L., & Zenk, R. (1994). Cultural sensitivity in multicultural counseling: A perceptual schema model. *Journal of Counseling Psychology, 41,* 125–136.

Stewart, E. C. (1981). Cultural sensitivities in counseling. In P. B. Pedersen, J. G. Draguns, W. J. Lonner, & J. E. Trimble (Eds.), *Counseling across cultures* (Rev. ed., pp. 61–86). Honolulu: University of Hawaii Press.

Terrell, F., & Terrell, S. L. (1981). An inventory to measure cultural mistrust among Blacks. *Western Journal of Black Studies, 5,* 180–184.

Terrell, F., & Terrell, S. L. (1984). Race of counselor, client sex, cultural mistrust level, and premature termination from counseling among Black clients. *Journal of Counseling Psychology, 31,* 371–375.

Thompson, C. E., Worthington, R., & Atkinson, D. R. (1994). Counselor content orientation, counselor race, and Black women's cultural mistrust and self-disclosures. *Journal of Counseling Psychology, 41,* 155–161.

Watkins, C. E., Jr., Terrell, F., Miller, F. S., & Terrell, S. L. (1989). Cultural mistrust and its effects on expectational variables in Black client-White counselor relationships. *Journal of Counseling Psychology, 36,* 447–450.

Other Resources

Angelou, M. (1993). *Wouldn't take nothing for my journey now.* New York: Random House.

Bonner, L. B. (1990). *Good hair: For colored girls who've considered weaves when the chemicals became too ruff.* New York: Crown Trade Paperbacks.

Jordan, J. (1992). *Technical difficulties.* New York: Vintage Books.

Tarpley, N. (Ed.). (1995). *Testimony.* Boston: Beacon Press.

Vanzant, I. (1993). *Acts of faith: Daily meditations for people of color.* New York: Simon & Schuster.

Vanzant, I. (1995). *The value in the valley: A Black woman's guide through life's dilemmas.* New York: Simon & Schuster.

8

COUNSELING AFRICAN AMERICAN MALE YOUTH AND MEN

Courtland C. Lee and Deryl F. Bailey

Much attention has been focused on the changing face of manhood in the United States. With the approach of the 21st century, American men find themselves constantly evaluating and revaluating their role and meaning in society. They are besieged from all sides with messages about and images of what it means, or should mean, to be a man. On one hand, feminists call upon men to be more sensitive and share their masculine privilege (Ehrenreich, 1984), and male writers advocate that men get in touch with and celebrate primal or mythic images of manhood (Bly, 1990; Keen, 1991). On the other hand, Madison Avenue exhorts men to "just do it." The often conflicting nature of these images and messages has left many men confused about the nature of manhood and the essence of masculinity (Doyle, 1983; Emerson, 1985; Merton, 1986; Pleck, 1981).

For African American men these images and messages concerning manhood are often distorted by compelling data suggesting that, as a group, they are in a state of psychosocial crisis. Evidence from both popular and social science literature has indicated that African American males constitute a population at risk (Cordes, 1985; Dent, 1989; Gibbs, 1988; Johnson & Watson, 1990; Jones, 1986; McCall, 1994; Monroe, 1987; Parham & McDavis, 1987; Randolph, 1990; Salholz, 1990; Weathers, 1993; Wright, 1992).

In 1990 the National Urban League released a report on the status of the African American male (Johnson & Watson, 1990) that offered a disturbing portrait of African American male life. According to the report, African American males have a shorter life span than any other population group in America due to a disproportionate vulnerability to disease and homicide. In every age group, African American males are significantly more likely to be victims of violent crime than are White men or women of either race. Among youths ages 14 to 17, the African American male victimization rate is 65.9 per 100,000 in the population, compared to the White male rate of 8.5 per 100,000 (U.S. Department of Justice, 1986).

The Urban League report also pointed out that structural changes in the labor market and discriminatory hiring practices create wide gaps between the earnings of African American and White men, and a disproportionate number of African American men live in poverty. Significantly, unemployment rates for African American males are 2.3 times higher than for White males, and in 1988, less than one third of African American males between the ages of 16 and 19 had jobs (Holister, 1989; U.S. Bureau of the Census, 1990).

The Urban League report further pointed out that the negative self-image internalized by many African American males in combination with the negative attitudes of authority figures toward African American males and increases in violence and drug abuse have resulted in a disproportionate involvement of African American males with the criminal justice system. In 1988, for example, African American males accounted for 47% of all persons incarcerated in state prisons and 41% of inmates in city, county, and local jails. These percentages are significant given that African American men make up only 5% of the United States population (U.S. Bureau of the Census, 1991). In addition, 39.8% more African American males are involved in the criminal justice system than are enrolled in higher education (Mauer, 1990).

Central to the challenges confronting African American males are significantly low levels of educational attainment (Green & Wright, 1991; Johnson & Watson, 1990; Narine, 1992; Reed, 1988; Wright, 1992). Data on the educational attainment of African American male youth from a variety of sources present a profile of widespread failure (Johnson & Watson, 1990; Narine, 1992; National Black Child Development Institute, 1990; Patton, 1995; Reed, 1988; Select Committee on Children, Youth, and Families, 1989; Subcommittee on Investment, Jobs, and Prices, 1991; Subcommittee on Select Education, 1990). What is evident from this profile is that African American males tend to experience massive alienation from the educational process. In school systems throughout the country, achievement, aspiration, and pride are stifled in many African American male youth.

It is apparent that African American males face major psychosocial hurdles. Although many achieve significant economic, educational, and social success, African American men often face a series of significant challenges to such success across the life span. These challenges can take a heavy toll, often manifesting in significant levels of stress and depression (Evans & Evans, 1995; Gary, 1985; Gary & Berry, 1985; Jones & Gay, 1982, 1983).

This chapter offers direction for counseling with African American male youth and men. Many of the ideas and concepts presented in chapter 7 for counseling with African American women and girls have applicability here, but the historical and social challenges that confront African American males are unique. Thus this chapter first overviews historical and cultural perspectives. The chapter next describes issues and provides a framework for counseling African American male youth, and then explores issues and presents a framework for counseling African American men. Two in-depth case studies illustrate crucial issues and strategies.

Historical and Cultural Perspectives on Counseling African American Males

Responsive counseling with African American males, at any age, must be predicated on an understanding of the historical and cultural context that shapes the psychosocial development of this client group. Professional counselors must possess not only solid intervention skills but also knowledge of the historical forces that have impacted on African American male development. Likewise, they must appreciate the dynamics of African American culture and their influence on optimal mental health.

Historically, unlike his White male counterpart, achieving masculine privilege in the United States has not been a birthright for the African American male (Genovese, 1974; Hernton, 1965; Lee, 1990; Staples, 1983). Social and economic forces throughout American history have combined to keep African American males from assuming traditional masculine roles (Staples, 1983; Wilkinson & Taylor, 1977). This process has been an integral part of the dynamics of oppression and racism that have pervaded the Black experience in America (Grier & Cobbs, 1968; Thomas & Sillen, 1972). Beginning with the slavery experience, the African American male has been an object of fear (Grier & Cobbs, 1968; Hilliard, 1985; Staples, 1978). He, and his implied physical prowess and leadership ability, have been perceived as a significant threat to the social order and economic power structure. Both during the era of slavery and in the succeeding decades, the American power structure has initiated various social and economic actions that have resulted in the subordination of the African American male and the virtual elimination of his masculine advantage in the larger society (Staples, 1978; Taylor, 1977). The racism inherent in such actions has operated to impede the sex role socialization of African American males and has kept them, in many instances, from realizing even the most basic aspects of masculine privilege and power, namely life-sustaining employment and the ability to support a family (Staples, 1978).

The historical persistence of barriers to manhood has significantly impacted the psychosocial development of African American males (Crawley & Freeman, 1993). The general inability to fulfill masculine roles has made rage, frustration, powerlessness, and hopelessness pervasive themes in their developmental dynamics. These themes are often evident in antisocial and self-destructive behavior patterns (Cordes, 1985; Gary, 1981; McGhee, 1984). In a society where a man's worth (and ultimately his manhood) have seemingly been judged by his ability to accumulate a degree of wealth and power, the African American male's general inability to obtain little of either has had serious consequences for his psychosocial development.

Scores of African American men have developed the survival strategies, coping mechanisms, and forms of resistance to overcome societal barriers successfully, but it must be understood that systemic forces have historically been stacked against their psychosocial development (Chestang, 1980; Hilliard, 1985; Madhubuti, 1990). For this reason, counseling with African American male youth and men must be based on an understanding of the historical context in which their psychosocial development occurs. Such development is complex and challenging in a society that has historically placed the African American male at social and economic risk.

The cultural context of the Black experience has, however, served to nurture the socialization and psychosocial development of male youth and men, even though American society has characteristically stifled the expression of African American manhood. According to African American scholars, African American cultural experience has a positive relationship with optimal mental health and psychosocial development for men and male youth (Akbar, 1991; Crawley & Freeman, 1993; Hare & Hare, 1985; Lee, 1996; Majors & Bilson, 1992; Oliver, 1989) because African American male development and socialization is enhanced in a cultural environment characterized by rudimentary African- and African-American-oriented philosophical assumptions. These assumptions constitute cultural traditions among African Americans that place a high premium on kinship, cooperation, mutual respect, commitment, and spirituality.

The assumptions have thus contributed to the development of positive attitudes, values, and behaviors among African Americans, often despite the social pressure of racism and oppression in the larger American society. Significantly, from an early age, African American males are generally socialized into these cultural traditions—the foundation of optimal African American male socialization and mental health—in the home and larger African American community (Allen, 1981; Barnes, 1991; Crawley & Freeman, 1993; Lee, 1991; Majors & Bilson, 1992; Staples, 1983). The traditions form the meaning of psychosocial development and help African American males interpret the larger American social milieu. Counseling intervention with African American males, therefore, should be predicated on an appreciation of their cultural context and its crucial role in promoting psychosocial development.

Counseling African American Male Youth

Issues to Consider in Counseling With African American Male Youth

The psychosocial development of African American male youth needs to be interpreted within the context of psychosocial issues that may impede development of this client group. Counselors who work with African American male youth need to understand and be sensitive to these crucial psychosocial issues, which include negative environmental stressors, additional developmental tasks, and a lack of role models. The effects of these impediments to psychosocial development in childhood and adolescence can often be seen in negative and self-destructive attitudes, behaviors, and values among young African American males. Results include educational underachievement, unemployment, delinquency, substance abuse, homicide, and incarceration in disproportionate numbers (Cordes, 1985; Gibbs, 1988). Working with an awareness of these issues will allow counselors to develop effective intervention strategies that promote education and social empowerment for African American male youth.

Negative environmental stressors.   African American male youth may be extremely vulnerable to social forces and negative societal expectations. Society has far too often indoctrinated African American male youth with the belief that their future is limited to athletics, entertainment, prison, or the morgue (Cordes, 1985; Gibbs, 1988; Jones, 1986). The expectations of poor academic performance, drug use, violence, teenage fatherhood, and disrespect for authority in many instances become self-fulfilling prophecies for young African American males. What is not often considered, however, is that these represent secondary responses to negative environmental stressors for many African American male youth. These environmental stressors include cultural insensitivity and a generally oppressive system that fears the empowerment of African American male youth (Patton, 1995).

According to Patton (1995), the responses of African American male youth to these stressors have been identified as dysfunctional cultural adaptations and can include fathering a child out of wedlock, disrespecting women, and adopting a macho image. Such behavioral responses represent functional and immediate reactions to systemic insensitivity toward African American males. In their attempt to attain manhood, young African males often employ these adaptations without understanding why or realizing their possible self-destructive nature.

When working with African American male youth, counselors need to be aware of the context in which such behaviors occur. Counselors must understand the nature of these reactions and adaptations and their direct relationship to the socioeconomic status, social injustices, and educational constraints that often confront young African American males. An awareness of the relationship among environmental stressors (social, economical, political, and educational limitations), the challenges generated by these stressors, and the resulting secondary adaptations will help counselors to help many African American male youth address the issues confronting them. Thus although counselors may not be able to alleviate the environmental stress caused by cultural insensitivity and an oppressive system, they can effectively help African American male youth attain workable solutions to their often self-destructive secondary adaptations.

Additional developmental tasks. Theorists and researchers have suggested that major aspects of human development unfold in a series of life stages and are influenced by both heredity and environment (Erikson, 1950; Havighurst, 1972; Kohlberg, 1966; Piaget, 1970). As individuals progress through the life stages, they must master a series of developmental tasks. Mastery of tasks at one stage of life influences success with those in succeeding stages. Conversely, failure to master developmental tasks at one stage can negatively influence success in later stages.

For young African American males, successfully completing these early developmental stages and tasks has often been problematic due to a complex set of historical and social factors. In many instances, these factors interact in such a manner that African American male youth are forced to deal with additional developmental tasks in their psychosocial development (Crawley & Freeman, 1993). These tasks are most directly influenced by race, ethnicity, and culture. These tasks are often negatively impacted by the convergence of environmental forces (Lee, 1996; Madhubuti, 1990; Majors & Bilson, 1992), including extreme environmental stress in home, community, or school during the crucial early years of life (Hilliard, 1985; Myers & King, 1980). Successful completion of developmental tasks can, for example, be hampered by school experiences distinguished by ineffective teaching strategies as well as predetermined negative views on African American male youth and their learning potential on the part of educators (Lee, 1996; Washington & Lee, 1982). Thus instead of developing the sense of industry that comes with mastering fundamental skills in reading, writing, and computing during the all-important elementary school years, many young African American male students experience a sense of frustration with the teaching-learning process, which lays the groundwork for future academic and social failure.

Because African American male youth are often prevented from mastering both the crucial universal and race-specific developmental tasks in childhood and adolescence, this lack of mastery negatively influences their academic, career, and social success in the later stages of life (Lee, 1994, 1996). It is not unusual, therefore, for African American males to reach adolescence with a basic mistrust of their environment, doubts about their abilities, and confusion about their place in the social structure. This makes developing an identity during the crucial boyhood-to-manhood transition of the adolescent years extremely problematic.

Lack of role models. The social reality that many African American male youth may have to engage in the process of identity formation with minimal or no positive adult male role modeling compounds the issues. Significantly, identity formation during adolescence is a process in which youth develop aspects of their personal and social identities by selecting and identifying with various role models. Given the historical social and economic limitations placed on Black manhood in America, the range of adult African American male role models available to adolescent males may often be severely restricted. The developmental passage to adulthood can thus become a confusing experience for many African American male youth because the evolution of gender-appropriate roles and behaviors for African American men has often been stifled by historical and social powerlessness.

A Framework for Counseling With African American Male Youth

The psychosocial challenges that confront African American male youth suggest a pressing need for programmed intervention on the part of professional counselors. Such initiatives must focus on helping these youth develop the attitudes, behaviors, and values necessary to function at optimal levels.

Counseling may need to be provided through culture-specific empowerment experiences. These experiences should develop the attitudes and skills necessary for academic achievement, foster positive and responsible behavior, provide opportunities to analyze the image of African American men critically, expose participants to African American male role models, and develop a sense of cultural and historical pride in the accomplishments of African American men.

Four guidelines provide the framework for culture-specific counseling with African American male youth in educational or community mental health settings:

- **Be developmental in nature.** Far too often the only counseling young African American males receive comes after they have committed an offense against the social order. Generally the goal of such an intervention is not development, but rather punishment. Counseling should focus on helping African American male youth to meet challenges that often lead to problems in school and beyond in a proactive manner.
- **Provide for competent adult African American male resources as appropriate.** Only African American men can teach African American male youth how to be men. By virtue of attaining adult status as African Americans and males, they alone have the gender and cultural perspective to address the developmental challenges facing African American male youth accurately. Although African American women and individuals of both sexes from other ethnic backgrounds can play a significant role in helping to empower young African American males, it is only an adult African American man who can model the attitudes and behaviors of successful African American manhood. As necessary, therefore, efforts should be made actively to recruit, train, and support competent African American men to serve as facilitators or consultants in counseling interventions.
- **Incorporate the strengths of Black families.** Counseling initiatives for African American male youth must be based on an appreciation of the historical strength of the African American family. Such an appreciation is critical because much of the social science literature presents the generally pathological view of African American family life rather than the long-standing alternative view that disputes pathological notions of Black fam-

ily life. This alternative view reveals a legacy of continuity, hard work, kinship, love, pride, respect, and stability in the evolution of African American families—despite the history of discrimination, racism, oppression, and poverty that has characterized much of the African American experience. In the face of extreme environmental hardship, scores of African American families have found the inner resources to cope effectively, promote the positive development of children, and prevail ultimately across generations. Promoting family involvement in counseling with African American male youth, therefore, should be approached with the understanding that this institution is a strong and viable force for enhancing psychosocial development.

- **Incorporate African/African American culture.** Counselors should find ways to incorporate African and African American cultural dimensions into interventions for male youth. Culture-specific approaches to counseling transform basic aspects of African American life, generally ignored or perceived as negative in a traditional psychoeducational framework, into positive developmental experiences. For example, African and African American art forms (e.g., music, poetry, and graphic expression) and culture-specific curriculum materials can be incorporated into counseling.

The Case Study of Michael

The case study presented here illustrates many of the issues confronting counselors when working with African American male youth.

Michael is a 16-year-old African American male. He is the second oldest of three children. His mother is an elementary school teacher, and his father is a supervisor with an industrial firm. Michael and his family have lived in a White upper-middle-class suburban neighborhood for the past year. Prior to this they lived in an African American lower-middle-class neighborhood in a nearby city.

Michael has a history of negative educational experiences that began in preschool. His preschool teacher read continuously from a particular series of books that did not include any positive African American characters. When other children asked the teacher why Michael's skin was another color, the teacher explained that "He was left in the oven too long." Many mornings, Michael cried when it was time to leave for school.

Michael's dislike for school intensified as he got older. Despite this, he still managed to earn A's in elementary school until he reached fourth grade. At this time his grades started slipping, and his teachers started complaining about Michael's aggressive behavior toward his classmates. Because of his behavior and his teacher's inability to handle him, Michael was referred and placed in the Behavioral-Emotional Handicapped (BEH) class. He remained in this class through the remainder of elementary school and into middle school. Despite protest from Michael's parents, his counselor and teachers continued to push for the BEH placement.

A few months after his middle school BEH placement, Michael's parents noticed a major change in his attitude and circle of friends. These new friends had been labeled as *trouble makers*. Whenever Michael tried to do well in his school work, his peer group accused him of "acting White." He then became disruptive in school in order to earn their respect.

Case analysis.   The issues in Michael's case are characteristic of those confronting many African American male youth in contemporary schools. The school years for many young African American males are often characterized by dissimilarity and imbalance. Confronted daily with attitudes, behaviors, and values of educators, who in many instances are unaware of or insensitive to African American culture, bright and capable boys such as Michael can become alienated from the educational process at an early age. A review of this case makes it is easy to understand how African American male youth become negatively labeled and ultimately consigned to special education tracks.

Michael's middle school issue is typical of a growing phenomenon particularly evident among adolescent African American males. Because of peer accusations of acting White by getting good grades in school, many African American males question the value of academic achievement. Within the peer group, achieving academically is often viewed as adopting White values and forsaking Black culture. There is often tremendous pressure on African American students not to sell out in the eyes of their peers. This often means performing poorly in school in an attempt to stay in favor with the peer group.

Michael is feeling confused and alienated. His friends have communicated to him the message that somehow because he attempts to work hard in school he is no longer acting Black and is becoming White. It is obvious that peer relationships are extremely important to Michael and that he would rather be accepted by his friends than continue to do well in school.

Culturally responsive counseling practice with Michael.   Michael currently needs support to deal with the intense peer pressure he is experiencing. The counselor should be very forthright with Michael and process his perceptions of academic achievement. He needs to understand that by achieving in school he does not have to compromise his African American identity. The counselor should explore with Michael the historical importance of education to African Americans. The counselor might discuss with him the fact that he has the potential to be a role model for his siblings by working hard in school.

It is important for Michael to understand the concept of being bicultural. The counselor should explain to him that it is important to learn to "walk the walk and talk the talk" when he is in the classroom. This does not mean that he has become White, but that he has merely learned appropriate behavior for the American macroculture. He must be led to see that when he is in African American social and communal settings he can freely express his blackness.

The counselor may also want to explore with Michael the nature of friendship. They should talk about the unconditional nature of friendship and the fact that true friends are supportive no matter what an individual does.

Such guidance might come in the form of a culture-specific counseling intervention. One approach might be to get Michael and other adolescent African American boys in the school involved in a developmental rites-of-passage experience. For example, a multisession developmental group counseling experience for adolescent African American males has been developed by Lee (1996) within the context and spirit of a traditional African ritual known as *manhood training*. In this ritual, adolescent boys were isolated from their families for an extended period of time and given rigorous physical and mental training conducted by respected older males. The purpose of the training was to develop the attitudes and skills necessary for assuming the responsibilities associated with, and considered important in, the masculine role. If a boy successfully completed this training, he was formally acknowledged as a man among his people and accorded the rights and responsibilities that went with being a man.

This multisession developmental group counseling experience helps to redirect the focus of counseling strategies from remediation to development. It provides the opportunity for counselors to help young African American males develop the attitudes and skills to effectively meet environmental challenges that often lead to problems in the school setting and beyond.

A significant feature of the experience is the use of selected African and African American art forms (e.g., music, poetry, and graphic expression) and culture-specific curriculum materials as educational aids in the counseling process. Incorporating such curriculum materials and aesthetic dimensions into counseling interventions with African American students is a way to facilitate personal and social growth (Lee, 1989; Lee & Lindsey, 1985; Pasteur & Toldson, 1982) and strengthen body, mind, and soul. This strengthening is accomplished not only through developing an understanding and appreciation of the Black man in African and African American history and culture but also through developing achievement motivation, developing positive and responsible behavior, and modeling positive African American male images.

Given the importance of role modeling, an adult African American male presence is crucial for this counseling experience. Concerted efforts should be made to include competent African American males as group leaders or resource people.

Such an experience will assist Michael in developing a new attitude and improving skills necessary for academic achievement. Also, he will begin to analyze his image of himself as a young African American man critically, develop a sense of positive brotherhood with the other members of the group, and gain a sense of cultural and historical pride in the accomplishments of African and African American men.

It is also important for the counselor to consult with Michael's parents. The counselor should reconsider his or her support for Michael's BEH placement. Often African American students are placed in such classes both because of biased perceptions on the part of educators and because of culturally biased psychoeducational assessment procedures. The counselor should stand ready, therefore, to assist Michael's parents in challenging and reviewing the assessment criteria used to place him in BEH classes.

In addition, the counselor should be prepared to intervene with educators to effect institutional change for his benefit. Many of Michael's difficulties throughout his school career can be attributed to educators who lacked an understanding of the dynamics of growing up both African American and male and their implications for the learning process. In acting as a student advocate, the counselor should facilitate an awareness among his or her professional colleagues of the systemic factors that impinge upon the educational development of African American students. Consulting with teachers to help them delineate and challenge any stereotypes they may have acquired about African American males and their expectations of them may be important. Advocacy may also entail helping teachers find ways to integrate the accomplishments of African American culture into the curriculum and to emphasize the contributions of African American males in instructional plans.

Summary.   Michael's case demonstrates that counseling African American male youth requires an understanding of the crucial aspects that impact their psychosocial development. Counseling practice for promoting Michael's educational and personal-social development must be conducted on a series of levels. Not only is culturally responsive counseling with African American male youth necessary, but also intervention into major aspects of their environment may be required.

Counseling African American Men

Issues to Consider in Counseling With African American Men

Although much has been written about counseling men in recent years, very little of this literature has focused on specific issues of counseling with African American men. The literature has suggested that although there are issues common to counseling all men (Moore & Leafgren, 1990; Scher, Stevens, Good, & Eichenfield, 1987), the unique psychological and social pressures on African American men make mental health intervention with this client group particularly challenging (Gary, 1985; Gary & Berry, 1985: Jones & Gay, 1982, 1983; Lee, 1990; Washington, 1987). In order to provide a framework for counseling African American men, a number of important issues need to be considered. These include racism, problems of aggression and control, cultural alienation, self-esteem, dependency, and help-seeking attitudes and behaviors (Gary, 1985; Gary & Berry, 1985; Jones & Gay, 1982, 1983).

Racism as a precipitating factor of mental health challenges for African American men. When discussing important issues in counseling with African American men, it is important to stress that, as a client group, they differ significantly in terms of their socioeconomic status, educational attainment, lifestyles, and value orientations. However, all African American men share the common reality of racism (Gary, 1985; Gary & Berry, 1985; Jones & Gay, 1983). Reactions to this oppressive dynamic may differ, but its persistence significantly impacts the quality of life for African American men and should be considered as a significant factor in both problem etiology and counseling intervention (Gary, 1985; Gary & Berry, 1985; Jones & Gay, 1983).

The stresses of daily life are compounded for African American men by both overt and covert racism. As mentioned previously, racism operates, in many instances, to limit African American men from a full measure of life-sustaining employment and the ability to support a family (Jones & Gay, 1983; Staples, 1978). In addition, racism has spawned a number of negative stereotypes about African American manhood. (Gibbs, 1988; Jones & Gay, 1983; Majors & Bilson, 1992; Oliver, 1984; Staples, 1978).

The historical persistence of racism has significantly impacted the mental health of adult African American males. The general inability to fulfill masculine roles totally has made anger, frustration, diminished self-esteem, and depression pervasive mental health issues for African American men (Gary, 1985; Gary & Leashore, 1982; Hilliard, 1985; Jones & Gay, 1983; Washington, 1987).

Significantly, African American men have developed a number of ways of coping with and adapting to the dynamics of racism and its inherent challenges, many of which may manifest themselves as presenting issues in counseling. Several of these are discussed in the following paragraphs.

Problems of aggression and control. The problems that African American men experience with aggression and control often present themselves in one of three ways. First, African American men may exhibit too much control over their anger, frustration, or other strong emotions, resulting in repression or suppression of such affect. Second, they may exhibit too little control over such emotions. In this case, they often demonstrate limited or immature coping skills. Third, African American men may engage in inappropriate channeling processes in which they direct strong emotions inward. Such channeling processes can often lead to stress-related illness such as hypertension (Myers, Anderson, & Strickland, 1989) or maladaptive behaviors including substance abuse (Redd, 1989).

Cultural alienation/disconnection. Often perceiving themselves to be marginalized or powerless in American society, many African American men cope with their anger, frustration, or sense of hopelessness by disconnecting from meaningful personal relationships or roles valued by society. Such disconnection often leads to cultural alienation. With a limited sense of interconnectedness and a perceived sense of rejection by many sectors of society, the attitudes, behaviors, and values of many African American men often reflect significant disengagement from the world of work, family, and community. This cultural alienation often leads to an identity built on an outlaw or outsider image.

Self-esteem issues. The general inability to fulfill masculine roles totally often contributes to diminished self-esteem among many African American men. An internalized negative self-image generally results when African American men perceive that they are socially or economically handicapped by negative stereotypes or exclusion from a full measure of employment opportunities. Such perceptions may lead to concerted and often misdirected efforts to assert manhood and attain a sense of self-esteem. In many instances, such efforts result in maladaptive or antisocial behaviors.

Dependency issues. The dimensions of coping and adaptation among African American men can often be related to issues of dependency. African American men may relieve environmental or interpersonal stress by developing unhealthy or unproductive dependencies. For example, the release of anger, frustration, or other negative affect may be associated with a dependency on drugs or alcohol. Similarly, the release of such affect may be linked to dependency on a process. This might be seen among men whose problem-solving or coping behavior consists of a relatively constant process of maladaptive or violent behavior.

Help-seeking attitudes and behaviors among African American men. In considering issues of counseling with African American men, it is important to examine their help-seeking attitudes and behaviors. Consistent with the literature on counseling men in general, African American men, as a rule, do not seek counseling. In many cases, African American men consider the need to seek traditional counseling as an admission of weakness or as "unmanly." Although this is a phenomenon that can be observed among men from a number of racial or ethnic groups, it takes on a different dimension for African American men. For many of them, doing anything that seems unmanly can threaten a masculine self-concept already diminished by society's views and stereotypes of African American manhood. As a rule, therefore, African American men are generally socialized not to open up to strangers.

African American men often find nontraditional counseling, however, within community kinship networks (Taylor & Chatters, 1989). For example, many men seek out family members or close and trusted friends for help with problem resolution or decision making. They may also seek the guidance of a minister or other religious leader associated with the Black church. In addition, African American men have traditionally found nontraditional counseling services in community centers of male social activity such as barbershops, taverns, or fraternal/social organizations. These are places where men engage in informal conversation and significant male bonding. Such centers allow men to informally, and often indirectly, discuss personal issues with trusted confidants in a nonthreatening atmosphere.

In many instances, African American men are referred for counseling by some societal agent—judge, social worker, or probation officer—after they have committed some offense against the social order. Counseling, therefore, becomes for these men a forced process, and the implicit goal is rehabilitation or punishment. Many other African American men also approach the counseling process with apathy, suspicion, or hostility. The resistant attitude about counseling may be a defense mechanism among many African American males (Majors & Nikelly, 1983; Vontress, 1971, 1995). Because they generally view counseling as an activity conducted by agents of a system that has rendered them virtually powerless, the counseling process can seem to be just one more infringement on African American manhood (Lee, 1990).

A Framework for Counseling With African American Men

The issues just discussed may present barriers to effective counseling with African American men, but they also provide the basis of a framework for effective intervention with this client group. Among key guidelines that comprise this framework are the following:

- **Develop rapport.** Given the possible degree of alienation or distrust of the counseling process, it is important to find ways to make an initial personal connection with African American male clients. Counselors may need to adopt an interpersonal orientation when counseling with African American men. Such an orientation places the primary focuses on the verbal and nonverbal interpersonal interactions between counselor and client as opposed to counseling goals or tasks (Gibbs, 1980).
- **Pace the engagement of the actual counseling process.** It is important to pace the counseling relationship and be mindful not to engage in therapeutic work too rapidly with many African American men. The process is often more effective if it evolves naturally from a personal relationship, based on openness and trust that emerges between the counselor and the client.
- **Prepare to self-disclose.** It is important that a counselor be prepared to self-disclose, often at a deep and personal level, to an African American male client. A counselor's willingness forthrightly to answer direct, and often intimate, questions about his or her life increases credibility and promotes rapport with many African American men in counseling. A counselor should only

self-disclose, however, to the level of his or her comfort about revealing personal information to a client.

- **Encourage introspection.** Given cultural alienation or disconnection among many African American men, a counselor may need to foster a climate that encourages client introspection. The veneer of aloofness, strength, and control characteristic of alienation among African American men may preclude the sharing of intimate feelings that is generally a major aspect of the counseling process. Counselor credibility and openness can promote a climate that will facilitate an introspection process with many African American male clients.

- **Explore spirituality.** Counseling with African American men can often be enhanced if a counselor can engage clients in an exploration of how they approach living and dying (i.e., spirituality). Helping clients to explore their sense of spirituality or personal meaning in life can provide a focus for processing issues of alienation, anger, or frustration. Such an existential/philosophical exploration can be facilitated only when rapport and trust have been established.

- **Be racism sensitive.** Counseling with African American men must be predicated on a sensitivity to the dynamic of racism. Although there is a great deal of variation in the effects of racism on the psychosocial development of African American men, its influence on the quality of their lives cannot not be overstated. A culturally responsive counselor, therefore, should factor this variable into problem etiology and resolution as appropriate. It is important to avoid discounting clients' perceptions of how this dynamic impacts their lives.

- **Conduct psychoeducational counseling.** Counseling should be viewed as an educative process for many African American men. The primary focus of the process may need to be developing new skills or behaviors to deal more effectively with social and economic challenges.

The framework for a counseling process with African American men can be seen in five crucial stages. The stages are similar in their structure and content to a framework advanced by Gibbs (1980) for conceptualizing the initial response of African American consultees to the use of mental health consultation. Gibbs suggested the importance of considering an interpersonal orientation in mental health interventions with African Americans. This clinical orientation focuses on process rather than content in interpersonal interactions. Adopting such an orientation requires interpersonal competence, that is, the ability to evoke positive attitudes and to obtain favorable responses to one's actions. Culturally responsive counseling with African American men, therefore, is predicated on promoting an interpersonal orientation. The following five stages imply interpersonal competence on the part of a counselor.

Stage 1—Initial Contact/Appraisal.   Upon entering counseling, many African American men will be aloof, reserved, passive-aggressive, or openly hostile. Conversely they may be superficially pleasant and appear to acquiesce to the counselor's wishes. Underlying such behavior may be a lack of trust in or hostility toward the counselor and the therapeutic process. At this stage, therefore, personal authenticity on the part of counselor is critical. It is essential that an African American male client see the counselor from the outset as genuine or as "being for real."

Stage 2—Investigative.   Equalitarian processesing characterizes this stage. In specific terms, this may consist of attempts on the part of an African American male client to minimize any social, economic, professional, or educational distinctions he perceives between himself and the counselor. A client may seek to relate to the counselor on a level that minimizes degrees, licenses, and other forms of professional identification. An African American male client may check out the counselor by investigating possible areas of personal commonality that exist between them. It is important, therefore, that a counselor become comfortable with stepping outside of his or her professional role to interact with an African American male client at such a level of personal commonality.

Stage 3—Involvement.   It is at this stage that an African American male client often decides whether he can identify with the counselor as a person. This decision is generally predicated on open and honest self-disclosure on the part of the counselor. At this stage of the counseling process a client often engages in an identification process that is characterized by asking the counselor personal questions. The degree to which a counselor is able to get personal and engage in self-disclosure with an African American male client can often promote a sense of trust and facilitate movement into a working counseling relationship.

Stage 4—Commitment. An African American male client generally makes a decision about whether or not he can trust and work with a counselor at this stage. This decision is usually based on his evaluation of the counselor as an open and honest individual that he can relate to on a personal level.

Stage 5—Engagement. At this final stage the client makes a decision that the counselor is for real and can be trusted. This is the working stage in which the counselor and client engage in the process of counseling.

The Case Study of Curtis

The case study presented here highlights some of the possible issues and challenges associated with counseling African American men.

Curtis is a 50-year-old African American male. He is currently a midlevel manager with a major electronics firm. He is married with three children. His wife is a middle school teacher in an urban public school system. Curtis and his family live in a middle-class suburb of a major city. His oldest child is a student at a prestigious university, and his other two children attend secondary school.

Curtis grew up in a working class neighborhood in a large city. His father worked two manual labor jobs to support Curtis, his mother, and his younger brother and sister. Today, Curtis's sister is a nurse who is married and lives with her family in a distant city. His brother became involved in drugs during adolescence and is now serving time in a nearby prison for manslaughter.

When he graduated from high school, Curtis enlisted in the Marine Corps and served a tour of duty in Vietnam, where he was wounded and received the Purple Heart. Upon his discharge from the Marines, Curtis got married and started his family. He also enrolled in college part time. After 6 years of working full time in a factory and attending college part time, Curtis received a BS degree in electrical engineering. He was then hired as a management trainee by the electronics firm. He was the only African American hired as a management trainee.

Recently, Curtis's performance at work has been slipping. He appears at work looking tired and, according to his boss, often seems detached from his coworkers. Suspecting problems at home, Curtis's boss suggests that he talk with the firm's employee assistance counselor.

Curtis is extremely reluctant to talk with the counselor. He initially attends the counseling sessions because he feels that has been ordered to do so. Curtis gradually reveals to the counselor, however, that he has recently been under a great deal of stress. His father passed away several years ago, and now he finds that he must take care of his mother, who is beginning to have health problems. This, in addition to paying college tuition for his oldest child and addressing the needs of his two younger children, has begun to strain his relationship with his family. Curtis says he and his wife are constantly arguing over finances and other family matters. He also never seems to have time for his children and seems to be constantly yelling at them.

However, he is most upset because he has watched younger White males with less experience than his advance beyond him in the management of the firm. In many instances, Curtis was responsible for the initial training of these men. When he has discussed his progress in the company with his supervisor, he has been told that these younger employees attended better training programs and that their knowledge of the electronics field is more current. This is despite the fact that his performance evaluations have always been outstanding. He claims he has watched White men in the company form networking groups that have generally excluded him. He knows that the key to advancement in the firm lies in being a part of one of these groups. Curtis reluctantly confides to the counselor that he has begun drinking to deal with his stress, fears, anger, and frustration.

Case analysis.   Curtis is an African American man dealing with a significant amount of stress in his life. His anger, frustration, fears, and perceptions of racism have actually moved him beyond stress to a state of distress. Ironically, he did what the system expects and sought the so-called *American dream.* He got an education, honorably served his country in a time of crisis, found gainful employment, worked hard, raised a family, and joined the ranks of the middle class. His achievements refute many of the statistics and stereotypes associated with Black men in contemporary American society.

Despite his accomplishments, however, Curtis perceives that he has not been able to participate fully in or cash in on the American dream. Although his financial and family challenges are characteristic of many middle-class American men, the dynamics associated with his ethnicity play a major role in Curtis's perceptions. Despite his qualifications and job performance, he has been unable to feel fully integrated into his work setting. More importantly, he has not been afforded the opportunity to advance in a manner commensurate with his job performance.

Curtis considers his failure to move up the corporate ladder a reflection of how he, as an African American, is viewed and treated in the workplace. It is obvious that he has reached the infamous glass ceiling that confronts many ethnic minorities and women in the workplace. It is a barrier that is characterized by racial or gender insensitivity and exclusion in the workplace. This unseen but pervasive barrier generally stifles both talent and career goals. It can also have a damaging effect on many aspects of an individual's life. For African Americans, this barrier to career advancement has fostered significant amounts of anger among members of the middle class (Cose, 1993; Thomas, 1993). This is certainly the case with Curtis.

Significantly, Curtis's anger, frustration, and associated stress have begun to affect the quality of his home and family life. His perceived inability to fulfill his multiple masculine roles of provider and head of his family have severely impacted upon his well-being.

As is often the case with African American men in counseling, the major presenting issue in Curtis's case is anger. He is angry at a system that has thwarted his ability to reach his full potential. Curtis appears to have channeled this anger and the other strong emotions associated with it inward, which has no doubt precipitated his drinking. As his level of stress rises, he attempts to cope by disconnecting from his environment, both at home and in the workplace.

It is obvious that being constantly passed over for career advancement has severely impacted Curtis's self-esteem. As family pressures increase, his ability to fulfill increasing responsibilities as a provider is in direct proportion to his inability to advance professionally. Curtis's career stagnation is particularly hard on him because, in his perception, the only thing blocking his advancement is the color of his skin.

Culturally responsive counseling practice with Curtis.   At the outset, in Stage 1—Initial Contact/Appraisal, it was important to gain Curtis's trust and allay his fears about talking about personal issues to a stranger. The counselor wanted Curtis to see him as a person first and mental health professional second. The counselor adopted an interpersonal approach that was focused more on the relationship between the two of them then any specific counseling goals. The counselor engaged Curtis in conversation about a variety of nonthreatening issues (e.g., sports, events in the community, the firm's ranking in the electronics field).

Stage 2—Investigative got underway as Curtis and the counselor continued to talk over the first few sessions, and it became obvious that they had much in common. The counselor was forthcoming with information about his own family origins, educational background, and military experience. It turned out that Curtis and the counselor shared similar political views, religious views, and opinions about the local sports teams. Several times Curtis asked direct questions about the counselor's home and family life. The counselor although not altogether comfortable in revealing such information, was generally open and honest with Curtis. Curtis had not yet revealed anything of any substance related to his anger and frustrations, but he and the counselor established a solid personal relationship. This was evidenced by the fact that Curtis began to refer to the counselor as *my man.*

Curtis and the counselor shared much in common. If this had not been the case, however, it would have been important for the counselor to be open with Curtis in a personal way. Finding ways to equalize the status of client and counselor is an important aspect in establishing a counseling relationship with many African American men.

Stage 3—Involvement was reached as Curtis began to reveal his anger at the firm's promotion policies. As he spoke, his anger became increasingly evident. It was important at this point for the counselor to let Curtis tell his story and vent his anger. As his story unfolded, Curtis periodically turned to the counselor and asked, "You understand what I'm saying?" or "You see where I'm coming from?" This was Curtis's way of checking to see if the counselor was really hearing what was being said. It was important for the counselor to answer these questions in a forthright and often personal way. In other words, Curtis needed to hear from the counselor, "Hey man, I've been there."

Stage 4—Commitment began after several sessions when it was obvious to Curtis that the counselor was someone he could definitely talk to and possibly work with. Curtis proclaimed that the counselor was "all right!" With this stamp of approval, he proclaimed that he was ready to work with the counselor on finding concrete solutions to the challenges facing him. In Curtis's words, it was "time to take care of some business."

Stage 4—Engagement started at this point because of the personal nature of the professional relationship that had been established between the counselor and Curtis. The counselor now encouraged Curtis to explore meaning in his life. He asked Curtis to consider how he saw himself as a human being, as a man, and as an African American. The counselor encouraged Curtis to consider what gave his life meaning as an African American man. Curtis talked about the importance of family, God, and work to his life. Curtis claimed that all of these things were important to him because things were so bad for Black men in general.

As the meaning and purpose of his life became more focused for Curtis, the counselor helped him to see the interrelatedness of his challenges: He now bears the financial responsibility not only for his children but also for his ailing mother. Career advancement could no doubt make this responsibility easier to bear. However, the glass ceiling appears to be preventing him from moving up the corporate ladder to greater economic reward. All of this contributes to his sense of anger and frustration, which affects his relationships both at home and work. It also has him questioning his worth as a man. Curtis was now ready to engage in a plan of action.

His first step was to admit that he was drinking too much and that this excessive behavior could not effectively relieve his stress. The counselor helped him to engage in a concrete problem-solving process. The primary goal was to find ways to channel his strong emotions more effectively. Curtis and the counselor explored a variety of options.

Curtis decided that one way to deal with the drinking and relieve stress was to get some exercise. He had played some basketball in high school and had put a net in his driveway for his children's recreation many years ago. In the past he had enjoyed shooting hoops with his kids. The counselor suggested that he might find time to shoot baskets again with his two younger children. This could not only provide him with exercise but could also help him to reconnect with his children.

His wife and children went to church on a regular basis, but Curtis did not. He and the counselor discussed the possibility that spiritual direction within the African American religious tradition might be important in dealing with his challenges. The counselor strongly supported Curtis's decision to attend church again with his family on a regular basis. The counselor and Curtis considered ways that this could become important family time, and how part of family time could include talking about and planning for family challenges with his wife.

A particularly difficult family issue, and one that heretofore had not been discussed, was Curtis's relationship with his incarcerated brother. Curtis visited his brother several times a year, but had minimal contact with him. When talking about his brother, Curtis got extremely emotional. He experienced tremendous guilt with respect to his brother. He discussed his regret at not having spent more time with his brother when they were both younger. Curtis felt that if he had spent more time as a role model or mentor for his brother, perhaps his brother could have avoided getting into trouble.

He made a commitment that part of his family time was to entail visiting his brother on a regular basis. Curtis planned to use his visits with his brother as a time to reestablish his relationship with him and possibly help him plan for his life after incarceration.

With respect to his work situation, Curtis discussed with the counselor the possibility of confronting his supervisor about his perceptions concerning racism in the firm's promotion practices. Curtis rehearsed with the counselor what he might say to the supervisor about his concerns. His goal was to be able to state his perceptions about the promotion practices in a calm, logical, but forceful manner.

The counselor at this point also decided to engage in some advocacy efforts on Curtis's behalf. He helped Curtis network with several local civil rights associations that could serve as a resource in his efforts to impact the firm's promotion policies. He promised to help Curtis locate and work with a lawyer in preparing a discrimination suit against the firm if that became necessary. The counselor also coordinated some training sessions on diversity issues in the workplace for the firm's management team.

As a result of his efforts and the threat of external legal and political action, Curtis was eventually promoted to an upper level management position. His family-focused efforts also improved the quality of his home life. He had found important new ways to channel his anger. His drinking behavior moderated significantly. After terminating the formal relationship with counselor he periodically dropped by the counselor's office whenever he was feeling stressed out and needed to talk.

Summary. In cases like Curtis's, a culturally responsive counselor needs to address the challenges associated with issues such as those confronting Curtis with intervention at the interpersonal and systemic levels. The first level of intervention involves the direct service to the client. There is much that a culturally responsive counselor can do to help empower a client such as Curtis to challenge his stress, fears, anger, and frustrations effectively. Such service delivery must be predicated, however, on an understanding and appreciation of the culture-specific issues that may hinder or facilitate responsive counseling with African American men.

In addition to direct client intervention with a client such as Curtis, a culturally responsive counselor may need to intervene into the work setting to effect institutional change. In this case, the counselor readily assumed the role of advocate for Curtis. As an advocate, the counselor intervened within the firm on behalf of Curtis, and indirectly other minority employees, in a way that was designed to eradicate both overt and covert racism.

Conclusion

Within the panorama of the changing face of manhood in America, the realities of African American males often stand out in a striking and often troublesome manner. The challenges confronting Michael and Curtis do not represent the experience of all African American male youth and men. However, these two cases do highlight the issues facing scores of African American male youth and men in contemporary society. The future status of African American males depends, in some measure, on the ability of counselors to help empower this client group for maximum psychoeducational achievement and meaningful, productive lives. This requires not only an understanding of the social and cultural context that frames African American male realities but also a willingness to expand the boundaries of counseling practice.

References

Akbar, N. (1991). *Visions for Black men*. Nashville, TN: Winston-Derek.

Allen, W. R. (1981). Moms, dads, and boys: Race and sex differences in the socialization of male children. In L. E. Gary (Ed.), *Black men* (pp. 99–114). Beverly Hills, CA: Sage.

Barnes, E. J. (1991). The Black community as a source of positive self-concept for Black children: A theoretical perspective. In R. L. Jones (Ed.), *Black psychology*. (3rd ed., pp. 667–692). Berkeley, CA: Cobb & Henry.

Bly, R. (1990). *Iron John: A book about men*. Reading, MA: Addison-Wesley.

Chestang, L. W. (1980). Character development in a hostile environment. In M. Bloom (Ed.), *Life span development* (pp. 40–50). New York: Macmillan.

Cordes, C. (1985, January). At risk in America: Black males face high odds in a hostile society. *APA Monitor*, pp. 9, 10, 11, 27.

Cose, E. (1993). *The rage of a privileged class: Why are middle-class Blacks angry? Why should America care?* New York: HarperCollins.

Crawley, B., & Freeman, E. M. (1993). Themes in the life views of older and younger African American males. *Journal of African American Male Studies, 1,* 15–29.

Dent, D. (1989, November). Readin,' ritin,' and rage: How schools are destroying Black boys. *Essence*, pp. 54–59, 114–116.

Doyle, J. A. (1983). *The male experience*. Dubuque, IA: W. C. Brown.

Ehrenreich, B. (1984, May 20). A feminist's view of the new man. *New York Times Sunday Magazine*, pp. 36–39.

Emerson, G. C. (1985). *Some American men*. New York: Simon & Schuster.

Erikson, E. (1950). *Childhood and society*. New York: Norton.

Evans, R. C., & Evans, H. L. (1995). Coping: Stressors and depression among middle-class African American men. *Journal of African American Men, 1,* 29–40.

Gary, L. (1985). Correlates of depressive symptoms among a select population of Black males. *American Journal of Public Health, 75,* 1220–1222.

Gary, L. E. (Ed.). (1981). *Black men*. Beverly Hills, CA: Sage.

Gary, L. E., & Berry, G. L. (1985). Depressive symptomatology among Black men. *Journal of Multicultural Counseling and Development, 13,* 121–129.

Gary, L. E., & Leashore, B. R. (1982). High-risk status of Black men. *Social Work, 27,* 54–58.

Genovese, E. (1974). The slave family, women—a reassessment of matriarchy, emasculation, weakness. *Southern Voices, 1,* 9–16.

Gibbs, J. T. (1980). The interpersonal orientation in mental health consultation: Toward a model of ethnic variations in consultation. *Journal of Community Psychology, 8,* 195–207.

Gibbs, J. T. (Ed.). (1988) *Young, Black, and male in America: An endangered species.* New York: Auburn House.

Green, R.L., & Wright, D.L. (1991, March). *African American males: A demographic study and analysis.* Paper presented at the National Workshop of the W. K. Kellog Foundation, Sacramento, CA.

Grier, W. H., & Cobbs, P. M. (1968). *Black rage.* New York: Basic Books.

Hare, N., & Hare, J. (1985). *Bringing the Black boy to manhood: The passage.* San Francisco: Black Think Tank.

Havighurst, R. J. (1972). *Developmental tasks and education* (3rd ed.). New York: McKay.

Hernton, C. (1965). *Sex and racism in America.* New York: Grove.

Hilliard, A. G. (1985). A framework for focused counseling on the African American man. *Journal of Non-White Concerns in Personnel and Guidance, 13,* 72–78.

Holister, R. G. (1989). *Youth employment and training programs.* Washington, DC: National Academy Press.

Johnson, J. M., & Watson, B. C. (Eds.). (1990). *Stony the road they trod: The African American male.* Washington, DC: National Urban League.

Jones, B., & Gay, B. (1982). Survey of psychotherapy with Black males. *Journal of American Psychiatric Association, 139,* 1174–1177.

Jones, B., & Gay, B. (1983). Black males and psychotherapy. *American Journal of Psychotherapy, 37,* 77–85.

Jones, K. M. (1986). Black male in jeopardy. *Crisis, 93,* 16–21, 44–45.

Keen, S. (1991). *A fire in the belly: On being a man.* New York: Bantam Books.

Kohlberg, L. (1966). Moral education in the schools: A developmental view. *School Review, 74,* 1–30.

Lee, C. C. (1989). Counseling Black adolescents: Critical roles and functions for counseling professionals. In R.L. Jones (Ed.), *Black adolescents* (pp. 293–308). Berkeley, CA: Cobb & Henry.

Lee, C. C. (1990). Black male development: Counseling the native son. In D. Moore & F. Leafgren (Eds.), *Problem solving strategies and interventions for men in conflict.* Alexandria, VA: American Association for Counseling and Development.

Lee, C. C. (1991) Counseling blacks: From theory to practice. In R. L. Jones (Ed.), *Black psychology* (3rd ed., pp. 559–576). Berkeley, CA: Cobb & Henry.

Lee, C. C. (1994). Adolescent development. In R. Mincy (Ed.), *Nurturing young Black males: Challenges to agencies, programs, and social policy* (pp. 33–44). Washington, DC: Urban Institute Press.

Lee, C. C. (1996). *Saving the native son: Empowerment strategies for young Black males.* Greensboro, NC: ERIC Counseling and Student Services Clearinghouse.

Lee, C. C., & Lindsey, C. R. (1985). Black consciousness development: A group counseling model for Black elementary school students. *Elementary School Guidance and Counseling 19,* 228–236.

Madhubuti, H. (1990). *Black men: Obsolete, single, dangerous? Afrikan American families in transition: Essays in discovery, solution, and hope.* Chicago: Third World Press.

Majors, R., & Bilson, J. M. (1992). *Cool pose: The dilemmas of Black manhood in America.* New York: Lexington Books.

Majors, R., & Nikelly, A. (1983). Serving the Black minority: A new direction for psychotherapy. *Journal of Non-White Concerns in Personnel and Guidance, 11,* 142–151.

Mauer, M. (1990). *Young Black men and the criminal justice system: A growing national problem.* Washington, DC: The Sentencing Project.

McCall, N. (1994). *Makes me wanna holler: A young Black man in America.* New York: Random House.

McGhee, J. D. (1984). *Running the gauntlet: Black men in America.* New York: National Urban League.

Merton, A. (1986). Father hunger. *New Age Journal, 94,* 22–29.

Monroe, S. (1987, March). Brothers. *Newsweek,* pp. 54–66.

Moore, D., & Leafgren, F. (Eds.). (1990). *Problem-solving strategies and interventions for men in conflict.* Alexandria, VA: American Association for Counseling and Development.

Myers, H. F., Anderson, N. B., & Strickland, T. L. (1989). A biobehavioral perspective on stress and hypertension in Black adults. In R. L. Jones (Ed.), *Black adult development and aging.* Berkeley, CA: Cobb & Henry.

Myers, H. F., & King, L. M. (1980). Youth of the Black underclass: Urban stress and mental health. *Fanon Center Journal, 1,* 1–27.

Narine, M. L. (1992). *Single-sex, single-race public schools: A solution to the problems plaguing the Black community?* Washington, DC: U.S. Department of Education.

National Black Child Development Institute. (1990). *The status of African American children: 20th Anniversary Report 1970–1990.* Washington, DC: Author.

Oliver, W. (1984). Black males and the tough guy image: A dysfunctional compensatory adaptation. *Western Journal of Black Studies, 8,* 201–202.

Oliver, W. (1989). Black males and social problems: Prevention through Afrocentric socialization. *Journal of Black Studies, 20,* 15–39.

Parham, T., & McDavis, R. (1987). Black men, an endangered species: Who's really pulling the trigger? *Journal of Counseling and Development, 66,* 24–27.

Pasteur, A. B., & Toldson, I. L. (1982). *Roots of soul: The psychology of Black expressiveness.* Garden City, NY: Anchor Press/Doubleday.

Patton, J. M. (1995). The education of African American males: Frameworks for developing authenticity. *Journal of African American Men, 1,* 5–27.

Piaget, J. (1970). *Science of education and the psychology of the child.* New York: Onion Press.

Pleck, J. H. (1981). *The myth of masculinity.* Cambridge, MA: MIT Press.

Randolph, (1990, August). What can we do about the most explosive problem in Black America—the widening gap between women who are making it and men who aren't? *Ebony,* p. 52.

Redd, M. L. (1989). Alcoholism and drug addiction among Black adults. In R. L. Jones (Ed.), *Black adult development and aging.* Berkeley, CA: Cobb & Henry.

Reed, R. J. (1988). Education and achievement of young Black males. In J. T. Gibbs (Ed.), *Young, Black, and male in America: An endangered species.* New York: Auburn House.

Salholz, E. (1990, December). Short lives, bloody deaths: Black murder rates soar. *Newsweek,* p. 116.

Scher, M., Stevens, M., Good, G., & Eichenfield, G. A. (1987). *Handbook of counseling and psychotherapy with men.* Newbury Park, CA: Sage.

Select Committee on Children, Youth, and Families, U.S. House of Representatives. (1989). *Barriers and opportunities for America's young Black men.* Washington, DC: U.S. Government Printing Office.

Staples, R. (1978). Masculinity and race: The dual dilemma of Black men. *Journal of Social Issues, 34,* 169–183.

Staples, R. (1983). *Black masculinity: The Black male's role in American society.* San Francisco: Black Scholar Press.

Subcommittee on Investment, Jobs, and Prices, Joint Economic Committee, U.S. Congress. (1991). *The economic status of African Americans.* Washington, DC: U.S. Government Printing Office.

Subcommittee on Select Education, Committee on Education and Labor, U.S. House of Representatives. (1990). *Hearing on the Office of Educational Research and Improvement.* Washington, DC: U.S. Government Printing Office.

Taylor, R. J., & Chatters, L. M. (1989). Family, friend, and church support networks of Black Americans. In R. L. Jones (Ed.), *Black adult development and aging.* Berkeley, CA: Cobb & Henry.

Taylor, R. L. (1977). Socialization to the Black male role. In D. Y. Wilkinson & R. L. Taylor (Eds.), *The black male in America: Perspectives on his status in contemporary society.* Chicago: Nelson-Hall.

Thomas, A., & Sillen, S. (1972). *Racism and psychiatry.* Seacacus, NJ: Citadel Press.

Thomas, C. (1993). *Black and blue: Profiles of Blacks in IBM.* Atlanta, GA: Aaron Press.

U.S. Bureau of the Census. (1990). *Statistical abstracts of the United States: 1989.* Washington, DC: U.S. Government Printing Office.

U.S. Bureau of the Census. (1991). *Statistical abstracts of the United States* (11th ed.). Washington, DC: U.S. Government Printing Office.

U.S. Department of Justice, Bureau of Justice Statistics. (1986). *Correctional population in the United States—1986.* Washington, DC.

Vontress, C. E. (1971). *Counseling Negroes.* New York: Houghton Mifflin.

Vontress, C. E. (1995). The breakdown of authority: Implications for counseling young African American males. In J. G. Ponterotto, J. M. Casas, L. A. Suzuki, & C. M. Alexander (Eds.), *Handbook of multicultural counseling* (pp. 457–472). Thousand Oaks, CA: Sage.

Washington, C. S. (1987). Counseling Black men. In M. Scher, M. Stevens, G. Good, & G. A. Eichenfield (Eds.), *Handbook of counseling and psychotherapy with men* (pp. 192–202). Newbury Park, CA: Sage.

Washington, V., & Lee, C. C. (1982). Teaching and counseling Black males in grades K to 8. *Black Caucus: Journal of the National Association of Black Social Workers, 13,* 25–29.

Weathers, D. (1993, December). Stop the guns. *Essence,* pp. 70–71, 132–137.

Wilkinson, D. Y., & Taylor, R. L. (1977). *The Black male in America: Perspectives on his status in contemporary society.* Chicago: Nelson-Hall.

Wright, W. (1992). The endangered Black male child. *Educational Leadership, 49,* 14–16.

9

UTILIZING AND MAXIMIZING THE RESOURCES OF THE AFRICAN AMERICAN CHURCH:
Strategies and Tools for Counseling Professionals

Bernard L. Richardson and Lee N. June

Professional counselors who want to be effective in African American communities must discover and become proficient in using nontraditional methods of service delivery (June, 1986, 1988; Lee, 1990). June (1986), for example, suggested an aggressive outreach strategy that utilizes indigenous helping resources. Therefore, effective counseling practice with African Americans must incorporate those institutions, organizations, and strategies that are consistent with their cultural and life experiences.

The African American church is an indigenous institution that counseling professionals can turn to in providing counseling services to African Americans (Boyd-Franklin, 1989; June, 1986; Richardson, 1989). In this chapter the term *African American church* is used in a generic sense to describe the traditions of those religious institutions in African American communities represented by a variety of Christian denominations. Smith (1982) described the African American church as having been born in bondage. "It was, from its inception, a servant church embedded and engaged in the anguish and freedom of an oppressed people" (p. 15). Slavery and then segregation denied African Americans access to the full rights and privileges accorded other Americans. The church was the only institution that African Americans had to meet their emotional, spiritual, and material needs. Today, the church remains at the center of community life, attending to the social, spiritual, and psychological needs of scores of African

155

Americans. No other institution claims the loyalty and attention of African Americans as does the church. Boyd-Franklin (1989) described the church as a "multifunctional community institution" serving the needs of a disenfranchised population. The significance of the church among African Americans has important implications for providing mental health services. Many associate traditional counseling settings with institutional or individual racism. Settings perceived as oppressive or racist may promote a defensive posture among many African Americans, which may hinder therapeutic progress (Katz, 1985; Sue, McKinney, Allen, & Hall, 1974). The African American church offers a familiar and supportive environment for counseling. In this environment, individuals may confront a full array of issues that affect their lives in an open and honest way.

Lincoln and Mamiya (1990) estimated the Black church membership at 23.7 million. They further stated that based on various indices of church membership, approximately 78% of the African American population claimed church membership and have attended at least once in the last 6 months. They further noted that Blacks tend to have higher rates of church attendance than White Protestants (44% to 40%). Malone (1994) estimated the annual income of the Black church to be $1.7 billion. These indicators suggest the important influence of the church on the lives of scores of African Americans.

African American Religion and Spirituality: Their Role in Mental Health

God and religious institutions are prominent in the lives of the majority of Americans. Bergin (1980) noted that polls have indicated that 90% of the general public believe in a divine being. However, he further stated that only 50% of psychologists do.

There are many reasons why the African American church should be considered as a vehicle for providing mental health services. One important reason is related to the role of religion and spirituality in the lives of African Americans (Frazier, 1963; Mbiti, 1969). Boyd-Franklin (1989) noted that "Some of the most cogent historical and psychological experiences of Black Afro-Americans and their families are strongly rooted in religious and spiritual background and experience" (p. 91).

The church is, therefore, the key symbol and the vehicle of expression of religion and spirituality for many African Americans. Ironically, it is this spiritual and religious orientation that may be at the root of why the African American church has not been utilized by many counseling professionals, who may have a conscious or unconscious desire to stay clear of religious or spiritual issues and symbols in the treatment process. Many counselors are not trained to deal with such issues and thus often ignore religion and spirituality as therapeutic concerns even when initiated by clients. This failure to consider the issues of religion and spirituality in counseling, especially when they play such an important role in the lives of many African Americans, will undoubtedly result in less than successful outcomes. Therefore, counseling professionals who work with African Americans must be sensitive to the role that religion and spirituality play in many of their clients' lives. This does not mean that a counselor must be formally trained in theology to work with those African Americans for whom religion and spirituality are important. To be sensitive within this context means a willingness to explore with clients the role that these issues play in their lives as well as to demonstrate a respect for and some level of understanding of the worldview that emanates from the religious belief.

Knox (1985) documented, in her work with African American alcoholics and their families, that spiritual beliefs have become a part of the survival system of African Americans. She argued that these "coping methods" should be explored just as any other psychosocial area in the assessment process. Accordingly, Lovinger's (1984) insight about the role of religion in the lives of clients is especially relevant for working with African Americans. He noted that

... a patient's religious belief and experiences contain important meanings about past experiences and can characterize the quality of a patient's relationship with others. When these issues emerge in therapy, they can aid therapy if approached with interest and respect. None of this requires any change in the therapist's own attitudes toward religion, other than relinquishing (if held) that religion is silly or meaningless. No phenomena can be usefully approached this way. (pp. xi–xii)

The proclivity toward religion and spirituality does not mean that African Americans are not amenable to psychological interpretations and insights. Often observed in counseling African Americans in both pastoral and secular situations is that many interpret the events of their lives theologically as well as psychologically. For example, the following was related at the close of an initial session in a pastoral context by an African American client who was himself a mental health worker:

This session made me realize that I am now ready to deal with some of the issues that I have been resisting for some time. I wish the process didn't have to be so painful. I guess it is true that it sometimes hurts to grow. I wonder what God is trying to teach me by this trial?

Accordingly, the authors agree with Smith (1982) that many African Americans seek out certain counselors because of their religious and pastoral identification.

It must be acknowledged that the reluctance of many counseling professionals to engage in any dialogue concerning religious or spiritual beliefs is most likely due to a fear that they can not or could not integrate the information into their own understanding of human behavior rather than to any disregard for the clients' belief. However, such a fear on the part of the counselor can lead to unsuccessful therapeutic outcomes in counseling situations in which a client's religious belief is counterproductive to positive mental health. Counseling professionals should consider enlisting the aid of the church and clergy in working through this type of impasse. Particularly when a mental health professional feels that a client's belief is counterproductive to positive mental health, he or she should consult with a clergyperson. The counseling professional should not assume that the client's belief is supported by the client's pastor or church. After consulting with the client's pastor, the counselor might recommend that the client receive instruction from the church about particular beliefs. A counselor should be as comfortable consulting a member of the clergy about a client's religious belief and its possible effect on the helping process as consulting a physician about a physical condition that might affect medical treatment. This kind of collaborative relationship will enhance the quality of care counseling professionals provide.

The Role of African American Clergy

At the center of the church is the African American clergy, who have traditionally been recognized as major leaders in their respective communities (Hamilton, 1972; Woodson, 1921). In attending to spiritual needs, they have had and still have a significant influence on mental health intervention. Often the pastoral counseling activity has represented the only resource available to address emotional and psychological crises (Washington, 1964). An important aspect of the clergyperson's role that has important implications for mental health practitioners is that of pastoral initiative. Historically, clergy are expected to go where the people are and intervene when necessary on their own initiative and without specific invitation (Switzer, 1986). Further, with their entree to homes, clergy are able to discover problems in their early stages (Switzer, 1986).

Another important aspect of the counseling that clergy perform is that they usually have prior relationships with those who seek them out for counseling. Therefore, clergy often may have an understanding of the family dynamics and living conditions of their parishioners. The unique role of African American clergy also affords them the opportunity to provide counseling that is proactive and preventive. Through activities such as educational programs, sermons, and interaction in organizations and business meetings, the clergy, unlike other professionals, have an ongoing opportunity to educate people about potentially harmful situations in the community and potentially harmful individual behaviors. In discussing the role of clergy in crisis intervention, Switzer (1986) suggested that the clergyperson is unique in that no other professional has the kind of "platform or organizational context" in which to engage in sound education for mental health and problem solving. With the support of pastors and church leaders, the resources of the church can be available to counseling professionals. Thus counseling professionals have tremendous opportunities to be an instrumental part of the proactive and preventive aspect of the African American church. For example, workshops on such topics as addiction, parenting, male/female relationships, education, racism, and sexism are greatly needed. With the assistance and the cooperation of the pastor, counseling professionals can provide preventive counseling services to these communities.

The Need for Partnership With Clergy

The clergy's role is unique and the mental health professional may not be able to duplicate their strategies and techniques. However, mental health practitioners in partnership with clergy can use the unique resources of the African American church to offer more comprehensive, aggressive, and indigenous outreach programs in African American communities. Nowhere is this more evident than in the area of referral. The counseling professional who has developed a working relationship with an African American pastor has access to a referral system that can enhance the relationship between counselor and client. A person is more likely to participate in counseling and feel more comfortable with a counselor who has the respect and trust of his or her pastor and church community.

Considering the importance of counseling services, it is a cause for concern that the majority of these services aimed at African American communities historically have not had working relationships with churches and clergy. Boyd-Franklin (1989), drawing from her work with African American families, noted with amazement that mental health practitioners routinely contact clinics, hospitals, or counselors who have previously worked with clients but not pastors. She further noted that when a family counselor recognizes the significance of religious values for a client and is aware of the resources of the African American church, four types of intervention are possible: (1) involving a clergyperson as a consultant, cocounselor, or integral part of the treatment process; (2) mobilizing the resources of the Black church network to help a family in crisis; (3) utilizing or deploying church networks as support for a family during times of illness, death, or loss; and (4) helping isolated African American families cut off from their original networks to create new ones.

A popular notion exists that the reason for the absence of working relationships between African American clergy and mental health professionals is that members of this clergy are not supportive of mental health professionals. It is believed that African American clergy are threatened and fear the loss of parishioners who might seek only psychological solutions to their problems. Research evidence has suggested, however, that African American clergy hold favorable attitudes toward mental health professionals (Richardson, 1989). An important implication of this research is that the possibility exists for African American clergy and mental health professionals to work together in partnership to foster the social, spiritual, and psychological well-being of people in African American communities.

Intervention Strategies Using the Resources of the African American Church

The African American church provides counselors with a setting that can facilitate various intervention strategies. Two modes of intervention can be used in counseling African Americans: intervention that focuses on the church as a support system and intervention that addresses systemic problems that affect African Americans (Gunnings, 1976). These intervention strategies, which can utilize and maximize the many resources within the African American church, are discussed in this section.

Intervention That Focuses on the Church as a Support System

True religion has an element of increasing self-esteem. Increasing self-esteem is critically important when it has been negatively affected by the forces of racism and oppression, which is often the case with African Americans. The African American church is in a powerful position to bolster the self-esteem of its members, and historically, the church has been a primary source for the development of African American self-esteem. The African American church provides avenues of self-expression and efficacy via church titles and responsibilities, and via its theology or conception of God. Individuals who find their level of self-efficacy diminished by limited opportunities and who have jobs that do little to enhance self-esteem gain a strong sense of self-respect and community recognition as a result of positions they hold in African American churches.

The communal aspect of working within the church serves to strengthen individual and group identity. The heritage of African Americans lends credence to this cultural phenomenon. In his research on West African civilization, Mbiti (1969) maintained that group membership is the preeminent source of identification in the development of a sense of self for Africans. Nobles (1980) has stressed the importance of the African philosophical notion of kinship or collective unity as an important foundation for African American mental health intervention. Within this context, counselors must see and use the African American church as a support system for individuals facing various life challenges. For example, the church could be an important helping resource for individuals recently released from prison, or for others needing assistance in adjusting to community life.

The African American church has always emphasized the need for strong families and, as part of its religious tradition, provides teachings and programs that support family life. The African American church, therefore, can also be utilized as a support system in the treatment of African American families. Boyd-Franklin (1989) argued that it is important for counselors to understand the concept of the church family as it relates to African Americans. She noted that for many African Americans the church functions as an extended family and for single mothers as a surrogate family. She also noted that the African American church provides role models for young people and also serves a social function by providing families the opportunity to mingle. It is significant to note that many African American parents who live in all-White neighborhoods and whose children attend predominantly White schools seek out African American churches not only for spiritual edification but also for the positive African American identity that the churches instill in children.

Counselors can utilize these unique resources in working with African American families. Boyd-Franklin (1989) suggested that counselors should identify the church as a social support resource for isolated families who have a religious orientation. She noted that some African American families entering community mental health centers are "socially isolated and emotionally cut off from their extended families," and that assisting isolated African American families in identifying and locating a new church network could be a significant intervention. Boyd-Franklin rightly cautioned that this intervention is not for everyone and stated that "it should be made only if it appears syntonic with the family's belief systems and earlier experiences" (p. 91).

Even though the church can be a potent supportive resource, mental health professionals have traditionally considered it to be an institution that is noncompromising and holds a narrow perspective on morals and values. Those that hold this view often fail to recognize that in certain cases, the identification with the church can appropriately reinforce an individual's moral and ethical belief system. As an example, clergy, working in concert with counseling professionals, can offer alternatives and support to people contemplating and/or engaging in self-destructive and community-disruptive economic enterprises such as the illegal drug trade. Such alternatives and support might include church-sponsored community forums that offer testimonials by former addicts and drug dealers who can point out the short- and long-term negative effects of selling drugs.

Intervention That Addresses Systemic Problems Affecting African Americans

The African American church has historically played a key role in fostering social change at the community and societal levels (Smith, 1982). The civil rights movement of the 1960s and the leadership of Dr. Martin Luther King, Jr., attest to the role of the African American church and clergy in social change. Thus the counselor who works within the context of the African American church can educate clients about how systemic problems affect their lives and can also be part of the process that seeks to change these conditions. Counselors working in African American communities should seek to empower their clients to challenge and confront racist and oppressive structures and policies that unjustly govern their lives. Counselors should also be willing to be advocates on behalf of clients. The church is a vehicle that counselors can use to help them become effective advocates and to assist them in empowering clients. For example, counselors can identify clients who have been victimized by unfair hiring practices, discrimination in housing, inadequate educational facilities, or inadequate health care. They can then refer these clients to pastors and church leaders who can in turn help them organize and collectively confront oppressive systems and practices using the church as a base of operations. The use of the church, the support of pastors, and the identification with other victims of systemic injustice can give clients a sense of control over their lives.

Guidelines for Working Within a Church Context

Although the proposal that counseling professionals should enlist the resources of the African American church in providing mental health services to African American communities has been made (Richardson, 1989; June, 1986), this is a new concept for most counseling professionals, and some direction is needed in establishing working relationships with African American churches. The guidelines that follow are based on the authors' experience and represent suggestions for facilitating the development of such relationships and enhancing counselor effectiveness.

1. Earn Acceptance

Some well-meaning counseling professionals come into the church believing that they will be immediately accepted because of their education or their professional accomplishments. However, they soon find that it takes more than credentials to be accepted as helping professionals within the African American church. To earn acceptance, counseling professionals must be perceived as being sincere and trustworthy, as not flaunting professional status, and as having a genuine interest in the betterment of African Americans. Hunt (1988) rightly stated that "it is not what you know but who you are and how you use the information about a person's cultural characteristics that eventually allows the client to trust" (p. 116). With other conditions being right, when these attributes are perceived, the word quickly spreads among church members that the counselor is a professional who is "down to earth and easy to talk to"—a description that is a sign of acceptance within the African American church community.

2. Explore Personal Beliefs

If counselors are to be sensitive to the role of spiritually and religion in the lives of clients, they must examine their own beliefs. Counselors should determine what aspects of their personal religious beliefs (or nonbeliefs) could interfere with being competent in working with certain problems. This is especially important in handling such delicate racial issues as abortion and homosexuality. More personal beliefs, such as those concerning spiritual healing, also require counselors to possess a certain spiritual affinity with the concept in order to be effective. Counselors should not attempt to undertake this process alone but should explore their attitudes toward religion and spirituality with a clergyperson or religious professional. When the counselor's attitude is negative or when there is a core value conflict, referring the client to another counselor may be appropriate.

3. Develop a Relationship With Pastors

In the African American church tradition is a great deal of respect for the office and authority of the pastor. Therefore, regardless of how skillful the counselor is, all efforts to use the African American church as a therapeutic ally will fail unless positive relationships are developed with pastors. An excellent way to meet and establish contact with pastors is through ministerial alliances or pastors conferences. Most communities have such alliances or conferences at which clergy meet regularly to discuss clerical and community concerns, and these alliances and conferences can provide counseling professionals with an opportunity to meet African American clergy from various denominations. Rather than merely articulating their skills and concerns, however, counseling professionals should use the alliances and conferences as an opportunity to demonstrate them concretely. Presenting a workshop on a relevant problem confronting African Americans, such as the problems facing youth, could be an excellent way to showcase counseling expertise.

4. Establish and Maintain a Relationship With Local Churches

After developing a relationship with the pastor of a local church, the next step is to be introduced to a local congregation. Again, the workshop format is a dramatic and efficient way to present counseling skills to the African American church community. Workshops on topics such as addiction, parenting, peer pressure, male/female relationships, racism, and prejudice are usually well received in church settings. If the workshop is successful, individual counseling referrals usually follow.

It is also possible for mental health professionals, in collaboration with the host church, to establish a counseling center on site. Such a model has been outlined by Solomon (1990).

5. Become Acquainted With the Religious Tradition of the Local Church or Denomination

The religious traditions of the African American church are represented by various denominations. These include African Methodist Episcopal Zion, African Methodist Episcopal, Baptist, Congregational, Church of God in Christ, Church of God, Seventh Day Adventist, Apostolic, Lutheran, Episcopal, and Roman Catholic. In addition, an increasing number of African Americans follow Islam. Counseling professionals need to have some knowledge of these denominations and religions because of possible therapeutic and/or customary issues that may affect a client's ability to function. Counseling professionals can become familiar with the religious beliefs and practices of various Christian denominations by requesting denominational handbooks from pastors and by taking a survey course on American religion. An excellent source for background information on the African American church is *The Black Church in the African American Experience* (Lincoln & Mamiya, 1990). Information on Islam can be obtained by contacting the leader of a Muslim congregation or by taking a course on world religions.

In becoming familiar with the various traditions, counselors should pay close attention to local church and denominational laws as well as attitudes toward the role of women in the church and society, attitudes toward divorce and remarriage, prohibitions against drugs and alcohol, and teachings on abortion, homosexuality, healing, and health practices. These issues may become therapeutic issues or the focus of counseling.

6. Become Acquainted With the Field of Biblical Counseling

Over the last few decades, increasing attention has been given to developing theories and techniques of Christian and biblical counseling. Many churches and pastors have been trained in principles of biblical counseling, and an increasing number of Black parishioners are seeking such counseling. Several Black churches have set up their own counseling centers and have regular counseling hours. Thus mental health professionals need to become acquainted with this field, its literature, and these types of counseling resources.

Representative materials that give good general overviews of the field include *The Psychology of Counseling* (Narramore, 1960), *Christian Counseling: A Comprehensive Guide* (Collins, 1988), *Effective Biblical Counseling* (Crabb, 1977), *Basic Principles of Biblical Counseling* (Crabb, 1975), *Competent to Counsel* (Adams, 1970), *The Christian Counselor's Manual* (Adams, 1973), and *The Integration of Psychology and Theology* (Carter & Narramore, 1979).

Writings that are more African American oriented include *Biblical Counseling With African Americans* (Walker, 1992). Others are by Edward Wimberly, one of the more prolific writers on pastoral counseling, and his book *Pastoral Care in the Black Church* (1979) and particularly his chapter "Pastoral Counseling and the Black Perspective" (1989) are must readings.

Additional materials that can give mental health professionals a perspective on how counseling, mental health, and other pertinent issues are perceived and conceptualized within the Black church include *The Black Family: Past, Present and Future* (June, 1991), *How to Equip the African American Family* (Abatso & Abatso, 1991), *Reclaiming the Urban Family* (Richardson, 1995), *From Holy Power to Holy Profits* (Malone, 1994), and, as already mentioned, *The Black Church in the African American Experience* (Lincoln & Mamiya, 1990).

7. Develop and Nurture a Collaborative Research Program

Counselors who have shown a genuine interest in the Black church and have developed effective relationships could further aid both the mental health field and the congregation by developing a collaborative research agenda. According to Cook (1993),

Collaborative research efforts between mental health counseling researchers and African American churches can advance the knowledge of mental health resources within the church, and can assist churches in using their resources in productive ways that will benefit the surrounding communities. (p. 320)

The areas that Cook (1993) suggested as ripe for research are individual interventions, individual counseling practices, collaboration with African American clergy, group interventions, and outreach interventions. Her article also discussed the issues surrounding access to African American churches, such as gaining entry, negotiating collaborative relationships, and selecting appropriate methodologies.

Conclusion

The emergence of counseling professionals who recognize cultural diversity has initiated a search for new skills, innovative strategies, and appropriate techniques for delivering mental health services to African American communities. The African American church, with its rich history, continuing significance, and great influence in African American communities, can be a valuable resource, an avenue of service delivery and cooperative research. Those counseling professionals who wish to gain access to the full range of African American clients will be wise to seek out the African American church.

The strategies put forth in this chapter necessitate that counselors serve as advocates of social change, as consultants, as mediators, as research collaborators, and as continual learners. Counselors are also encouraged to develop alliances with African American religious professionals and to become familiar with their literature and counseling techniques. Further, counselors need to become more aware of personal biases, fears, and skill deficits that could prevent them from embracing indigenous resources such as the African American church. Counselors who are willing to meet these challenges will build a foundation that could ultimately lead to the discovery of new strategies and techniques for mental health practices in African American communities.

References

Abatso, G., & Abatso, Y. (1991). *How to equip the African American family.* Chicago: Urban Ministries.

Adams, J. (1970). *Competent to counsel*. Grand Rapids, MI: Baker.

Adams, J. (1973). *The Christian counselor's manual*. Grand Rapids, MI: Zondervan.

Bergin, A. (1980). Psychotherapy and religious values. *Journal of Consulting and Clinical Psychology, 481*, 95–105.

Boyd-Franklin, N. (1989). *Black families in counseling*. New York: Guilford Press.

Carter, J. D., & Narramore, B. (1979). *The integration of psychology and theology*. Grand Rapids, MI: Zondervan.

Collins, G. R. (1988). *Christian counseling: A comprehensive guide* (Rev. ed.). Dallas, TX: Word.

Cook, D. A. (1993). Research in African American churches: A mental health counseling imperative. *Journal of Mental Health Counseling, 15*, 320–333.

Crabb, L. J. (1975). *Basic principles of biblical counseling*. Grand Rapids, MI: Zondervan.

Crabb, L. J. (1977). *Effective Biblical counseling*. Grand Rapids, MI: Zondervan.

Frazier, E. F. (1963). *The Negro church in America*. New York: Schocken Books.

Gunnings, T. S. (1976). *A systemic approach to counseling*. East Lansing, MI: Michigan State University.

Hamilton, C. V. (1972). *The Black preacher in America*. New York: William Morrow.

Hunt, P. (1988). Black clients: Implications for supervision of trainees. *Psycho-Counseling, 24*, 114–119.

June, L. N. (1986). Enhancing the delivery of mental health and counseling services to Black males: Critical agency and provider responsibilities. *Journal of Multicultural Counseling and Development, 14*, 39–45.

June, L. N. (1988, November). *Psychotherapy (mental health counseling) and the Black church*. Paper presented at the International Congress on Christian Counseling, Atlanta, GA.

June, L. N. (Ed.). (1991). *The Black family: Past, present, and future*. Grand Rapids, MI: Zondervan.

Katz, J. H. (1985). The sociopolitical nature of counseling. *The Counseling Psychologist, 13*, 615–624.

Knox, D. H. (1985). Spirituality: A tool in the assessment and treatment of Black alcoholics and their families. *Alcoholism Treatment Quarterly, 2*, 31–44.

Lee, C. C. (1990). Black male development: Counseling the "native son." In D. Moore & F. Leafgren (Eds.), *Problem solving strategies for men in conflict.* Alexandria, VA: American Association for Counseling and Development.

Lincoln, C. E., & Mamiya, L. H. (1990). *The Black church in the African American experience.* Durham, NC: Duke University Press.

Lovinger, R. J. (1984). *Working with religious issues in therapy.* New York: Aronson.

Malone, W., Jr. (1994). *From holy power to holy profits.* Chicago: African American Images.

Mbiti, J. S. (1969). *African religions and philosophies.* Garden City, NY: Anchor Books.

Narramore, C. M. (1960). *The psychology of counseling.* Grand Rapids, MI: Zondervan.

Nobles, W. (1980). African philosophy: Foundations for Black psychology. In R. L. Jones (Ed.), *Black psychology* (pp. 23–36). New York: Harper & Row.

Richardson, B. L. (1989). Attitudes of Black clergy toward mental health professionals: Implications for pastoral care. *Journal of Pastoral Care, 43,* 33–39.

Richardson, W. (1995). *Reclaiming the urban family.* Grand Rapids, MI: Zondervan.

Smith, A. (1982). *The relational self.* Nashville, TN: Abingdon Press.

Solomon, B. B. (1990). Counseling Black families at inner city church sites. In H. Cheatham & J. B. Stewart (Eds.), *Black families: Interdisciplinary perspectives.* New Brunswick, NJ: Transaction.

Sue, S., McKinney, H., Allen, D., & Hall, J. (1974). Delivery of community mental health services to Black and White clients. *Journal of Consulting and Clinical Psychology, 42,* 594–601.

Switzer, D. K. (1986). *The minister as crisis counselor.* Nashville, TN: Abingdon Press.

Walker, C. (1992). *Biblical counseling with African Americans.* Grand Rapids, MI: Zondervan.

Washington, J. R. (1964). *Black religion: The Negro and Christianity in the United States.* Boston: Beacon Press.

Wimberly, E. P. (1979). *Pastoral care in the Black church.* Nashville, TN: Abingdon Press.

Wimberly, E. P. (1989). Pastoral counseling and the Black perspective. In G. S. Wilmore (Ed.), *African American religious studies.* Durham, NC: Duke University Press.

Woodson, C. G. (1921). *The history of the Negro church.* Washington, DC: Associated.

The Asian American Experience

Americans of Asian descent trace their cultural origins to countries such as Cambodia, China, Japan, Korea, and Vietnam. Each Asian American ethnic group has its own unique cultural history and traditions. However, some dynamics are rooted in centuries-old Asian religious traditions and play a major role in shaping the cultural values of Asian Americans, regardless of ethnic background. These dynamics must be appreciated if culturally responsive counseling is to occur with Asian American clients and include factors such as moderation in behavior, self-discipline, patience, and humility. Many of these behaviors and values are dictated by family relationships that emphasize honor and respect for elders.

10

COUNSELING STRATEGIES FOR CHINESE AMERICANS

David Sue

The largest Asian Pacific Island group living in the United States is comprised of approximately 1,700,000 Chinese Americans (Ong & Hee, 1993). About two thirds of them are either foreign born or recent immigrants. Because of the relaxation of immigration quotas, the number of Chinese Americans will continue to increase. The continuing influx of immigrants indicates the importance of gaining a knowledge of Chinese culture. The Chinese in America are a heterogeneous group. There are people from mainland China, Hong Kong, and Taiwan. In addition, many refugees and immigrants from Southeast Asia are of Chinese origin. Because of this, Chinese Americans may differ both in terms of language and socioeconomic status. Differences in acculturation also exist among foreign born and American born Chinese Americans. This chapter, however, focuses on their commonalities in experiences and traditions rather than these differences.

A pervasive view is that Chinese Americans are a highly successful group with few problems. This view is reflected in articles such as "To America With Skills" (1985) and "Asian Americans: Are They Making the Grade?" (1984). It is true that Chinese Americans are well represented in higher education at the undergraduate and graduate school levels, but included in these data are the graduate students from Asian countries who stay in the United States for advanced degrees (Wang, 1993). It is also true that many Chinese Americans are well educated, but others have very low educational levels. A close examination of the statistics reveals a bimodal distribution: one group is highly successful and acculturated, and the other is poor, lives in poverty, and is traditional in orientation (Kitano & Daniels, 1988; Sue & Sue, 1990). Compared to White Americans, nearly four times as many Chinese Americans have less than 4 years of schooling (Nishi, 1982). English proficiency continues to be a problem. Three quarters of Chinese students have a bilingual background. The inability to communicate well in English contributes to low self-esteem and self-consciousness (Kiang & Lee, 1993).

Even among college-educated Chinese Americans, academic success has not led to commensurate rewards. Salaries are less than might be predicted according to educational levels, and Chinese Americans are underrepresented in managerial and supervisory positions (Ong & Hee, 1993; Sue & Okazaki, 1990). In addition, the careers of Chinese Americans are constricted; most are engineers or work in other technical occupations (McLeod, 1986). Studies of Chinese American men and women at several universities also show few entering into the social sciences (Sue, Ino, & Sue, 1983; Sue, Sue, & Ino, 1990) or the field of education (Ong & Hee, 1993).

This chapter first considers Chinese American cultural values, including filial piety, stress on family bonds and unity, roles and status, somatization versus psychologization, control over strong emotions, and academic and career orientation. These values are contrasted with Western values, and their impact and implications discussed. A case study is provided to illustrate the influence of these values. The chapter concludes with an exploration of Chinese American personality studies and assertiveness, and guidelines for providing assertiveness training for Chinese Americans.

Chinese American Cultural Values and Their Impact

Values have a tremendous impact in terms of how we view the world, what we consider to be right, the standards we uphold, and the way we assess and evaluate situations. However, these values are influenced by acculturation. Leong and Tata (1990) found that highly acculturated Chinese American children are more likely to value self-actualization than those with low acculturation. Some values and traditions change at different rates. For example, Chen and Yang (1986) found that Chinese American adolescents' attitudes toward dating and sex become more similar to those of White adolescents with acculturation, but that the Confucian values of loyalty, conformity, and respect for elders remain. The continuing arrival of Chinese from Asian countries to the United states ensures the survival of traditional cultural values.

Filial Piety

Filial piety is a strong value in Chinese American families and represents the obligations, respect, and duty that a person has to his or her parents. Parents are obeyed and held in high esteem. Allegiance to them is primary and expected from male offspring even after they have married and begun a family of their own. Many Chinese tales for children reflect the theme of filial piety. One such story tells of a destitute couple whose husband's parents were living with them. Because there was not enough food for everyone, the couple decided to bury their youngest child. In digging the grave, they discovered gold (Tseng & Hsu, 1972). Their choice of sacrificing their child for the parents demonstrated the reward for filial piety.

In Western culture, although parents are also honored, the emphasis on the nuclear family and independence reduces the importance of the family of origin. In fact, obligation to children is often stressed. It is their feelings and desires that are paramount. As Hsu (1953) observed, "The most important thing to Americans is what parents should do for their children: to Chinese, what children should do for their parents" (p. 75).

In a study of child-rearing practices among Chinese and Caucasian American parents, Chinese mothers were rated higher on parental control than Caucasian American mothers, reflecting the "parents are always right" notion of Confucian philosophy (Lin & Fu, 1990). In Chinese families, the parents often choose their children's careers. For example, Taiwanese college students were more likely to report being influenced by their parents for a particular field of study, whereas White American college students indicated being influenced in career choice by peers and friends (Kuo & Spees, 1983). Obeying parents is emphasized in Chinese American families as an indication of filial piety, leaving little room for self-determination.

Such situations may lead to conflict, especially among Chinese Americans who have become more acculturated and exposed to the notion of personal choice. In one sample of 24 Chinese students (including both foreign born and American born) seeking counseling, nearly all of them indicated stress associated with filial piety. Pressure to meet parental obligations and expectations clashed with individual goals and desires (Bourne, 1975).

In working with individuals who experience conflict between filial piety and individual goals, the counselor could help the clients identify the reasons for their stress. Chinese clients often do not know the source of their conflict other than it involves their parents. Being able to understand that this conflict is connected with differences in cultural expectations may lead the way to resolution. The parents define love for the family in terms of having their offspring follow their direction. Exposure to Western values of self-determination and independence often produces conflicts in family relationships.

Stress on Family Bonds and Unity

Among Chinese Americans, child-rearing practices are focused on emphasizing the importance of family ties and obligations, not on helping individuals separate and become independent. Individual growth is not the accepted norm (Jung, 1984). Praise is given for actions that are seen as benefiting the family, and guilt-inducing techniques are used to maintain discipline. Children are expected to retain emotional ties with the mother and a respectful attitude toward the father, even when they become adults. An individual who agonizes over career choices because of concern over upsetting parental wishes might be seen as being overly dependent according to the Western perspective. Expecting and assisting the Chinese client to become more independent without considering the cultural implications, however, may lead to even greater conflict.

Roles and Status

Communication patterns among Chinese Americans are based on cultural tradition and flow down from those of higher status. Men and elders are accorded greater importance than women or younger individuals. In a family, the father makes the major decisions with little input from others (Sue & Sue, 1990). A well-functioning family is one that adheres to prescribed communication rules. Negotiations and democratic discussions to arrive at decisions, which are typical of White American families, may be foreign to many Chinese American families (Jung, 1984; Saner-Yiu & Saner-Yiu, 1985). Indeed, such discussions may be seen as challenges to the authority figure, the father.

These role prescriptions make it necessary to alter traditional forms of therapy. For example, family counseling might seem to be an ideal modality for Chinese families, but family therapy is based on the Western perspective on what constitutes a well-functioning family. For example, Bowen (1978) believed that dysfunctional families are the result of fused identities and overemotional dependence, and that family members should be helped to develop greater independence and differentiation. This approach, however, conflicts with the Chinese American practice of maintaining interdependent family ties. Other possible problems with some forms of family therapy include an emphasis on expressing emotions to one another freely, egalitarian role relationships, confrontational methods, role-playing, and little focus on environmental issues affecting the family such as economics, prejudice, and acculturation conflicts (Sue, 1994). Without modification, family therapy could threaten the traditional roles and values of the Chinese culture.

Does this mean that family counseling should not be used in working with Chinese American families? With some modification, family therapy can be useful. Shon and Ja (1982) indicated that it is first important to identify possible family issues. The father may feel threatened about his status in this country because of role reversals. He may have to depend on his children to translate for him. His wife may have assumed the role of breadwinner. As a reaction, he may demand greater compliance to his wishes. Because the mother is responsible for socializing the children, it is a reflection of poor parenting if they become rebellious or overly acculturated. She has to mediate between the dictates of her husband and the demands of her children.

If the mother has done her job well, the children will be respectful and provide for her in her old age. The greatest responsibility is placed on the eldest son. He is expected to help raise his younger siblings and to be a role model for them. He inherits the family leadership upon the death of the father and is expected to provide financial and emotional support for his mother. Daughters are expected to help in the household. Fewer demands are placed upon them because they become members of the husband's family when they marry.

Ho (1987) made the following suggestions when dealing with a Chinese American family in a counseling situation: Promote differences in roles by addressing the father and mother first. Reframe or relabel statements family members make. If a child becomes angry, restate the issue in terms of parental expectations. Do not encourage the child to communicate strong negative feelings to the parents. Promote filial piety by gently reminding parents of the necessity of being positive role models for their children. Focus on the use of positive and respectful feelings between family members.

Somatization Versus Psychologization

In general, Chinese Americans perceive problems as difficulties with health. Discomfort and disturbance are expressed in terms of somatic complaints, such as headaches. In fact, symptoms of physical illnesses are believed to cause psychological problems, and for example, having a headache may result in feelings of depression. In contrast, White Americans have a psychosomatic perspective. That is, physical symptoms and illnesses are often thought to be the result of psychological states.

In working with Chinese Americans, it is a mistake to discount physical complaints. They are real problems. Both physical and psychological or family concerns have to be dealt with. One approach might be to inquire about the physical symptom and inquire about its impact on individual or family functioning. Physical or medical treatments can be used with suggestions for improvement in other aspects of the client's life. The effectiveness of the intervention is based on the alleviation of both physical and psychological symptoms.

Control Over Strong Emotions

In traditional Chinese culture, emotional expression is restrained to prevent challenges to tradition and order. This is not to say that

Chinese Americans do not show a variety of emotional reactions. Like other human beings, they can be angry, sad, happy, jealous, confident, or anxious. However, these displays do not typically occur outside the family. Feelings are not openly expressed except in the case of young children. Parents rarely show signs of physical affection, such as holding hands or saying, "I love you" (Shon & Ja, 1982), and instead, love is acknowledged through behaviors that benefit the family and its members. Children are rarely praised directly for their contributions. Parents express pride indirectly by telling friends or other siblings about the achievements or work of a particular offspring.

White Americans believe that the expression of feelings is healthy and leads to better adjustment. In counseling, the Western focus on the expressing emotions may present difficulties for the Chinese American client, especially when negative emotions are aired. The Chinese American client may lack the experience to identify, acknowledge, or communicate emotional states.

Forcing Chinese clients to express emotions directly will meet with resistance and be counterproductive. Instead, the emphasis should be on the indirect expression of positive and respectful feelings. Because love, respect, and affection are shown through behaviors, one approach might be to make the following statement: "We do different things to show that we care for our family. I would like to learn from you the ways you have of caring for your family" (Ho, 1987). Such an approach focuses on behavior, is respectful, and is indirect.

Academic and Career Orientation

In most Chinese families, there is great stress on academic achievement (Chen & Stevenson, 1989). This may be present even if the parents have received only a few years of formal education. But it is not individual achievement that is desired: rather the work is for the enhancement of the family. The emphasis on academics is reflected in the statistic that Chinese Americans complete a college education at a rate nearly double that of the average in the United States (Sue & Okazaki, 1990). Paradoxically, the academic success of Chinese Americans has led to the revision of standards by certain institutions of higher education to reduce the number of admissions to Asian Americans (Wang, 1993).

Achievement comes at a price, however. Sue and Zane (1985) reported that foreign-born Chinese American university students achieved higher grade point averages but accomplished this by taking reduced course loads, studying more hours per week, and limiting their career choices. Partly because of this the students reported greater anxiety, loneliness, and feelings of isolation than did other college students.

Parental pressure to succeed academically can be great. Anything less than an A may be considered inferior and an indication that the student no longer cares for the family. There is also pressure to choose a career that the parents approve of. Chinese American students continue to go predominantly into the scientific fields and not into the social sciences. Counselors must be careful to expose Chinese Americans to a wide range of career options.

The Case Study of David Chan

The case study presented here illustrates the importance of Chinese American cultural values and their influence in the counseling process.

David Chan is a 21-year-old student majoring in electrical engineering. He first sought counseling because he is having increasing study problems and was receiving failing grades. These academic difficulties became apparent during the first quarter of his senior year and were accompanied by headaches, indigestion, and insomnia. Because he had been an excellent student in the past, David felt that his lowered academic performance was caused by illness. However, a medical examination failed to reveal any organic disorder.

During the initial interview, David seemed depressed and anxious. He was difficult to counsel because he responded to inquiries with short but polite statements and seldom volunteered information about himself. He avoided any statements that involved feelings and presented his problem as a strictly educational one. Although he never expressed it directly, David seemed to doubt the value of counseling and needed much reassurance and feedback about his performance in the interview.

After several sessions, the counselor was able to discern one of David's major concerns. David did not like engineering and felt pressured by his parents to go into this field. The counselor felt that David was unable to take responsibility for any of his actions, was excessively dependent on his parents, and was afraid to express the anger he felt toward them.

Using the Gestalt "empty chair technique," the counselor had David pretend that his parents were seated opposite him. The counselor had David express his true feelings toward them. Although ventilating true feelings was initially very difficult, David was able to eventually do so under constant encouragement by the counselor. Unfortunately, the following sessions with David proved non-productive in that he seemed more withdrawn and guilt ridden than ever (Sue & Sue, 1990, p. 259).

In analyzing this case, what thoughts and hypotheses about David and the counseling process might a culturally responsive counselor entertain?

David's counselor values openness and the elaboration of personal feelings. This is a Western value, perhaps not shared by the client. Instead, David might be more comfortable with the Chinese American cultural values of restraint of feelings. His "short and polite" statements might reflect respect for elders and authority. David's cultural background might hinder the discussion of personal problems with outsiders.

The techniques the counselor used may be culturally inappropriate. "Expressing your feelings to parents" in the empty chair technique may ask the client to violate the basic cultural values of filial piety, stress on family bonds and unity, and control over strong emotions. David's withdrawal and apparent depression may have been the result of guilt he experienced after the therapeutic intervention. Indirect and subtle strategies might have been more effective with this client.

The counselor needs to understand that restraint of strong feelings, the stigma of personal problems, and cultural conflicts with his family may be the basis for the headaches, insomnia, and indigestion reported by David. It might be wise to address the physical symptoms first and design treatment strategies for them before proceeding to the inter- and intrapersonal conflicts.

Western culture values taking responsibility for one's life (individual responsibility and decisions); Chinese culture values a family decision. The family is harmonious, and one is part of the family, not separate from it. To infer that David is avoiding responsibility and is "excessively dependent on his parents" is a serious distortion of cultural values. This case demonstrates clearly how Chinese American values such as filial piety, stress on family roles and status, somatization, control of feelings, and pressures to excel may strongly influence the counseling process.

Personality Studies and Assertiveness

On paper and pencil tests, Chinese Americans score high on deference, self-restraint, abasement, external locus of control, and need for structure. They also show a lower tolerance for ambiguity, lower dominance, and lower aggression (Abbott, 1976; Fenz & Arkoff, 1962; Sue & Kirk, 1972). Chinese American boys are more cooperative and have a more external locus of control than White American children (Cook & Chi, 1984). These characteristics seem to make sense in terms of the cultural values and traditions just presented. Chinese children and adolescents also report greater fear of criticism and failure than comparison groups (Dong, Yang, & Ollendick, 1994). Some groups of Chinese Americans describe themselves as quiet and nonassertive. They report being uncomfortable in situations in which an evaluative component is present (Sue, Ino et al., 1983; Sue, Sue et al., 1990). Interestingly, during a presentation by the author of research on Asian Americans, the Chinese American students attending voiced many questions and were quite responsive. However, when asked if they participated in classroom discussions at the university, few indicated that they did. Most saw the value of assertive training.

There is some controversy over whether or not these personality characteristics reflect cultural values or are responses to racism (Sue & Morishima, 1982). Tong (1971) contended that many findings result from situational factors rather than personality characteristics. In other words, Chinese Americans learn to be nonassertive in White American society as a survival mechanism not because of cultural values. Within their own group and society they may display assertiveness. Sue, Ino et al. (1983) did find some evidence for the influence of situations on the assertiveness of Chinese American male students.

Guidelines for Chinese American Assertiveness Training

As just indicated, Chinese American men and women often feel uncomfortable in social situations and believe that they lack assertiveness. Many voice an interest in assertiveness training. Guidelines for group assertiveness training are as follows:

1. **Conduct pregroup screening in 15-minute individual meetings with prospective group members.** During this time, explain the procedures and approaches used in the group. Determine client expectations and assess the appropriateness of assertive training group work for the individual. Some group leaders believe that having homogeneous members (same sex, same generational status) is important in the smooth operation of the groups. This has not been found to be necessary, although individuals who actively reject their own cultural identity may be screened out.

2. **In the first group meeting, present information about the purpose of the group, the materials that will be covered, and the techniques that will be employed.** Discuss and stress the importance of confidentiality. Begin personal introductions with the group leader, who serves as a model. To reduce anxiety, designate the order for the rest of the group for the introductions.

3. **In subsequent sessions, focus on culture and racism.** Discuss the roots of nonassertiveness of Chinese Americans. Share child-rearing patterns and family experiences and discuss, for example, the use of shame and guilt in the members' own families. Discuss why these and other values were important in Chinese American development. Point out that in Chinese culture nonassertiveness has often been viewed positively, that being quiet and respectful indicate filial piety. Discuss feelings of being a person of color in America and its possible impact on assertion. Discuss stereotypes and prejudice. Ensure active participation by directing specific questions to individuals. Bring up and define the idea of assertiveness. Discuss its advantages and disadvantages with respect to both traditional Chinese and Western values. In general, members of these groups agree that assertiveness is useful in American society.

4. **Discuss situational assertiveness.** Point out that an individual may be assertive in some situations but not in others. Share experiences in which assertive behaviors have been exhibited, such as with friends or siblings. Point out that individuals can decide to be assertive with professors, classmates, and employers but remain deferential to parents and relatives if they so desire.

5. **Ask group members to write down on paper some situations in which they have difficulty being assertive.** Suggestions can be

gained from the assertion questionnaire completed earlier. Consider cultural contexts. If more assertion is desired with parents, have group members brainstorm to come up with suggestions that are respectful and culturally appropriate. Make the distinction between nonassertiveness, aggression, and assertiveness. Provide demonstrations of these behaviors for different situations. Elicit feelings and thoughts after each performance. The group leader should model each procedure first and then structure an easy situation for each participant.

6. **Have each group member choose from his or her list a simple assertive response to practice outside the group setting.** Practice the situation first in the group. Discuss cognitions and affect about the situation. Acknowledge possible consequences, both positive and negative. Employ cognitive approaches that reframe or focus on task performance and realistic appraisal. Practice use of the minimal effective response to achieve the desired goal, and discuss alternative responses. Ask group members to try out their assertive responses outside of the group. Assign the easiest tasks first. Ask group members to note their feelings and thoughts during the assertion.

7. **Discuss homework assignments and cognitive coping strategies used.** Ask group members to share what has worked for them. Give more complex assignments, and assess progress.

8. **In final group sessions, ask group members to summarize their understanding of the factors associated with nonassertiveness, their evaluation of their own progress, and suggestions for improvement in the program.**

With some modifications, this basic format for the group assertiveness training can be used to discuss issues such a filial piety, conflicts over acculturation, sex-role conflicts and expectations, and career options.

Conclusion

Chinese Americans represent a growing and heterogeneous population. It is currently the largest Asian group in the United States, of whom the majority are foreign born. Because of this, counselors and other mental health professionals need to become aware of the possible impact of cultural values on the process of counseling. Specifically, counselors have to become aware of their own worldview and assumptions about what constitutes successful counseling when working with Chinese American clients. Issues such as independence, the necessity of eliciting emotional reactions, and equality of relationships must be seen from a cultural perspective. Group experiences can be highly effective with Chinese Americans, especially when cultural influences on behavior are discussed.

References

Abbott, K. A. (1976). Culture change and the persistence of the Chinese personality. In G. De Vos (Ed.), *Responses to change: Society, culture, and personality* (pp. 87–119). New York: Van Nostrand.

Asian Americans: Are they making the grade? (1984, April 2). *U.S. News and World Report.*

Bourne, P. G. (1975). The Chinese student: Acculturation and mental illness. *Psychiatry, 38,* 269–277.

Bowen, M. (1978). *Family therapy in clinical practice.* New York: Aronson.

Chen, C., & Stevenson, H. W. (1989). Homework: A cross-cultural examination. *Child Development, 60,* 551–561.

Chen, C., & Yang, D. (1986). The self-image of Chinese American adolescents. *Pacific/Asian American Mental Health Research Center Review, 3/4,* 27–29.

Cook, H., & Chi, C. (1984). Cooperative behavior and locus of control among American and Chinese American boys. *Journal of Psychology, 118,* 169–177.

Dong, Q., Yang, B., & Ollendick, T. H. (1994). Fears in Chinese children and adolescents and their relations to anxiety and depression. *Journal of Child Psychology and Psychiatry, 35,* 351–363.

Fenz, W. D., & Arkoff, A. (1962). Comparative need patterns of five ancestry groups in Hawaii. *Journal of Social Psychology, 58,* 67–89.

Ho, M. K. (1987). *Family therapy with minorities.* Newbury Park, CA: Sage.

Hsu, F. L. K. (1953). *Americans and Chinese: Two ways of life.* New York: Abelard-Schuman.

Jung, M. (1984). Structural family therapy: Its application to Chinese families. *Family Process, 23,* 365–374.

Kiang, P. N., & Lee, V. W. (1993). Exclusion or contribution? In *The state of Asian Pacific America* (pp. 25–48). Los Angeles, CA: LEAP

Asian Pacific American Public Policy Institute and UCLA Asian American Studies Center.

Kitano, H. H. L., & Daniels, R. (1988). *Asian Americans: Emerging minorities*. Englewood Cliffs, NJ: Prentice Hall.

Kuo, S. Y., & Spees, E. R. (1983). Chinese American student lifestyles: A comparative study. *Journal of College Student Personnel, 42*, 407–413.

Leong, F. T. L., & Tata, S. P. (1990). Sex and acculturation differences in occupational values among Chinese American children. *Journal of Counseling Psychology, 37*, 208–212.

Leong, F. T. L., Wagner, N. S., & Kim, H. H. (1995). Group counseling expectations among Asian American students: The role of culture-specific factors. *Journal of Counseling Psychology, 42*, 217–222.

Lin, C-Y. C., & Fu, V. R. (1990). A comparison of child-rearing practices among Chinese, immigrant Chinese, and Caucasian American parents. *Child Development, 61*, 429–433.

McLeod, B. (1986). The Oriental express. *Psychology Today*, pp. 48–52.

Nishi, S. M. (1982). The educational disadvantage of Asian and Pacific Americans. *Pacific/Asian American Mental Health Research Center Review, 1*, 4–6.

Ong, P., & Hee, S. J. (1993). The growth of the Asian Pacific population: Twenty million in 2020. In *The state of Asian Pacific America* (pp. 11–24). Los Angeles, CA: LEAP Asian Pacific American Public Policy Institute and UCLA Asian American Studies Center.

Saner-Yiu, L., & Saner-Yiu, R. (1985). Value dimensions in American counseling: A Taiwanese-American dimension. *International Journal for the Advancement of Counseling, 8*, 137–146.

Shon, S. P., & Ja, D. Y. (1982). Asian families. In M. McGoldrick, J. K. Pearce, & J. Giordano (Eds.), *Ethnicity and family therapy* (pp. 208–228). New York: Guilford Press.

Sue, D. (1994). Incorporating cultural diversity in family therapy. *The Family Psychologist, 10*, 19–21.

Sue, D., Ino, S., & Sue, D. M. (1983). Nonassertiveness of Asian-Americans: An inaccurate assumption? *Journal of Counseling Psychology, 30*, 581–588.

Sue, D., Sue, D. M., & Ino, S. (1990). Assertiveness and social anxiety in Chinese-American women. *Journal of Psychology, 124*, 155–164.

Sue, D. W., & Kirk, B. A. (1972). Psychological characteristics of Chinese-American college students. *Journal of Counseling Psychology, 6*, 471–478.

Sue, D. W., & Sue, D. (1990). *Counseling the culturally different: Theory and practice* (2nd ed.). New York: Wiley.

Sue, S., & Morishima, J. K. (1982). *The mental health of Asian Americans*. San Francisco: Jossey-Bass.

Sue, S., & Okazaki, S. (1990). Asian-American educational achievements: A phenomenon in search of an explanation. *American Psychologist, 45,* 913–920.

Sue, S., & Zane, N. W. S. (1985). Academic achievement and socioemotional adjustment among Chinese university students. *Journal of Counseling Psychology, 32,* 913–920.

To America with skills. (1985, July 8). *Time,* pp. 42–44.

Tong, B. R. (1971). The ghetto of the mind: Notes on the historical psychology of Chinese-America. *Amerasia Journal, 1,* 1–31.

Tseng, W., & Hsu, J. (1972). The Chinese attitude toward parental authority as expressed in Chinese children's stories. *Archives of General Psychology, 26,* 28–34.

Wang, L. L-C. (1993). Trends in admissions for Asian Americans in colleges and universities. In *The state of Asian Pacific America* (pp. 49–60). Los Angeles, CA: LEAP Asian Pacific American Public Policy Institute and UCLA Asian American Studies Center.

11

COUNSELING JAPANESE AMERICANS:
From Internment to Reparation

Satsuki Ina

A fter the Japanese attack on Pearl Harbor on December 7, 1941, President Franklin D. Roosevelt issued Executive Order 9066, which enabled the military, in absence of martial law, to circumvent the constitutional safeguards of American citizens of Japanese descent. The order authorized the mass evacuation of 110,000 Japanese Americans—without due process of law—from the West Coast into internment camps for 1 to 5 years. Although the order was implemented as a "military necessity," it has since been documented that these "grave injustices were perpetrated in spite of the fact that our government had in its possession proof that not one Japanese American, citizen or not, had engaged in espionage, not one had committed any act of sabotage" (Weglyn, 1976, p. 29). It has also been documented that the decision to create concentration camps, bounded by barbed wire and guard towers, was, in fact, a result of hysteria, racism, and economic exploitation (Weglyn, 1976).

Almost 50 years after this bleak period in American history, through the indefatigable efforts of leaders and advocates of the Japanese American community, the Civil Liberties Act of 1988 was passed. Popularly known as the Japanese American Redress Bill, this bill mandated Congress to pay each victim of the internment $20,000 in reparation for a most grievous error perpetrated on Americans of Japanese descent.

The following story, written by a 45-year-old Japanese American woman who participated in an intensive group therapy session that focused on the internment experience during World War II, captures the quiet trauma of an internment camp experience and the impact of this event on later development.

Once upon a time there was a little soldier girl who grew up surrounded by barbed wire. She was scared, and so were her mommy and daddy and brother. But they all marched together and pretended to be unafraid. The father wrote poems about guard towers and guns while the brother played with his toy tank made with broken checkers for wheels. Then one day, the little soldier girl's daddy was taken away, and no one could pretend to be unafraid anymore. No one knew where her daddy was. And when she grew up she kept searching for her daddy. She often recognized him because he always went away when she needed him. And she still today sleeps in her soldier clothes, trying to be unafraid.

Like the other participants in the intensive group therapy session, the woman who told this story presented the classic image of the successful Japanese American. She was highly educated and had a successful career with all the outward appearances of the so-called *model minority*. And yet, like the others in the group, she suffered from the invisible consequences of low-grade depression and psychosomatic illness. Lack of spontaneity, low risk taking, workaholism, and difficulty in interpersonal relationships were issues with which all participants in the group were able to identify.

The psychological consequences of having been born a political prisoner in her own country was something this woman was reluctant, and yet compelled, to explore within the safety of a supportive group of men and women who had also been *Children of the Camps*. This term, coined by the author, is used to identify individuals who were either born or spent some portion of their formative years in the U.S. internment camps during World War II.

In this chapter an intensive therapy process is presented in detail as a means of highlighting the social, political, and cultural issues that affect the psychological development of Japanese American clients. The chapter first provides essential background information by discussing traditional Japanese values and norms as well as the acculturation variable, which often depends on generation. The focus then turns to intervention strategies and the group therapy process.

Traditional Japanese Values and Norms

A brief sketch of significant cultural variables may help to clarify the process and content issues in counseling Japanese Americans. (To acquire an in-depth understanding of the matrix of traditional Japanese values and norms that influence the Japanese American personality and family structure, see the resources listed at the end of the chapter.) Although there are variations due to social class, geographical origin, and generation in the United States, some common themes can be identified in terms of cultural values and norms.

Much of traditional Japanese culture can be traced to the philosophical precepts of life based in Confucianism, which arrived in Japan with Buddhism in the sixth century. Within this system of thought, the individual is superseded by the family, specific hierarchical roles are established for all family members, and rules of behavior and conduct are formalized. An individual's adherence to this code of conduct is a reflection not only on the immediate family but also on the extended kinship network.

Within the nuclear family, as Shon and Ja (1982) have described, the father is the leader and decision maker. His authority is unquestioned. He enforces family rules and is the primary disciplinarian. The welfare of the family rests squarely on the father's shoulders, and the successes or failures of the family and its individual members are viewed essentially as the father's responsibility. The mother's traditional role is that of the nurturant caretaker of both her husband and children. Because the mother is clearly the emotionally devoted, nurturant parental figure, the strongest emotional attachments tend to be with the mother.

Highly developed feelings of obligation govern many of the interpersonal relationships of Japanese Americans. Shame and loss of face are frequently used to reinforce adherence to prescribed sets of obligations. The interdependent quality of relationships suggests that harmony in these relationships is best achieved through proper conduct and attitudes. The often unspoken obligatory reciprocity within relationships is a serious consideration in the life of a Japanese American. Respect and obedience to parents and others in authority positions reflect the indebtedness of the individual and serve to express affection and gratitude.

In a social structure where interdependence is so highly valued, the fear of losing face can be a powerful motivating force for conforming. The withdrawal of the family's, community's, or society's confidence and support, and the exposure of one's wrong actions for all to see, is a profound shaming experience to be avoided at all costs.

Harmonious interpersonal relationships are maintained by avoiding direct confrontation. Therefore, much of the communication style of the Japanese American is indirect and is characterized by talking around the point. Problem solving occurs within the prescribed family structure. There is a strong dictum that problems be kept within the family and solved there. The ability to endure hardships, demonstrate unflagging loyalty, and sacrifice for the good of the whole is often called upon for resolution of problems.

The Acculturation Variable

Empathic understanding of a client's experience is based on the principles of similarity and identification. Therefore, it is essential that counselors avoid projecting their unconscious stereotypes onto the culturally different client. Such benevolent blindness can lead the counselor to discount or deny differences in values, behavior, family structure, and communication style that can serve as rich resources for change and growth. To minimize the dangers of assumed similarities or differences, a careful evaluation of the extent to which the Japanese American client has adopted American mainstream values, attitudes, and behaviors must be made.

Japanese Americans typically identify themselves in terms of numbers of generations since immigrating to the United States. Issei, the first generation, are currently in their 80s and older. They are the immigrant group that arrived in the United States during the late 1800s. Targeted by the Oriental Exclusion Act of 1924, issei were prohibited from gaining citizenship or owning land (Kitagawa, 1967). Today they are the elderly in the community and the least likely cohort group to utilize Western mental health services. Due to the language barrier and traditional Japanese values of shame associated with having emotional problems, the issei are more likely to cope with personal problems by relying on their religious beliefs and drawing on the cultural coping mechanisms of stoicism, privacy, fatalism, and family support (Maykovich, 1972). Issei interned in the camps during the war typically did not talk about the shame and humiliation they experienced, nor of the guilt they felt about their children who had to be imprisoned because of their parents' nationality (Kiefer, 1974). Traditional loyalty, propriety, and fear of retribution were also likely factors that inhibited complaining or being openly critical of the government (Kitagawa, 1967). A recent study by Kiyoko Hallenberg (1988) of the Japanese American elderly who had experienced internment indicates that 55% of the subjects interviewed hardly ever talked about the internment even after 15 years, and that 42% rarely talked about it more than 40 years later.

Nisei, the second generation, currently range in age from 60 to 80 years. They are the American-born children of the issei. Educated in American schools, this cohort group tends to reflect a more bicultural approach to life. Some are bilingual, but due to the internment experience, most felt the social and familial press to acculturate and adopt American ways so as to ensure success and acceptance in the larger community. The questioned loyalty and assimilability of Japanese Americans raised by the wartime hysteria intensified the urgency to become "good Americans." Consequently, this generation of Japanese Americans, encouraged by their immigrant parents, were deeply committed to educational and professional achievement as the mechanism for being accepted by the dominant culture. Thus the unconscious influence of Japanese culture on the nisei personality may be more prominent than outwardly acknowledged.

In the group process, nisei and sansei (the third generation) participants were asked to rate themselves on a scale of *very Japanese* to *very American*. Nisei tended to rate themselves in the *very American* range, as did their sansei counterparts. Although nisei participants were older than the sansei, and therefore during their early years were raised in a closed Japanese cultural system within the camps, they tended to deny the impact of this early Japanese socialization on their self-perception. However, in the discussion that followed regarding traditional Japanese values and coping styles, nisei participants often expressed surprise at how Japanese they really were.

Sansei, the third generation, are now approximately 40 to 60 years old. They may have been born in the camps or are likely to have experienced the reentry process after the internment as young children. This generation is, almost without exception, English speaking only. Though more fully acculturated, the intense striving to be good Americans has been perpetuated in sansei. Although national loyalty was no longer an issue, sansei in the group reflected the divided loyalty between familial expectations and personal desires.

Several sansei participants in the group talked about their dissatisfaction with their jobs. In the discussion, it became clear that for some, their original career choice was fostered more by parental definitions of success and the more accessible or socially appropriate career paths for Asian Americans than by personal preference. For example, when asked to describe any persistent problems in his life, a 45-year-old dentist reported, "I have difficulty handling paper work, official forms, bookkeeping, business information, and documents. I am easily distracted from priority work. I procrastinate. I am tentative and unclear as to my life's primary work." Although initially he was unable to label his feelings and understand the roots for his chronic state of depression, with the support of the group, he was eventually able to recognize the depth of his feelings of obligation to his parents as well as his guilt for resenting his role as the dutiful son. Angry feelings surfaced as he described the faceless oppression that plays a part in his psychic dilemma.

This sansei client was surprised to discover the extent to which he adheres to the values of filial respect and avoidance of losing face. His experience as a child internee, the possible internalized anxiety that his parents felt during the trauma of internment, and the subsequent discrimination and displacement led him to choose an acceptable career to ensure his security and status in society. "It's hard work being Japanese, and it's damn painful to be a minority."

This sansei client also demonstrates how important it is for counselors to be sensitive to the conscious and unconscious cultural identification processes operating in the Japanese American client. It is incumbent upon counselors to have a working knowledge of traditional Japanese values and norms and to use this cultural information as the background from which each client emerges as a unique individual. McGoldrick, Pearce, and Giordano (1982) suggested that cultural information is best used as a filter to determine the extent to which cultural factors contribute to the presenting problem and as a resource in choosing clinical interventions.

The counselor's ability to appreciate the impact of social, cultural, and familial processes can help the client understand the source of his or her pain as well as enable the client to make more conscious choices about staying within or stepping outside of cultural and societal boundaries. A culturally responsive counselor will thoroughly explore the possible social and psychological consequences of the client's choices.

In addition to generational identification as issei, nisei, and sansei, other acculturation indicators can provide a general sense of degree of acculturation. For example, rural Japanese American communities tend to be more traditional in contrast to urban communities, which have been disturbed by urban renewal efforts. Affiliation with specific ethnic, social, civic, and religious organizations can be a helpful indicator. Peer group affiliation in schools and dating preferences also help to determine the degree of acculturation. It is important to keep in mind, however, that the influences of culture and racial discrimination are often more unconscious than conscious, and the counselor will do well to explore these issues jointly with the client. Assessing the degree of acculturation enables the counselor to clarify the presenting problem and to select appropriate culture-specific interventions.

The Presenting Problem

Human problems are at once unique and universal. What brings the client into therapy, however, is the inappropriate or ineffective ways in which he or she is coping with a problem. For ethnic minority clients, it is essential that these coping styles be understood in terms of both their cultural and defensive overlay. The counselor's ability to attend to the personal, cultural, and defensive variables that influence the client's coping style enable the counselor to understand the backdrop for the presenting problem.

William Grier and Price Cobbs in their classic text, *Black Rage* (1968), described the concept of the paranorm, which can be applied to all minority group members who have been victims of racial bigotry and oppression. As a psychological defense against the dehumanizing effects of racism, minority subgroups develop a norm of appropriate paranoia against which they check their perceptions of safety and trust.

Although ferreting out how much of the client's coping style is cultural, defensive, or uniquely individual is impossible, two types of errors in understanding the presenting problems could bring the therapeutic process to a standstill. The first error is to assume that cultural or defensive factors are insignificant in influencing the client's coping style. The second error is to assume the client's coping style can be explained completely by cultural or defensive factors, without consideration for individual uniqueness. Thus the workaholism some group participants describe will only be superficially understood if the clients' historical experience of being viewed as unassimilable as a race is not explored. Japanese Americans who experienced the confinement possess a group consciousness that should not be minimized. Fear of failure for this group is understandably high. The counselor's task is to facilitate the client's awareness of this socially imposed defense mechanism to enable him or her to see the problem in a contextual as well as uniquely personal framework.

The participant whose story of a little soldier girl introduces this chapter further illustrated this point in speaking of her difficulty in finding lasting relationships with men. She typically picked men who tended to be emotionally unavailable to her. As an adult, she consciously understood that her father was taken away suddenly in the middle of the night and incarcerated in a separate prison for suspected dissidents. In the course of the group process, however, she realized that as a child she experienced her father's disappearance as abandonment and felt overwhelmed by the anguish and fear of her mother who was left alone to care for two small children behind barbed wires.

This early childhood trauma was then exacerbated not by a dysfunctional family's no-talk rule but by cultural mandates that discouraged discussion about what was internalized as a shameful experience. Maintaining dignity in the face of the loss of their personal freedom was a challenging and precarious balance for

Japanese American internees. As a coping style influenced by Japanese culture and reinforced by the larger society's amnesia about the camps, silence was used in an effort to heal the injury. The consequences of both the cultural and defensive coping mechanism are depicted in Hallenberg's study (1988), which found a significant relationship between not talking about the internment and chronic depression. The group helped the woman challenge her mistaken belief that somehow she was unlovable and that was why her father left her. She was also able to recognize how the silence into which she withdrew mirrored the silence of her parents, the community, and the government regarding her internment experience.

Intervention Strategies

In working with Japanese American clients, the entire range of clinical interventions may be considered for treatment. However, the counselor who has assessed the degree of acculturation, cultural constraints and prescriptions, and defense mechanisms against racism will be better able to make a sensitive choice of intervention. To minimize resistance in a cross-cultural therapeutic relationship, it is recommended that the interventions selected serve to challenge, not conflict with or negate, existing coping mechanisms. Consequently, the counselor must be willing to adapt interventions to the client's need. This requires the counselor to have a wide repertoire of clinical interventions from which to choose.

To better understand the psychological effects of the internment experience on Japanese Americans, a clinical analogy may be appropriate. Like the incest victim in a dysfunctional family, American citizens of Japanese descent were singled out and their fundamental rights to due process were violated by the very arm of the government designated to protect those rights. The social amnesia and denial subsequent to the internment further traumatized the victims and led to internalized shame and repressed anger. Not unlike the child victim who manages to cope by developing psychic barriers against vulnerability (Courtois, 1988), Japanese Americans as a group committed themselves to being good citizens and made every effort to be accepted by the larger society. After years of suppressing and denying the anger because of the dependency on the perpetrator, clients in this classic "incest bind" can experience symptomatic behaviors.

The examination of a group experience for Japanese Americans who experienced internment follows. Important stages of the group experience—creating a safe environment, telling your story, identifying developmental needs, expressing the unexpressed, grieving the losses, and terminating—as well as critical issues are explored. Replication issues are also discussed.

Creating a Safe Environment

As the group experience began, the facilitator acknowledged and opened for discussion the cultural prohibitions against disclosing family problems and openly expressing feelings. The reluctance to reopen the painful experience of the internment required an extensive trust-building process. Participants were encouraged to be aware of their physical and emotional boundaries, and the facilitator modeled, with respect, each person's right to say "no." This was particularly crucial for people whose rights had been so blatantly violated. Participants were told that any level of self-disclosure was acceptable, and every member agreed to honor confidentiality for the material presented by the group.

Telling Your Story

Like the incestuous family's "secret," the unacknowledged crime against the Japanese Americans was rationalized with euphemisms, including *wartime hysteria, protective custody,* and *national security.* Consequently, many of the victims themselves, culturally primed to respect authority and shamed by the experience, kept the story of their internment to themselves. Rather than complaining and revolting, they practiced silent endurance. Until recently, when reparation became imminent, very little about the camp experience was acknowledged in the classroom, in the media, or in government policy. For the participants, then, telling their story, talking about what they experienced and how they coped, was the beginning of the healing process. To have others in the group mirror back empathic acceptance, without judgment, served as an invaluable intervention in empowering the victim.

Prior to the session, each person was asked to talk to at least one other family member about his or her intention to participate in this group. This served not only to prepare the participants emotionally but also to begin effecting a challenge to the no-talk rule to which the family may have adhered.

Often, implicit in the minority experience is the absence of acknowledgment and validation by the majority power structure. Just as in the family, when this validation is not provided, self-doubt prevails. Thus the facilitator's role was to model and support, emphatically and affirmatively, the acknowledgment of each participant's story. Participants were asked to bring photographs of themselves, share stories that were told about them, and describe what happened to their family. The participants expressed shame in terms of loss of face. Therefore, assisting the participant to look into the faces reflecting acceptance and understanding served as a powerful shame-reduction intervention. This section of the workshop was given no time limit. It was completed only after each person felt that he or she had finished.

Identifying Developmental Needs

Participants were encouraged to identify their developmental tasks and needs at the time of the internment and to consider how those tasks and needs were affected by the internment. Many participants were able to understand for the first time what it must have been like for their parents to have children behind barbed wire fences. One of the significant issues that surfaced was the disorganization of family roles and rules with the imposition of the military superstructure upon the family. Just the very physical structure of the barracks and mess hall affected family privacy, communication, and control. In addition, participants described the pervasive fear and anxiety that gripped their parents as they attempted to raise a family in a prison compound surrounded by tanks and armed guards standing on watch towers.

Using the Adlerian Early Childhood Recollections process (Dinkmeyer, Pew, & Dinkmeyer, 1979), participants reexperienced that period of their development and identified what it was that they needed from their parents at the time. The group was then asked to respond to each individual's needs with verbal affirmations as the participant returned to the early experience, but this time with an empowered parental source. Cultural injunctions against violating filial piety carry a heavy burden of guilt. Therefore, during the debriefing, the facilitator actively reframed blaming of parents for their child's unmet needs as limitations compounded by external forces.

One woman described the images that came up for her as she regressed to her early infancy. She was born in the camps. She recalled that as she looked up from her straw mat "crib" she saw her parents' faces. Rather than being joyful at her birth, she realized that what she saw were faces that were fearful and anxious. She wept as she recognized that her arrival was not a welcome blessing. She realized that her need for security was only tenuously provided because her parents were likely to have been ambivalent about having an offspring when their own security was in question. With the help of the group, she further realized that the egocentric "child" decided that somehow she was the source of her parents' fear and anxiety.

Themes that emerged from these early recollections and consequent decisions included issues of trust, abandonment, powerlessness, fear of risk, pessimism, and self-discounting. Participants were able to relate these issues to current persistent problems in their work and love relationships.

Expressing the Unexpressed

Having identified the source of the hurt that had been so long buffered by culturally and socially induced guilt and shame, the participants were encouraged to express the emotions that had been suppressed so long. Anger directed at parents could be identified; anger directed at an amorphous government that had violated their right to freedom, however, was difficult to identify and justify. It was expressed as anger without a target, as a diffuse, unlabeled rage.

Because of cultural prescriptions of emotional constraint, anger release techniques were presented in progressive steps of intensity from passive to more active forms of release. Participants were invited to participate at a level that was just over their comfort zone and no more. The first step was to discuss the effects of suppressed emotions on the body and the relationship of this suppression to somatic illnesses and depression. Participants were then encouraged to relate their experiences to these concepts. The next step was to listen to music written and performed by Japanese Americans that expressed the trauma and humiliation of the internment experience. This process enabled participants to hear the feelings of others poignantly and emotionally expressed. For many, this released tears and feelings of affirmation.

Each step progressively intensified the release of feelings. To reduce anxiety about the public display of emotions, people were paired up for each exercise, and partners were instructed to affirm and nonverbally support the other person's feelings. Most preferred to pair up and go to separate rooms to have some privacy. Participants were then encouraged to move their bodies using Bioenergetic (Lowen, 1975) movements and to vocalize their feelings.

Debriefing was extensive, and inhibitions were discussed and acknowledged. The facilitator explained that reluctance or refusal to participate was honored as a choice and was not a sign of emotional inadequacy. Participants were assured that no judgment or clinical assessment would be assigned as a result of their choices. For all victims, choice without judgment is crucial to the healing process.

Grieving the Losses

As anger gave way to sadness, participants identified their grief over their losses. One man said, "When my parents lost their freedom, I guess I lost some of my childhood." Participants recalled discussion about material losses, but rarely about emotional losses. Children grew up or were born into a family environment in which parents had lost the dignity of self-determination. Though most of the internees faced the situation with courage, the experience took away 2, 3, and sometimes 4 years from the lives of innocent people. Participants were encouraged to identify ways to continue to heal the wounds of the inner child. Personal work, family work, and even political work were discussed.

Personal work was the need to acknowledge the losses that the child had experienced and to work to fulfill unmet needs. One man said, "I really need to let the child in me play joyfully and without guilt." Another woman said, "I'd like to let the fearful child in me have new experiences."

Family work included discussion of the detrimental effects of the no-talk rule, and how beginning to talk to parents and learning about their experiences could help participants integrate these feelings and experiences into their personal history. Discovering how parents had coped, and how the internment had affected their relationships and their feelings about their children, were all issues that remained cloaked in silence for members of the group.

At the political level, of course, the pending monetary reparation of $20,000 for all the surviving internees was discussed. Many participants felt that the reparation represented a symbol of the long-awaited acknowledgment of the crime against Japanese Americans. The guilt and loss of face shrouded in government silence could now be lifted and guilt assigned to the appropriate perpetrator. Foremost, acknowledgment and a formal apology would facilitate the healing of an insidious wound.

Terminating

The group grew very close. A simulated family had been created in which the pain could be identified, shared, and validated. The grief work could be completed, and the participants could move forward in their development. For most, the group experience was just the beginning of a therapeutic journey. One participant closed the final session with, "Now, maybe I can really do something with my freedom!"

Replication Nuts and Bolts

In attempting to replicate this group experience, it is highly recommended that at least one of the facilitators be a member of the Japanese American community because of the highly sensitive nature of the issues involved and the cultural constraints against involving outsiders. A facilitator who has also been an internee can facilitate some of the more difficult processes through self-disclosure and role modeling. Ideally, a male and female cotherapy team would be helpful. Because fewer men than women are likely to participate, the presence of a male role model can serve to validate the different gender perspectives. A small group size—five or six—can serve to minimize the public quality of the group and also allow each member as much time as needed to tell his or her story and express the deeply buried emotions that are likely to surface. A tight, safe context is essential for trauma victims; therefore, a weekend intensive with a 1-month and 6-month follow-up was adopted in order to prevent time disruption and screen out possible dropouts.

Because it is not generally acknowledged by the Japanese community or the community at large that people suffer today from the consequences of the internment, this group experience is not likely to be one that a participant will want to publicize. Therefore, participation is more likely to be enhanced by working within the community through notifying key people such as clergy persons, education and medical personnel, and social service providers who can, by word of mouth, inform people about such a group experience.

As with other groups, it is essential that the group leader conduct an individual intake to assess the psychological well-being of potential participants. Due to the social, cultural, and political influences that have caused much of the emotions around the internment experience to be suppressed, it is important that individual members possess the necessary ego strength to process intense emotions and that they have a relatively supportive environment to which they will return. Because an essential feature of the healing process is the ability to bond and experience acceptance, individuals with personality disorders that could interfere with this process are referred for individual therapy to deal with internment issues.

Conclusion

Because the evacuation of the Japanese Americans in 1942 occurred on the West Coast of the United States and Canada (Daniels, 1971; Weglyn, 1976), not every Japanese American client will have the direct experience of the internment as did those participating in the group discussed in this chapter. This description of the group experience, however, can help counselors to understand the acculturation process, cultural constraints and resources, and defensive strategies for coping with racism and discrimination when working with Japanese American clients. Additionally, the group process presented in this chapter can serve to demonstrate methods for modifying traditional interventions to make them culturally appropriate for the Japanese American client.

Implications of the internment experience on subsequent generations of Japanese Americans need to be addressed. Possible clinical issues to be considered include the intergenerational effects of cultural coping mechanisms with respect to the trauma of internment.

References

Courtois, C. A. (1988). *Healing the incest wound: Adult survivors in therapy.* New York: Norton.

Daniels, R. (1971). *Concentration camps USA: Japanese Americans and World War II.* New York: Holt, Rinehart & Winston.

Dinkmeyer, D. C., Pew, W. L., & Dinkmeyer, D. C. (1979). *Adlerian counseling and psychotherapy.* Monterey, CA: Brooks/Cole.

Grier, W. H., & Cobbs, P. M. (1968). *Black rage.* New York: Basic Books.

Hallenberg, K. (1988). *Internment experience of the Japanese American. Elderly and their emotional development.* Unpublished master's thesis.

Kiefer, C. W. (1974). *Changing cultures, changing lives.* San Francisco: Jossey-Bass.

Kitagawa, D. (1967). *Issei and nisei. The internment years.* New York: Seabury Press.

Lowen, A. (1975). *Bioenergetics.* New York: Penguin Books.

Maykovich, M. (1972). *Japanese American identity dilemma.* Tokyo: Waseda University Press.

McGoldrick, M., Pearce, J. K., & Giordano, J. (Eds.). (1982). *Ethnicity and family therapy.* New York: Guilford Press.

Shon, S. P., & Ja, D. Y. (1982). Asian families. In M. McGoldrick, J. K. Pearce, & J. Giordano (Eds.), *Ethnicity and family therapy* (pp. 208–228). New York: Guilford Press.

Weglyn, M. (1976). *Years of infamy: The untold story of America's concentration camps.* New York: Morrow Press.

Additional Resources

Armor, J., & Wright, P. (1989). *Manzanar.* New York: Vintage Books.
Broom, L., & Reimer, R. (1949). *Removal and return: The socioeconomical effects of the war on the Japanese Americans.* Berkeley: University of California Press.
Chuman, F. F. (1976). *The bamboo people: The law and Japanese Americans.* Chicago: Japanese American Citizens League.
DeVos, G. A. (1955). A qualitative Rorschach assessment of maladjustment and rigidity in acculturating Japanese Americans. *Genetic Psychology Monograph, 52,* p. 51.
Doi, T. (1973). *The anatomy of dependence.* Tokyo: Kodansha International.
Exec. Order 9066, 7 Fed. Reg. 1407 (1942). As of March 31, 1942, Pub. L. No. 503, 18 U.S.C. §47(a) (1942).
Grier, W. H., & Cobbs, P. M. (1968). *Black rage.* New York: Basic Books.
Guterson, D. (1995). *Snow falling on cedars.* New York: Vintage Books.
Hosokawa, B. (1969). *Nisei: The quiet Americans.* New York: Morrow Press.
Ishigo, E. (1972). *Lone Heart Mountain.* Los Angeles: Anderson, Ritchie, & Simon.
Kashima, T. (1980). Japanese American internees' return, 1945 to 1955: Readjustment and social amnesia. *Phylon* (The Atlanta University), *41*(2), 107–115.
Kikumura, A. (1981). *Through harsh winters: The life of a Japanese immigrant woman.* Novato, CA: Chandler & Sharp.
Kitano, H. (1969). *Japanese Americans: The evolution of a subculture.* Englewood Cliffs, NJ: Prentice-Hall.
Kogawa, J. (1983). *Obasan.* Harmondsworth, England: Penguin Books.
Nishi, S. M., Bannai, L., & Tomihiro, C. (1983). Bibliography on redress: Wartime relocation and internment of Japanese Americans. *P/AAMHRC Research Review, 2*(1), 6–8.
Ogawa, D. M. (1971). *From Japs to Japanese: The evolution of Japanese American stereotypes.* Berkeley, CA: McCutchan Press.
Okubo, M. (1946). *Citizen 13660.* New York: Columbia University Press.
Sone, M. (1953). *Nisei daughter.* Seattle: University of Washington Press.

Sue, S., & Morishima, J. K. (1982). *The mental health of Asian Americans*. San Francisco: Jossey-Bass.

Sue, S., & Wagner, N. N. (1973). *Asian-American psychological perspective*. Palo Alto, CA: Science and Behavior Books.

Takaki, R. (1989). *Strangers from a different shore*. Boston: Little, Brown.

Thomas, D. S., & Nishimoto, R. S. (1946). *The spoilage*. Berkeley: University of California Press.

Tsukamoto, M., & Pinkerton, E. (1987). *We the people*. Elk Grove, CA: Laguna.

Wake, M. N. (1983). Acculturation and clinical issues affecting the mental health of Japanese Americans. *P/AAMHRC Research Review*, 2(4), 5–7.

Wilson, R. A., & Hosokawa, B. (1980). *East to America: A history of the Japanese in the United States*. New York: Morrow Press.

Yamamoto, J., Machizawa, S., & Steinberg, A. (1986). The Japanese American relocation center experience. *P/AAMHRC Research Review*, 5(3/4), 17–20.

12

COUNSELING AMERICANS OF SOUTHEAST ASIAN DESCENT:
The Impact of the Refugee Experience

Rita Chi-Ying Chung, Fred Bemak,
and Sumie Okazaki

Background

Since 1975, more than 1.5 million Southeast Asians have fled from their homes and sought refuge in the United States. The mass exodus of Southeast Asian refugees, prompted by political turmoil and genocide has caused them to become one of the fastest growing ethnic groups in the United States. This population consists of five main Southeast Asian groups: Cambodians, Chinese-Vietnamese, Hmong, Laotians, and Vietnamese. The refugees have settled in every state in the United States but are especially concentrated in California, Texas, and Washington, DC.

It is important to distinguish between refugee and immigrant status. Murphy (1977) differentiated between "forced versus free," or involuntary versus voluntary migration. According to this definition, refugees are forced to leave their country of origin and are displaced from their countries by events outside of their control, such as war or genocide, because it is dangerous to remain in their home countries and impossible to continue their customary way of life. The refugee population is therefore distinguished from other migrants such as immigrants or sojourners due to their involuntary and sudden departure. As is characteristic of refugees in general, the Southeast Asian refugees were ill prepared for the sudden departure from their familiar world and faced uncertainty, confusion, high risk for personal safety, and complete disruption of their normal lives. Such chaos often caused the loss of personal identity as well as the loss of reference groups such as family, community, culture, and country (Bemak & Greenberg, 1994).

Southeast Asian refugees entered the United States in primarily two main waves, with each wave having different demographic characteristics and experiences before and after migration. The first wave of Southeast Asian refugees left Vietnam prior to the fall of Saigon in 1975 and entered the United States directly or from refugee camps for the next few years. During the fall of Saigon, due to their close association with the United States and/ or South Vietnamese forces, these refugees were assisted by the American government and hastily evacuated by helicopters or sea-lifts. This first wave was mainly Vietnamese and tended to be relatively well educated and able to speak some English.

The second main wave of Southeast Asian refugees entered the United States between 1978 and 1980 and consisted of Cambodians, Hmong, Laotians, and Vietnamese. The second wave of refugees escaped from their homes by sea or made hazardous journeys through the jungle. Those from Vietnam left in small, overcrowded, and unseaworthy boats. The boat people frequently encountered brutal attacks by sea pirates, and many were subjected to severe violence, or were raped or killed (Chung & Okazaki, 1991). The Cambodians, Hmong, and Laotians escaped by land through the jungle, crossing mine fields and avoiding ambushes by military soldiers. They encountered tropical diseases, death, hunger, starvation, and exhaustion. Further compounding the trauma, the escape from countries of origin for many of those in the second wave did not result in an immediate resettlement to a host country. Instead these groups of refugees were forced to wait in overcrowded and unsanitary refugee camps in nearby countries such as Thailand, the Philippines, or Hong Kong for months or even years before they were permanently resettled in the United States. In contrast to the first wave, the second wave refugees generally tended to be less educated with no prior English-language skills. Furthermore, many, especially those from the rural areas, had little or no exposure to Western culture prior to arriving in resettlement countries.

The first wave of Southeast Asian refugees tended to adjust more successfully than the second wave because of the premigration differences. Because they managed to escape before the fall of Saigon, they were exposed to less premigration trauma, and they were better educated and possessed more wealth and resources (Nguyen, 1982). As the political repression intensified in Cambodia, Laos, and Vietnam after 1975, many in the second wave experienced human atrocities and genocide and were victims of incarceration, torture, beatings, sexual abuse, rape, and starvation. Many also witnessed killings and torture or were forced to commit human atrocities themselves. These atrocities were not only confined to countries of origin but also occurred during their escape and in the refugee camps.

This chapter first dicusses the psychosocial adjustment and adaptation of Southeast Asian refugees, their cultural belief systems, and their barriers to mental health services and use of traditional methods. The chapter then looks at counseling services and provides an in-depth exploration of the Multi-Level Model as an approach to psychotherapy with refugees and a case study illustrating the model's use.

Psychosocial Adjustment and Adaptation

Two major factors are associated with Southeast Asian refugees' psychosocial adjustment and adaptation in the United States. One factor is the amount of premigration trauma experienced in home countries during the escape process and in the refugee camps. Mollica, Wyshak, Coelho, and Lavelle (1985) classified the different types of premigration trauma for refugees into four general categories: deprivation (e.g., food and shelter), physical injury and torture, incarceration and reeducation camps, and witnessing killing and torture. The second factor is the level of difficulties experienced after the actual resettlement in adjusting to a country with a culture significantly different from their home country (e.g., Bemak, 1989; Chung & Kagawa-Singer, 1993; Lin, Masuda, & Tazuma, 1982; Lin, Tazuma, & Masuda, 1979; Westermeyer, 1986).

The emotional survival mechanism used by the Southeast Asian refugees to cope with experiences of torture, rape, and other human atrocities prior to migration was to act "dumb" (Mollica & Jalbert, 1989). In order to survive, individuals had acted as if they were deaf, dumb, foolish, confused, or stupid. They had also learned to comply with orders obediently without question or complaint because they knew that appearing smart resulted in a torture or execution. The fear of being killed or tortured has remained for many refugees who continued to act dumb after resettling in the United States. They continue to be afraid to speak up or show their true feelings (Mollica & Jalbert, 1989). Such behavior among the refugees, which originally served as survival skills, may appear to be aversive, antisocial, or even pathological when viewed within the culture of the host country (Stein, 1986).

Studies have found group differences among the Southeast Asian populations with respect to psychological distress. Cambodians have been found to experience more psychological distress compared to other groups (Chung & Kagawa-Singer, 1993; Mollica, Wyshak, & Lavelle, 1987). This has been attributed to the Cambodian refugees' experience of the genocide orchestrated by the Pol Pot regime. The Vietnamese and Chinese-Vietnamese have been found to be the least distressed compared to the other groups, which Chung and Kagawa-Singer (1993) found was associated with higher levels of education, better English language skills, the fact that some had managed to arrive with financial assets, and access into the already established Chinatown communities in the United States.

Resettlement in a foreign country poses additional challenges for Southeast Asian refugees. Premigration trauma may be exacerbated by hardships experienced after resettlement. For example, Amerasian refugees (often with Vietnamese mothers and American fathers) frequently experienced strong racism in Vietnam. Their hopes that such discrimination will end are often shattered as they find themselves once again facing prejudice and racism in the United States. Some Amerasian youths have responded aggressively and sometimes violently, resulting in legal problems. Tayabas and Pok (1983) found that problems with adjustment were more accentuated during the initial 1- to 2-year resettlement period during which refugees commonly focus on meeting their basic needs of housing and employment. Bemak (1989) described a three-phase developmental model of acculturation associated with successful adjustment and adaptation to the host country. In the first phase, the refugee attempts to use skills to master the new environment and establish security and psychological safety. The second phase follows after the successful completion of phase one and is the integration of former skills that were developed in the home country with the newly acquired skills learned in the host country. Phase three is achieved when the refugee develops a growing sense of the future. It is only after the mastery of culture, language, and a sense of psychological safety that the refugee begins to plan for future attainable goals and implement strategies to achieve those goals.

During resettlement, refugees may become motivated to recover what has been lost as they attempt to rebuild their lives. However, they may also encounter a loss of control over decision making with regard to basic life issues such as the geographical location of where they will live in the resettlement country, job opportunities, and social networks. These difficulties may hinder their enthusiasm to acculturate and create emotional and psychological problems as they begin to confront the loss of their culture and identity. Tasks such as catching a bus, handling money, and going shopping, which were routine tasks in their home countries, may become major ordeals in the process of acculturation (Chung & Okazaki, 1991).

It is common for refugees to experience survivor's guilt after resettlement (Brown, 1982; Lin, Masuda, et al., 1982; Tobin & Friedman, 1983). They are haunted by the guilt of successfully escaping from their home country while leaving family, relatives, and friends behind in a politically volatile country. Many refugees have little or no information regarding those they left behind. The lack of knowledge about their safety and well-being adds to the already existing guilt. Furthermore, survivor's guilt intensifies as the refugee becomes more successful in the resettlement country.

To rebuild one's life in a foreign country is a difficult task. A high percentage of Southeast Asian refugees remain dependent on welfare even after being in the United States for a long period of time (Chung & Bemak, 1995), largely due to unemployment. Acquiring a job poses particular difficulties for refugees because educational training and skills obtained in their home country are most often not transferable to resettlement countries. This may cause a dramatic change in socioeconomic status, causing some refugees to take jobs for which they are overqualified. Chung and Bemak (1995) indicated that there was a tendency for refugee men to remain unemployed and welfare dependent while waiting for a suitable position that will match their skills because taking just any employment may result in downward mobility and loss of status. Although refugees make remarkable progress in their adjustment, only a small percentage regain their former socioeconomic status (Lin et al., 1979; Lin, Masuda et al., 1982).

English language skills play an important part in refugee adjustment and are a key to gainful employment. However, for those who are illiterate in their own language, learning English proves to be a challenge. Chung and Kagawa-Singer (1993) found that attendance in English as a second language (ESL) classes was significantly associated with distress in this population. Furthermore, emotional and mental fatigue as well as memory and concentration difficulties due to premigration trauma may also inhibit learning performance in ESL (Mollica & Jalbert, 1989).

Resettlement for Southeast Asian refugees also creates changes in the family structure. Due to high rates of unemployment and underemployment among Southeast Asian men, it is often necessary for women to work in order to provide adequate financial family support. While refugee men may experience a downward turn in their socioeconomic status, women may experience upward mobility in their socioeconomic status (Chung, 1991). Working outside of the home and community and being exposed to American culture, refugee women may begin to question their traditional cultural gender roles and seek more independence. Such shifts in roles and attitudes frequently cause marital conflicts.

Role shifts also occur within the Southeast Asian refugee family. As is common among immigrants, children and adolescents tend to acculturate faster than their parents. Attending school and having exposure to nonrefugee children through ESL or other classes, children are apt to learn the English language and the American customs faster than their parents. This often results in a shift in family dynamics, with the children assuming the role of a language and cultural translator for their parents. When this happens, the children frequently witness a transformation of their parents from previously competent, autonomous caretakers to depressed, overwhelmed, and dependent individuals. Confidence in their parents as caregivers and providers is inevitably undermined, and the traditional family structure may change dramatically as a result. Furthermore, some children may experience feeling ashamed of their parents in the resettlement country because their parents lack English language skills, dress "funny," and behave according to non-Western manners and customs. There may also be embarrassment to speak publicly in their mother tongue with parents or family members because peers in the resettlement country may laugh at them.

Another area of change within families may be in child-rearing practices. Usual disciplinary measures used before migration such as corporal punishment may be prohibited by the different laws in the resettlement country. This issue presents a serious dilemma for Southeast Asian refugee parents, who may already feel diminished in their status as parents and constricted in raising their children in ways that have been culturally acceptable for generations. Intergenerational conflict between parents and children may also occur regarding issues such as dating, marriage, curfew, and/or parental supervision. Many refugee children face the difficult position of bridging two worlds—acculturating and adopting the customs and behaviors of their host country peer group while maintaining the role as a child in a traditional family. In attempts to keep their child from adopting patterns of behavior and values incongruent with traditional values and beliefs, some refugee parents try to maintain a strict traditional upbringing. Despite this, many parents experience the loss of traditional authority and control as their children become more outspoken and challenge their authority and the "old culture."

Paralleling the home experience are the difficulties faced in schools by many refugee children and adolescents. They may experience racial tension manifested in being punched, mimicked, harassed, or robbed by non-Asian students (Huang, 1989). The norms regulating classroom and school behavior are usually different than those in their home countries. Children wishing to participate in extracurricular activities may have difficulties because their Asian refugee parents see educational success as a tool for upward mobility and can not understand this "foreign activity" that does not emphasize studying or the relevance of extracurricula activities. These issues, combined with the desire to belong socially, may generate both internalized and externalized tensions and conflicts for refugee children and adolescents.

Cultural Belief Systems

Studies suggest that Southeast Asian refugees express depression and other psychological problems in a manner that is consistent with their cultural belief systems (e.g., Chung & Kagawa-Singer, in press; Lin et al., 1979). These studies have indicated that Southeast Asian refugees, like other Asian populations, tend to express psychological distress as neurasthenia, which is comprised predominantly of somatic symptoms (e.g., headaches, weakness, pressure on the chest or head) but with some depression, anxiety, and psychosocial dysfunction. Mental illness is highly stigmatized in most Asian cultures, and the expression of neurasthenic symptoms may be a culturally sanctioned method of expressing psychological distress (Cheung, 1982; Chung & Kagawa-Singer, 1996; Kleinman, 1982). In many Asian cultures, mental illness is seen as a reflection on the entire family line, including ancestors and future offspring. If it is known that an individual within a family has a mental health problem, the individual's family is seen as undesirable, and the marriageability of family members is dramatically reduced. The manner in which Asians express psychological distress through somatic symptoms may allow the individual to seek help regarding physical complaints, thereby avoiding the stigma of seeking help for mental health problems. However, it is important to acknowledge that although many Southeast Asian refugees exhibit distress through somatic channels, they are also capable of discussing their problems in psychological terms (Cheung, 1982; Kinzie et al., 1982; Mollica et al., 1987).

Southeast Asian refugees' conceptualization of mental health differs from the Western framework. Refugees' help-seeking behavior reflects their perception of the problem, which in turn influences expectations for treatment. How can a Western psychotherapist be effective with this population if there is disparity regarding the conceptualization of mental illness between therapist and client? It is critical for the psychotherapist to be aware of and understand the client's conceptualization of problems within the context of the client's culture, and employ culturally sensitive therapeutic interventions and skills (Kagawa-Singer & Chung, 1994; Kleinman, Eisenberg, & Good, 1978; Kleinman & Good, 1985; Pedersen, 1988). Furthermore, the psychotherapist must acknowledge the fact that many Southeast Asian refugees are unfamiliar with Western mental health concepts because few had ever been exposed to mental health treatment in their home countries (Lin & Masuda, 1983). Indeed, there were no psychiatrists in Laos, South Vietnam had only a handful in 1975, and it is doubtful that

there were mental health professionals in Cambodia. Consequently, when Southeast Asian refugees seek help from Western
psychotherapists, they expect a medical approach and quick symptom relief. Given their view of mental illness as akin to physical
disorders, they often request injections or medication (Chung &
Okazaki, 1991).

Even so, many Southeast Asian refugees reject Western practices
and prefer traditional healing practices that involve belief in possession, soul loss, and witchcraft. Rituals for exorcism, performed
by shamans and Taoist priests in Vietnam (Hickey, 1964) and by
Buddhist monks in Laos and Cambodia (Westermeyer, 1973), consist of calling back the soul of individuals believed to be suffering
from soul loss and asking local guardian gods for protection. For-
tune-telling with cards and coins, the Chinese horoscope, and phy-
siognomy (palm reading and reading of facial features) are also
popular methods of treatment.

A major influence on the Southeast Asian belief system is
Chinese medical practices. Cambodians, Hmong, and Vietnamese
regularly use Chinese folk remedies, including herbal concoctions
and poultices, forms of acupuncture, accupressure and massage,
and the dermabrasive practices of cupping, pinching, rubbing, and
burning (Nguyen, Nguyen, & Nguyen, 1987). Because mental illness is seen as a disturbance of the internal vital energy, acupuncture is often used as a remedy for depression and psychosis.

Although religious beliefs differ among Southeast Asian refugee
groups, health and mental health practices are influenced by religious and medical practices. For example, Vietnamese religious
beliefs combine Buddhism, Taoism, and Confucianism. Further,
Vietnamese values share commonalities with Chinese cultural concepts such as filial piety, ancestor worship, interpersonal relationships based on hierarchical roles and reciprocal obligations, high
regard for education, a strong family orientation, and loss of face.
Theravada Buddhism, in which the attainment of spiritual enlight-
enment is valued over the achievement of material success, plays
a central role in every aspect of a Cambodian's life. Laotians
strongly believe in animism (the belief in supernatural, gods, demons, and evil spirits) as an essential part of everyday life. Illnesses
are commonly treated by the shaman through practices such as
string tying, in which a cord is tied around the wrist to enable a
person to communicate with the spirit of decreased ancestors, or

to prevent the loss of a sick person's soul. The string may be perceived as a symbol of a patient's spiritual wholeness and his or her social and familial support system (Muecke, 1983).

Barriers to Mainstream Mental Health Services and Use of Traditional Methods

Due to premigration trauma, many Southeast Asian refugees are at high risk for developing severe psychological problems. Many studies have stated the serious need of mental health services for this population (e.g., Gong-Guy, 1987; Kinzie & Manson, 1983; Mollica et al., 1985), and some studies have revealed a high incidence of depression and posttraumatic stress disorder (PTSD) (Kinzie, Frederickson, Ben, Fleck, & Karls,1984; Mollica et al., 1985). A number of older Cambodian refugee women have reported incidences of nonorganic blindness in which the degree of subjective visual impairment was found to be significantly related to the number of years the women experienced in the internment camps, starvation, physical and sexual abuse, forced labor, and witness of the execution of significant others (Rozee & Van Boemel, 1989). Although the need for mental health services is great, only a small percentage of this group utilizes mainstream mental health services or even those services targeting Asian clients (Sue, Fujino, Hu, Takeuchi, & Zane, 1991).

The main reason for the low utilization of mainstream mental health services is that these services are not culturally responsive (Kagawa-Singer & Chung, 1994; Sue et al., 1991). When refugees enter mainstream mental health services, the environment is unfamiliar to them. There may be not only a language barrier between the client and psychotherapist but also cultural differences in both verbal (e.g., tone and volume of the speaking) and nonverbal (e.g., eye contact and personal space) behaviors. For example, if the therapist should happen to put his or her feet up on a stool with the sole of the feet facing the Southeast Asian refugee client or pat the head of a child, it will be considered extremely offensive. The therapist may not be aware of the effect of this nonverbal behavior. Poor accessibility may also be a hindrance to the utilization of mainstream mental health services (Lin, Inui,

Kleinman, & Womack, 1982). Clinics and private offices are often located in places that can not easily be reached, and using public transportation to get to these places may be a difficult task for Southeast Asian refugees, especially those individuals with poor English skills. Simple tasks such as working out a bus timetable, a bus route, or the payment may be highly stressful. Furthermore, many refugees may be unaware of the types and availability of mental health services (Van Deusen, 1982).

When considering or providing mainstream mental health services for Southeast Asian refugees, the cultural frame of reference must be kept in mind. Southeast Asian refugees' help-seeking behavior is influenced by culturally based attitudes (Van Deusen, 1982; Vignes & Hall, 1979). For example, traditional beliefs, superstitions, and the belief in the supernatural are common barriers to mainstream mental health care (Tung, 1983). This population instead often relies on indigenous healers and folk medicine (Egawa & Tashima, 1982; Muecke, 1983; Yeatman & Dang, 1980). Chung and Lin (1994) found that many Southeast Asian refugees reported concurrent utilization of both traditional and Western mainstream health care methods. This population of refugees in Chung and Lin's study reportedly preferred to use traditional methods, and their utilization of mainstream services in the United States was a reflection of the unavailability of traditional methods. Such behavior may suggest a desperate need for health and mental health services in this population.

Counseling Refugees

In view of the cultural beliefs and preference for the traditional health care methods, it is crucial that psychotherapists work cooperatively with bilingual/bicultural mental health professionals, community leaders, elders, and traditional healers (e.g., spiritual leaders, monks, priests, herbalists, and shamans). Bilingual/bicultural mental health professionals are not just interpreters or translators but serve as specialized mental health professionals who are familiar with both Western models of mental health and the unique medical and psychological worldview of Southeast Asian cultures. Bilingual/bicultural mental health professionals play an important role because they not only bridge the language gap and interpret subtle cultural messages between clients and therapist but also help establish a culturally sensitive treatment environment.

Because language differences pose a major barrier to help seeking for Southeast Asian refugees, using trained translators and interpreters is essential in areas where bilingual/bicultural mental health professionals are not available. Training of translators and interpreters is imperative to facilitate effective interventions and to minimize inaccuracies in communications. For example, an untrained Southeast Asian translator may be too embarrassed to tell the Western-trained psychotherapist that certain questions may be culturally offensive to the Southeast Asian client. Sometimes inadequately trained translators may answer for the refugee client, interpreting what they believe to be the "right" answer or a respectful response. Problems can also arise due to confidentiality, poor paraphrasing of questions, and inadequate translation of problems and psychological terms into the client's language.

Even with accurate translations, misdiagnoses may occur because of cultural misunderstandings. In one instance, a Southeast Asian man was committed to a psychiatric institution and was heavily medicated because his sponsor reported that he kept referring to seeing dead relatives and speaking with them. What the sponsor failed to realize was that referring to the dead is a common and accepted behavior among people from Southeast Asian cultures (Chung & Okazaki, 1991).

Many of the principles for counseling Asian Americans also apply to Southeast Asian refugees. In order to be effective, psychotherapists need to maintain both ascribed and achieved credibility with their clients in order to continue with the counseling process and avoid premature termination (Sue & Zane, 1987). Ascribed credibility is determined by the psychotherapist's status (e.g., age, education, or gender), whereas achieved credibility or gaining the trust and confidence of the client is determined by the psychotherapist's competency in the therapy sessions. Therefore, if the psychotherapist initially has a low ascribed credibility, he or she can acquire credibility by being culturally aware and sensitive. To achieve trust and credibility, psychotherapists need to be aware of the Southeast Asian refugee client's premigration history, postmigration adjustment issues, cultural belief systems pertaining to health and mental health, and the potential concurrent use of traditional and Western methods of health care.

Refugee clients are frequently preoccupied, especially in earlier sessions, with resolving problems associated with basic needs and services rather than with working on more serious mental health concerns. This may result in refugee clients requesting help for social services such as an assistance with housing, employment, and welfare. Responding to these requests rather than discounting them as inappropriate in the process of psychotherapy will develop trust and credibility. Psychotherapists should be aware that the client's need to address these problems may be associated with personal desperation and fear concerning basic needs, which may overshadow other therapeutic issues. Because these social problems about daily living are often presented to psychotherapists rather than to other social service providers, there is a need for a linkage between existing resettlement programs, social and human service providers, and the mental health and counseling services. It is important that psychotherapists understand the refugee client's unfamiliarity with the Western psychotherapeutic method of talk therapy and the low credibility ascription of talk therapy. Subsequently, one way of beginning counseling sessions with the refugee client is to discuss everyday survival issues, such as asking clients about their employment situation, housing, and income. These discussions over critical life issues are natural ways to lead into the pressing psychological problems, which are often associated with premigration trauma and postmigration adjustment issues. The general aims of a psychotherapist working with Southeast Asian clients should be to (a) alleviate hopelessness, (b) instill in clients faith in themselves and hope for the future, (c) identify existing coping strategies, (d) explore new alternative coping strategies, and (e) help clients attain a sense of mastery and confidence over their lives.

The Multi-Level Model (MLM): An Approach to Psychotherapy With Refugees

In order to provide psychotherapy for Southeast Asian refugees effectively, the psychotherapist must be culturally sensitive and understand the individuals' and families' worldview, premigration history and experience, and the extent of identification with their culture of origin. This requires not only the knowledge of Western counseling and psychotherapy techniques but also the ability to incorporate such theories into a multicultural counseling framework. To work effectively with refugees, it is also necessary to understand the factors associated with severe trauma and to take a multidisciplinary approach that incorporates constructs in psychology, counseling, anthropology, psychiatry, public health, social work, and sociology.

In order to address the complexity of these diverse bases of knowledge and skills, Bemak, Chung, and Bornemann (1996) have designed a comprehensive approach to counseling refugees called the Multi-Level Model. The MLM takes into account the intricacy of the refugee's historical background, past and present stressors, the acculturation process and the psychosocial ramifications of adapting to a new culture while providing a psychoeducational approach that includes cognitive, affective, and behavioral interventions. Cultural foundations and their relation to community and social processes are critical in this model. The MLM includes the following four levels: Level I—Mental Health Education; Level II—Individual, Group, and/or Family Psychotherapy; Level III—Cultural Empowerment; and Level IV—Indigenous Healing. The four levels are interrelated, and there is no fixed sequence for their implementation, so that they may be used simultaneously or independently. Although each level can be viewed as an independent unit, working with a client on all levels is essential to attain the desired goals of psychotherapy. The treatment planning emphasizing or using any one level or combination of levels must be based on the assessment of the psychotherapist. Use of this model does not require additional funding or resources, but rather the model allows the psychotherapist to assume different and more diverse roles as a helper.

In Level I—Mental Health Education, the focus is on the psychotherapist educating clients about mainstream mental health services. Many refugees are not familiar with the types of services available or with the process of mental health treatment. Thus the psychotherapist must educate the client about issues such as the norms of behavior in the physical environment of the mental health clinic, the purpose of the intake assessment, the roles and expectations for the client and the psychotherapist, the role of the interpreter, the types and use of medications, and the appointment system. Such information helps the Southeast Asian refugee client understand the nature of a therapeutic relationship and formulate expectations for psychotherapy.

Level II—Individual, Group, and/or Family Psychotherapy builds on the traditional Western techniques of psychotherapy. The psychotherapist must make an assessment about the individual's needs and then determine which type of psychotherapy (individual, group, or family) will be most suitable for the particular client. Although traditional Western techniques are foreign to Southeast Asian refugee clients, these traditional methods of individual and family therapy are also effective with Asian clients (Zane & Sue, 1991). In particular, some specific techniques have been identified to be effective in working with this population. For example, the psychotherapist may take a more directive and active role during counseling sessions with Southeast Asian refugees (Kinzie, 1985). Cognitive-behavioral interventions have also been recognized as being helpful with Southeast Asian refugees (Bemak & Greenberg, 1994; Egli, Shiota, Ben-Porath, & Butcher, 1991), and both De Silva (1985) and Mikulas (1981) have suggested that cognitive-behavioral intervention may be effective with refugees because of its compatability with Buddhist beliefs. However, Beiser (1987) maintained that cognitive-behavior interventions are helpful to this population because the techniques assist them to reorient to the present rather than to maintain a painful preoccupation with the past memories or to worry about an uncertain future.

Other techniques that can be incorporated into MLM Level II are storytelling and projective drawing. Pynoos and Eth (1984) described how these techniques can assist children who have experienced trauma regain control over their response to the traumatic event. Bemak and Timm (1994) demonstrated the efficacy of employing dream work in the therapeutic process with refugees. Other techniques that may be used in individual counseling include gestalt, relaxation, role-playing, and psychodrama.

Although group therapy has not been used extensively as a therapeutic intervention with Southeast Asian refugees, several studies have pointed toward its effectiveness with this population. Friedman and Jaranson (1994) have indicated that highly traumatized refugees find solace in group therapy. Kinzie et al. (1988)

have instituted a 1-year therapy group for Southeast Asian refugees that incorporates discussions about somatic symptoms, cultural conflicts, and loss, with the group structure allowing for flexibility with therapy session times and duration. The group approach may naturally lend itself to include psychoeducational information sessions (MLM Level I), traditional group psychotherapy (MLM Level II), and cultural empowerment group meetings (MLM Level III).

For Southeast Asian refugees, family is an important part of the culture and all aspects of the individual's life. This suggests that family therapy is a natural means of focusing on systemic rather than individual problems. It is important to note that given the emphasis on extended rather than nuclear family, family therapy for this population may include members of the extended family. Mental health professionals have stated the importance of family therapy with refugees, explaining that the roots, experiences, and subsequent family system problems with acculturation make family counseling an ideal intervention strategy (Bemak, 1989; Lee, 1989). Psychotherapists who use family therapy must have a clear understanding and knowledge about the cultural background and traditional relationships in the family.

Level III—Cultural Empowerment provides another important dimension in the healing of the refugee client. Cultural empowerment consists of assisting Southeast Asian refugee clients gain a better sense of environmental mastery. Frequently, the psychotherapist unfamiliar with a multicultural framework may focus exclusively on mental health concerns and neglect basic issues of adaptation in daily life. But many psychotherapists find themselves faced with refugee clients who are initially more interested in working on survival issues, such as housing and employment. The refugees may be trying to understand and make sense of their new environment, rather than discussing psychosocial adjustment and interpersonal issues. As mentioned earlier, it is important to address these issues as fundamental concerns before exploring other psychological problems. Cultural empowerment directly addresses these adjustment issues. Psychotherapists must therefore be sensitive to the difficulties inherent in adjusting to a new culture and provide case management through assistance and guidance that will lead to a sense of empowerment for the refugee clients. In MLM Level III—Cultural Empowerment, the psychotherapist is not expected to be a case manager for the client but rather to assume the role of cultural guide in order to provide the client with relevant information about how the American social service system works, and answer questions about the host culture. In addition, by serving as a cultural broker, the psychotherapist may educate the refugee client about the legal system governing certain practices that may be misunderstood by social agencies. For example, school teachers and police have often mistaken coin rubbing, an Asian traditional medical treatment method that leaves bruises on the skin, for child abuse (Nguyen, Nguyen, & Nguyen, 1987). The practice of coin rubbing is believed to bring negative energy, the cause of physical and emotional problems, out of the body and restore balance to body, mind, and spirit.

In Level IV—Indigenous Healing, the psychotherapist integrates Western and traditional healing methodologies. The World Health Organization (1992) described how an integration of indigenous healing with Western traditional healing practices resulted in more effective outcomes. Such integration may be best accomplished in cooperation with indigenous healers who are known to refugee community members. As indicated previously, Chung and Lin (1994) found that Southeast Asian refugees prefer to utilize traditional methods of healing rather than Western psychotherapy and that a large percentage of this population concurrently use both traditional and Western methods. Psychotherapists working with this population must not only acknowledge that their clients may prefer traditional practices or want to combine traditional and Western methods, but also must be willing to integrate the refugee clients' healing methods with the Western treatment techniques. To this end, the psychotherapists of Southeast Asian refugees will benefit from approaching and working cooperatively with healers or community elders in the treatment (Chan, 1987; Hiegel, 1994). Note that not all traditional healers are legitimate, and that it is important to use community members to assist in identifying legitimate healers.

The Case Study of Mrs. N

The case study and sample treatment plan using the MLM presented here illustrate the complex issues involved in counseling Southeast Asian refugee clients.

Mrs. N is a 48-year-old Vietnamese woman who came to the United States in 1982 in a mass exodus from Southeast Asia. Her husband had worked for the U.S. government during the Vietnam War, and after the fall of Saigon in 1975 he was placed in a reeducation camp run by the North Vietnamese. Although Mrs. N does not know the details of her husband's camp experience, she had heard that people placed in such camps were forced to work as laborers under harsh conditions and were regularly tortured. According to an official, her husband died of unknown causes while in the camp.

Upon learning about her husband's death, Mrs. N and her two children (at the time ages 1 and 3) fled Vietnam on a small boat. Because of terrible travel conditions and the lack of adequate hygiene and nutrition, Mrs. N's 1-year-old baby died on the boat. Mrs. N and her 3-year-old daughter finally arrived in Thailand, where they stayed in a refugee camp hoping to gain entry into the United States as refugees. The living conditions in the camp were poor, and Mrs. N and her daughter shared a tent with two other families. After a year and a half of waiting, a church in San Diego, California, became her sponsor, and Mrs. N and her daughter relocated to the United States.

It has been over a decade since Mrs. N and her daughter moved to the United States. Her daughter, now a teenager, appears to be well adjusted with a number of Vietnamese and non-Vietnamese friends. However, Mrs. N continues to have many problems. She still has frequent nightmares about the war atrocities she witnessed and the deaths of her husband and her baby. Mrs. N doesn't share anything about her background or bad dreams with others. Apart from attending special ceremonies and occasional parties, she remains quietly by herself or with two other single Vietnamese women her own age. Having taken many ESL courses, Mrs. N's English skills have improved, and she holds a job as a janitor in a local office building. She often feels sad and has frequent thoughts of ending her life. She explains that the only reason for staying alive is her daughter. Mrs. N came to the clinic on the recommendation of a Vietnamese coworker who was familiar with mental health treatment.

MLM Level I—Mental Health Education.   Although Mrs. N came to the clinic through a referral of a friend, the psychotherapist (Dr. A) wanted to assess her understanding and expectations about counseling. Dr. A quickly determined that the friend who had referred Mrs. N had provided a good overview about the counseling process. One area that needed clarification was Dr. A's role as a psychotherapist. Mrs. N had assumed that Dr. A would be directive in "telling her what to do to feel better." Dr. A carefully explained the collaborative nature of counseling and how she would assist Mrs. N to gain a better understanding of her experiences.

MLM Level II—Individual, Group, and/or Family Psychotherapy.
In the assessment of Mrs. N it was clear to Dr. A that she was
experiencing a posttraumatic stress disorder (PTSD) and depression. Dr. A decided that initially Mrs. N could benefit from individual short-term therapy to address her PTSD and depressive
symptoms. As Dr. A heard Mrs. N describing her loneliness and
lack of companionship, Dr. A thought about the Vietnamese culture and Mrs. N's background. Exploring with Mrs. N about her
days in Vietnam, Dr. A learned that Mrs. N had many friends and
an active social life in Vietnam. Mrs. N commented, "I really
enjoyed this time . . . there was always someone to talk with then."
Based on an understanding that the Vietnamese culture emphasizes
family and community, combined with the fact that Mrs. N was
lonely, Dr. A recommended that upon completion of short-term
individual psychotherapy, Mrs. N should continue her treatment
through group counseling to deal with unresolved issues related to
leaving her home country, losing her husband and a child, and
adapting to a new culture.

MLM Level III—Cultural Empowerment. At the clinic, Dr. A was
also conducting an open membership group for refugee women
who had lost family members. Dr. A felt that the format, shared
experiences with peers, and interpersonal communication provided by this group should be beneficial for Mrs. N. The group
therapy sessions were comprised of bereavement and grief counseling sessions. The structure of the group also allowed for an
exploration of issues relevant to its members' experience so that
in later sessions Mrs. N could explore her forced migration from
Vietnam and the problems of adapting to a new culture. The group
sessions incorporated MLM Level III—Cultural Empowerment,
which focuses on psychoeducational training to enhance acculturation skills. Topics such as difficulties in adjusting to a foreign
culture; strategies for adaptation; cognitive, emotional, and behavioral responses to cultural and identity loss; and available resources were presented and discussed during the group sessions.
Furthermore, Dr. A had established a relationship with one of the
Vietnamese community leaders who works in a resettlement
agency, and they periodically meet to discuss the general themes
emerging in the group (maintaining confidentiality) related to cultural realities for widowed Vietnamese women.

MLM Level IV—Indigenous Healing.   Dr. A believed that it was important to learn about the Vietnamese culture because she had been identified by the Vietnamese community as a professional with cultural sensitivity and with an openness to the traditional healing methods important to the Vietnamese community. Although Dr. A was not a Buddhist and did not understand many of the religious practices, she understood from her previous clients and contacts with the community leader that there were practices in the Buddhist religion that may play an important role in the healing process. Despite her Western training as a psychotherapist, she was open to incorporating traditional healing as a curative element to help her Vietnamese clients. Thus Dr. A determined that if Mrs. N believed in traditional practices, MLM Level IV—Indigenous Healing could be introduced at any time during the individual or group therapy. In fact, the Vietnamese community leader had told Dr. A about special ceremonies done by Buddhist monks that gave peace to the deceased. In the counseling sessions, Dr. A explored whether Mrs. N believed in this practice and whether she would be interested in participating in the ceremony with a Buddhist monk. Mrs N responded, "I am afraid to finally 'let go' but I think it would be best for everyone if I did."

Conclusion

The support and integration of cultural healing practices in conjunction with Western psychotherapy practices are instrumental in providing culturally sensitive treatment. The case of Mrs. N can be viewed as typical for many Southeast Asian refugees. The implementation of the MLM provides an important framework for working with the Southeast Asian refugees. The model does not require the psychotherapist to work sequentially on each level and does not necessitate additional resources or funding. (For a more in-depth understanding of the MLM regarding such issues as the concurrent usage of multiple levels of the MLM, incorporation of bilingual/bicultural mental health workers in the psychotherapeutic process, gaining crosscultural understanding and awareness, skill development in cross-cultural work, and selection of individual, group and/or family therapy as a method of treatment, see

Bemak, Chung, Pedersen, & Bornemann, in press.) Utilizing the MLM assists in expanding the psychotherapist's role to incorporate culturally sensitive intervention strategies specific to Southeast Asian refugees.

References

Bemak, F. (1989). Cross-cultural family therapy with Southeast Asian refugees. *Journal of Strategic and Systemic Therapies, 8,* 22–27.

Bemak, F., Chung, R. C-Y., Pedersen, P. B., & Bornemann, T. H. (in press). *Multicultural counseling with refugees: A case study approach to innovative interventions.* Newbury Park, CA: Sage.

Bemak, F., Chung, R.C-Y., & Bornemann, T. (1996). Counseling and psychotherapy with refugees. In P. Pedersen, J. Draguns, W. Lonner, & J. Trimble (Eds.), *Counseling across cultures* (4th ed., pp. 243–265). Thousand Oaks, CA: Sage.

Bemak, F., & Greenberg, B. (1994). Southeast Asian refugee adolescents: Implications for counseling. *Journal of Multicultural Counseling and Development, 22*(4), 115–124.

Bemak, F., & Timm, J. (1994). Case study of an adolescent Cambodian refugee: A clinical, developmental, and cultural perspective. *International Journal of the Advancement of Counseling, 17,* 47–58.

Beiser, M. (1987). Changing time perspective and mental health among Southeast Asian refugees. *Culture, Medicine, and Psychiatry, 8,* 22–27.

Brown, G. (1982). Issues in the resettlement of Indochinese refugees. *Social Casework, 63,* 155–159.

Chan, F. (1987, April). *Survivors of the killing fields.* Paper presented at the Western Psychological Association Convention, Long Beach, CA.

Cheung F. H. (1982). Psychological symptoms among Chinese in urban Hong Kong. *Social Science and Medicine, 16,* 1339–1334.

Chung, R. C-Y. (1991, August). *Predictors of distress among Southeast Asian refugees: Gender and group differences.* Paper presented at the Asian American Psychological Association Convention, San Francisco.

Chung, R. C-Y., & Bemak, F. (1996). The effects of welfare status on psychological distress among Southeast Asian refugees. *The Journal of Nervous and Mental Disease, 184*(6), 346–353.

Chung, R. C-Y., & Kagawa-Singer, M. (1993). Predictors of psychological distress among Southeast Asian refugees. *Social Science and Medicine, 36*(5), 631–639.

Chung, R. C-Y., & Kagawa-Singer, M. (1996). Southeast Asian refugees' symptom expression. *Journal of Nervous and Mental Disease, 183*(10), 639–648.

Chung, R. C-Y., & Lin, K. M. (1994). Help-seeking behavior among Southeast Asian refugees. *Journal of Community Psychology, 22,* 109–120.

Chung, R. C-Y., & Okazaki, S. (1991). Counseling Americans of Southeast Asian descent: The impact of the refugee experience. In C. C. Lee & B. L. Richardson (Eds.), *Multicultural issues in counseling: New approaches to diversity* (pp. 107–126). Alexandria, VA: American Association for Counseling and Development.

De Silva, P. (1985). Buddhism and modern behavioral strategies for the control of unwanted intrusive cognitions. *The Psychological Record, 35,* 437–443.

Egawa, J. E., & Tashima, N. (1982). *Indigenous healers in Southeast Asian refugees communities.* San Francisco: Pacific Asian Mental Health Research Project.

Egli, A., Shiota, N., Ben-Porath, Y., & Butcher, J. (1991). Psychological interventions. In J. Westermeyer, C. Williams, & A. Nguyen (Eds.), *Mental health services for refugees.* Washington DC: U.S. Government Printing Office.

Friedman, M., & Jaranson, J. (1994). The applicability of the posttraumatic stress disorder concepts to refugees. In A. J. Marsella, T. Bornemann, S. Ekblad, & J. Orley (Eds.), *Amidst peril and pain: The mental health and well-being of the world's refugees* (pp. 207–288). Washington DC: American Psychological Association.

Gong-Guy. (1987). *The California Southeast Asian Mental Health Needs Assessment.* Unpublished manuscript, San Francisco Asian Community Mental Health Services.

Hickey, G. G. (1964). *Village in Vietnam.* New Haven, CT: Yale University Press.

Hiegel, J. P. (1994). Use of indigenous concepts and healers in the care of refugees: Some experiences from the Thai border camps. In A. J. Marsella, T. Bornemann, S. Ekblad, & J. Orley (Eds.), *Amidst peril and pain: The mental health and well-being of the world's refugees* (pp. 293–310). Washington, DC: American Psychological Association.

Huang, L. N. (1989). Southeast Asian refugee children and adolescents. In J.T. Gibbs & L.N. Huang (Eds.), *Children of color: Psychological interventions with minority children.* San Francisco: Jossey-Bass.

Kagawa-Singer, M., & Chung, R. C-Y. (1994). A paradigm for culturally based care in ethnic minority populations. *Journal of Community Psychology, 22,* 192–208.

Kinzie, J. D. (1985). Overview of clinical issues in the treatment of Southeast Asian refugees. In T.C. Owan (Ed.), *Southeast Asian mental health: Treatment, prevention, services, training, and research* (pp. 113–135). Washington, DC: National Institute of Mental Health.

Kinzie, J. D., Leung, P., Bui, A., Ben, R., Keopraseuth, K. O., Riley, C., Flect, J., & Ades, M. (1988). Group therapy with Southeast Asian refugees. *Community Mental Health Journal, 23*(2), 157–166.

Kinzie, J. D., Frederickson, R. H., Ben, R., Fleck, J., & Karls, W. (1984). Posttraumatic stress disorder among survivors of Cambodian concentration camps. *American Journal of Psychiatry, 141*(5), 645–650.

Kinzie, J. D., & Manson, S. (1983). Five years' experience with Indochinese refugee psychiatric patients. *Journal of Operational Psychiatry, 14*(3), 105–111.

Kinzie, J. D., Manson, S., Do, V., Nguyen, T., Anh, B., & Pho, T. (1982). Development and validation of a Vietnamese language depression rating scale. *American Journal of Psychiatry, 139*(10), 1276–1281.

Kleinman, A. (1982). Neurasthenia and depression: A study of somatization and culture in China. *Culture, Medicine, and Psychiatry, 6*, 117–190.

Kleinman, A., & Eisenberg, L., & Good, B. (1978). Culture, illness, and care. *Annals of Internal Medicine, 88*, 251–258.

Kleinman, A., & Good, B. (1985). *Culture and depression: Studies in the anthropology and cross-cultural psychiatry of affect and disorder.* Berkeley: University of California Press.

Lee, E. (1989). Assessment and treatment of Chinese American immigrant families. *Journal of Psychotherapy, 6*(102), 99–122.

Lin, K. M., Inui, T. S., Kleinman, A. M., & Womack, W. (1982). Sociocultural determinants of the help-seeking behavior of patients with mental illness. *Journal of Nervous and Mental Disease, 170*(2), 78–85.

Lin, K. M., & Masuda, M. (1983). Impact of the refugee experience: Mental health issues of the Southeast Asians. In *Bridging cultures: Southeast Asian refugees in America* (pp. 32–52). Los Angeles: Special Services for Groups, Asian American Community Mental Health Training Center.

Lin, K. M., Masuda, M., & Tazuma, L. (1982). Adaptational problems of Vietnamese refugees: Part III. Case studies in clinic and field: Adaptive and maladaptive. *Psychiatric Journal of University of Ottawa, 7*(3), 173–183.

Lin, K. M., Tazuma, L., & Masuda, M. (1979). Adaptation problems of Vietnamese refugees: II: Life changes and perception of life events. *Archives of General Psychiatry, 37*, 447–450.

Mikulas, W. (1981). Buddhism and behavior modification. *The Psychological Record, 31,* 331–342.

Mollica, R. F., & Jalbert, R. R. (1989). *Community of confinement: The mental health crisis on Site Two: Displaced persons' camps on the Thai-Kampuchean border.* Boston: Committee on World Federation for Mental Health.

Mollica, R. F., Wyshak, G., Coelho, R., & Lavelle, J. (1985). *The Southeast Asian psychiatry patient: A treatment outcome study.* Boston: Indochinese Psychiatric Clinic.

Mollica, R. F., Wyshak, G., & Lavelle, J. (1987). The psychosocial impact of war trauma and torture on Southeast Asian refugees. *American Journal of Psychiatry, 144*(12), 1567–1572.

Muecke, M. A. (1983). Caring for Southeast Asian refugees in the U.S.A. *American Journal of Public Health, 73*(4), 431–438.

Murphy, H. B. (1977). Migration, culture, and mental health. *Psychological Medicine, 7,* 677–681.

Nguyen, D. L., Nguyen, P. H., & Nguyen, L. H. (1987). *Coin treatment in Vietnamese families: Traditional medical practice vs. child abuse.* Unpublished manuscript. Long Beach, CA: Long Beach Community Mental Health Agency.

Nguyen, S. (1982). Psychiatric and psychosomatic problems among Southeast Asian refugees. *Psychiatric Journal of the University of Ottawa, 7*(3), 163–172.

Pedersen, P. (1988). *A handbook for developing multicultural awareness.* Alexandria, VA: American Association for Counseling and Development.

Pynoos, R., & Eth, S. (1984). Children traumatized by witnessing acts of personal violence: Homicide, rape, or suicide behavior. In S. Eth & R. Pynoos (Eds.), *Posttraumatic stress disorder in children* (pp. 17–44). Washington, DC: American Psychiatric Press.

Rozee, P. D., & Van Boemel, G. (1989). The psychological effects of war trauma and abuse on older Cambodian refugee women. *Women and Therapy, 8*(4), 23–50.

Stein, B. N. (1986). The experience of being a refugee: Insights from the research literature. In C. L. Williams & J. Westermeyer (Eds.), *Refugee mental health in resettlement countries* (pp. 5–23). Washington, DC: Hemisphere.

Sue, S., Fujino, D., Hu, L., Takeuchi, D., & Zane, N. (1991). Community mental health services for ethnic minority groups: A test of cultural responsive hypothesis. *Journal of Consulting and Clinical Psychology, 59*(4), 533–540.

Sue, S., & Zane, N. (1987). The role of culture and cultural techniques in psychotherapy: A critique and reformulation. *American Psychologist, 42*(1), 37–45.

Tayabas, T., & Pok, T. (1983). The arrival of the Southeast Asian refugees in America: An overview. In *Bridging cultures: Southeast Asian refugees in America* (pp. 3–14). Los Angeles: Special Services for Groups, Asian American Community Mental Health Training Center.

Tobin, J. J., & Friedman, J. (1983). Spirits, shamans, and nightmare death: Survivor stress in a Hmong refugee. *Journal of Orthopsychiatry, 53*, 439–448.

Tung, T. M. (1983). Psychiatric care for Southeast Asians: How different is different? In T. C. Owan (Ed.), *Southeast Asian mental health: Treatment, prevention, services, training, and research* (pp. 5–40). Washington DC: National Institute of Mental Health.

Van Deusen, J. (1982). Part 3. Health/mental health studies of Indochinese refugees: A critical overview. *Medical Anthropology, 6*, 213–252.

Vignes, A. J., & Hall, R. G. W. (1979). Adjustment of a group of Vietnamese people to the United States. *American Journal of Psychiatry, 136*(4A), 442–444.

Westermeyer, J. (1986). Migration and psychopathology. In C. L. Williams & J. Westermeyer (Eds.), *Refugee mental health in resettlement countries* (pp. 39–59). Washington, DC: Hemisphere.

Westermeyer, J. (1973). Lao Buddhism, mental health, and contemporary implications. *Journal of Religion and Health, 12*, 181–187.

Yeatman, G. W., & Dang, V. V. (1980). Cao Gio (coin rubbing): Vietnamese attitudes toward health care. *Journal of American Medical Association, 247*, 1303–1308.

World Health Organization. (1992). *Refugee mental health: Draft manual for field testing.* Geneva, Switzerland: Author.

Zane, N., & Sue, S. (1991). Culturally responsive mental health services for Asian Americans: Treatment and training issues. In H. Myers, P. Wohlford, P. Guzman, & R. Echemendia (Eds.), *Ethnic minority perspectives on clinical training and services in psychology* (pp. 47–58). Washington, DC: American Psychological Association.

13

ISSUES AND STRATEGIES IN COUNSELING KOREAN AMERICANS*

Dosheen Toarmino and Chi-Ah Chun

A sian Americans have been perceived as the model minority and have received more positive attention from mainstream America than any other ethnic minority group. Paradoxically, this stereotypical representation of Asian Americans has resulted in an underestimation of their needs. Korean Americans, as an Asian ethnic group, share this predicament. The issues Korean Americans encounter have rarely been brought to public awareness, and they usually are not examined separately from Asian Americans as a whole.

The 1992 Los Angeles riots exposed the unique sociopolitical conditions of Korean Americans. The psychological ramifications of living under such conditions are tremendous. Yet studies concerning the mental health issues and status of Korean Americans are lacking. Only recently have counselors and psychologists begun to recognize the magnitude of mental health issues faced by this ethnic group. This chapter first provides information on the culture, sociodemographics, and immigration history of Korean Americans to form the context for understanding the mental health issues of Korean Americans. The chapter then highlights mental health issues pertinent to Korean Americans, including their mental health status and barriers to mental health service utilization, in terms of both inter- and intraethnic differences. Case examples are presented to illustrate these issues and the diversity among Korean Americans. The chapter concludes with a discussion of culturally responsive treatment, including a concept framework,

*The preparation of this chapter was supported in part by the National Research Center on Asian American Mental Health: NIMH R01 MH 44331.

specific techniques and strategies, and culturally consistent modalities.

Immigration History and Sociodemographic Profile

Since the Shufeldt Treaty in 1882, there have been three waves of Korean immigration to the United States. During the first wave, more than 7,000 Koreans migrated to Hawaii to be plantation workers. Initially, economic factors were the primary reason for immigration. However, in 1910, Korea was declared a Japanese colony, and as a result, most Koreans decided to stay in America for political reasons. More than 80% of these immigrants were male (Houchins & Houchins, 1976). Therefore, more than 1,000 females entered the United States as mail-order brides until the 1924 Immigration Law closed the door on immigration from Asian countries (Yang, 1979). The second wave of immigration took place between 1951 and 1964, during and after the Korean War when a select and limited number of the Korean population—wives of American soldiers, war orphans, and students—came to the United States. Thus this second immigrant group was more heterogeneous as compared to the first (Kitano, 1991).

These two earlier immigration waves were characterized by a very small number of Koreans who entered America individually rather than as family units. However, after the 1965 Immigration and Naturalization Act, about 30,000 Koreans immigrated to the United States, and the pattern of immigration changed dramatically. This third wave of immigrants, more educated than the two earlier groups, tended to come from urban areas and consisted mostly of families. The reasons for this immigration and subsequent immigration include better employment, educational opportunities, and a chance to be reunited with family (Kim & Condon, 1975).

The majority of the third wave of immigrants settled in metropolitan areas including Los Angeles, New York, and Chicago. Approximately one third of all Korean Americans are concentrated in the Los Angeles area. Korean Americans in these metropolitan areas have developed large communities with organizations such as churches, temples, and hospitals that serve mainly Korean

Americans. According to the 1990 census, there are approximately 800,000 Korean Americans in the United States, which represent about 11% of all Asian Americans. Due to the short immigration history, approximately 70% of Korean Americans are foreign born, a considerably higher percentage than that of Japanese and Chinese Americans (U.S. Bureau of the Census, 1991).

Cultural Values

Discussing Korean cultural values separately from philosophy and religion is difficult, if not impossible. In Korea, Confucianism (as well as Buddhist teachings and shamanism) has had a great deal of influence on people's values throughout history. The philosophy of Confucius and his disciples is still practiced and seen as common sense by Korean people. According to Confucianism, human dignity is one of the most important qualities that differentiates humans from other animals, and this sense of dignity can only be achieved through relations to other human beings.

Human relations in Korean families are exemplified through three basic hierarchy-defining relations: between sovereign and man, between father and son, and between husband and wife (Rohner & Pettengill, 1985). Within the family, roles are also strictly defined according to gender and age. The oldest male, usually the father, is respected as an authority, protector, and provider for the family. Although the father tends to be less directly involved in child rearing, he usually presides over children as a strict disciplinarian. Conversely, females take a more submissive position both inside and outside of the family. Mothers are viewed as nonauthoritative but nurturing figures; and because respect is also based on age, there is hierarchical structure among siblings (Rohner & Pettengill, 1985).

These basic human relations are practiced not only within the family but also in other parts of Korean society such as government, work place, and even in relations that are not confined to these systems. These defined human relations imply a twofold obligation: those in a superior position should grant assistance to those who are dependent upon them while the dependents must practice subordination and obedience. This relationship creates an interdependent network among the family and other people in Korean society (Shon & Ja, 1982).

The emphasis on human relationships is often illustrated through collectivism, which places the group over the individual (Abbott, 1976; Goldstein, 1988). Collectivism in Korea is commonly supported by ideas and practices such as self-discipline of and dedication by the individual. The family stands at the center of the social unit, and the sacrifice of individuals is not uncommon in order to maintain harmonious relations within the family (Kim & Choi, 1994). Therefore, interpersonal values and other personal characteristics such as being patient and attentive to others' needs rather than to one's own are adhered to in Korean societies (Choi, Kim, & Choi, 1993). For the sake of harmonious relationships, withholding direct expression of personal opinions or feelings is considered an important virtue among Koreans. The emphasis on sensitivity to others' needs can be found in the Korean word *nunchi*, which is directly translated as *sensing the eyes* and is a common quality among Koreans. If one possesses *nunchi*, he or she is good at reading the feelings and state of mind of others by observing their nonverbal cues. The communication style of Americans is explicit, whereas communication among Koreans is more implicit. That is exemplified with the practice of *nunchi* in Korean culture.

The collectivistic dimension of Korean culture, therefore, is contradictory to the American cultural value of individuality (Yun, 1976). Individualism holds *self* as an independent entity; collectivism holds *self* as an extension of a particular group. Promotion of self over group is considered a socially acceptable quality in American culture, whereas an individual's needs are often suppressed in the name of harmony in Korean culture. Individual creativity is also encouraged as a virtue in an individualistic society; conformity is considered a virtue in a collective society.

Notable in Korean culture is the concept of *palzza*, which refers to the fate by which life unfolds. A person is born with certain *saju*, which is largely determined by astrological data that depends on birth time, date, and year. *Saju* determines what kind of *palzza* one will have. *Palzza* can also be read by the person's physical features such as the configuration of the face and the shape of the hands. A person with good *palzza* leads a comfortable life without much effort on his or her part; a person with rough *palzza* will have things go wrong even when they are guaranteed to go right.

Palzza is an interesting concept because it may help Koreans to accept hardship, personal tragedy and misfortune. Such acceptance makes it easier for many Koreans to let things go, and to go on with their lives. But the concept of *palzza* can also debilitate a person if he or she feels helpless and trapped in life. In general, however, attributing misfortune to *palzza* may be an important coping skill for many Korean Americans.

In summation, Confucianism (together with Buddhism and shamanism) underlies the traditional Korean culture. All influence how Koreans view life, interact with others, and deal with difficulties. Many of the traditional Korean values and beliefs have been retained by Korean immigrants to the United States and passed on to subsequent generations. The interaction between Korean and American values and beliefs have many ramifications, including the dynamics of mental health.

Mental Health Status of Korean Americans

The psychological toll of juggling two diametrically opposed cultures can be substantial. Korean immigrants often experience rejection or animosity for exhibiting behaviors that are rewarded in Korea but are often ignored or punished in this new environment. In addition, they may have to acquire new sets of behavioral repertoires to embrace both cultures. Like all other immigrant groups, Korean Americans live with the reality that they are subject to a great deal of stress, including cultural conflict, racism, and adjustment problems (Nah, 1993).

Studies on the mental health status of Asian Americans have found that Korean Americans fare worse than most other Asian ethnic groups and European Americans. For example, Aldwin and Greenburger (1987) found that Korean American college students are more depressed than their European American counterparts. Kuo (1984) also found that Korean Americans were more depressed than other Asian Americans and European Americans. Similarly, a study of Canadian Korean immigrants (Noh & Atkinson, 1992) found them more depressed than nonimmigrant North Americans in Canada. All these studies attributed the poor mental health status of Korean Americans, at least partly, to the adjustment or acculturation difficulties of immigrants.

Due to the short immigration period, the majority of Korean Americans are first generation immigrants who are still struggling to build a new life (U.S. Bureau of the Census, 1991). As a result, adjustment problems may be the most frequently experienced psychological difficulty (Abe & Zane, 1990; Kuo, 1984). However, as the level of acculturation to mainstream society increases, the level of psychological adjustment in Korean Americans appears to improve. Research indicates that Korean Americans who have lived in the United States longer tend to be happier than the more recent immigrants (Hurh & Kim, 1990; Sasao & Chun, 1994).

Adjustment may be particularly difficult during the early years of resettlement (Hurh & Kim, 1990; Kuo, 1984; Weeks & Cuellar, 1983). For many new arrivals, high expectations for the land of opportunity are not met (Shon & Ja, 1982). For example, relocation to America often results in lower socioeconomic status as compared to what many immigrants had established in their homeland (Kim, 1980; Yu, 1983). In addition, the education received in Korea is often not recognized; and due to language difficulties, immigrants' abilities as professionals are frequently underestimated.

Women who were housewives in Korea often have to take on a new role as a second provider for the family in order to secure financial stability. This shift in role fosters changes in the family dynamics and often places a strain on relationships, especially between husband and wife (Light & Bonacich, 1988; Shon & Ja, 1982). The children of Korean immigrants also face many challenges growing up between two distinctively different cultures and often have difficulties finding ways to cope with such stress (Lee & Cynn, 1991).

Therefore, in addition to such common issues as cultural conflict, language barriers, lack of social support, racism, and minority status, both children and adults, as well as both sexes, encounter unique sets of issues as individuals and members of a family. Korean immigrants often experience dramatic environmental changes in their lives and must learn to cope with the reality that many of the cultural values and behavioral patterns that were useful in their native country are now irrelevant, misperceived, or ineffective (Kim, Kim, & Hurh, 1991). In addition to these challenges, Korean Americans encounter atypical issues that are founded on the power dynamics among ethnic groups. Asian Americans, mostly Japanese, Chinese, and Koreans, are viewed as the "middleman group" (Kitano, 1974). The middleman model purports a categorization of ethnic people based on power differences, and is illustrated by a dominant-subordinate stratification in America. According to this model, Asian Americans have served as a mediating influence between African Americans and European Americans. However, as Japanese and Chinese Americans have become more stabilized as ethnic groups, and have improved their social status closer to the dominant mainstream, Korean Americans, who are overrepresented in the small businesses, continue to serve the poor and subordinate minority and have become social and geographical buffers between the dominant and the subordinate (Kitano, 1991). Korean Americans, therefore, have become scapegoats for the political and social distress in America, such as in the Los Angeles riots. Their geographical proximity to high crime areas has made many Korean Americans the target of criminal activity. These social and geographical situations exacerbate a stressful living and working environment for many Korean immigrants (Min, 1990).

Barriers to Mental Health Service Utilization

Despite the findings that clearly indicate significant mental health needs among Korean Americans, especially the immigrants, research has found that Korean Americans, like other Asian Americans, are less likely to seek help from mental health professionals in times of distress (Atkinson & Gim, 1989; Hatanaka, Watanabe, & Ono, 1975). Several factors are believed to hinder mental health service utilization by Korean Americans. One is that Korean Americans share beliefs similar to other Asian Americans regarding mental illness. They believe that sanity can be maintained as long as unpleasant thoughts are avoided through the exercise of willpower (Root, 1989). According to cultural values, psychological problems are private matters, and talking openly about these problems with strangers is considered a personal weakness or a disgraceful act (Root, 1989). In addition, mental illness is viewed as having a genetic rather than a social origin. Thus use of mental health services is connected with personal shame and social stigma (Ahn-Toupin, 1980).

A second barrier to using mental health services is that although Korean Americans believe in having control of internal events, such as morbid thoughts, they are more likely to practice acceptance of external events, such as environmental stressors. Korean Americans also often see environmental stress as a part of human suffering and endurance of anguish as their given fate (Kang, 1990).

The cultural differences in the manifestation or presentation of psychological problems are a third barrier. Korean Americans often have difficulty in identifying problems as psychological, particularly when they are accompanied by somatic symptoms. According to Yu and Cypress (1982) and Kuo (1984), because of the physical manifestation of psychological problems, Korean Americans tend to consult medical practitioners rather mental health professionals. For example, *hwa-byung*, which is prevalent among elderly Korean women, illustrates this phenomenon (Lin, 1983; Lin et al., 1992). *Hwa-byung*, which is directly translated as *fire illness*, is accompanied by somatic symptoms—such as headache, chest pain, heat sensation, and epigastric mass—as well as psychological symptoms—such as flushing, anxiety, irritability, insomnia, and difficulty in concentration (Lin, 1983). Although *hwa-byung* is perceived as a physical illness in Korean culture, its onset is pervasively psychological in nature, and it shares similar symptoms with depressive disorder in the Western diagnostic criteria (Lin, 1983). Therefore, it is possible that Koreans present their problems as physical rather than psychological because it is more socially acceptable to talk about being physically ill than emotionally ill.

A fourth cultural factor that may discourage the use of mental health services among Korean Americans lies in help-seeking behaviors. Korean Americans are more likely to consult with family members or close friends about their problems than to seek help from professionals (Ahn-Toupin, 1980; Atkinson & Gim, 1989). When this close circle of people is unable to help with the problems, Korean Americans often turn to the spiritual figures such as Buddhist monks, or fortune-tellers for advice. Consequently, those who finally seek help from the mental health professionals tend to be more psychologically disturbed than European Americans who seek help (Sue & Sue, 1977).

Final factors are the language barriers and unavailability of culturally responsive counselors that may also discourage Korean Americans from seeking professional help (Gim, Atkinson, & Kim, 1991). Studies have shown that a common language between counselors and clients facilitates rapport building and lowers premature termination of treatment (Dolgin, Salazar, & Cruiz, 1987; Leong, 1986; Marcos & Alpert, 1976; Sue, 1988). Therefore, Korean Americans who are not fluent in English may experience great frustration in expressing their feelings and may be afraid to seek service from people who do not speak their language. Treatment outcome studies on Asian Americans also found that an ethnic match between counselor and client prevents premature termination (Flaskerud & Liu, 1990; Sue, Fujino, Hu, Takeuchi, & Zane, 1991). A major implication of these findings is that ethnically matched counselors may be more culturally responsive to the needs of Korean Americans. Thus, short of an ethnic match, cultural responsiveness of mental health services appears to be a vital component for providing effective mental health services to Korean Americans.

Case Studies

The case studies presented here illustrate important mental health issues confronting Korean American men, women, and children.

The Case Study of Mr. G, a Korean American Man

A 40-year-old Korean American laundromat owner was referred for consultation by his gastroenterologist. Mr. G, married and the father of two children, was suffering from an ulcer that was presumably caused by his excessive drinking. Mr. G had moved to the United States 5 years previously. The primary reason for relocation was to continue his education (while in Korea, he taught history at a high school). However, due to language difficulties as well as financial reasons, he gave up his dream of education, and he and his wife started a laundromat. In order to reduce the overhead, Mr. G and his wife worked more than 60 hours per week. He seldom attended Korean church and refused to be involved in Korean American organizations because he thought "those Koreans gossip too much." In his spare time, he drank alone at home. Mr. G's drinking had gradually worsened during the last 3 years.

A year ago, during an argument with his wife, he became physically violent with her. Although he had had a few similar incidents while in Korea, this was the first time that the local police were called. In addition, a few months ago, he was visited by the state social services. His children, who are in third and fifth grade, reluctantly told their school counselor about their father's physical disciplinary methods. Mr. G, confused and embarrassed, had to justify his way of parenting. Under the circumstances, the state did not take any legal action. However, Mr. G had to give a written promise to refrain from similar incidents.

Recently, Mr. G has become more resentful toward his family. Despite his dream to provide the best education and more opportunities for his children, he feels that they have become more estranged from him. He gets angry when his children speak in English to each other because he cannot understand the content of the conversation. His wife also seems changed since she started to work at a nearby sandwich shop on the weekend. She has become more active and appears to be closer to the children. During the last few disputes, she has threatened to leave him if he does not stop drinking.

Mr. G showed up about 20 minutes late for his intake session. Throughout the session, he successfully avoided eye contact with the counselor and was reluctant to answer the questions. He told the counselor that he was suspicious because he could possibly be misdiagnosed as "crazy." He added that his mind functioned very properly. Mr. G expressed great regret about his relocation to America by saying it had cost him his family. He also revealed his feeling of being trapped and frustrated. However, he assumed that his stomach problem was the result of his drinking, but he denied its relationship to his stress. Toward the end of the session, Mr. G became very agitated about "keeping secret" referring to confidentiality and asked the counselor the location of the back door.

Korean American men are often at high risk for psychological problems. As described earlier, although modernization has slowly taken place, the patriarchal social order, which emphasizes the role of males as the head of the family and as the leaders of society, is still pervasive. When Korean men immigrate to the United States, much of their traditional male role is lost, and often they find themselves without power, both inside and outside of the family. Inside the family, the men frequently come to rely on their children for assistance, especially with respect to the language barrier. Furthermore, the economic hardship of immigration often necessitates that their wives find employment, which further threatens their leadership role as family breadwinner.

Outside of the family, the newly acquired minority status exposes them to a whole new array of experiences including discrimination and oppression. Thus, once again, their pride as an authority figure is undermined. Therefore, they often feel that the superior status assigned to them at birth has been taken away, and their manhood challenged. As a result, many Korean American men are left feeling extremely frustrated and resentful of their current life circumstances. The lack of social support as well as change in status exacerbates their psychological stress. Because Korean American men are at a high risk for social isolation, their spouses and children can easily become the target of their frustration and anger. This problem is often compounded by substance abuse, mostly alcohol.

The Case Study of Ms. C, a Korean American Woman

Ms. C, a 33-year-old Korean American woman, came to the Psychological Service Center after being discharged from a local psychiatric hospital. One month ago, she attempted suicide by overdosing on pain killers. During the intake session, she revealed that she and her husband had ended their 4-year marriage prior to her suicide attempt.

Ms. C came to the United States 4 years ago when she married a first generation Korean American immigrant. They were introduced by a mutual friend in Korea when her husband-to-be was there on business. He was operating a small travel agency in Los Angeles at the time. After relocation to America, Ms. C, persuaded by her husband, started to work as a cashier at a nearby Korean market. The job was too simple and unchallenging for Ms. C who has a business degree. However, due to her unfamiliarity with the new country as well as a language barrier, she was not able to find a job commensurate with her degree.

Two years ago, her father-in-law died, and her mother-in-law moved in with Ms. C and her husband. Initially, it seemed to be a good idea to Ms. C because she felt lonely and needed someone to care for her infant daughter while she was at work. After a few months, Ms. C found herself constantly working both at her job and at home.

It became apparent that Ms. C's mother-in-law, who was expected to be a helper, was becoming more of a burden. She passed housework onto Ms. C and began to interfere with the decision making between the couple. Ms. C became increasingly frustrated as she struggled to juggle the demands of her job, husband, baby, and mother-in-law. To make matters worse, whenever Ms. C had an argument with her mother-in-law, her husband took his mother's side and scolded Ms. C. Her husband then questioned Ms. C's moral conduct toward the elderly and blamed her parents for "poor upbringing." As the problems between the two women escalated, Ms. C became more resentful toward her husband as well as toward her marriage. Several months prior to her divorce, a frustrated Ms. C demanded that her mother-in-law should move out. The fight between Ms. C and her mother-in-law resulted in a spousal dispute.

Because Ms. C was newer in the Korean American community, relative to her mother-in-law, she felt isolated from other Koreans and believed that many people sided with her mother-in-law. A few months ago, her husband initiated and proceeded with the divorce. Ms. C, unfamiliar with American law, lost custody of her daughter. Since then, Ms. C has been severely depressed and has suffered from insomnia, shortness of breath, and chest pain, but no physical cause was found during a medical examination. Recently, she became very anxious whenever she ran into other Korean Americans in the community and thus began to spend most of her time at home. Last month the news of her husband's remarriage devastated Ms. C. She felt that she had now completely lost the chance of getting her family back together. She decided to end her life rather than having to live the rest of it alone as a divorcee.

As the case illustrates, many first generation Korean American women suffer from emotional problems due to stressful life circumstances and cultural conflicts. Through modernization in Korea, women's roles have gradually been changing. Yet their roles as a wise mother and subservient wife, *hynmoyangchuh*, are still held as a virtue and expected from them. The traditional place for women has been the home, and any kind of outside activity is strongly discouraged. The immigrant's life, however, often entails working both inside and outside the home for many Korean American women. Working outside the home, however, rarely reduces domestic responsibilities. Women are expected to fulfill their traditional responsibilities in addition to their newly acquired role as a joint contributor to family income. Furthermore, having to work for money can cause humiliation and shame for some women because it implies that their husbands are unable to fulfill the role of family breadwinner successfully (Sasao & Chun, 1994).

In addition to the roles of wife, mother, and breadwinner, many Korean American women also have the role of daughter-in-law. The intrafamilial tension and conflict between a mother-in-law and a daughter-in-law are viewed almost as a cultural tradition by many Koreans and Korean Americans. These tensions and conflicts are almost inevitable due to the hierarchical nature of the Korean family structure in which absolute submission is demanded from women. Traditionally, mothers-in-law have functioned as supervisors over the women who marry their sons. Their job is to keep their son's wives in line so that these women properly fulfill their responsibilities in the household. Despite acculturation, such family structure still remains, although its original form has been somewhat altered in contemporary Korean American families. In particular, many Korean Americans who immigrated in the1960s and 1970s, isolated from both American mainstream society and left out from rapid social changes in their native country, still adhere to the traditional values. Therefore, Korean American women who are married to Korean American men often find themselves in the midst of incessant conflicts with their mother-in-law. For highly acculturated Korean American women, the presence of such conflict may be more apparent in their marriage.

The Case Study of D, a Korean-American Child

A 17-year-old Korean American girl, D, who just graduated from high school with honors, was referred by her family physician after a series of panic attacks. She did not share these episodes with her family because she did not want to worry them. Her mother noticed one day that D was sweating and having difficulty breathing and took D to their family physician. During the physical examination, D reported she had been generally feeling anxious for many years and that the symptoms of anxiety worsened since her brother's death a year ago.

D was 9 years old when she moved with her family to the United States. Her father was a college professor in Korea and now operates a fast-food franchise. Her mother runs a small drug store in Korea-town. At first D had some difficulties adjusting to the new school system. D, who was a good student in Korea, had to repeat her grade due to her low English proficiency. D still remembers how kids in school often made fun of her accent.

In junior high school, as her English improved, her academic performance began to outshine those of many of her peers. However, D continued to have difficulties making friends in school. D became shy and socially withdrawn. She began to avoid being in a large crowd. Her biggest fear was being called upon to answer questions in class. When she is called upon, she begins to sweat heavily and cannot recall the information even though she remembered it just before she was called upon.

The only time D felt comfortable being in a crowd was when she taught preschoolers at her Sunday school. Thus, D hoped to become a preschool teacher in the future. However, her parents, who strongly believed academic success to be the key to success in life, felt D's career goal lacked status and strongly disapproved of D's extracurricular activities, which they felt took time away from studying. Her older brother's admission to medical school, however, shifted some of the parental expectation away from her. Relieved, D enrolled in a nearby community college.

A year ago, her older brother, who was her parents's pride, was killed in an automobile accident. It was a nightmare for the whole family, particularly for her parents. Her father had to be hospitalized because his heart condition deteriorated because of her brother's death. As a result, the family had to be very careful to avoid any subject that might upset the father. D was left to work out her grief alone and had to deal with the unspoken pressure that now she had to take the role as a first born. Her father began talking about D choosing premed as her college major.

D became confused and consulted with her school counselor, who encouraged her to pursue her own dream. The counselor's advice made logical sense to D, and yet it seemed almost impossible to contradict her parents' wish. Knowing how much her parents had sacrificed for their children, D truly did not want to disappoint them. She felt obligated to return her love to her parents by fulfilling their wish. Torn between her dream and the pressure from her parents, D became more and more withdrawn from her friends and family. At present, she feels helpless and misunderstood. She experienced her first panic attack after a hospital visit to her father. The subsequent panic attacks occurred mostly before D left home to visit her father in the hospital.

The children of Korean immigrants are the 1.5 generation, born in Korea but raised in the United States. Many in the 1.5 generation are bilingual and have been exposed to both cultures during their developmental years. They usually adapt to the new life in the United States and acquire a second language much faster than their parents. Differences in the rate of acculturation between parents and their children can result in conflict pertaining to lifestyle, attitudes, and cultural values (Lee & Cynn, 1991).

The generational and cultural conflicts often exacerbate the developmental stressors (Lee & Cynn, 1991). The Korean culture has a strong emphasis on the family. Children are often viewed as extensions of the parents themselves. At home their parents demand obedience, whereas their outside environment fosters independence. Korean parents often support their children financially throughout the school years. In return, the children are expected to succeed academically and to obtain occupations that have high status (Kim, 1980; Lee & Cynn, 1991). The high parental expectations, however, create a situation in which the children feel pressure to succeed (Aldwin & Greenberger, 1987).

Culturally Responsive Treatment

Understanding the cultural context in which a behavior occurs is crucial in the analysis of one's behavior. Attempting to determine whether a particular behavior is psychologically healthy or unhealthy, without reference to the context, is equivalent to asking a Kalahari Bushman to evaluate the value of a Christian Dior necktie in comparison to a gallon of water. A lack of understanding of a client's cultural background may lead to misdiagnosis because a particular behavior may be seen as pathological when, in actuality, the behavior simply reflects cultural differences (Uba, 1994). The culturally sensitive assessment is important for both identifying problematic behavior and providing adequate intervention for ethnic minority clients.

Conceptual Framework for Counseling
Korean American Clients

Sue and Zane (1987) examined the role of cultural knowledge and culture-specific techniques in psychotherapy of ethnic minority clients and proposed two basic processes—credibility and giving—that appear to underlie the cultural knowledge and techniques. *Credibility* refers to the "client's perception of the counselor as an effective and trustworthy helper" (p. 40). Two factors determine a counselor's credibility: The first is *ascribed status*, which refers to the position or role that a counselor is assigned by the client. Among Korean Americans, age, gender, education, training, and expertise of a counselor usually determine how much credibility is ascribed by the client. For example, a middle-aged White male counselor with a doctoral degree may have more ascribed credibility than a young Asian female counselor with a master's degree in the eyes of a Korean American client. The second factor, *achieved status*, is more directly related to a counselor's skills as reflected in his or her actions. Culturally responsive treatments and general therapeutic skills such as ability to build rapport can significantly enhance a counselor's credibility.

Sue and Zane (1987) suggested that underutilization of treatment might be primarily due to a lack of ascribed credibility assigned to the mental health profession in general; whereas premature termination might be the result of a lack of achieved credibility of the mental health professional the client encounters. Thus enhancing achieved credibility is critical in preventing premature termination by Korean American clients.

Achieved credibility of a counselor can be enhanced through the other process that Sue and Zane refer to as *giving* (Sue & Zane, 1987). Gift giving is "the client's perception that something was received from the therapeutic encounter" (p. 40). Counselors should be able to offer clients a "gift," a direct benefit of treatment, as early as the initial session to maintain the client's interest and motivation for treatment. Thus gift giving takes place when clients perceive the direct relationship between therapeutic work and alleviation of their problems, which increases the client's trust in the counselor's ability to help.

Culturally Responsive Techniques and Strategies for Korean American Clients

Many techniques and strategies have been proposed to remedy the high premature counseling termination rate among Asian Americans (Sue & Sue, 1977; Sue & Zane, 1987; Uba, 1994). Techniques and strategies that are applicable to Korean Americans are as follows.

What takes place during the initial session often determines whether the client will give the counselor a chance to work on his or her problems. For Korean Americans, counselors need to establish enough credibility to convince these clients that therapy can help them deal with their problems. Most Korean American clients are not familiar with the counseling process. Their lack of trust in the efficacy and method of counseling may become an obstacle in building rapport. In order to reduce the client's suspicion and to increase the counselor's credibility, it is important for the counselor to provide relevant information about the process and the credentials of the counselor.

Another strategy that may increase the counselor's credibility is conducting a brief yet accurate assessment. If the counselor devotes too much time to gathering background information, the client may become discouraged and mistakenly think that the rest of the counseling will have the same structure. Information that briefly focuses on the client's place of origin, family structure and values, birth order, available support systems, immigration history, communication style, and occupation and educational level prior to immigration is beneficial in making an accurate assessment in a short period of time.

Moreover, many foreign-born Asian Americans expect a quick diagnosis and some form of treatment benefit in the early stage of the therapy (Huang, 1991; Kim, 1985; Kinzie, 1989; Lin & Shen, 1991). During the initial session, this gift giving needs to take place. Gifts can be in the form of giving clients some explanations about their problems based on the information gathered during the session, even if they are tentative. Feeling understood and being able to place things in perspective can alleviate some of the client's stress and worries. In order to meet some of the client's expectations, focusing on symptom relief in the early stages may be helpful. Subsequently, all these tactics may provide the counselor with more opportunities to work on the client's underlying problems.

Culturally Consistent Counseling Modalities for Korean Americans

Traditionally, counseling/psychotherapy has been very much embedded in European American culture and thus is better designed to serve clients from that cultural background. For example, Western counseling approaches are predicated on lateral human relationships, individuation, independence, and self-disclosure. Conversely, Korean values emphasize hierarchical relationships, interdependence, self-control, and acceptance. Hence, the therapeutic needs of Korean Americans, which are combined with cultural values and the impact from immigration, may not be served effectively by the traditional approach. Given this, some mental health professionals suggest that directive, structured, and unambiguous therapeutic approaches may be more culturally compatible with Korean Americans than explorative, neutral approaches (Foley & Fuqua, 1988; Lee, 1988; Root, 1985). For example, Korean American clients may value an individual's willpower and ability to control morbid thoughts. If Korean American clients believe in exercising willpower as a means of psychological improvement, then a therapeutic method that coincides with their cultural expectation (such as a control-based cognitive therapy) is more likely to be effective than a culturally contradictory method (such as an insight-oriented therapy).

Family therapy can also work well in counseling Korean American clients, especially children. This is because problems are often embedded in family dynamics. Because of the hierarchical structure and the traditional value and belief system of Asian American families, the strategic-structural model of the family therapy model has been recommended for Asian American families (Kim, 1985). This model of family therapy focuses on concrete, external stressors rather than internal conflicts, teaches problem-solving techniques and active problem management, and helps the family to achieve concrete, external solutions.

Conclusion

Culturally, there is a great overlap among Asian American ethnic groups. Like other Asian Americans, Korean Americans are highly collectivistic and value individual sacrifice for the family as well as the larger society. Such a value and belief system often clashes with American individualism and becomes the source of much pain and struggle for many Korean immigrants. Korean Americans are a unique group in the sense that they are mostly comprised of recent immigrants and, as a group, are still in the process of resettling in this society. In addition, their atypical social status as middleman intensifies stressful living and working conditions. These environmental stressors have been documented, but the needs of Korean Americans have not yet been adequately addressed either by researchers or clinicians. Furthermore, even less is known about how they might be helped more effectively. This chapter has addressed some of these issues with the little that is known about Korean Americans. More systematic research on the mental health needs of and culturally responsive treatments for Korean Americans is clearly needed to address the mental health issues of Korean Americans adequately.

References

Abbott, K. (1976). Culture change and the persistence of the Chinese personality. In G. DeVos (Ed.), *Responses to change: Society, culture, and personality* (pp. 74–104). New York: Van Nostrand.

Abe, J., & Zane, N. (1990). Psychological maladjustment among Asian and White American college students. *Journal of Counseling Psychology, 37,* 437–444.

Ahn-Toupin, E. S. (1980). Counseling Asians: Psychotherapy in the context of racism and Asian American history. *American Journal of Orthopsychiatry, 50,* 76–86.

Aldwin, C., & Greenberger, E. (1987). Cultural differences in the predictors of depression. *American Journal of Community Psychology, 15,* 789–813.

Atkinson, D. R., & Gim, R. H. (1989). Asian American cultural identity and attitudes toward mental health services. *Journal of Counseling Psychology, 36*(2), 209–212.

Choi, S. C., Kim, U., & Choi, S. H. (1993). Indigenous analysis of collective representations: A Korean perspective. In U. Kim & J. W. Berry (Eds.), *Indigenous psychologies: Research and experience in cultural context* (Cross-cultural research and methodology series, 17, pp. 193–210). Newbury Park, CA: Sage.

Dolgin, D. L., Salazar, A., & Cruz, A. (1987). The Hispanic treatment program: Principles of effective psychotherapy. *Journal of Contemporary Psychotherapy, 17*(4), 285–299.

Flaskerud, J. H., & Liu, P. Y. (1990). Influence of therapist ethnicity and language on therapy outcomes of Southeast Asian clients. *International Journal of Social Psychiatry, 36*(1), 18–29.

Foley, J. B., & Fuqua, D. R. (1988). The effects of status configuration and counseling style on Korean perspective of counseling. *Journal of Cross-Cultural Psychology, 19*(4), 465–480.

Gim, R. H., Atkinson, D. R., & Kim, S. J. (1991). Asian American acculturation, counselor ethnicity, and cultural sensitivity and ratings of counselors. *Journal of Counseling Psychology, 38*(1), 57–62.

Goldstein, B. (1988). In search of survival: The education and integration of Hmong refugee girls. *Journal of Ethnic Studies, 16,* 1–27.

Hatanaka, H. K., Watanabe, W. Y., & Ono, S. (1975). The utilization of mental health services by Asian Americans in Los Angeles. In W. H. Ishikawa & N. H. Archer (Eds.), *Delivery of services in Pan Asian communities* (pp. 33–39). San Diego, CA: San Diego State University, San Diego Pacific Asian Coalition Mental Health Training Center.

Houchins, L., & Houchins, C.-S. (1976). The Korean experience in America, 1903–1924. In N. Hundley (Ed.), *The Asian American* (pp. 129–156). Santa Barbara, CA: Clio Press.

Huang, K. (1991). Chinese Americans. In N. Mokuau (Ed.), *Handbook of social services for Asian and Pacific Islanders* (pp. 79–96). New York: Greenwood Press.

Hurh, W. M., & Kim, K. C. (1990). Adaptation stages and mental health of Korean male immigrants in the United States. *International Migration Review, 24,* 456–479.

Kang, S. H. (1990). Training and development of psychotherapy in Korea. *Psychotherapy and Psychosomatics, 53,* 46–49.

Kim, B. C. (1980). *The Korean American child at school and at home* (Technical report to the Administration for Children, Youth, and Families). Washington, DC: U.S. Government Printing Office.

Kim, B. C., & Condon, M. E. (1975). *A study of Asian Americans in Chicago: Their socioeconomic characteristics, problems, and services needs* (Interim report to the National Institute of Mental Health). Washington, DC: Department of Health, Education, and Welfare.

Kim, K. C., Kim, S., & Hurh, W. M. (1991). Filial piety and intergenerational relationship in Korean immigrant families. *International Journal of Aging and Human Development, 33*(3), 233–245.

Kim, S. (1985). Family therapy for Asian Americans: A strategic structure framework. *Psychotherapy, 22*(2), 342–348.

Kim, U., & Choi, S. H. (1994). Individualism, collectivism, and child development: A Korean perspective. In P. M. Greenfield & R. R. Cocking (Eds.), *Cross-cultural roots of minority child development* (pp. 227–257). Hillsdale, NJ: Erlbaum.

Kinzie, J. D. (1989). Therapeutic approaches to traumatized Cambodian refugees. *Journal of Traumatic Stress, 2,* 75–91.

Kitano, H. L. (1974). Japanese Americans: The development of middleman minority. *Pacific Historical Review, 43*(4), 500–455.

Kitano, H. L. (1991). *Race relation* (4th ed.). Englewood Cliffs, NJ: Prentice Hall.

Kuo, W. (1984). Prevalence of depression among Asian Americans. *Journal of Nervous and Mental Disease, 172*(8), 449–457.

Leong, F. T. (1986). Counseling and psychotherapy with Asian Americans: Review of the literature. *Journal of Counseling Psychology, 33*(2), 196–206.

Lee, E. (1988). Cultural factors in working with South Asian refugee adolescents. *Journal of Adolescence, 11,* 167–179.

Lee, J., & Cynn, V. (1991). Issues in counseling 1.5 generation Korean Americans. In C. C. Lee & B. L. Richardson (Eds.), *Multicultural issues in counseling: New approaches to diversity* (pp. 127–140). Alexandria, VA: American Association for Counseling and Development.

Light, I., & Bonacich, E. (1988). *Immigrant entrepreneurs: Koreans in Los Angeles, 1965–1982.* Berkeley: University of California Press.

Lin, K. M.(1983). *Hwa-byung:* A Korean culture-bound syndrome? *American Journal of Psychiatry, 140*(1), 105–107.

Lin, K. M., Lau, J. K., Yamamoto, J., Zheng, Y.-P., Kim, H-S., Cho, K.-H., & Nakasaki, G. (1992). *Hwa-byung:* A community study of Korean Americans. *Journal of Nervous and Mental Disease, 180*(6), 386–391.

Lin, K. M., & Shen, W. (1991). Pharmacotherapy for Southeast Asian psychiatric patients. *Journal of Nervous and Mental Disease, 179,* 346–350.

Marcos, L. R., & Alpert, M. (1976). Strategies and risks in psychotherapy with bilingual patients: The phenomenon of language independence. *American Journal of Psychiatry, 133*(11), 1275–1278.

Min, P. G. (1990). Problems of Korean immigrant entrepreneurs. *International Migration Review, 24,* 436–455.

Nah, K. H. (1993). Perceived problems and service delivery for Korean immigrants. *Social Work, 38*(3), 289–296.

Noh, S. R., & Atkinson, W. R. (1992). Assessing psychopathology in Korean immigrants: Some preliminary results on the SCL-90. *Canadian Journal of Psychiatry, 37,* 640–645.

Rohner, R. P., & Pettengill, S. M. (1985). Perceived parental acceptance-rejection and parental control among Korean adolescents. *Child Development, 56,* 524–528.

Root, M. (1989). Guidelines for facilitating therapy with Asian American clients. In D. Atkinson, G. Morten, & D. Sue (Eds.), *Counseling American minorities: A cross-cultural perspective* (pp. 116–128). Dubuque, IA: William C. Brown. (Originally published in 1985 in *Psychotherapy, 22,* 349–356)

Sasao, T., & Chun, C. A. (1994). After the Sa-I-gu Los Angeles riots: Correlates of subjective well-being in the Korean American community. *Journal of Community Psychology, 22*(2), 136–152.

Shon, S., & Ja, D. (1982). Asian families. In M. McGoldrick, J. Pearce, & J. Giordano (Eds.), *Ethnicity and family therapy* (pp. 208–229). New York: Guilford Press.

Sue, D. W., & Sue, D. (1977). Barriers to effective cross-cultural counseling. *Journal of Counseling Psychology, 24,* 420–429.

Sue, S. (1988). Psychotherapeutic services for ethnic minorities: Two decades of research findings. *American Psychologist, 43*(4), 301–308.

Sue, S., Fujino, D. C., Hu, L.-T., Takeuchi, D. T., & Zane, N. W. S. (1991). Community mental health services for ethnic minority groups: A test of the cultural responsiveness hypothesis. *Journal of Consulting and Clinical Psychology, 59*(4), 533–540.

Sue, S., & Zane, N. (1987). The role of culture and cultural techniques in psychotherapy: A critique and reformulation. *American Psychologist, 42*(1), 37–45.

Uba, L. (1994). *Asian Americans: Personality patterns, identity, and mental health* (1st ed.). New York: Guilford Press.

U.S. Bureau of the Census. (1991). *Asian and Pacific Islander population in the United States: 1990* (Current Population Reports, Series P-20, No. 142-C-01). Washington, DC: U.S. Government Printing Office.

Weeks, J. R., & Cuellar, J. B. (1983). Isolation of older persons: The influence of immigration and length of residence. *Research on Aging, 5*(3), 369–388.

Yang, E.-S. (1979, March 10). *Korean community, 1903–1970: Identity to economic prosperity.* Paper presented at Korean Community Conference, sponsored by Koryo Research Institute, Los Angeles.

Yu, E. Y. (1983). Korean communities in America: Past, present, and future. *Amerasia Journal, 10*(2), 23–51.

Yu, E., & Cypress, B. (1982). Visits to physicians by Asian/Pacific Americans. *Medical Care, 20*(8), 809–820.

Yun, H. (1976). The Korean personality and treatment considerations. *Social Casework, 57*(3), 173–178.

The Latino American Experience

atino is a sociological/political term that identifies a culture shared by several ethnic groups in the United States, including Mexicans, Puerto Ricans, and Cubans as well as other ethnic groups with origins in Central and South America. Latino culture developed as a result of the fusion of Spanish culture (brought to the Americas by missionaries and soldiers) with Native indigenous cultures and African (the result of the slave trade) cultures in Mexico, South America, and the Caribbean Basin. Commonality among Latino American ethnic groups is found in the use of the Spanish language, the influence of Roman Catholic traditions, and strong kinship bonds between family members and friends. However, there is a wide variety within each Latino American group based on variables such as degree of acculturation, socioeconomic status, language preference, and generation in the United States.

255

14

COUNSELING INTERVENTIONS WITH LATINAS

Sandra I. Lopez-Baez

The term *Hispanic* is used by government institutions and the media to label those individuals who reside in the United States and who were born in or trace the background of their families to one of the Spanish-speaking Latin American (Central and South America) nations, the Caribbean, or Spain (Marin & Marin, 1991). However, this designation is not a self-identifier used by individuals within this population. Many prefer to use their country of origin to identify their nationality. Members of this cultural group recognize the term *Latino/Latina* as a more accurate descriptor of their Latin American origin.

The U.S. Census Bureau reports the Latino/Hispanic population to be 22.8 million or approximately 9% of the total U.S. population (Montgomery, 1994). The rapid growth of this group—an increase of 53% in the 10-year period 1980 to 1990—is of great significance. If the present growth trend continues, predictions are that the Latino population will reach 30 million by the year 2010 (Chapa & Valencia, 1993).

Latinos are a composite of heterogeneous groups, a fact that should be understood by professionals involved in the delivery of mental health services. Further, each Latino population is composed of groups of people with distinct historical, political, economic, and racial differences (Amaro & Russo, 1987), including people of Mexican, Puerto Rican, Cuban, and Central and South American origin. Marin and Marin (1991) have contended that Latinos are of no one race, but belong to all human races. These authors have described Latinos as racially mixed, as combining European Whites, Native indigenous groups, and African Blacks. Thus Latino identity lies in the shared sense of ethnicity, not in racial heritage.

257

Although the terms *Latino* and *Hispanic* are used interchangeably in the literature to refer to this population, the term *Latina* can be used as a word that stands by itself to refer to women of Latino/Hispanic origin (Arredondo, 1991). This chapter examines important issues to consider when counseling with women from this cultural group by exploring their cultural values and then presenting the case studies of Carmen and Conchita.

Latinas and Their Cultural Values

Latinas are as diverse a group as the population they represent. They number 11 million, or 1 out of every 14 women in the United States. Latinas share commonalities as well as differences in language preference and ability, degree of cultural traditionalism, and relationship between ethnic identity and degree of acculturation. Significantly, they have become active participants in a growing female workforce (Amaro & Russo, 1987; Arredondo, 1991; Johnston & Packer, 1987; Vazquez, 1994).

In order to intervene in a responsive manner with women from this client group, counselors must understand values fostered by the Latino culture. The importance of developing culturally sensitive mental health services is recognized by mental health policy makers (Amaro & Russo, 1987). This importance is reflected in the fourth edition of the *Diagnostic and Statistical Manual of Mental Disorders (DSM-IV)* (American Psychiatric Association [APA], 1994), which incorporates gender and cultural considerations in an effort to ensure its appropriate use with diverse populations and to avoid discrimination due to gender or cultural differences. By addressing cultural variations and their impact upon diagnosis, *DSM-IV* not only acknowledges the importance of cultural background and gender in assessment, diagnosis, and treatment planning but also promotes discussion of culture-specific mental health problems, the use of culturally sensitive assessment, and counseling interventions.

A particularly salient culture-specific value among Latinos is *familism* (Marin & Marin, 1991; Sabogal, Marin, Otero-Sabogal, Marin, & Perez-Stable, 1987; Vazquez, 1994). Familism is the strong identification with and attachment to both nuclear and extended family members, and this value produces strong feelings of loyalty, reciprocity and solidarity among members of a family. Three value orientations accompany familism: a perceived obligation to provide material and emotional support to the members of the extended family, the reliance on relatives for help and support, and the perception of relatives as behavioral and attitudinal referents. For Latinos, familism includes not only the extended family composed of blood relatives but also those considered kin because they are in close relationship and actively involved with the family. This family orientation is frequently misunderstood by counselors unfamiliar with this cultural value. Thus when a Latino client seems unwilling to discuss family issues with the counselor on the first visit, such familism-produced reluctance may be misinterpreted as dependence, immaturity, enmeshment, inability to take the initiative, uncooperativeness, and even paranoia.

Collectivism is also a central value to Latino culture (Marin & Marin, 1991). This value emphasizes interdependence, field sensitivity, conformity, mutual empathy, willingness to sacrifice for the welfare of others, and trust of members of the group. Latinos prefer nurturing, loving, intimate, respectful relationships to confrontational, superordinated ones. Group orientation, rather than a focus on the individual, tends to be the norm. When these traits are misconstrued as maladaptive, they can become symptoms such as lack of boundaries, inability to be assertive, resistance to therapeutic change, passivity, or a passive-aggressive stance.

Understanding cultural values is vital in order to avoid misdiagnosis of behaviors arising from the client's culture of origin. However, although it is true that cultural norms in the United States differ from those found in Latino culture, they are not necessarily incompatible. The challenge for many Latinos is to find balance in the process of acculturation so that they can retain Latino identity while adapting to the macroculture of the United States.

Because U.S. culture often devalues reliance on the extended family system and collectivism, Latinas face unique problems when attempting to acculturate (Comas-Diaz, 1987; Espin, 1982). Separation from the family, individualism, and a competitive attitude are primarily macroculture values. Cooperation, collectivism, and strong family ties sustain Latinas throughout their endeavors. A significant loss in social support, kinship bonds, and close friendships are a reality when Latinas try to fit into the macroculture.

Latinas also face the extra burden of dealing with the sociopolitical reality of prejudice in the macroculture and often become disoriented when they encounter minority status (Smart & Smart, 1995). If in their country of origin racial mixtures were the norm, they often possess a majority mind-set when arriving in the United States. To be labeled *minority* may be quite a shock. Related issues of race, skin color, facial features, and oppression may be confusing to Latinas who grew up in countries with tolerance and acceptance of a wide variety of racial mixes as cultural values. The loss of status, and the adjustment required, can precipitate both anxiety and depression. These symptoms when accompanied by stress can result in adjustment disorder, or more severe mental disorders.

Cultural values related to gender roles are another source of acculturation problems. Latinas in the United States often must confront the dilemma of either adopting traditional culturally dictated gender roles, or facing the threat of losing their ethnic identification (Long & Martinez, 1994). Particularly Latinas who are professionals must deal with the challenge of balancing middle-class U.S. culture, with its stress on individual achievement outside the home, and Latin culture, with its traditional emphasis on home and family. The price of not attaining the right balance can be both marginality because of loss of ethnic identity and internal conflict because of loyalty divided between family and work.

The common perception of distinct gender roles for Latinos and Latinas has not found support in the research literature (Marin & Marin, 1991), however. The stereotypical portrayal of Latino men as strong and in control, as the only providers for their families, and as exhibiting the popular domineering machismo traits has not been fully documented. Neither have Latinas been found to be submissive, dependent, or lacking in power and influence in the nuclear family. Couples and families attain a balance of power and influence that allows spouses to fulfill their gender roles in a harmonious way. To an outsider, a husband's attempt to protect his wife may be seen as a dominant attitude colored by possessiveness. But when interpreted in light of the appropriate cultural context, the behavior may be part of the couple's agreement to keep their cultural system in balance.

Because of the need to understand and accommodate cultural values, areas to explore when working with a Latina client include self-descriptor related to country of origin, language preference and ability, length of stay in the United States, migrational history of the client and her family, nuclear and extended family composition, reason for referral, and expectations from the counselor. Remember that the client's perception of the helping process may be very different from that of the counselor. Latinas may view a counselor as an external agent who represents a confusing and often oppressive societal system. They may also expect a helper to be similar to a member of the family support system who provides advice as well as information.

Case Studies and Interventions

The case studies of Carmen and Conchita presented in this section illustrate issues and interventions to consider in counseling Latinas.

The Case Study of Carmen

Carmen is a professional woman in her mid-30s, divorced with two children. She has lived in the mainland United States for 2 years, after leaving Puerto Rico in search of a better job opportunity. Carmen lives with her two children in an upwardly mobile middle-class neighborhood. She is the only one in her family to have left the island. Her children spend summers with their grandparents and uncles back in Puerto Rico. During the Christmas holidays she and the children also visit the family in Puerto Rico. Carmen sought counseling because of stress-related feelings of depression and anxiety. She was referred by her family physician.

As a single mother, Carmen has many responsibilities to shoulder in caring for her children and working full time. The past 2 years had been taxing but she had managed successfully. She reports that now "things" seem to be falling apart. She has difficulty sleeping, is experiencing anxiety at work and guilt over her children's adjustment problems at school, and is feeling depressed. At times she battles strong urges to take the children and return home to Puerto Rico where her family could be actively involved in caring for the children while she works. Yet if she returns home, finances will be limited and she will have to admit defeat to herself and her children.

Carmen's initial question was "What is happening to me?" Things seemed to be working well and suddenly her life started to unravel. Carmen was not fitting into her new environment and felt distant from her familiar homeland. She inquired about the counselor's ethnic background and immigration experience. The counselor readily offered this information and shared with Carmen her own feelings of isolation and marginality. This exchange of information between counselor and client allowed for the establishment of a warm and close relationship that addressed Carmen's need for *simpatia*—for establishing positive, close affiliations with others based on empathy for their feelings (Marin & Marin 1991). Though this manner of relating to a client may appear highly personal in that the counselor reveals self-information, it is recommended as a way to establish rapport with many Latina clients.

Validation of Carmen's feelings and discussion of the acculturation process made up the bulk of the first three counseling sessions. Her "cultural fatigue" stemmed from the process of adaptation to new cultural norms and rules that she had to decipher on her own (Smart & Smart, 1995). The children were learning cultural norms faster than their mother, which created some tension at home. Carmen was past the initial stages, and the novelty of her move had worn off. She had transitioned into questioning her decision to leave Puerto Rico while adjusting to the new culture. She reported feeling "bombarded" with the language, sights, sounds, and stimuli from the environment. This is a common complaint, particularly from individuals whose primary language is not English. Home becomes a safe haven in which the culture of origin is an anchor.

Another issue was Carmen's distance from extended family support systems. This created a sense of isolation for her. American culture had no equivalent system to fill this void. Often a family of choice can provide some support when a family of origin is lacking. For Carmen, the Catholic church might be considered as an institution that could bring the sense of family she needs. However, her divorced status was an issue to consider when enlisting the assistance of the church. Locating an understanding priest whose parish had a strong Latino presence proved to be an effective family alternative for Carmen. The parish had Latino members at various stages of acculturation who were supportive of Carmen and her issues.

A delicate issue that emerged in the course of counseling with Carmen centered around an incident in which someone referred to her as a *non-White*. She reported anger and shame at being labeled in such an unfamiliar manner. She perceived this label as somehow being derogatory. Significantly, many Latinos experience disorientation when labeled *minority* in the United States (Espin, 1987). For Latinos, racial mixtures are the norm in their countries of origin. Diverse combinations of skin color and facial features are acknowledged, but the words used do not carry sociopolitical implications, nor are they generally used to devalue people. Discussion of this issue, and validation of Carmen's feelings along with acknowledgement that discrimination due to skin color is an every day reality in the United States, was an important aspect of the counseling process. Carmen's sense of indignation brought on by her understanding of racial issues empowered her to work toward educating people in her community. She joined the PTA at her children's school and insisted that the students there receive some form of multicultural education.

As she began to better understand her process of acculturation, her symptoms decreased. She succeeded in balancing the two cultures, which allowed her and her children to move closer to bicultural status. New alternatives for coping took the place of the symptoms, and counseling was terminated.

The Case Study of Conchita

Conchita is a 22-year-old woman who is the daughter of Mexican immigrants. Her parents left Mexico seeking a better life for their four children. Both parents work at a local manufacturing plant and have made enough money to have some modest savings. Conchita's relatives are still in Mexico, and she and her family visit them as often as possible.

As the oldest of the children, Conchita has a lot of responsibility for her siblings as well as a share of household duties. This is because her mother works outside the home. Conchita also works part time at a bookstore and attends the local community college. Her grades are dropping, so the college counselor has called her to his office concerned that Conchita might lose her scholarship. Tearfully, Conchita expressed that she couldn't take it much longer. Her life felt like a dead end. She has no friends, has no one to help her, and is feeling anxious about having to transfer to a 4-year institution in order to complete her studies. She has not discussed this with her parents for fear that they will ask her to quit school. She told her counselor that she was experiencing *nervios* and is afraid of going crazy. Because of his concern that she might be suicidal, the counselor referred Conchita for evaluation and therapy to an outside mental health facility.

Conchita was evaluated by a psychiatrist who found her not suicidal but experiencing extreme distress. She was referred for mental health counseling. Conchita's first concern dealt with whether she was "crazy" because she was getting so much medical attention. It was explained to her that the team approach used by this group of practitioners seemed to work best for clients, and that from this point on, she will be working with a counselor who will see her on a regular basis. Conchita described herself as both *Latina* and *Americana*, but at times, she felt like neither.

In establishing rapport with Conchita, it was important to assess her life situation accurately in light of her perceived identity as both *Latina* and *Americana*, a combination that at times seemed incompatible. Bicultural individuals must frequently adjust areas of functioning in order to attain an optimal balance that allows them to operate successfully in two cultures simultaneously. Significantly, the counselor assigned to Conchita's case also identified herself as a bicultural individual. This facilitated the forming of a common bond. Salgado de Snyder (1987), based on her research regarding age of migration, has suggested that those individuals who migrate after age 14 (late immigrants) experience higher levels of stress than those who migrate prior to that age (early immigrants). The importance of cultural context in which childhood and adolescent socialization takes place can determine successful adaptation to a new environment. Because Conchita had moved to the United States by her sixth birthday, her schooling had given her many strengths, such as fluency in both Spanish and English, and an experience of two cultural contexts. Her personal integration of both of these contexts needed her attention and was addressed in several counseling sessions.

Conchita had a tremendous amount of responsibility in her family and was dreading going away to college and defaulting on her home responsibilities. This weighed heavily on her mind. Talking to her parents about her feelings did not seem feasible because she knew how hard they worked to provide for the family. Stress, guilt, anxiety, and fear of separation formed a constellation of symptoms for Conchita. These symptoms can also be part of a culture-specific syndrome addressed in *DSM-IV* and labeled *nervios*.

Nervios translates to distress and refers to a general state of vulnerability to stressful life experiences brought on by difficult circumstances (APA, 1994). In the macroculture of the United States it parallels an adjustment disorder (APA, 1994) because its symptomatology is similar. However, *nervios* is different in that it also implies a general weakness of the nerves that makes the person incapable of coping with difficult stressful situations and thus requires extra care and attention. Adjustment disorder is considered a time-limited condition that subsides after the stressor terminates, but *nervios* is seen as a long-term condition that individuals endure throughout most of their lives. *Nervios* exemplifies the belief that mental and physical conditions are linked together, not unlike the notion of somatization. The difference is the concept that mind, body, and spirit are one, that symptoms impact the whole not just one part. Of particular importance is the fact that the process of acculturation is ongoing, requiring periodic adjustments as the individual's life circumstances change.

Validation of Conchita's life situation was important in counseling. Her strength in successfully managing many different demands at home, school, and work needed to be reinforced to dispel the notion of weak *nervios*. Exploration of her internal strengths, such as resilience, allowed Conchita to see all that she was accomplishing despite the demands placed on her. The pain of divided loyalties between love for her family and the need to move on in her schooling presented a theme all too common with Latinas. Conchita's *respeto* (respect) for her parents kept her from discussing important issues with them. As they had no available extended network of kin, the resources within the family system seemed extremely taxed.

It was necessary to urge Conchita to talk to her parents about school and her need to move in order to complete her studies. A meeting with Conchita, her parents, and the counselor was suggested to discuss these issues. Conchita chose to talk to her parents first, then suggested that they all meet with the counselor to discuss options and alternatives. In Latino culture, the concept of familism is evidenced by sustained parental involvement in the lives of their children. Both of Conchita's parents were present for counseling. They were curious about the counselor's involvement with their daughter's concerns, the process of counseling, and the issues that

Conchita had already discussed with the counselor. Conchita's parents were very supportive of their daughter's effort to attain a college education, although the process was unfamiliar to them. The counseling process prompted a discussion of possible alternatives to provide support to Conchita and her family. A variety of community groups and agencies available to help the family adjust to Conchita's transition were suggested as options.

Conchita left for college where her siblings visited her often. Her parents were proud of having a daughter in college who was interested in pursuing graduate studies. She kept in touch with her counselor through occasional letters. She referred to her counselor as *madrina de estudios* (godmother of my schooling). This implied the inclusion of the counselor into Conchita's kinship network.

Conclusion

The delivery of culturally responsive counseling services, as both case studies suggest, is contingent upon the counselor's knowledge and understanding of the populations he or she serves. Latinas' cultural background is unique and diverse. Information about country of origin, ethnic identification, degree of acculturation, and the kinship network are important areas of knowledge for understanding a Latina client's reality. Such knowledge prevents the possibility of misdiagnosing culturally relevant processes as pathological.

References

Amaro, H., & Russo, N. F. (1987). Hispanic women and mental health: An overview of contemporary issues in research and practice. *Psychology of Women Quarterly, 11,* 393–408.

American Psychiatric Association. (1994). *Diagnostic and statistical manual of mental disorders* (4th ed.). Washington, DC: Author.

Arredondo, P. (1991). Counseling Latinas. In C. C. Lee & B. L. Richardson (Eds.), *Multicultural issues in counseling: New approaches to diversity* (pp. 143–156). Alexandria, VA: American Association for Counseling and Development.

Chapa, J., & Valencia, R. R. (1993). Latino population growth, demographic characteristics, and educational stagnation: An examination of recent trends. *Hispanic Journal of Behavioral Sciences, 15,* 165–187.

Comas-Diaz, L. (1987). Feminist therapy with mainland Puerto Rican women. *Psychology of Women Quarterly, 11,* 461–474.

Espin, O. (1987). Psychological impact of migration on Latinas: Implications for psychotherapeutic practice. *Psychology of Women Quarterly, 11,* 489–503.

Johnston & Packer. (1987). *Workforce 2000: Work and workers for the 21st century.* Indianapolis, IN: Hudson Institute.

Long, V. O., & Martinez, E. A. (1994). Masculinity, femininity, and Hispanic professional women's self-esteem and self-acceptance. *Journal of Counseling and Development, 73,* 183–186.

Marin, G., & Marin, B. V. (1991). *Research with Hispanic populations.* Newbury Park, CA: Sage.

Montgomery, P. A. (1994). *The Hispanic population in the United States: March 1993* (U.S. Bureau of the Census Current Population Reports, Series P20, No. 475). Washington, DC: U.S. Government Printing Office.

Sabogal, F., Marin, G., Otero-Sabogal, R., Marin, B. V., & Perez- Stable, E. J. (1987). Hispanic familism and acculturation: What changes and what doesn't? *Hispanic Journal of Behavioral Sciences, 9,* 397–412.

Salgado de Snyder, V. N. (1987). Factors associated with acculturative stress and depressive symptomatology among married Mexican immigrant women. *Psychology of Women Quarterly, 11,* 475–488.

Smart, J. F., & Smart, D. W. (1995). Acculturative stress of Hispanics: Loss and challenge. *Journal of Counseling and Development, 73,* 390–396.

Vazquez, M. J. T. (1994). Latinas. In L. Comas-Diaz & B. Greene (Eds.), *Women of color* (ch. 4). New York: Guilford Press.

15

LA FAMILIA FERNANDEZ
Directions for Counseling Cuban Americans

Silvia Echevarria Rafuls and
Martha Gonzalez Marquez

Sometimes I wonder what it's like never to be an immigrant. I have friends who were born and raised here, and they have a different perspective and different views. My personality is completely shaped by this process of being an immigrant. It's fundamental. . . . I'm caught up in that in-between. It's very uncomfortable. It's a generation that's not totally Cuban, not totally American, but right in between, and you have to identify with the two sides. You never know which one you are.

—MIGUELL (IN SHORRIS, 1992, P. 471)

For over three decades the plight of exiled Cubans has been widely known in the United States. To date, the waves of Cuban exiles continue to present serious challenges for the immigrants themselves, the exiled communities in which they hope to settle, the policy makers charged with the task of regulating immigration and settlement, and the service delivery systems instrumental in the Cubans' process of adaptation to a new country. As mental health professionals, we are part of the service delivery system that may encounter clients like Miguell, who describe immigration as a fundamental part of their being. As has been suggested in migration and acculturation literature, the experience of immigration goes beyond the event (Falicov, 1988; Karrer, 1989; Sluzki, 1979). It is a process that impacts families throughout generations.

In this chapter, the authors build upon the description of characteristics and special problems of Cubans and Cuban Americans in this book's first edition (Gonzalez, 1991) by presenting a family-oriented systems perspective that places clients within the multidimensional context of family, community, and therapeutic sys-

269

tem. This is done through the case example of the Fernandez family (La Familia Fernandez), and the discussion of the family through the Framework for Cultural Awareness (Marquez, 1992), which illustrates an approach to therapy with Cuban Americans from a culturally based, resource-oriented perspective. The guiding assumptions underlying this framework and interventions with La Familia Fernandez are addressed through description and case transcript. The cornerstone of this framework lies in the self-referent work required of the counselor(s) who work with culturally diverse clients. That is, the Framework for Cultural Awareness (Marquez, 1992) is based upon the belief that practitioners need continually to address their own individual issues toward diversity as part of their work with clients if they are to be culturally sensitive. This aspect of the framework is described and illustrated through the counselors' dialogue about their own culturally-based issues in relation to La Familia Fernandez. The summary then discusses the impact of this approach with this and other families as it develops further conceptually and in practice.

Although the Framework for Cultural Awareness is used to illustrate work with Cuban American clients in this chapter, the framework's core orientation to self-of-therapist issues in relation to others makes it useful in working with diversity and clients from a variety of cultures. Further, even though this chapter uses one case example to exemplify Cuban American families, within-culture variations must not be ignored (Karrer, 1989). The uniqueness of families and variation within groups should not be disregarded by viewing all Cuban American families through the experience of La Familia Fernandez (whose true name has been changed for reasons of confidentiality). Specificity falls short of accomplishing the task of culturally sensitive practice if counselors apply the same approach with all families they encounter of the same ethnic/racial group.

La Familia Fernandez: A Review of Cuban American Culture Through Their Experiences

Orlando Fernandez contacted a local university-affiliated family therapy center in his community (Southeastern United States) for reasons related to "problems at home." As he informed us of his family, he described a three-generation household made up of himself (41); his wife of 18 years, Miriam (40); their three children Antonio (17), Orlando, Jr. (15), and Natalia (9); and his in-laws, Ernesto (72) and Ana (66) Gomez. Mr. Fernandez specifically requested a Spanish-speaking counselor and an evening appointment time. For many Cuban/Cuban American families, it is important to have a Spanish-speaking counselor for the fullness of expression that it offers them and for the sake of including family members who do not speak English. These reasons were behind Mr. Fernandez's request: Spanish was the language spoken in the home; neither of his in-laws spoke English; Miriam spoke adequate English but was more comfortable speaking Spanish. The children did, however, speak English to each other, sometimes using it as a way to draw a boundary between themselves and the adults in the family. The family's requests could be accommodated because several counselors were fully bilingual in Spanish and English and evening times were available.

The obvious differences in the use of language in the Fernandez household exemplifies how culture can influence the family members, their interactions, and their life together as a family. In order to gain an understanding of the family's developmental process and of how their differing views affect their perceptions of mental health, it is important to address the role of culture within the context of the family's migration history. As Falicov (1988) and others have asserted, issues of migration and political history are an integral part of a family's culture (Breunlin, Schwartz, & MacKune-Karrer,1992; McGoldrick, Pearce, & Giordano, 1982.) In La Familia Fernandez, the issue of migration itself was an unsettled one between the generations. Ernesto, Miriam's father, still believed that leaving Cuba was a sign of cowardice. His preference as a strong anti-Castro supporter was to remain in Cuba in order to rebel against Castro's regime. He left only because Ana was determined to take their children and leave without him.

The decision to leave one's country and familiar culture is not made lightly. In one of the first studies of Cubans in exile, Fagen, Brody, and O'Leary (1968) observed that "people go into self-imposed exile only when they have experienced the effects of changes in economic arrangements, social structure, or political order in extremely personal and negative ways" (p. 76). They also pointed out that even then, many individuals remain reluctant to leave the society and culture of which they feel a part (p. 7). It is difficult to take a contextualized approach with immigrant clients without some understanding of their migration experience and history. Sluzki (1979) and Karrer (1989) have emphasized the trangenerational impact of migration and pointed out that any long-term delay in the family's adaptive process can become readily apparent when a second generation is raised in the country of adoption. That which may have been avoided in the first generation has a way of reappearing in the second, generally in the form of conflict between generations (Gonzalez, 1988, 1991; Sluzki, 1979). In their programmatic research and clinical efforts with Cuban American families in Dade County, Florida, Szapocznik and his associates at the Spanish Family Guidance Clinic have found that the acculturation process has often resulted in family disruption in these families (Kurtines & Miranda, 1980; Szapocznik & Kurtines, 1989; Szapocznik, Scopetta, Kurtines, & Aranalde, 1978). This body of work has substantiated the view that family therapy with Cuban American clients needs to deal with disruptive acculturative differences that may occur between family members. This can be addressed by utilizing the Framework for Cultural Awareness (Marquez, 1992).

Orlando Fernandez: Migration History

Orlando came to the United States with his parents and younger sister in 1962. He was 8 years old and his sister was 5. Like so many other Cuban families during the 1959–62 wave of immigrants, their lifestyle changed drastically from one day to the next. Orlando's family had to start all over again after they lost the clothing business his parents worked so hard for in Havana. The shift from upper middle to lower socioeconomic status was deeply felt by Orlando's family in their adjustment to this country. Orlando believed losing everything left a permanent scar of insecurity within his hardworking father, who never strived again for any job other than factory work. The family's hopes and dreams were left for Orlando and his sister to fulfill. Education became very important as a way out of their losses. Orlando eventually became an elementary school science teacher, and his sister became a nursing instructor with her master's degree.

Miriam Fernandez: Migration History

Miriam came to the United States with her parents and two older brothers in 1973 through one of the last Freedom Flights. Miriam's family took longer to emigrate from Cuba because of her father's reluctance to leave, which placed them at greater risk of securing a way out of Cuba. Miriam arrived here at 18 years of age, much later than Orlando did. Even though she had completed the equivalence of a high school education in Cuba, she was required to attend high school in Miami to learn to speak English and to obtain her high school diploma. English did not come as easily to her as it had for Orlando, who was able to learn it at a much younger age. Orlando and Miriam were high school sweethearts. Soon after high school, Miriam went on for her nursing degree and became an R.N. She and Orlando married as soon as they both obtained their college degrees in 1977.

Miriam's father is disabled and is retired as an electrician. Her mother worked only out of necessity for a few years after arriving in the United States. After her father's second heart attack 10 years ago, Miriam asked that her parents move into their home. Although Orlando wanted to be of help, and believed in "family coming through when needed," he knew this could be stressful and could have some long-term repercussions—which they were now experiencing. Intergenerational tension and differences were evident in their developmental process as a family.

Culturally Based Aspects of the Family's Developmental Process

La Familia Femandez brought to therapy issues surrounding boundaries and space, cohesion and autonomy. Orlando and Miriam were experiencing differences in how to deal with Orlando Jr.'s wishes to participate in activities contrary to their beliefs. This had the whole family in an uproar because Miriam and Orlando were also feeling pressure from the Gomezes, who had very strong beliefs about what they should do with Orlandito's (Orlando Jr.'s) behaviors. Based on their own upbringing, Miriam and Orlando could articulate the type of limitations they thought were appropriate for this stage of adolescent development. However, because of the complexity of influences from their host culture, the couple experienced a dilemma with regard to their course of action.

This dilemma, their uncertainty, and lack of results in dealing with Orlando Jr.'s recent rebellious behavior at home precipitated Orlando's call for therapy. Each of the family members held their own perspective about Orlando Jr.'s behaviors. Orlando Jr. was himself bothered by his parents' "restricting" views that he not spend time away from home on weekend outings, among other activities, that he found his peers were able to take part in and he could not. From Miriam's perspective, Orlando Jr. was too young to do many of the things he was asking to do, like going away for weekends without adult supervision. Likewise, Orlando thought that weekend outings without supervision were not appropriate for Orlando Jr. at his age, and he also disapproved of the friends that he went with. Both parents also feared that he might have been abusing drugs, even though Orlando Jr. denied it. From Antonio's perspective, he trusted that his younger brother could handle the weekend outings and should be allowed to begin exploring curiosities outside the protected home front. Natalia, as the only daughter, knew that if her parents were that protective about her brother, there was no way that they could approve of her doing the same, even at a much later age. As grandparents, Ernesto and Ana could not believe that their daughter and son-in-law could even consider other options when it came to this issue. For them it was clear that this was not to be allowed: "Children belong in their home at night and should not be out there with strangers." In fact, the grandparents could not understand how a counselor could help them with this issue.

The Family's Culturally Based Perceptions of Mental Health

One of the basic issues La Familia Fernandez struggled with was who to seek help from for their family difficulties. Because he had more exposure to the American culture since he arrived as a youngster, and because of the environment at his employment, Orlando's view of seeking a counselor was normal within the popular culture. He was frequently advised by his students' parents that they were in counseling for family problems. In addition, at faculty meetings, teachers often discussed students' progress as therapy improved their home situation. Teachers also recommended meetings with school counselors as needed.

Miriam, however, was taught that family struggles should be dealt with by the family, including the extended family. In her more traditionally based perspective, quite similar to that of her parents, the older generation was highly respected for its wisdom and insight, especially surrounding family values. The younger generations should seek the advice of the elders and heed their recommendations. Indeed, it was not uncommon for children to go directly to grandparents for advice. However, this was not the case with Miriam's children.

For Miriam's family, religion was an additional factor related to seeking outside assistance. Miriam was raised according to the Roman Catholic tradition. An element of her mother's expression of their religion was her belief that obstacles can frequently be overcome through prayer and renewed devotion to the church. The Gomezes believed that assistance could be sought by talking with clergy or with a medical physician who might a have a "cure." Thus the Gomezes were reluctant and disapproving of Orlando's decision to seek therapy. They were supportive and pleased, however, that the counselors requested they attend sessions.

Miriam herself was somewhat torn in her own beliefs about therapy. A part of her still resonated with the religious belief that prayer and devotion could help, but she had more exposure than her parents to the host culture and the normalization of therapy. Miriam's medical training as a nurse also prompted her to see therapy as more acceptable, and she strongly connected with biological causes. From her medical perspective, discussion about psychotropic treatment was not unusual, and therefore it was not surprising that she inquired about medication for Orlando Jr. as she spoke of their struggles with him.

The dissonance between Miriam's own family's belief system about help seeking and her more acculturated views clearly made Miriam uncertain about therapy being an appropriate avenue. Ultimately, however, she went along with Orlando's decision. Orlando generally had the final say in all major family decisions, and although Miriam sometimes took issue with this traditional gender role, she generally heeded her husband's wishes as her mother did her father's. As part of her socialization in this respect, relinquishing some of her power also meant that her husband was ultimately responsible for the decisions made for the family as a whole. In a way this was a relief to her, especially when outcomes were not as expected.

The different views that family members had about help seeking, the gender-related issues between Orlando and Miriam, and their conflict with Orlando Jr. exemplify some of the intergenerational and acculturative dissonance that can occur among family members in immigrant families. From a culturally based view, the task was to help the family sort through all the many layers and dimensions within which their conflicts were embedded.

Theoretical Assumptions Guiding Clinical Practice With Cuban American Families: The Framework for Cultural Awareness

To increase awareness of the importance of culture in therapy, and to help and to guide work with La Familia Fernandez, the counselors used the Framework for Cultural Awareness (Marquez, 1992). In its systemic orientation, one of the underlying assumptions of the framework is that families and their situations are contextual in nature. That is, families bring with them a number of interconnected variables that occur within different dimensions of lived experience and influence their situation. For instance, from an individual perspective, clients experience internal and biologically influenced processes that they may struggle with or that they may celebrate in terms of who they are (Breunlin et al., 1992). Within a family context, individuals are also affected by their interpersonal relationships with other family members. This interrelatedness occurs within the dimensions of shared history, the language they speak with each other, the roles they are assigned in relation to their age and gender, their spiritual and/or religious beliefs, and their level of education. From a community/societal perspective, individuals within families are also influenced by their place of residence in terms of climate, region, and community; their work and school environments; and the sociopolitical climate in which they live. This multidimensional view of a family's complexity was illustrated in the description of La Familia Fernandez in order to present how some of these variables inevitably become part of therapy.

A second assumption of the Framework for Cultural Awareness is that neglecting to include and incorporate these contextual variables or issues in therapy is both disrespectful and potentially dangerous. Focusing primarily on the problem or on the solution might only help to devalue their unique life experiences by assuming all families are similar or are simply attempting to assimilate to the host culture.

A third assumption underlying the Framework for Cultural Awareness is that the counselor adds an additional layer of context and diversity to the family's life experience and inevitably to the therapy. A counselor becomes a part of the system to be examined and negotiated in therapy (Becvar & Becvar, 1993). The counselors' own culture, history, gender, migration experiences, biases, and assumptions affect the conversation in therapy, the direction of therapy, and the change process (Karrer, 1989). Because of this assumption, the framework focuses heavily on the self-of-the-therapist and ways in which therapists can increase cultural awareness for themselves and, as a result, for their clients.

A fourth assumption within this framework is that the family, its presenting problem, the culture, the counselor, and therapy itself are all involved in a systemic relationship. Therapy and all its related variables are viewed as a cybernetic system influencing one another and at the same time being recursively influenced by each other. Although the field of marriage and family therapy has moved well beyond the traditional definitions of systems theories, a general systemic epistemology envelopes the framework. The primary difference is the expansion of the cybernetic model to include culturally based influences in the families as well as gender issues and issues of power differentials and the sociopolitical climate (Hare-Mustin, 1987; Carter & McGoldrick, 1988).

A final assumption is that cultural experience should be normalized by validating families within the context of uniqueness and strengths. As McGoldrick (1982) asserted, "there is a common tendency for human beings to fear, and therefore reject, that which they can't understand" (p. 4). Clinically this leads to labeling that which is different as *inappropriate*, *bad*, or *crazy*. Because ethnic families fall within this range of possible difference, they can easily be pathologized for cultural factors. In an effort to stay away from pathologizing tendencies, the resource-oriented nature inherent in the original framework has now been enhanced by clarifying this as a stated assumption. The addition is primarily based on research with Latin American families in therapy in which in-depth resource-based interviews were conducted with the Latino families and their counselors (Rafuls, 1994). A major finding was that resource-oriented interviewing had a positive influence on how families perceived themselves and how counselors viewed their ability to change.

Tenets of the Framework for Cultural Awareness are as follows:

1. **Adopt a broader perspective about culture.** Broadening one's view about culture leads to further cultural awareness and tends to reduce occurrences of stereotyping by preparing the counselor to deal with social changes and problems that exist. A wider view also reduces the view of cultural issues as deficits for families and as specialty issues. Overall, the journey toward cultural awareness involves broadening of perspectives on many levels.

   In describing clinical cases, counselors frequently list only demographics as important information. In this light, La Familia Fernandez might only have been described in a short paragraph with names, ages, household members, and presenting problem. As mental health fields progressed, counselors began also to include ethnicity and race as important information. Unfortunately, many training programs and clinics end their definition of culture there. This framework instead encourages the counselor to consider a broader lens that is ever evolving as more is learned about family diversity and uniqueness. La Familia Fernandez, as described earlier, is replete with cultural similarities and differences both within their own family and within their host culture. A counselor neglecting the inner turmoil that Miriam experiences about the appropriateness of therapy as a helping option might, for example, arrive at erroneous assumptions concerning her motivation. This chapter's description of La Familia Fernandez reflects a multidimensional definition of culture that is not static but evolving.

2. **Become continuously more self-aware.** Cultural awareness and sensitivity toward others starts with an awareness of self. This includes an examination of one's assumptions, values, biases,

and cultural context. This process seems to be fluid and never finished. It can also be anxiety provoking or fear producing because facing one's biases and deficiencies in any situation is difficult. Knowing one's identity and the process toward identity formation is vital to understanding others as well.

Becoming aware of one's own cultural background assumes that the counselors are in the process of adopting a broader perspective of culture. The personal process of gaining more awareness of one's culture can take on many forms, as the counselors' dialogues in the next section about, for example, migration histories, bicultural experiences, and gender-related roles and messages illustrate.

3. **Interact with others.** Immersion and/or experience with diversity leads to increased cultural awareness. Experience with people of diverse cultures provides the chance to experience those cultures as they are lived. Working with or being associated with diversity increases one's knowledge base about others. It can also break down barriers toward the insensitive tendency to stereotype. Dialogue about cultural issues can elucidate myths and assumptions and alleviate some of the emotional discomfort that sometimes accompanies such an exploration. Organizing with groups who are committed to furthering cultural awareness can speed up the process and punctuate its importance.

4. **Examine individual personal experiences.** Learning to be culturally aware is a personal process. Searching for more cultural awareness involves much more than simply reading a book or engaging in an exercise. Each individual has his or her own set of unique life experiences, values, and beliefs that he or she must organize and process in his or her own way. Individuals must examine and interpret their own experiences with culture, prejudice, and oppression in order to learn from their own life. How each individual decides to give meaning to his or her experiences is a personal and unique endeavor.

The overarching connecting element of this framework involves the interpretation individuals ascribe to the first three tenets and how they shape, and are shaped, by individual personal experiences. Thus in their mutually recursive relationship these tenets shape each other. Individual personal experience is as strongly influenced by perspective, awareness, and interaction with others as perspective, awareness, and interactions with others influence individual personal experiences—as Figure 15-1 illustrates.

As evidenced with La Familia Fernandez, migration took on a different meaning for different members of the family based on their own individual personal experiences around that issue. For instance, Ernesto Gomez resisted migration and was not pleased to come to the United States. Yet his wife and children viewed migration as a refuge. Thus their individual personal experiences of the same event were quite different and had dissimilar long-

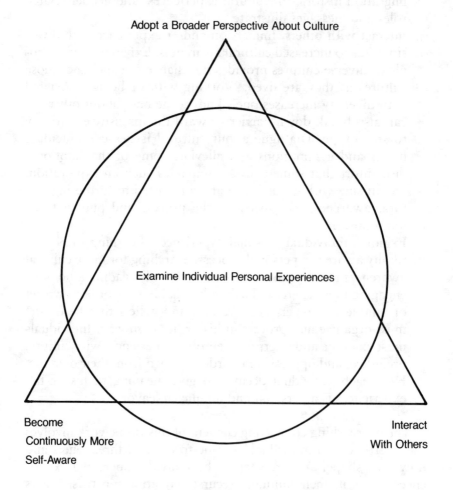

Figure 15-1 *Framework for Cultural Awareness*

term implications for each of them in terms of acculturation. Furthermore, just as there were differences and similarities among each of the family members' experiences of migration, there were the counselors' own contrasting experiences of migration to consider as they worked with this family. Much like La Familia Fernandez, one of the counselors emigrated from Cuba with her family as a young child for political reasons and the other counselor was born in the States from Colombian parents that migrated here for increased opportunity.

Many counselors learn about cultural differences and similarities only through their own personal experiences. For many, these experiences are broad and can indeed contribute to the understanding and progress of therapy. However, for others, relying on their own life experiences may be too narrow a base to draw from. In such a case, working with clients from other cultures is one form of increasing contact, as is forming discussion groups with other professionals from diverse backgrounds. This part of the process is illustrated in the counselors' discussions of La Familia Fernandez in terms of their relationship with the Cuban culture and other Hispanic and Latin American cultures, both on a personal level and professional level, in the following section.

Putting the Framework of Cultural Awareness into Practice With a Cuban American Family

One of the first things that counselors do within this framework is to discuss definitions of culture in an attempt to broaden lenses with regard to what may be meaningful to a family. Meaningfulness is viewed in terms of the dimensions of culture specified earlier, which are based on what is known about the family's experience.

From the limited information obtained from the intake form, pertinent cultural issues in La Familia Fernandez seemed to include migration history, gender-related issues, and differing levels of acculturation. Later, after the first session, it was clear that political affiliation and sentiments as well as spiritual and religious beliefs were other dimensions of the family that also needed to be discussed. In the dialogues that follow, the counselors discuss La

Familia Fernandez, as thoughts occurred, before and after the first session, and later in terms of interventions. (Word repetitions have been deleted to make the dialogues easier to read.) Throughout contacts with La Familia Fernandez the counselors' thoughts about them were shaped by their own experiences of nationality, migration, acculturation, language, appearance, and setting.

Counselors' Dialogue Before the First Session With the Family

Nationality and migration.   As the counselors discussed their own nationality and migration experiences in contrast to La Familia Fernandez, counselor 1 (Silvia Echevarria Rafuls), a Cuban immigrant herself at the age of 5 in 1962, could identify strongly with the parents in the family, especially with Orlando's bicultural dilemmas. However, counselor 2 (Martha Gonzalez Marquez), born to Colombian parents in the States, could identify more strongly with the issues faced by the children in the family.

The initial dialogue about this family led the counselors to wonder about several aspects of this family, such as the father making the initial call, the family's living arrangement and how that came to be, their request for a Spanish-speaking counselor and what that was about, and some thoughts about their approach as co-counselors. In addition, the two counselors wondered about the family's migration history and what motivated them to immigrate to the United States. This dialogue serves as a basis for discussing counselors' assumptions and biases regarding the family.

Counselor 2: One of the assumptions that I think I have going into working with this La Familia Fernandez is that since they're Cuban, a Cuban family, I assume that they migrated here out of political refuge, to get away from the political situation in Cuba. I'm not sure that would be the case so I don't want to stereotype, but I think that would be something to wonder about out loud with them, and also to inquire as to what their sentiments are about that, if that is the case.

Counselor 1: Yet on the other hand, they may think it would be ignorant for us to take a position of wondering whether that was the case or not because most Cubans are here (Counselor 2 giggles) probably for that reason. You know what I'm saying? They may just kind of think, well where have you been for the last 30-something years? I mean being Cuban, I could see them wondering why wouldn't we understand that that's why they're here? Why else would they be here?

Counselor 2: Being Colombian, people frequently mistake that my family is here for similar reasons, because of political influences. I think there are counselors that assume that a person who's Hispanic or Latin American is here in the States fleeing a political . . . situation.

Counselor 1: Mm hmm. And in your family's case that was not true?

Counselor 2: In my family's case that was not true. Well, maybe we could present it to the family just like that, I'm not Cuban, yet I am Latin American, and my family arrived for different reasons and I don't want to make assumptions. And then you can share with them, not wanting to disrespect them [by asking the question].

Counselor 1: Okay. Or to say that it was a question for you but it was less of a question for me.

Counselor 2: Okay, that's a good way . . .

Appearance, setting, and language.   At this point in the dialogue, the counselors continued to talk about the family members' perceptions of the counselors as two professional Latin American women and how it might be for the family to not have a male counselor as part of the cotherapy team. The counselors wondered about the family's assumptions in relation to the counselors' use of language and the way the counselors looked (i.e., Latin versus non-Latin), and how comfortable the family might feel in the agency environment.

Counselor 2: So what else about us might [we consider]. . .

Counselor 1: We don't have an accent.

Counselor 2: Neither of us.

Counselor 1: No.

Counselor 2: Pretty strange.

Counselor 1: What about our appearance, does that influence the system in any way?

Counselor 2: Yes. . . Well I think we both look Latin. . . .

Counselor 1: Yeah, I agree—with our dark hair and dark eyes and olive skin. . . .

Counselor 2: Just in terms of how La Familia Fernandez might feel here, one thing that I think might be inviting for them is the fact that we have posters in our office from Nicaragua, Colombia, and Cuba and Rio. . . .

Counselor 1: Yeah, that is nice.

Counselor 2: And in our waiting room we have . . .

Counselor 1: Spanish magazines?. . .

Counselor 2: Yeah, which I think will make them feel more comfortable.

From the clients' level of comfort the counselors moved to their own level of comfort regarding their use of language. They discussed how different it might be for them to conduct the sessions with La Familia Fernandez in Spanish rather than in English, not only in terms of their own language experience but also in terms of supervision because none of their supervisors at the time spoke Spanish.

Counselor 2: Are we going to be freer without someone monitoring our language?. . .

Counselor 1: Would speaking Spanish in therapy be freer as well? I wonder if it would be freer perhaps emotionally, or whatever.

Counselor 2: That brings up a really good point on how do you and I feel differently speaking Spanish than we do speaking English, because I do feel different speaking Spanish than I do speaking English.

Counselor 1: What's the distinction for you?

Counselor 2: Honestly, sometimes when working with families speaking in Spanish there are times when I feel like I'm being authoritative.

Counselor 1: Interesting!

Counselor 2: Yeah, and I don't feel like that as much when I'm speaking in English.

Counselor 1: I can relate to that.

Counselor 2: Can you?

Counselor 1: Yes, I can see myself being much more formal maybe, or hierarchical or. . . .

Counselor 2: . . . In therapy. Now personally, when I speak in Spanish I feel a lot more casual, very conversational.

Counselor 1: So in this case . . . it would be interesting to note that, just to see, because the parents are just a little bit older than I am, and sort of the same generation. You know, I can relate to them as immigrant children, and having grown up here, especially the father, I think I'm more like the father than I am like the mother.

Counselor 2: Because he. . . .

Counselor 1: [because] of acculturation.

Counselor 2: . . . because he arrived here as a child?

Counselor 1: . . . Right, and probably learned English rather quickly. I wonder if speaking Spanish, or the experience of Spanish speaking for the father and myself based on that, as opposed to the mother who came much older, connects my experience closer to his.

Counselor 2: Well you know that's interesting because I might be able to relate with the children more on that level . . . and you know what might be . . . an obstacle—or a resource, actually—is that they're at an age where in my personal experience, and also in my experience with clients of similar ages, is that . . . the appreciation for your biculturalness isn't there yet. It's a dilemma in your teenage years, about where to belong in your host culture.

Counselor 1: With the kids, you mean?

Counselor 2: With the kids. And it wasn't until I was an adult, or much later, that I appreciated the biculturalness, and developed better my conversational skills and things like that.

Counselor 1: I remember . . . as a teen, you're mostly trying to be American.

Counselor 2: Right. . .

Counselor 1: So you might find yourself relating more with the kids based on your acculturation experience.

Counselor 2: Perhaps, but I have, like I've said, moved from there as an adult, which most people do, so that would be a very interesting aspect to explore. Again, these are all assumptions that I think we can't let blind us, but that might guide us in ways to expanding . . . the session . . . I wonder too if another issue might be rates of acculturation. . .

Counselor 1: Well, I can see my parents in the grandparents of La Familia Fernandez in terms of rates of acculturation. I can see a lot of them in there. And I can see . . . [myself closest to] the Dad's experience.

Counselor 2: So, we're assuming that the grandparents still hold on to much of the cultural traditions.

Counselor 1: This is again assumptions, but I think that Spanish speaking has more to do with the grandparents than the parents. . . . Anyway, I think these are all good points we need to keep in mind when we first meet them.

By broadening perspective through dialogue such as this, counselors make room for the impact that cultural elements of a family's life have upon everyday experience. The counselors found themselves examining broad contexts of culture through a constant process of thinking of their experience in relation to the family's and the family's to theirs.

Counselors' Dialogue After the First Session With the Family

During the session, attended by the whole family, what had brought them to therapy was discussed. Each family member described his or her perspective of the presenting problem. The different views, the counselors believed, were related to distinctive levels of acculturation. The dialogue that follows led the counselors to further clarification about the interrelatedness of the framework's tenets and how individual personal experience shapes and is shaped by broadened perspective, self-awareness, and interaction with others. Counselor 2 gave an example of the difference that exists between her individual personal experience and that of two of her siblings' experiences of biculturalism, which thus affects their outlooks on others' experiences of acculturation.

Counselor 2: My siblings and I, for example, have a similar upbringing in terms of having been born in this country, yet all three of us have had very different individual personal experiences with our biculturalism, so that may affect our outlook [of our clients' acculturation experiences]. . . . So one of the things I would be curious about with La Familia Fernandez is, especially for the kids and supposedly Orlando Jr. who is the identified patient in this family, . . . what is his individual personal experience of . . . being a multicultural or bicultural youth?

Counselor 1: Mm hmm.

Counselor 2: How is he experiencing that right now?

Counselor 1: And what would that have to do with his rebelliousness?

Counselor 2: I would wonder if Orlando Jr. is in part rebelling— of course this is in his parents' eyes that he's rebelling—by virtue of the fact that this is what all of the other teens are doing in his cohort and this is a norm in his culture, or because he doesn't want to adhere to what his parents or his culture of origin says he needs to adhere to, or because he does not want to be a coward like his mother's family was to leave Cuba.

Counselor 1: Or simply maybe because he may feel like it's more American to be out for the full weekend, versus be more Cuban-like to keep him at home.

Counselor 2: Yeah!

Counselor 1: And obviously we're kind of saying that based on the different cultural experiences that they had, based on age and gender, exposure to their host culture, and so on and so forth, that that all creates different individual personal experiences for them. So if it's tied into (pause) what's going on now that Orlando Jr. is the one that's acting out the most in the family, at least in the most bothersome way right now to the family members, what is it about this happening now?

Counselor 2: Mm hmm.

Counselor 1: If we broaden our perspective enough to take into account that each of them have their own experience, if you will, which they could each tell us, have a different story about.

Counselor 2: Right, that's true. . . go ahead!

Counselor 1: What is it about this point in time, right now? And you know, by broadenening perspective we're looking at everything that has come before that. And that includes how it was for Orlando to be a young man here in the States, during the time back in the 60s and the 70s, and how it was for let's say the other older male [in the household], how was it for him to be a young man in Cuba, at his [Jr.'s] age? And so I'm trying to make a transgenerational link of time, place, and history, how that creates a different individual personal experience for each of them . . . and so I'm wondering, then, if one of the ways to go with this would be as growing young men who at the time the issue is that of becoming independent, and in this case being your own man.

Counselor 2: Mm Hmm.

Counselor 1: . . . In a way, we could tie those three individual personal experiences, that of being, or becoming a young man.

Counselor 2: Mm hmm.

Counselor 1: With all the three men in this family.

Counselor 2: That would be very interesting.

Counselor 1: And to look from not only how it was different, but how it's also similar.

Counselor 2: That would be a lovely way to help them connect.

Counselor 1: Mm hmm.

Counselor 2: Since especially at this time in their lives they're feeling distant from each other.

Rather than focusing on Orlando Jr.'s rebelliousness and addressing his behavior as that alone, this discussion led the counselors to think about his rebelliousness within the dimensions of culture and development. This in turn led the counselors toward interventions that would address Orlando Jr.'s rite of passage of becoming a man within his current context, and how his experience related to his father's and grandfather's experiences of the same.

Interventions

The Framework for Cultural Awareness presents a way of thinking about clients rather than a way of "doing something with them," but interventions can illustrate how the theory behind the framework might present itself in therapy. Two interventions that took place with La Familia Fernandez are presented here, first through actual session dialogue and then by an explanation of outcomes. Major themes that emerge are also described.

Intervention 1—Three men in the family (session three).

Counselor 1: We have been thinking about the uniqueness of your situation and how each of you might have a part in influencing it. I was struck by the opportunity that is available, especially for the men in this family, to share some of your personal experiences of the transition to adulthood. From my own experience, I am aware of the differences between men and women in the Cuban culture and the expectations that are placed upon us. What kind of things can each man in this family share with Orlando Jr. regarding his journey into adulthood?

Grandfather: Well . . . um . . . from the time I was a young boy, I was told what would be expected of me. . .

Orlando: Were you actually told?

Grandfather: Well, I guess not . . . I guess I was . . . I don't know. Maybe shown. Men were supposed to stay near the home and keep an eye out for the whole family, brothers, sisters, mothers, everyone. We were always to find ways to make living easier both financially and physically.

Orlando: I remember only a little of that. Maybe because we lost so much in the move here to the States. I remember not seeing my father a lot. He worked long hours to try to make it better for us. (Long pause) I suppose that is similar to what Ernesto is talking about. My father showed us through example what was important. However, I also remember learning quite a bit from my peers, their families, and . . . well . . . just the environment.

Hearing the men tell their stories in the third session broadened their own, as well as the women's, perspectives about the men in the family and all that is involved in their process of developing into men. Orlando Jr. was able to appreciate the similarities in struggles and concerns that existed among all four men in the family (Antonio, his older brother was included in the discussion), despite their differences. The conversation continued with the boys becoming more and more engaged in their father's and grandfather's stories about their lives. Orlando Jr. was initially hesitant but later asked many questions. Both older men also spoke of the unspoken messages they received from their families and from their environment about gender roles. Highlights of this session were not only the storytelling but also the reactions from the listening members. Miriam was especially surprised and animated upon hearing her husband's experience. The session was concluded with an invitation to continue such discussions at home. Also interesting to note was that as the counselors talked about this intervention within the context of becoming a man, Counselor 2 pointed out that this terminology sounded different in English than it did in Spanish by stating, "I think that in English, or in this society, it's leaning toward some negative connotation, but in Spanish it's not like that." Because the counselors were conducting therapy in Spanish, she was not as uncomfortable with its use because in Spanish it emphasizes development ("Disraeli como hombre"), whereas in English it could lead to stereotypical heterosexual notions of manhood that are more related to being tough, rather than growing into responsibility or maturity. In a later session, the counselors explored the same issue with the women in the family as the men listened.

Intervention 2—Celebrations (session five).   Because the counselors noticed how different levels of acculturation were disruptive to La Familia Fernandez, they wanted to explore ways in which the family could maintain the ties to their values and their traditions and still go forward. How could they celebrate both cultures?

Counselor 2: (looking at Orlando Jr.) I am curious about several issues raised here so far and I would like to discuss them. I am interested in finding out what elements of your lives are affecting the situation with Orlando Jr. So far, it seems as though one is that your family is trying to deal with two different cultures. Another is that different members of the family are at different places of combining the two cultures. What do you think about these points?

Orlando: Hum...I never thought about those problems in that way. In my mind, there aren't necessarily two different cultures...maybe because I've been combining them for so long myself...I've been here since I was 8.

Miriam: That's exactly how I've been feeling for years! In my mind there are two very different cultures. I guess that is also affecting all of us now . . . especially since Orlando and I sometimes have difficulty deciding what is right for our family in a lot of areas.

Counselor 1: How is it that you can use your individual experiences of combining two cultures as a model for your children, and what might they gain by hearing what your experiences were about?

The family responded by telling us about rituals and celebrations that brought them together as a family, and elements of both cultures were represented. This intervention allowed the counselors to provide a forum for La Familia Fernandez in which they were able to share both their traditional and nontraditional values. Additionally, the children were able to observe how it was possible for them to be part of both cultures. The counselors also addressed how the family members were already exemplifying both sets of values and how it affected each of them as they did so.

Major themes.   From the intervention excerpts, several major themes relating to the Framework for Cultural Awareness become apparent. Not all have been openly discussed yet, but they have arisen. One is that the broad perspective of culture allows identification of several aspects affecting the family's situation. The grandparents have strongly made reference to the cultural differences in parenting and discipline. Additionally, Miriam has alluded to her own inner conflict with the cultures, and Orlando has shared his experience of a lack of conflict. Another theme is that the children have openly discussed their sense of isolation and discomfort with the bicultural nature of their experience. Orlando Jr. especially expressed a desire to become more "American," even though this could mean being disloyal to his own family. Yet another is that, from a resource-based standpoint, the parents' personal experiences as children/young adults are used in assisting the family in finding their own strengths. Utilizing a member's own journey in combining cultures as a resource was a method counselor 2 developed after embarking on her own self-awareness and interacting with other diverse groups, both tenets of the framework. The sessions concluded with an exploration of the positive aspects associated with their biculturalism and an invitation to take note of other benefits their situation entitles them to—and thus with a celebration of their multicultural experience.

Summary

This chapter describes one way of working clinically with a Cuban American family based upon a systemic, resource-oriented framework for cultural awareness. The discussion of La Familia Fernandez presents some of the cultural factors that may impact Cuban Americans throughout their acculturative experiences following migration. Migration is viewed as a process beyond the actual event that could potentially affect families throughout several generations. The counselors' thoughts about the family's experiences and the counselors' own biases and assumptions about La Familia Fernandez are presented through excerpts of actual transcripts from the dialogues that took place before and after sessions with the family.

The Framework for Cultural Awareness is applicable to a variety of clients, regardless of their presenting problem or background, because of its broadened view of culture. Within this framework, culture is viewed as a construct made up of multiple dimensions that is uniquely experienced by individuals within the context of their environment. This broadened, self-referent view of culture does not expect clinicians to be experts within each of the dimensions, but rather encourages genuine openness, self-awareness, and motivation for an understanding of others.

A major factor to consider is the relationship between the culture of the counselor and the culture of the client. With La Familia Fernandez, coincidentally one of the counselors was from a similar cultural background in terms of country of origin and migration history. The other counselor was similar to the family within the dimensions of language, acculturation (of the children), and general Latin American traditions. What if such a coincidence had not occurred?

The Framework for Cultural Awareness still applies to counselors whose cultural background is dissimilar from their clients' because of its focus on broadening cultural perspective and its emphasis on interaction with others from differing backgrounds and experiences. As clinicians allow themselves to encounter diversity, they enter into a process of awareness that can bring them closer to the client's experiences.

References

Becvar, R. J., & Becvar, D. S. (1996). *Family therapy: A systemic integration* (3rd ed.) Boston: Allyn & Bacon.

Breunlin, D. C., Schwartz, R. C., & MacKune-Karrer, B. (1992). *Metaframeworks: Transcending the models of family therapy.* San Francisco: Jossey-Bass.

Carter, B., & McGoldrick, M. (1988). *The changing family life cycle: A framework for family therapy* (2nd ed.). Boston: Allyn & Bacon.

Fagen, R. R., Brody, R. R., & O'Leary, T. J. (1968). *Cubans in exile: Disaffection and the revolution.* Stanford, CA: Stanford University Press.

Falicov, C. J. (1988). Learning to think culturally. In H. A. Liddle, D. C. Breunlin, & R. C. Schwartz (Eds.), *Handbook of family therapy training and supervision.* New York: Guilford Press.

Gonzalez, G. M. (1988). Cuban Americans. In N. A. Vacc & J. Wittmer (Eds.), *Experiencing and counseling multicultural and diverse populations* (2nd ed., pp. 263–288). Muncie, IN: Accelerated Development.

Gonzalez, G. M. (1991). Cuban Americans: Counseling and human developmental issues, problems, and approaches. In C. C. Lee & B. L. Richardson (Eds.), *Multicultural issues in counseling* (pp. 157–170). Alexandria, VA: American Association for Counseling and Development.

Hare-Mustin, R. T. (1987). The problem of gender in family therapy. *Family Process, 26*(1), 15–27.

Karrer, B. M. (1989). The sound of two hands clapping: Cultural interactions of the minority family and the therapist. In G. W. Subway, B. M. Karrer, & K. V. Hardy (Eds.), *Minorities and family therapy* (pp. 209–237). New York: Haworth Press.

Kurtines, W. M., & Miranda, L. (1980). Differences in self and family role perception among acculturing Cuban American college students: Implications for the etiology of family disruption among migrant groups. *International Journal of Intercultural Relations, 4,* 167–184.

Marquez, M. G. (1992). *Cultural awareness in the field of marriage and family therapy: A qualitative analysis of multiple perspectives.* Unpublished doctoral dissertation, Purdue University, West Lafayette, IN.

McGoldrick, M. (1982). Ethnicity and family therapy: An overview. In M. McGoldrick, J. K. Pearce, & J. Giordano (Eds.), *Ethnicity and family therapy* (pp. 3–30). New York: Guilford Press.

McGoldrick, M., Pearce, J. K., & Giordano, J. (Eds.). (1982). *Ethnicity and family therapy.* New York: Guilford Press.

Rafuls, S. E. (1994). *Qualitative resource-based consultation: Resource-generative inquiry and reflective dialogue with four Latin American families and their therapists*. Unpublished doctoral dissertation, Purdue University, West Lafayette, IN.

Shorris, E. (1992). *Latinos: A biography of the people*. New York: Norton.

Sluzki, C. (1979). Migration and family conflict. *Family Therapy Process, 18*, 379–390.

Szapocznik, J., & Kurtines, W. M. (1989). *Breakthroughs in family therapy with drug-abusing and problem youth*. New York: Springer.

Szapocznik, J., Scopetta, M. A., Kurtines, W. M., & Aranalde, M. A. (1978). Theory and measurement of acculturation. *Inter-American Journal of Psychology, 12*, 113–130.

16

ASSESSING AND COUNSELING CHICANO(A) COLLEGE STUDENTS:
A Conceptual and Practical Framework[1]

Madonna G. Constantine and Augustine Barón

In 1990, the Chicano(a)[2] population was estimated to be about 13.3 million, up from 2.1 million in 1960. The number of Chicano(a)s in the United States rose from 1.2% in 1960 to 5.4% in 1990, an increase of 350% in 30 years (Aguierre & Martinez, 1993; Griffith, Frase, & Ralph, 1989; National Council of La Raza, 1990). In light of the rapid rise in the number of Chicano(a)s in the United States, it appears that Mexican Americans may be in prime positions to influence major social, economic, and political policy well into the 21st century.

However, educational attainment data do not provide an encouraging forecast for Chicano(a)s. Specifically, in terms of completion rates for 4 or more years of college, Mexican Americans are behind in comparison to other Latino(a) groups (20.2% for Cubans, 9.7% for Puerto Ricans, and 5.4% for Mexican Americans) and in comparison to Asians (39.9%), Whites (28.5%), and African Americans (11.4%) (Aguirre & Martinez, 1993; U.S. Bureau of the Census, 1991). Thus although the Mexican American population constitutes one of the most rapidly increasing Hispanic ethnic groups, it is also one of the least educated (Barón & Constantine, 1997). Enrollment data for higher education institutions

---

1. This chapter is based in part on concepts presented in Barón (1991) and Barón and Constantine (1997).

2. The terms *Mexican American* and *Chicano(a)* are used interchangeably in this chapter, although there are connotational meanings for each that have important psychological implications, as will be discussed later.

during fall 1992 (Chronicle of Higher Education Almanac, 1994) indicated that approximately 954,000 Hispanic students were registered in U.S. colleges, representing 6.5% of the college population. Determining the exact number of Chicano(a)s in higher education is difficult because of collapsed demographic categories across Hispanic subgroups, but researchers have estimated that Chicano(a)s typically comprise about 60% of the total Hispanic enrollment (Astin, 1982; U.S. Bureau of the Census, 1987).

Given the educational attainment figures, successful matriculation in higher education is a major achievement for many Chicano(a)s. Although numerous studies have attempted to identify academic predictors of success for Chicano(a) college students (e.g., Duran, 1983; Humphreys, 1988; Lunneborg & Lunneborg, 1986; Willie, 1987), the literature has indicated that personal, nonacademic factors are frequently more reliable predictors of persistence in college than standardized test scores. These factors consist of positive self-esteem, leadership ability, community involvement, ability to conduct a realistic self-appraisal, understanding and dealing effectively with racism, development of long-range goals rather than relying on short-term ones, and availability of a strong support person (Arbona & Novy, 1990; Pennock-Roman, 1988; Sedlacek, 1987; Sedlacek & Brooks, 1976; Tracey & Sedlacek, 1984, 1985, 1987; Young, 1992). For Mexican Americans seeking postbaccalaureate degrees, several psychological factors have been noted to be strong predictors for success: parents' work ethic, strong emotional support from family, strong maternal role model (for female students), and demonstration of gratitude for family by working diligently and obtaining a degree (Aguirre & Martinez, 1993; Cortese, 1992; Fiske, 1988; Gandara, 1982; Madrid, 1988).

Because these psychosocial and cultural factors are critical, the role of mental health services on a college campus seems crucial in the retention and graduation of Chicano(a)s. Many counseling centers offer a range of services that are designed to support students in sustaining academic persistence. Often the largest component of a counseling center is its clinical services domain (i.e., individual and group therapy).

This chapter presents some of the knowledge and skills that are useful in assessing and intervening with Chicano(a) college students who present for mental health counseling. Three primary psychosocial/cultural constructs, together with a fourth unifying construct, that we have found useful in client conceptualization and treatment planning are discussed as they apply to the counseling concerns of Chicano(a) college students. Also discussed are appropriate assessment methods and a case study that illustrates how the constructs may be assessed via a counseling interview and how they can guide treatment planning.

Core Psychosocial/Cultural Constructs

The decades of the 1980s and 1990s have been a time of rapidly developing theory and research in the area of multiculturalism. A variety of concepts have been developed and investigated that are proving useful in conceptualizing counseling dynamics with cultural minorities. In counseling Chicano(a) college students, there are three constructs, in particular, that are important to consider in addressing their mental health concerns: acculturation, ethnic identity development, and gender role socialization (Barón & Constantine, 1997). A fourth construct—interactive culture strain—helps to conceptually synthesize various dimensions inherent in the three core constructs.

Acculturation

Rogler, Malgady, and Rodriguez (1989) have defined acculturation as a process in which the attitudes, values, beliefs, customs, and behaviors of a minority group are changed toward those of the majority group as a result of continued exposure to the dominant culture. This process is considered to be somewhat complex because it can be bidirectional (Casas & Vasquez, 1989); that is, it can be reversed, and the rate of acculturation can be halted, decreased, or increased depending upon a number of factors (Barón & Constantine, 1997).

Mendoza and Martinez (1981) have presented a model of acculturation that demonstrates the complexity of acculturation outcomes and processes. Their model illustrates changes that may occur across the primary modalities of beliefs, emotion, and behavior. They identify four primary acculturation processes:

1. cultural resistance, whereby there may be active and/or passive resistance to incorporating dominant cultural patterns (i.e., lack of acculturation in one or more modalities);
2. cultural shift, which is the substitution of one set of patterns for those of the dominant culture (i.e., replacing new cognitions, affects, and/or behaviors while extinguishing the prior ones);
3. cultural incorporation, which is the adaptation of patterns representative of both one's own culture and the dominant culture (i.e., retaining both cultures at once); and
4. cultural transmutation, the alteration of certain elements from both cultures to create a third, unique, hybrid pattern (e.g., religious practices that fuse Christian and indigenous spiritual practices).

In terms of counseling and psychotherapy, acculturation represents an important construct in issues related to the following phenomena: client dropout rates (Miranda, Andujo, Caballero, Guerrero, & Ramos, 1976), content and extent of self-disclosure (Castro, 1977), willingness to seek professional help (Ruiz, Casas, & Padilla, 1977), overall success of therapy (Miranda & Castro, 1977), preferences for an ethnically similar therapist (Sanchez & Atkinson, 1983), and likelihood of seeking particular mental health services (Atkinson, Casas, & Abreu, 1992; Lopez, Lopez, & Fong, 1991; Ponce & Atkinson, 1989). Acculturation has often been assessed through the use of paper and pencil instruments. Some of these instruments have included the Measure of Acculturation for Chicano(a) Adolescents (Olmedo, Martinez, & Martinez, 1978), the Bilingualism/Multiculturalism Experience Inventory (Ramirez, 1991), the Acculturation Rating Scale for Mexican Americans (Cuellar, Harris, & Jasso, 1980), the Behavioral Acculturation Scale (Szapocznik, Scopetta, & Tillman, 1979), and the African American Acculturation Scale (Landrine & Klonoff, 1994, 1995).

Many of these measures can be valuable in clinical practice and may be appropriate for use within a screening battery. These instruments are intended to evaluate extent of acculturation, usually along a dimension ranging from traditional/unacculturated, to balanced/bicultural, to acculturated/assimilated. Research has demonstrated that unacculturated individuals, for example, often prefer therapists who are ethnically similar; bicultural individuals may not have a strong preference; and acculturated individuals are inclined to favor therapists of the dominant culture (Atkinson, Casas, & Abreu, 1992; Ponce & Atkinson, 1989). Such preferences are also, in part, determined by clients' ethnic/racial identity development.

Thus acculturation status has important implications in the area of client expectations regarding such aspects as therapist background, length of treatment, and acceptability of certain interventions (Barón & Constantine, 1997). The information that therapists may glean from the assessment of acculturation is best utilized to make decisions about client assignment to a counselor and setting appropriate therapeutic goals and interventions. For example, research has revealed that less acculturated clients are more likely to expect clear, concrete outcomes from a few sessions of therapy (less than three) provided by a directive, active therapist. Conversely, a more acculturated client is more likely to prefer a focus on broad personal developmental criteria in longer term treatment by a less directive therapist (Atkinson, Casas, & Abreu, 1992; Ponce & Atkinson, 1989).

Ethnic Identity Development

A unifying concept across most of the models of ethnic/racial identity development includes hypothesized stages, phases, or "ego statuses" (Helms, 1994; 1995) that ethnic/racial minorities can experience as they deal actively with issues of cultural diversity. Typically, this involves movement from a place where these individuals harbor negative stereotypes and thoughts about their own group to a place where they have internalized healthier self-esteem and cultural pride. Ideally, the outcome of the stages or phases should reflect an appreciation of cultural differences as manifested by all individuals, not just their own group.

Although many of these stage or phase models have been criticized as restrictive and not always valid, certain aspects are worth highlighting for clinical practice. For many students, college is a time when they may examine and amend some of their long-held beliefs and attitudes, particularly with regard to interacting with culturally different individuals. As counselors, we frequently notice a change in attitudes as Chicano(a) students study the history of their group for the first time in an in-depth manner. Experiencing frustration and anger over the injustices that are discovered through such study moves the students along some of the stages that the identity development models purport to capture. One of the changes may manifest itself in the ethnic labels used by the students. For example, terms such as *Hispanic* or *Mexican American* frequently signify a beginning stage of ethnic awareness or identity. As the students advance to higher stages, they may adopt the label *Chicano(a)*, *Latino(a)*, or *Hispano(a)* as a way of demonstrating a heightened awareness of their group identity because the terms have an ideological valence (Barón, 1991; Barón & Constantine, 1997). Chicano(a) college students at more advanced stages or phases may also be more prone to searching out an ethnically similar therapist in the belief that only someone from their own ethnic group can fully understand the Chicano(a) experience. Similarly, they may have a desire to immerse themselves into "all things Chicano(a)." Thorough understanding of developmental stage models related to ethnic/racial identity can enable counselors to use this information effectively to interpret their clients' thoughts, feelings, and actions more accurately. By raising and processing the broader, social context in which ethnic/racial minorities exist, a greater appreciation of the dynamics between internal and external forces can be achieved. Such insight may also help counselors to identify their clients' strengths rather than focus solely on pathological phenomena.

Gender Role Socialization

Over the past few decades, the concepts of sex role differences and gender role socialization have received increasing attention in the literature, largely due to the advent of the women's movement. With regard to Mexican American culture, there has been much dialogue about Chicano(a) culture's undue emphasis on the "elevated" status of males and the subsequent double standards that tend to affect women negatively. The Spanish term *machismo* has been used in American society to denote a kind of hypermasculinity or male chauvinism. The original meaning of the term, however, represented several positive connotations in Chicano(a) culture, some of which included chivalry, gallantry, courtesy, charitability, and courage; it is unfortunate that the positive references to the term *machismo* have been lost in the translation (Barón, 1991; Barón & Constantine, 1997). Due to generational differences, many younger Chicano(a)s may not be aware that these other elements are part of the cultural concept of manhood. A compounding issue also exists in that many non-Chicano(a)s may harbor stereotypical notions about Chicano(a)s possessing excessive amounts of male chauvinism and sexism (Barón, 1991).

To the degree that a Chicano(a) student has been reared with conservative, traditional views of male/female relationships, these notions are likely to be challenged significantly in a college or university environment, particularly if the overall social climate is overwhelmingly nontraditional. Several important questions are often raised by Chicano(a)s on college campuses in the area of gender role socialization. For example, what does it mean to be a Chicano or Chicana? By whose cultural standards will this definition or perception be judged? How will one deal with negative reactions from peers? What personal and/or professional aspirations are legitimate to have? Can one be gay, lesbian, or bisexual and still be considered "manly/masculine" or "womanly/feminine"? Many Mexican American clients struggle with these and many other questions related to gender roles based, in part, on culturally based beliefs about appropriate gender role behavior. Because the college years are frequently a vital period of exploring dating relationships and establishing ongoing romantic relationships and career goals, gender role issues are raised readily in work with Chicano(a) clients. One means of assessing gender role attitudes and beliefs is through the use of traditional sex role measures such as the Bem Sex-Role Inventory (Bem, 1974) and the Personal Attributes Questionnaire (Spence, Helmreich, & Stapp, 1974). Such instruments may provide beneficial information for counselors in order to identify clients' inter- and intracultural conflicts about female/male attitudes and beliefs.

Interactive Culture Strain

When individuals attempt to integrate various developmental challenges related to acculturation, ethnic/racial identity development, and gender role socialization, the existence of differences in the levels of awareness and progression across all the dimensions of the three psychosocial/cultural constructs may result in emotional distress or conflict (Barón & Constantine, 1997). This phenomenon can be labeled *interactive culture strain*. This construct captures some of the psychological and developmental demands faced by a Chicano(a) college student or any minority student. There is an intrinsic interactive strain because clients' developmental level in any one dimension affects the remaining areas. Chicano(a) students may be experiencing a variety of psychological changes across the three psychosocial/cultural constructs. Much counseling work with such clients centers around the identification and management of this subsequent interactive culture strain. The case study included in the next section further discusses this concept.

Assessing the Core Psychosocial/Cultural Constructs Through the Clinical Interview

For mental health professionals to become competent and successful within the context of their counseling, it is important that they develop culturally appropriate clinical assessment and intervention procedures in working with their clients (American Psychological Association, 1993). This notion is especially relevant when dealing with the core psychosocial/cultural constructs of acculturation, ethnic/racial identity development, and gender role socialization. Although there are several ways in which these core constructs can be measured (e.g., through the use of acculturation scales, ethnic/racial identity development scales, and sex role inventories), many counselors may not have these types of measures at hand. It may also prove difficult or challenging to administer and score paper and pencil instruments to Chicano(a) clients early in the counseling relationship, particularly before a sufficient level of rapport is established. This is why many counselors may rely largely on the clinical interview to evaluate these important variables.

A standard clinical interview may provide a context for gathering important information related to the core psychosocial/cultural constructs, in addition to gleaning relevant data about other phenomena in clients' lives. Clinical or diagnostic interviews are comprised of several basic components that include, but are not limited to, a history and assessment of the presenting problem(s); family, social, and occupational/academic histories; information about previous ways that clients may have coped (successfully and unsuccessfully) in attempting to address the presenting concern(s); clients' resources for addressing presenting issues (e.g., personal characteristics, familial and peer relationships, social functioning, economic standing); and goals for treatment (Barón & Constantine, 1997).

A conceptual framework to assess the core cultural concepts of acculturation, ethnic/racial identity, and gender role identity for Chicano(a) college students within the context of this type of interview is illustrated in Figure 16-1. This framework highlights the three core psychosocial/cultural constructs along with inquiry dimensions that may provide counselors access to the assessment of cognitions, emotions, and behaviors associated with each construct. Although the framework has not been empirically validated, it is based on collective clinical knowledge and experiences with Chicano(a) college students and other ethnic/racial minorities. Each of the core psychosocial/cultural constructs, however, has received extensive attention in the literature and has received varying degrees of empirical validation. The authors' contribution in the form of this framework is an attempt to join together the three constructs under the broader notion of interactive culture strain to assist in conceptualizing the mental health needs of Chicano(a) college students and other similar minorities.

The framework dimensions can be integrated into a standard clinical interview, and may be assessed in any order deemed appropriate by the counselor. The purpose of this type of assessment is to determine whether clients may be experiencing difficulties related to the core constructs presented earlier, and to ascertain their effect on clients' presenting problems. The incorporation of this type of framework within a clinical interview may also lead to a more open dialogue between counselors and their clients about cultural differences (e.g., race/ethnicity, gender), and how these may impact the psychotherapy relationship. This framework can also serve as a vital initial therapeutic intervention and has important implications for treatment planning and ongoing intervention. Evaluating and understanding the psychological impact

Figure 16-1. *Examples of Assessment Dimensions Across the Three Psychosocial/Cultural Constructs**

Core Cultural Constructs	*Examples of Assessment Dimensions*
Acculturation	1. Generational status in the U.S. (e.g., first or second generation) 2. Primary language spoken to communicate with others 3. Degree of affiliation with majority culture (e.g., composition of peer network, Anglicization of name) 4. Role conflicts with regard to familial expectations 5. Value systems, customs, and orientations (particularly with regard to religion, political affiliation) 6. Level of involvement in cultural traditions or activities
Ethnic/Racial Identity	1. Ethnic group label used when asked about own ethnicity 2. Ways ethnicity has affected life 3. Ethnicities or races of members of peer support system 4. Affiliations with clubs or organizations that reflect one's own ethnic group representation and/or ideology 5. Awareness of Chicano(a) history and heritage 6. Ability to recognize and confront racial or ethnic oppression 7. Other internalized issues of oppression or racism related to ethnic identity (e.g., feeling shame about having an accent, being "too dark")
Gender Role Socialization	1. Gender role definitions within family of origin 2. Gender role expectations within family of origin 3. Socialization with regard to gender role affiliation (i.e., androgyny vs. specific sex role) 4. View of male-female relationships (e.g., romantic, work, social) 5. Awareness of gender-based differences in relationships (e.g., communication styles) 6. Impact of gender role socialization on choice of academic major or career

*Note. From "A Conceptual Framework for Conducting Psychotherapy With Mexican American College Students," by A. Barón and M. G. Constantine (1997), in *Psychological Interventions and Research With Latino Populations*, edited by J. Garcia and M. C. Zea, Boston: Allyn & Bacon. Copyright 1997 by Allyn & Bacon. Adapted by permission.

of each of the core cultural constructs enables counselors to maximize the likelihood of achieving successful counseling outcomes
with Chicano(a) clients. In addition, the framework is intended to
evaluate the various areas of interactive culture strain that may be
occurring in a client's life.

The Case Study of Luis

The case study presented here illustrates the use of the assessment
framework with a Mexican American college student during
an initial clinical interview and over the course of a counseling
relationship.

Luis (a pseudonym) was an 18-year-old, third generation Chicano freshman
who was majoring in computer science at a large, southwestern university. He
came to the university counseling center for an intake appointment to address
adjustment and transition issues related to his recent commencement of college
and chronic stress and anxiety since coming to the university. On his intake
form, Luis indicated that his racial/ethnic affiliation was "White American."
His immediate family lived in a nearby state, and he reported feeling close to
them. Luis was the oldest of four siblings "who look up to me. They and my
parents expect me to do well in college." Luis claimed his parents had also
attended college and had long-standing expectations that he would major in
computer science and become a computer technician like his father. Luis'
mother was a homemaker. Luis reported feeling a great deal of pressure to
please his family "since I'm the oldest male in my family and I don't want to
embarrass my parents by flunking out of school." He requested individual
counseling sessions to "keep me from stressing out too much and to help me
feel better about being here."

**Assessing the core psychosocial/cultural concepts during the intake
session.** While obtaining information about Luis' presenting issues through the use of a semistructured clinical interview, his
counselor also queried him during the intake session about his
level of acculturation, primary ethnic or racial identity, and family-
of-origin socialization with regard to gender role issues in order
to ascertain information about the impact of these constructs on
his presenting concerns. In responding to questions about his acculturation level and his ethnic identity, Luis reported that he
considered himself to be White because his family, which had
emigrated from Mexico many years ago, "looked more White than

Mexican." Luis reported that most of his close high school friends were White. "I also had a couple of other friends who were Mexican, but I didn't hang out with them much. They didn't fit in too well with my close friends." Luis claimed his parents were disappointed in the fact that he chose to identify himself as White, and had expressed concern to him about the fact that he allowed his friends from high school to call him Louis. He also spoke of feeling guilty about his lack of interest in learning Spanish from his parents and his disinterest in maintaining "strong roots in the Mexican culture" because he wanted to "fit in with everybody else." Luis claimed that it felt foreign to him not to have a group of people with whom he could "hang out with" at the university because he had been very popular at his high school. He reported that, in his situation at college, he had been feeling as though "I don't belong here. Everybody seems smarter than me, especially some of the other White students." Luis noticed that many of the students in his classes formed study groups that seemed to exclude him. He disclosed that he felt isolated from many parts of the campus community, "even with the Chicano students on campus." He reported having maintained an A− average in high school, and was uncertain as to why he felt anxious about performing well in college and about his ability to make friends at college. When asked about the ways in which his ethnicity had affected his life, Luis replied, "It hasn't. I don't really see myself as Chicano. I'm just a regular person."

Luis also reported that during the first week of classes his first roommate (who was White) moved out of their dorm room to live with a friend who lived a few doors down from them. Luis was assigned another roommate who was also White. He claimed that his second roommate barely stayed in their room, and Luis had heard through a friend in his dorm that his second roommate felt "uncomfortable sharing a room with a Mexican guy." When Luis confronted his roommate about this situation, his roommate denied ever having said this, but stated that perhaps Luis would feel more comfortable next semester living with "somebody who's more like you."

Information ascertained about Luis' gender role socialization included Luis' disclosure that his parents were very traditional and had high expectations of him because he was the oldest and "the first male child" in his family. He reported having felt lifelong pressure from his parents to succeed academically and socially. He shared some feelings of resentment and anger about "being put in this situation because I'm the first-born male." Luis also asserted that the primary reason he wanted to major in computer science was because his father told him it was a good career and could provide financial stability to Luis and his future family. Near the end of the intake session, he and his therapist agreed to spend time during his counseling sessions dealing with his presenting problems and with issues related to the core cultural concepts that in many ways were closely tied to his presenting concerns.

Impact of the assessment on subsequent sessions.   Over the next several counseling sessions, Luis and his counselor explored his presenting concerns and the impact of his acculturation level, ethnic identity development, and gender role socialization on his presenting problems. He processed with his therapist the familial and peer conflicts he experienced with regard to his acculturation level and ethnic identification. Luis spoke about some of the difficulties he encountered in balancing the values, norms, and expectations of both the White and Chicano cultures. As counseling progressed, Luis began to gain insight about how he had previously attempted to resolve his discomfort and tension around "being different" by identifying as White person. He was also able to discuss the cognitive dissonance he had been experiencing in identifying himself as such, and he expressed an interest in learning more about aspects of Chicano culture. Luis subsequently joined a couple of Chicano organizations, which, he reported, helped him to feel more connected with fellow Chicano students on the campus. He also claimed that he began to feel more connected to a variety of ethnically and racially diverse students on the campus as he began to embrace his ethnic identity.

Through counseling, Luis was able to express anger about the ways he had been treated by several White students on the campus (e.g., in his dorm and his classes); and he explored ways he could potentially deal with and confront future problematic incidents on the campus, specifically with regard to his living and academic situations. He discussed one particularly successful resolution of a conflict with a peer on his dorm floor in which he invited dialogue about their ethnic differences and the impact of these differences on their perception of a racial incident. He reported having come away from this discussion with a sense of pride and empowerment about having taken ownership of his ethnic identity.

As counseling progressed, Luis also began to emerge with a greater awareness of the pressures he faced in living up to the expectations of his family related to his academic major and career options. He began to explore his feelings about this phenomenon, and near the end of his individual counseling sessions, Luis disclosed that he was seriously considering changing his major to sociology and was entertaining ways to inform his parents of his impending decision. Luis reported that, through counseling, he was becoming increasingly happy with his life and his choices, and he felt as though he was increasing his ability to be more congruent and genuine with others. He also expressed an interest in becoming a member of the Hispanic Student Support Group offered through the counseling center in order to work on his ethnic identity issues in a more in-depth fashion.

Discussion of the Case Study With Regard to the Core Psychosocial/Cultural Concepts

Luis is an example of a Chicano(a) college student who presented with different levels of awareness and development in terms of the core psychosocial/cultural concepts of acculturation, ethnic/racial identity, and gender role identity. As noted earlier, the existence of differences in the levels of awareness and development across the three concepts may result in interactive culture strain. This phenomenon appeared to be particularly salient in this case. It is not uncommon for Chicano(a) college students who seek counseling to present with varying levels of awareness and development with regard to each of these concepts. However, mental health professionals may make significant clinical errors (e.g., through misdiagnosis) or may inadvertently contribute to a client's distress if they attempt to generalize their assessment of only one of these concepts to one or both of the other concepts.

Luis' level of acculturation was labeled by his therapist as *high* (as opposed to either *low* or *moderate*) as evidenced by a combination of several acculturation dimensions. First, his family had moved to the United States many years ago (Luis was a third generation U.S. Chicano.). Second, Luis claimed he did not know

Spanish, nor did he have an interest in learning this language when his parents wanted to teach it to him. Third, he experienced some role and value conflicts with regard to his familial and cultural expectations, as his parents were disappointed that he did not wish to embrace aspects of the Chicano culture that they felt were important. Fourth, Luis seemed very strongly identified with White culture in terms of his friendships primarily with White peers. Fifth, he allowed his friends to Anglicize his name (to Louis) in an attempt to "fit in more." Near the end of counseling, however, he began to acknowledge the personal consequences of "being overly identified with White culture," and he began to make changes in himself and in his interpersonal relationships as he became increasingly identified with aspects of his ethnic heritage.

Relatedly, Luis appeared to have been at a beginning level of awareness of his ethnic identity. On his intake form, he identified himself as a "White American." He felt that the length of time his family had lived in the United States had "qualified" him to characterize himself as White. Initially, he also demonstrated a lack of awareness of the ways in which his ethnicity affected his life by minimizing or denying his ethnic identity. In addition, Luis' peer network consisted mostly of White friends and a few Chicano friends whom, he claimed, did not "fit in" with his White friends. Through counseling, he began to feel an increasing sense of pride in identifying as a Chicano student. He also began to feel less distressed, and was able to develop college friendships with a range of ethnically and racially diverse peers who seemed receptive to him, probably in large part because he was making attempts to be more genuine in pridefully embracing his ethnic identity.

At the beginning of counseling, Luis' gender role identity matched that of a more traditional masculine role orientation (as opposed to feminine or androgynous). His gender role socialization from his family of origin seemed to result in a somewhat constrictive and limiting gender role identity, which ultimately caused him anguish. Luis' gender role socialization clearly reflected the idea that there were stereotypical roles for both men and women with regard to career and financial issues. In his experience, men were cast in the role of breadwinner and were encouraged to have a financially stable career in order to care for their families. Luis saw this dynamic played out with his parents, and felt some distress about the pressure of having to make decisions about his future career based solely on his ability to provide financial resources for his future family. With the help of counseling, Luis was able to identify the impact of his gender role socialization on his choice of an academic major and his subsequent career aspirations. He was also able to see the relationship between this issue and the stress he experienced in trying to do well in an academic major in which he was not particularly interested. Through the examination of some of these gender role issues, Luis was eventually able to explore more personally congruent career options for himself, and emerged with a greater sense of his beliefs and values regarding his gender role identity.

The interactive culture strain experienced by Luis as he attempted to integrate the multiple levels of his awareness and development related to his degree of acculturation, ethnic identity development, and gender role socialization resulted in psychological distress. He experienced some adjustment problems related to the integration of these processes. Luis' acculturation level seemed to be a primary cultural dimension that determined his cognitive, affective, and behavioral experiences and that influenced these phenomenon in ways that became problematic for him. The difficulties he experienced certainly affected his ethnic identity development and gender role socialization, which led to a notable amount of interactive culture strain. As Luis became more grounded in his Chicano identity, he was able to view his decision to acculturate as a means of avoiding dealing with his ethnic identity. He also began to make more conscious choices to embrace his identity in a more prideful and personally congruent way.

Summary

As illustrated in the case study, the assessment of the psychosocial concepts of acculturation, ethnic identity development, and gender role socialization may serve an important function in understanding the impact of these cultural dimensions on the presenting concerns of Chicano(a) college students who present for counseling. Such assessment may play a critical role in diagnosis and treatment planning. Counselors who use this type of practical framework will find that they obtain potentially rich information that may help them to provide culturally sensitive and competent psychological interventions to Chicano(a) students and to other ethnic/racial populations as well.

References

Aguirre, A., Jr., & Martinez, R. (1993). *Chicanos in higher education: Issues and dilemmas for the 21st century* (ASHE-ERIC Higher Education Report No. 3). Washington, DC: George Washington University, School of Education and Human Development.

American Psychological Association. (1993). Guidelines for providers of psychological services to ethnic, linguistic, and culturally diverse populations. *American Psychologist, 48*, 45–48.

Arbona, C., & Novy, D. (1990). Noncognitive dimensions as predictors of college success among Black, Mexican American, and White students. *Journal of College Student Development, 31*, 415–422.

Astin, A. W. (1982). *Minorities in higher education.* San Francisco: Jossey-Bass.

Atkinson, D. R., Casas, J. M., & Abreu, J. (1992). Mexican American acculturation, counselor ethnicity and cultural sensitivity, and perceived counselor competence. *Journal of Counseling Psychology, 39*, 515–520.

Barón, A., Jr. (1991). Counseling Chicano college students. In C. C. Lee & B. L. Richardson (Eds.), *Multicultural issues in counseling: New approaches to diversity* (pp. 171–184). Alexandria, VA: American Association for Counseling and Development.

Barón, A., & Constantine, M. G. (1997). A conceptual framework for conducting psychotherapy with Mexican American college students. In J. Garcia & M. C. Zea (Eds.), *Psychological interventions and research with Latino populations* (pp. 108–124). Boston: Allyn & Bacon.

Bem, S. L. (1974). The measurement of psychological androgyny. *Journal of Consulting and Clinical Psychology, 42*, 155–162.

Casas, J. M., & Vasquez, M. J. T. (1989). Counseling the Hispanic client: A theoretical and applied perspective. In P. Pedersen, J. G. Draguns, W. J. Lonner, & J. E. Trimble (Eds.), *Counseling across cultures* (3rd ed., pp. 153–175). Honolulu: University of Hawaii Press.

Castro, F. G. (1977). *Level of acculturation and related considerations in psychotherapy with Spanish-speaking/surnamed clients* (Occasional Paper No. 3). Los Angeles: University of California, Los Angeles, Spanish Speaking Mental Health Research Center.

Chronicle of Higher Education Almanac [Special issue]. (1994). *Chronicle of Higher Education, 41.*

Cortese, A. (1992). Academic achievement in Mexican Americans: Sociolegal and cultural factors. *Latino Studies Journal, 3,* 31–47.

Cuellar, I., Harris, L. C., & Jasso, R. (1980). An acculturation rating scale for Mexican-American normal and clinical populations. *Hispanic Journal of Behavioral Sciences, 2,* 199–217.

Duran, R. (1983). *Hispanics' education and background.* New York: College Entrance Examination Board.

Fiske, E. (1988). The undergraduate Hispanic experience: A case of juggling two cultures. *Change, 20,* 29–33.

Gandara, P. (1982). Passing through the eye of the needle: High achieving Chicanas. *Hispanic Journal of Behavioral Sciences, 4,* 167–180.

Griffith, J., Frase, M., & Ralph, J. (1989). American education: The challenge of change. *Population Bulletin, 44*(4).

Helms, J. E. (1994). Racial identity and career assessment. *Journal of Career Assessment, 2,* 199–209.

Helms, J. E. (1995). An update of Helm's White and people of color racial identity models. In J. G. Ponterotto, J. M. Casas, L. A. Suzuki, & C. M. Alexander (Eds.), *Handbook of multicultural counseling* (pp. 181–198). Thousand Oaks, CA: Sage.

Humphreys, L. (1988). Trends in levels of academic achievement of Blacks and other minorities. *Intelligence, 12,* 231–260.

Landrine, H., & Klonoff, E. A. (1994). The African American acculturation scale: Development, reliability, and validity. *Journal of Black Psychology, 20,* 104–127.

Landrine, H., & Klonoff, E. A. (1995). The African American acculturation scale II: Cross-validation and short form. *Journal of Black Psychology, 21,* 124–152.

Lopez, S. R., Lopez, A. A., & Fong, K. T. (1991). Mexican Americans' initial preferences for counselors: The role of ethnic factors. *Journal of Counseling Psychology, 38,* 487–496.

Lunneborg, C., & Lunneborg, P. (1986). Beyond prediction: The challenge of minority achievement in higher education. *Journal of Multicultural Counseling and Development, 14,* 77–84.

Madrid, A. (1988). Missing people and others. *Change, 20,* 55–59.

Mendoza, R. H., & Martinez, J. L. (1981). The measurement of acculturation. In A. Barón, Jr. (Ed.), *Explorations in Chicano psychology* (pp. 71–82). New York: Praeger.

Miranda, M. R., Andujo, E., Caballero, I. L., Guerrero, C., & Ramos, R. A. (1976). Mexican American dropouts in psychotherapy as related to level of acculturation. In M. R. Miranda (Ed.), *Psychotherapy with the Spanish-speaking: Issues in research and service delivery.* Los Angeles: University of California, Los Angeles, Spanish Speaking Mental Health Research Center.

Miranda, M. R., & Castro F. G. (1977). Culture distance and success in psychotherapy with Spanish-speaking clients. In J. L. Martinez (Ed.), *Chicano psychology* (pp. 249–262). New York: Academic Press.

National Council of La Raza. (1990). *Hispanic education: A statistical portrait 1990.* Washington, DC: Author.

Olmedo, E. L., Martinez, J. L., & Martinez, S. R. (1978). Measure of acculturation for Chicano adolescents. *Psychological Reports, 42,* 159–170.

Pennock-Roman, M. (1988). *The status of research on the Scholastic Aptitude Test (SAT) and Hispanic students in postsecondary education.* Princeton, NJ: Educational Testing Service.

Ponce, F. Q., & Atkinson, D. R. (1989). Mexican American acculturation, counselor ethnicity, counseling style, and perceived counselor credibility. *Journal of Counseling Psychology, 36,* 203–208.

Ramirez, M. (1991). *Psychology of the Americas: Multicultural perspectives in personality and mental health.* New York: Pergamon.

Rogler, L. H., Malgady, R. G., & Rodriguez, O. (1989). *Hispanics and mental health: A framework for research.* Malabar, FL: Robert E. Krieger.

Ruiz, R. A., Casas, J. M., & Padilla, A. M. (1977). *Culturally relevant behavioristic counseling.* Los Angeles: University of California, Los Angeles, Spanish Speaking Mental Health Research Center.

Sanchez, A. R., & Atkinson, D. R. (1983). Mexican-American cultural commitment preference for counselor ethnicity, and willingness to use counseling. *Journal of Counseling Psychology, 30,* 215–220.

Sedlacek, W. E. (1987). Black students on White campuses: Twenty years of research. *Journal of College Student Personnel, 28,* 484–495.

Sedlacek, W. E., & Brooks, G. C., Jr. (1976). *Racism in American education: A model for change.* Chicago: Nelson-Hall.

Spence, J. T., Helmreich, R. L., & Stapp, J. The Personal Attributes Questionnaire: A measure of sex-role stereotypes and masculinity-femininity. *JSAS Catalogue of Selected Documents in Psychology, 4,* 127.

Sue, D. W., & Sue, D. (1990). *Counseling the culturally different: Theory and practice* (2nd ed.). New York: Wiley.

Szapocznik, J., Scopetta, M. A., & Tillman, W. (1979). What changes, what stays the same, and what affects acculturative change? In Szapocznik & M. C. Herrera (Eds.), *Cuban Americans: Acculturation adjustment and the family* (pp. 32–44). Washington, DC: COSSMHO.

Tracey, T. J., & Sedlacek, W. E. (1984). Noncognitive variables in predicting academic success by race. *Measurement and Evaluation in Guidance, 16,* 172–178.

Tracey, T. J., & Sedlacek, W. E. (1985). The relationship of noncognitive variables to academic success: A longitudinal comparison by race. *Journal of College Student Personnel, 26,* 405–410.

Tracey, T. J., & Sedlacek. W. E. (1987). Prediction of college graduation using noncognitive variables by race. *Measurement and Evaluation in Counseling and Development, 19,* 177–184.

U. S. Bureau of the Census. (1987). *The Hispanic population of the United States: March 1986 and 1987* (Advanced report, Current Population Reports). Washington, DC: U.S. Government Printing Office.

U.S. Bureau of the Census. (1991). *The Hispanic population in the United States, March 1990.* Washington, DC: U.S. Government Printing Office.

Willie, C. (1987). On excellence and equity in higher education. *Journal of Negro Education, 56,* 485–492.

Young, G. (1992). Chicana college students on the Texas-Mexico border: Transition and transformation. *Hispanic Journal of Behavioral Sciences, 14,* 341–352.

17

PUERTO RICANS IN THE COUNSELING PROCESS:
The Dynamics of Ethnicity and Its Societal Context

Jesse M. Vazquez

A lthough Puerto Rico has been a territory of the United States since 1898, many Americans still do not know, for example, where the island is geographically located, or that all Puerto Ricans have been American citizens since 1917, or that they are a racially heterogeneous population, or that Puerto Rican monetary currency is American currency, and so on. The degree of cultural illiteracy that exists among non-Puerto-Rican Americans about Puerto Rico and the Puerto Ricans is astounding. Unfortunately, the lay public knows far more about the negative Puerto Rican stereotypes than it does about matters cultural, political, historical, and psychological.

Puerto Ricans now constitute the second largest (Chicanos are the largest) ethnically distinct Latino group in the continental United States. Over 2.5 million Puerto Ricans live in the United States, and about 3.3 million still reside in Puerto Rico (U.S. Bureau of the Census, 1990). Although emigration from Puerto Rico to New York had been occurring since the early 1900s (and well before that under Spanish rule), the early and middle 1950s marked the most dramatic high point of the Puerto Rican migration to the United States. During that high watermark of migration, approximately 80% of the migrants settled in New York City (Fitzpatrick, 1987). Since that time, for well over 40 years, Puerto Ricans have continued to migrate not only to New York but also to other major urban centers in the northeastern and midwestern

315

parts of the United States (e.g., Boston, Chicago, Newark, Philadelphia, Trenton, and other urban centers across the country). New York City, however, continues to be home to the greatest number of Puerto Ricans in the continental United States, including Hawaii and Alaska. A significant colony of Puerto Ricans had taken root in Hawaii beginning in about 1902; Puerto Rican workers were sent to the Hawaiian Islands to cut sugar cane and pick pineapples (Centro de Estudios Puertorriqueños, 1977; Silva & Souza, 1982). According to recent estimates, one out of every eight New Yorkers is Puerto Rican, and Puerto Ricans make up approximately 12.6% of New York City's population (Rodriguez, 1989).

For many Puerto Ricans, however, the pattern of migration is circular (between the United States and Puerto Rico), a phenomenon that sustains cultural, linguistic, and family connections and loyalties. And according to Bonilla (1989), the circular migration—the dynamics and causes of which he places into the larger framework of an advanced international capitalism—is also creating a startling similarity in worldviews and problems shared between those who reside on the island and those who, for a time, find themselves in the United States. This phenomenon is greatly facilitated by Puerto Ricans' U.S. citizenship, ease of travel, and the island's political and economic connection with the United States as well as the place that Puerto Rico occupies in the larger network of the global economy.

The first person chronicles of the earlier migrants, the work of novelists, and the studies of historians, sociologists, anthropologists, and community activists reflect the toughness of spirit and intellect of those Puerto Ricans who served as the pioneers and formed the first *barrios* or colonies in New York City and in other cities throughout the United States (see Colon, 1982; Fitzpatrick, 1987; Iglesias, 1984; Mohr, 1985; Morales, 1986; Padilla, E., 1958; Padilla, F., 1987; Pantoja, 1989; Rivera, Edward, 1982; Rivera, Eugenie, 1987; Rodriguez, 1989; Sanchez-Korrol, 1994).

There is a history of struggle among Puerto Ricans, both on the island and in the United States. It is a struggle against the abuses and oppression of colonialism and imperialism of the Spanish and then the North Americans; it is a struggle to maintain a unique cultural heritage and identity amidst technological change and the overwhelming external and internal pressures to adopt and adapt to things American. For the Puerto Ricans in the United States, it is also a struggle to survive economically, culturally, linguistically, and psychologically. Counselors who choose to work with Puerto Rican clients must begin to appreciate the complexity and legacy of this social and historical reality. Unquestionably, the impact of these historical events has played a critical role in shaping the collective social, economic, and psychological worlds of the Puerto Ricans who continue to live on the island as well as those who have chosen to build communities in the United States.

Socioeconomics: Implications for Counselors

A small percentage of the Puerto Ricans in the United States have climbed out of poverty and into the so-called American mainstream, but the vast majority of Puerto Ricans in the United States continue to live at or below the poverty line. Incredibly, 30.9% of Puerto Rican families find themselves below the poverty level (U.S. Bureau of the Census, 1990).

Another statistical reality that continues to have significant implications for counselors in schools and social service agencies is that 39.6% of families in the Puerto Rican community are headed by females (U.S. Bureau of the Census, 1989). The following characterization, proposed by Reyes (1987), reflects the potential complexity of social, economic, and psychological distress brought about by specific external realities:

... the prototype of the Puerto Rican of today in the United States is a woman of 25 who dropped out of school, is the head of a household, is unemployed, and has two children to maintain and educate. This is so, in part, because the majority of Puerto Ricans are women (53.2%) and the median years of school completed by Puerto Ricans is 11.2. (p. 2)

Rodriguez (1989) has suggested that this kind of statistical profile does not portend the breakdown of the Puerto Rican family, as so many interpreters of these data might have us believe. It is critical that counselors who work within the Puerto Rican community suspend their own beliefs about what they consider a typical family as well as explore the sources of strength that keep these families together. However, the real issue, as Rodriguez noted, is not the increased number of female-headed households but poverty.

These issues represent aspects of the socioeconomic challenges that have a direct impact on the lives of Puerto Ricans and that in one form or another become the concerns of the counselor, even though they may seem far removed from the area of cultural beliefs, attitudes, and values of the Puerto Rican migrant. The challenges, by and large, are direct results of (a) the social and economic structure that exists in the United States; (b) the history of political, economic, and military control exercised over the people and resources of the island since the United States invaded and annexed Puerto Rico; and (c) the problems that spring from the fact that the "Puerto Ricans are both the only colonial group to arrive en masse, and the first racially heterogeneous group to migrate to the U.S. on a large scale" (Rodriguez, 1989, p. xiv). All of these conditions make for an environment guaranteed to create stress for the migrant who finds his or her way to an American metropolis. Counselors should be able to incorporate these kinds of observations into their work and to set them into a broader societal framework.

Racial/Ethnic Identity and Racism: Implications for Counselors

In one of the earliest community studies of Puerto Rican adaptation to life in an urban American setting, Padilla (1958) focused on the issue of racial and ethnic identity of Puerto Ricans in the United states. She noted that "both in Puerto Rico and in the United States social race is an important aspect of social life, but *race* is looked at, defined, and appraised in different ways in the two countries" (p. 69). This seemingly straightforward, yet complex, observation has been repeated many times in the literature since then, and has been linked to psychological stress in response to the chronic and persistent racism Puerto Ricans experience in the United States (Betances, 1971, 1972, 1973; Fitzpatrick, 1987; Longres, 1974; Martinez, 1986; Rodriguez, 1980, 1989).

If an individual is perceived to be phenotypically non-White in the United States, or if he or she is believed to be a member of an ethnic group (in this case Puerto Rican) that has been socially designated as non-White, all members of that group are then considered socially non-White regardless of within-group variability in phenotypes. Herein lies the psychological and social dilemma for many Puerto Ricans.

Puerto Ricans first identify culturally as Puerto Ricans and then secondarily proceed to make racial distinctions among a variety of physical traits, such as skin color, hair texture, thickness of lips, and nose configuration. Different combinations of these traits place the individual—phenotypically, that is—into one of several racially rooted categories, which as indicated are based on more than skin color: *blanco* (phenotypically White with a variety of Caucasian features), *trigueño* (brunette type, wheat color), *indio* (dark skin straight black hair), *morenos* (dark skin with a variety of Negroid or Caucasion features), and *negro* (equivalent to dark skinned Black people in the United States) (Rodriguez, 1989).

When forced to identify within the framework of the prevailing racial-social structure of the United States, many Puerto Ricans, particularly during the earliest stages of their migration, face stress and confusion while trying to fit into the Black-White dichotomy offered by the American racial and social framework. If an individual's primary anchor of identity is cultural, and he or she is forced to identify as either White or Black, that person is essentially being deprived of a personal sense of identity (Rodriguez,1989). This is especially confounding in families and in a population in which racial phenotypes are quite varied. If I identify as Black, or am identified as Black in a family that contains significant racial variation, what does that do to my sense of connection and identification as a member of that family? How do I feel about my lighter brother or sister who may have benefitted from this kind of perceptual distinction? Further, what is the emotional price paid when the experience is one that Rodriguez (1989) called *perceptual dissonance*? In such a case, the individual sees himself or herself in one way, and others see the individual quite differently. The experience, "particularly as it pertains to race, is clearly an unsettling process" (p. 76).

On an island where well into the latter part of the 19th century the merchants and landowners were primarily from Spain and other Western European countries, the "matter of color was also a matter of class" (Martinez, 1986, p. 39). According to Martinez, if "a non-White or racially mixed individual should rise in class status, then that person was accorded the deference of that class and the color disappeared" (p. 39). That is, racial identity, although not addressed directly, assumed less importance as measured against the individual's achievements as a university professor, accomplished musician, lawyer, engineer, or successful public servant.

Today, after nearly 100 years of an American presence on the island, and more than 40 years since the beginning of the huge migrations to the mainland, the matter of racial identity and confusion persists in expressions of how Puerto Ricans see themselves and how they are racially perceived and designated by non-Puerto-Ricans. For those who are involved in counseling Puerto Ricans, the issue of racial identity will be a repeated theme in the counseling process. Conflicts or uncertainty regarding racial intermarriage, incidents of racism and racial injustice, questions pertaining to racial/ethnic identity, and other related issues will continue to be raised in the counseling process as long as race and ethnicity continue to play a central role in the American social and political structure.

The Case Study of Nydia

The case study presented here illustrates the challenge in the counseling process of working with a client who specifically raises questions related to racial and ethnic identity.

Nydia is a 30-year-old Puerto Rican women, born in Puerto Rico, who at the age of 2 migrated with her family to the United States. Nydia sought counseling shortly after her non-Latino fiance made his first visit to meet her family. She came to me for counseling because she had heard that I was Puerto Rican and believed that I would be able to help her sort out the tension and fears that she was experiencing after her fiance's visit.

Although her fiance knew that Puerto Ricans were racially heterogeneous, he had no idea that this broad range of variability of racial phenotypes could also be seen within one nuclear family. He quickly identified some of the darker complected members in Nydia's family as Black and was quite taken aback by this observation. Up to that moment he had assumed (based on his American perception of race) that because Nydia was phenotypically White all of her siblings were also White. He asked her what she was: was she Black or was she White? As far as Nydia was concerned, she had always simply seen herself as a

Puerto Rican who happened to be phenotypically White with some darker and some lighter complected siblings and cousins. However, his subsequent persistent probing about Nydia's racial identity and pressing inquiries about her family's racial origins were sufficient to create a panic in her. Was he really telling her that this might be sufficient reason to call off their engagement? Nydia was concerned about her fiance's preoccupation with her racial identity; and she was also uncertain about her own racio/ethnic identity at this point. Although she never denied her identity as a Puerto Rican, she had never really come to terms with the complexity of her own racial identity.

After conducting a routine history, the counselor's approach was to encourage Nydia to examine her ethnic identity as a Puerto Rican woman in the United States. What did it mean to her to have grown up as a Puerto Rican in New York? What was it like for her? A detailed open exploration of the client's *ethnic self* or ethnic psychohistory will reveal a complex web of emotional experiences that ultimately allows the client an opportunity to examine more openly an aspect of the self that has heretofore remained vague, hidden, and undefined. This dynamic is quite common in American society. Although the American mythology espouses a so-called melting pot ideology, the real message we receive is that we must hide (or make little mention of) who we are ethnically. Americans are asked to deny racial or cultural contradictions, especially when they are apparent or experienced as painful. Those who are unable to grasp the reality of racial and ethnic identity in American society have a tendency to create a kind of new personal mythology about who they are ethnically and racially.

As a society, Americans rarely challenge their ethnic perceptions of self and others, and the societal myths that belie the trail of tears that is a central part America's racial and ethnic history. Instead, they manage to construct personal notions about who they are ethnically, and what other people think they are. Those who are members of the dominant society, particularly those who are considered White in this society, seem to have a greater tendency to accept an acculturated behavior pattern consistent with the core American society. However, people of color (and Puerto Ricans regardless of phenotype are placed in this category) who are still socially and economically marginal in the society are much more easily able to get in touch with this illusive ethnic self. Nydia was no exception. She began to look carefully at her family's migration history, the existence of racism in American society, and how a multiplicity of social and economic realities had shaped a good deal of her life. Her need to drop out of school, and her return to begin college again in her late twenties, were events that she reexamined from a variety of perspectives. She reevaluated her own personal success in a blue-collar career in light of the choices she had as well as in light of the limited and imposed choices available to her family and to thousands of other Puerto Ricans who had come to the United States in order to survive. Looking at specific critical incidents in her life through the lens of her ethnic self gradually allowed Nydia to begin to come to terms with who she is ethnically and racially. Eventually, Nydia was able to present effectively some questions of her own, which sought to clarify her fiance's racial belief system and some of his own preoccupations with race and racial identity.

A useful approach in cases like this in which ethnicity or ethnic identity plays a role in shaping affect and cognition is first to explore the structural and functional aspects of race and ethnicity in American society, and the impact of these on the development of the individual, and then attempt to connect these sociological and anthropological domains with the feelings, experiences, and meaning of these events in the life of the client. How has the client experienced these events? What is the meaning of these events in the client's life? A blend of cognitive, phenomenological, existential, and didactic (sociological, anthropological, and historical discourse) strategies allows the therapist to link the many layers of experience and external events that contribute to this kind of inner conflict.

The linkage between these domains is critical for movement in either the counseling process or in the educational process. There is no diagnosis because there is no identifiable disorder or disease process going on. However, there is distress that grows out of the client's perception of self (ethnically and racially), and others' perceptions of the client.

The often-heard comment, "that's funny, you don't *look* Puerto Rican" tells worlds about the perception of the speaker. If the Puerto Rican accepts the phrase, it can be assumed that there is confusion about the self in relation to others.

Martinez saw this racial identity confusion as a phenomenon that will continue to exist as long as Puerto Ricans "avoid or deny their reality in American society" (1986, p. 45). Rodriguez (1989), however, considered that the very ambiguity of racial and cultural identity can be viewed as a potential source of strength, and as a healthy sign of adaptation, that perhaps will pose a direct "challenge to the U.S. bifurcation of race" (p. 77). She found that many Puerto Ricans have been able to move back and forth between the White, Black, and Hispanic worlds. This, she suggested, "may be rooted in the ability to see oneself in a variety of ways" (p. 77). A new generation of Puerto Ricans may be emerging as truly tricultural, and perhaps bilingual or even trilingual. Is it a denial of a racial reality, or is it a forging of a new identity? Within the context of a rapidly changing racial and cultural America, this idea may begin to gain more meaning as racioethnic demographic balances shift in the 21st century.

Conclusion

Nydia's case raises a number of psychoculturally rooted issues that are frequently encountered when working with Puerto Rican clients. In order to serve the Puerto Rican client more effectively, the counselor must attend to a wide range of issues, including not only racial identity but also the importance of the continuity of language, implications of class, changing family patterns, and a societal structure that has shaped the migration and the life chances of Puerto Ricans in the United States and in Puerto Rico. In effect, the counselor must be fully prepared to explore issues that go well beyond the purview of the traditional counseling domain, and to use techniques and strategies that may challenge the current order of things.

Because of the central role of culture in the field of multicultural counseling, we should remain constantly vigilant and question the emerging literature that attempts to broaden our understanding of other groups but may reify cultural patterns or traits that may be situational and in the process of change. The cultural inventory approach, so common in much of the current counseling literature, enumerates traits or characteristics such as eye contact, kinetics, gender roles, and family patterns of Puerto Ricans and other ethnic groups in American society. But it is an approach that can hinder our attempts to help and in the final analysis reify and make static that which is by experience a most dynamic process. Understanding cultural patterns in a vacuum, without engaging in a more complex dialectical assessment of the client's world at that moment and historically, inevitably leads to the most superficial cultural pronouncements of a people.

Despite the strides that have been made in the last 20 years, we continue to read research literature that misinterprets cultural minutia and presents these as fixed unchanging phenomena. For example, some authors continue to distort the concepts of *machismo* and *marianismo* by presenting misleading and flattened descriptions of a complex set of behaviors that are shaped by a multiplicity of forces. Others propose that "passivity and docility" of Puerto Rican and other Latinos are still a part of the "character" of a people, and still others are preoccupied with trying to establish a pan-Hispanic psychological profile that defies the complex history of migration and immigration from the Caribbean and South and Central America. But Latinos in the United States are a complex people racially, culturally, politically, and historically, and to homogenize the Latino in psychological terms is misleading. Efforts to do so in a pseudoscientific way contributes to the oversimplification of experience. The rush to establish neat phases or stages in psychocultural development can do us more harm than good. Far better, as suggested, is to contextualize the issues at hand and to look at a broad range of factors contributing to the individual's behavior and to cultural and societal change.

Cultural observations, such as group identity, differing attitudes towards family, attitudes towards outsiders, and ideas of male dominance, can—if erroneously reported in the literature—have an adverse affect on the perceptions, strategies, and actions of counselors. This can be problematic, especially if these kinds of "cultural data" at one time or another are merged into the counseling process. Cultural data should never be seen as immutable. There is little argument with the idea that cultural specifics are valuable adjuncts in the counseling process; but how the cross-cultural practitioner validates, evaluates, and judiciously incorporates these observations into his or her intervention strategies warrants careful consideration.

Bock (1988), in his work in psychological anthropology, provocatively titled his prelude and postlude chapters with the following propositions: "All anthropology is psychological" and "All psychology is cultural." These seemingly paradoxical assertions are clearly intended to provoke consideration of the cultural roots of psychological thinking and practice, the psychological dimensions of all anthropological and social observations and conceptualizations, and their sources. This chapter on counseling Puerto Ricans should be seen simply as a guide to an approach, not a cookbook formula. It is suggestive of the complexities of the human experience and a snapshot of a people that continue to struggle in a rapidly changing world.

Counselors can anticipate working with Puerto Rican clients who may express a wide range of degrees of acculturation as well as with those who have a clear sense of who they are ethnically and racially. Many may adapt to the mainland simply as an accommodation for the sake of survival, whereas others may reassert their identity in forms that may be outmoded and perhaps dysfunctional in a postindustrial world. Still others will fashion new ways of assuring their future while holding on to what is valuable and enduring in their community of memory.

References

Betances, S. (1971). Puerto Rican youth: Race and the search for self. *The Rican, 1*(1), 4–13.

Betances, S. (1972). The prejudice of having no prejudice in Puerto Rico. Part I. *The Rican, 2*, 41–54.

Betances, S. (1973). The prejudice of having no prejudice in Puerto Rico. Part II. *The Rican, 3*, 22–37.

Bock, P. K. (1988). *Rethinking psychological anthropology: Continuity and change in the study of human action.* New York: Freeman.

Bonilla, F. (1989). La circulación migratoria en la década actual. *Boletín Del Centro De Estudios Puertorriqueños, 2*(6), 55–59.

Centro de Estudios Puertorriqueños. (1977). *Documents of the Puerto Rican migration: Hawaii, Cuba, Santo Domingo, and Equador.* New York: Research Foundation of the City University of New York.

Colon, J. (1982). *A Puerto Rican in New York and other sketches.* New York: International.

Fitzpatrick, J. P. (1987). *Puerto Ricans: The meaning of migration to the mainland* (2nd ed.). Englewood Cliffs, NJ: Prentice-Hall.

Iglesias, C. A. (1984). *Memoirs of Bernardo Vega: A contribution to the history of the Puerto Rican community in New York* (Juan Flores, Trans.). New York: Monthly Review Press. (Original work published as *Memorias de Bernardo Vega*, 1977).

Longres, J. F. (1974, February). Racism and its effects on Puerto Rican continentals. *Social Casework*, pp. 67–99.

Martinez, R. (1986). Puerto Ricans: White or non-White? *Explorations in Ethnic Studies: The Journal of the National Association for Ethnic Studies*, 9(2), 37–48.

Mohr, N. (1985). *Rituals of survival: A woman's portfolio*. Houston: Artes.

Morales, J. (1986). *Puerto Rican poverty and migration: We just had to try elsewhere*. New York: Praeger.

Padilla, E. (1958). *Up from Puerto Rico*. New York: Columbia University Press.

Padilla, F. (1987). *Puerto Rican Chicago*. Notre Dame, IN: University of Notre Dame Press.

Pantoja, A. (1989). Puerto Ricans in New York: A historical and community development perspective. *Boletín Del Centro de Estudios Puertorriqueños*, 2(5), 20–31.

Reyes, L. O. (1987). *Demographics of Puerto Rican-Latino students in New York and the U.S.* New York: Aspira.

Rivera, Edward. (1982). *Family installments: Memories of growing up Hispanic*. New York: Morrow.

Rivera, Eugenie. (1987). The Puerto Rican colony of Lorain, Ohio. *Boletín Del Centro De Estudios Puertorriqueños*, 2(1), 11–23.

Rodriguez, C. (1980) Puerto Ricans: Between Black and White. In C. Rodriguez, V. Sanchez-Korrol, & O. Alers. (Eds.), *The Puerto Rican struggle: Essays on survival in the U.S.* (pp. 20–30). New York: Puerto Rican Migration Research Consortium.

Rodriguez, C. (1989). *Puerto Ricans born in the U.S.A.* Boston: Unwin Hyman.

Sanchez-Korrol, V. E. (1994). *From colonia to community: The history of Puerto Ricans in New York City, 1917–1948*. Berkeley: University of California Press.

Silva, M. N., & Souza, B. C. (1982). The Puerto Ricans in Hawaii: On becoming Hawaii's people. *The Puerto Rican Journal*, 1(1) 29–39.

U.S. Bureau of the Census. (1989). *The Hispanic population in the United States: March 1988* (Current Population Reports, Series P-20, No. 438). Washington, DC: U.S. Government Printing Office.

U.S. Bureau of the Census. (1990). *The Hispanic population in the United States: March 1989* (Current Population Reports, Series P-20, No. 444). Washington, DC: U.S. Government Printing Office.

Resources

Community Agencies, Research Institutes, and Other Organizations

Aspira of New York, Inc., 332 East 149th Street, Bronx, NY 10451, (212) 292-2690.

Center for Puerto Ricans Studies (Centro de Estudios Puertorriqueños), Hunter College of the City University of New York, 695 Park Avenue, New York, NY 10021.

Hispanic Research Center, Fordham University, Bronx, NY 10458.

Institute for Puerto Rican Policy, 286 Fifth Avenue, Suite 805, New York, NY 10001-4512, (212) 564-1075.

Institute for the Puerto Rican/Hispanic Elderly, 105 East 22nd Street, New York, NY 10010.

Puerto Rican Council on Higher Education (% Center for Puerto Rican Studies), Hunter College of the City University of New York, 695 Park Avenue, New York, NY 10021.

Puerto Rican Family Institute, 116 West 14th Street, New York, NY 10011.

Puerto Rican/Hispanic Education Roundtable, Hunter College of the City University of New York, 695 Park Avenue, New York, NY 10021.

National Congress for Puerto Rican Rights, 160 West Lippincott, Philadelphia, PA 19133.

Additional References

Acosta Belen, E. (Ed.) (1979). *The Puerto Rican Woman*. New York: Praeger.

Canino, I. A., Earley, B. F., & Rogler, L. (1980). *The Puerto Rican child in New York City: Stress and mental health*. New York: Fordham University, Hispanic Research Center.

Comas-Diaz, L. (1982). Enriching self-concept through a Puerto Rican cultural awareness program. *Personnel and Guidance Journal, 60*(5), 506–508.

Comas-Diaz, L., Arroyo, A. L., Lovelace, J. C. (1982). Enriching self-concept through a Puerto Rican cultural awareness program. *Personnel and Guidance Journal, 60*(5), 306–307.

De La Cancela, V. (1988). Labor pains: Puerto Rican males in transition. *Centro Boletin, 2*, 41–55.

De La Cancela, V., & Zavala-Martinez, I. (1983). An analysis of culturalism in Latino mental health: Folk medicine as a case in point. *Hispanic Journal of Behavioral Sciences, 5*, 251–274.

Fernandez Olmos, M. (1989–1990). Growing up Puertorriqueña: The feminist bildungsroman and the novels of Nicholasa Mohr and Magali Garcia Ramis. *Centro Boletin, 2*, 56–73.

Fitzpatrick, J. P., & Gurak, D. T. (1979). *Hispanic intermarriage in New York City: 1975*. New York: Fordham University, Hispanic Research Center.

Garcia Coll, C. T., & de Lourdes Mattai, M. (1989). *The psychosocial development of Puerto Rican women*. New York: Praeger.

Gurin, G. (1986). Research issues: Drinking behavior, problems, and treatment among mainland Puerto Ricans. *Fordham University Research Bulletin, 9*(2), 1–7.

Perez, S. (1993, August). *Moving from the margins: Puerto Rican young men and family poverty* [Poverty Project]. Washington, DC: National Council of La Raza.

Rivera, A. N. (1984). *Hacia una psicoterapia par el Puertorriqueño*. Rio Piedras: CEDEPP.

Rivera-Batiz, F. L., & Santiago, C. (1994). *Puerto Ricans in the United States: A changing reality*. Washington, DC: National Puerto Rican Coalition.

Rogler, L. H., Santana Cooney, R., Constantino, G., Earley, B. F., Grossman, B., Gurak, D. T., Malgady, R., & Rodriguez, O. (1983). *A conceptual framework for mental health research on Hispanic populations*. New York: Fordham University, Hispanic Research Center.

Rodriguez, C. E. (1996) . Racial themes in the literature: Puerto Ricans and other Latinos. In G. Haslip-Viera & S. Baver (Eds.), *Latinos in New York: Communities in transition* (pp. 104–125). Notre Dame, IN: University of Notre Dame Press.

Rodriguez-Fraticelli, C. (1986). *Education and imperialism: The Puerto Rican Experience in higher education, 1898–1986*. New York: Hunter College of the City University of New York, Centro de Estudios Puertorriqueños.

Steward, J. H., Manners, R. A., Wolf, E. R., Padilla-Seda, E., Mintz, S. W., & Scheele, R. L. (1956) *The people of Puerto Rico: A study in social anthropology*. Urbana: University of Illinois Press.

Vazquez, J. M. (1975) *Expressed ethnic orientation and its relationship to the quality of student-counselor rapport as reported by Puerto Rican college students*. Unpublished doctoral dissertation, New York University.

Vazquez, J. M. (1977). Accounting for ethnicity in the counseling relationship: A study of Puerto Rican college students. *Ethnic Groups, 1*, 297–318.

Vazquez, J. M. (1986). The ethnic matrix: Implications for human service practitioners. *Explorations in Ethnic Studies: The Journal of the National Association for Ethnic Studies, 9*, 1–18.

Vazquez, J. M. (1988). Multicultural issues in career counseling: Puerto Ricans and other Latinos in the counseling relationship. *Career Development Specialists' Network, 2*(5), 4–5.

Westfried, A. H. (1985). *Three Puerto Rican families.* Salem, WI: Sheffield.

Zavala-Martinez, I. (1988). *En la lucha*: The economic and socioemotional struggles of Puerto Rican women. In L. Fulani (Ed.), *The psychopathology of everyday racism and sexism* (pp. 3–24). New York: Harrington Park Press.

Zavala-Martinez, I. (1994a). *Entremundos:* The psychological dialectics of Puerto Rican migration and its implications for health. In C. Lamberty & C. Garcia Coll (Eds.), *Puerto Rican women and children: Issues in health, growth, and development* (pp. 29–37). New York: Plenum Press.

Zavala-Martinez, I. (1994b). *¿Quien soy?* Who am I? Identity issues for Puerto Rican adolescents. In E. P. Salett & D. R. Koslow (Eds.), *Race, ethnicity, and self-identity in multicultural perspective* (pp. 89–116). Washington, DC: National Multicultural Institute.

The Arab American Experience

Dynamic international and social political events make it mandatory that Americans gain a greater understanding of the centuries-old cultural traditions of the Arabic-speaking world. Within the context of rapidly changing events taking place in that part of the world, Americans of Arab descent and their cultural traditions are gaining greater recognition in the United States. It is therefore incumbent upon professionals from every sector of American society to become more knowledgeable about important aspects of Arab and Arab American culture. As part of this, professional counselors must develop an understanding of the cultural dynamics associated with Arab American mental health and psychosocial development.

Arab Americans trace their cultural origins to the Middle East and northern Africa. They are a heterogeneous cultural group differing in ethnic background and religious affiliation. The most significant dynamics of Arab American culture that need to be considered in counseling are religion and family unity. The traditions of both Christian and Muslim religions influence basic attitudes, values, and behavior of Americans of Arab descent. Family unity is also a highly valued cultural dynamic among Arab Americans.

331

18

COUNSELING ARAB AMERICANS

Morris L. Jackson

A s a cultural group, Americans of Arab ancestry have received scant attention in the counseling literature. Professional counselors have had little access to information that addresses the important cultural and developmental issues of this group. Significantly, the U.S. Bureau of the Census in 1990 granted Arab Americans the option to write *other* as their cultural designation on census forms. This event truly signals the recognition of Arab Americans as a distinct cultural group in American society. History records that the first Arabic-speaking people came to American shores between 146 and 480 B.C. and were believed to be Phoenicians, people of the country known today as Lebanon (Boland, 1961). John Zogby, author of *Arab America Today: A Profile of Arab Americans*, estimates the number of Arab Americans to currently be in excess of 3 million (J. Zogby, personal communication, 1996).

Like other ethnic minority groups in American society, Arab Americans face daily challenges to their overall development and well-being. These challenges take the form of discrimination, stereotyping, and general negative reactions to them as an ethnic group. During the course of their development, Arab Americans encounter a crisis of cultural identity common to many minority groups in the United States.

This chapter first emphasizes the diversity of Arab Americans, explores important dynamics of their culture, such as religion and family, and considers racial-religious-ethnic identification issues. The chapter next discusses the counselor's challenge in providing mental health services to Arab Americans, including barriers to successful counseling and possible intervention strategies and techniques, and then presents a case study, which contains excerpts from counseling sessions, to illustrate and illuminate the challenge.

Diversity of Arab Americans

Although Americans of Arab ancestry are generally perceived to be a homogeneous group, it is important to recognize that they originally came from approximately 20 different countries in the Middle East and northern Africa. They form a heterogeneous group whose members differ in terms of race, religion, and political ideology. Writers and researchers who have traced the history and explored the diversity of Arab Americans in the United States include Hooglund (1987), McCarus (1994), Naff (1994), Orfalea (1988), and Pulcini (1993).

The arrival of people of Arab ancestry in America occurred during three distinct time periods (Orfalea, 1988). The first of these was from 1878 to 1925. Census data indicated that in 1910 there were approximately 100,000 Arab Americans in the United States. Most Arabs who arrived during this period came from Greater Syria, the territory that today includes Iraq, Israel and the Occupied Territories (formerly known as Palestine), Jordan, Lebanon, and Syria. These first Arab immigrants were Christians. They were laborers, factory workers, and peddlers who lived primarily in urban areas. The majority were poor and uneducated and sought refuge and contentment in building close-knit communities.

The second major period of Arab immigration to the United States was shortly after World War II. The people in this group differed sharply from the earlier immigrants in that they were primarily Muslim and better educated. According to Orfalea (1988), this was the beginning of the brain drain from Egypt and other North African countries, Jordan, Iraq, and Syria. This period also was marked by the surge in Palestinian refugees and exiles who felt that they were without a country. Other countries represented in this wave, but with smaller numbers of immigrants, were Lebanon and Yemen. This second wave of immigrants often found themselves alienated from their Arab peers and American counterparts because of their Muslim religion and its accompanying culture.

The third period of Arab immigration has been since 1966. This influx of people, approximately 250,000 individuals, is primarily the result of an easing of immigration regulations. This third group shares much in common with members of the second immigrant group. They are mostly Muslim, with the largest ethnic group being Palestinian, and primarily professionals or technical workers.

Essential to obtaining a comprehensive understanding of and perspective on this cultural group is appreciating that Arab Americans migrated to the United States from a variety of countries in the Middle East. The first Arab American immigrants arrived in the United States over a century ago, and today they represent a diverse cultural group with a growing impact in this country.

Arab American Culture

Any discipline that seeks to understand the dynamics of Arab American development must take into account the experiences that shape that development. Counseling strategies and techniques for Americans of Arab ancestry, therefore, must be predicated on an understanding of Arabic cultural dynamics and their important role in fostering attitudes, behaviors, and values. In a counseling context, the most significant aspects of Arab American culture that must be considered are religion and family.

Religion

Religion is a major vehicle by which Arab culture is transferred. Most Arab Americans are either Christians or Muslims. Those Americans of Arab ancestry who practice Christianity have found it somewhat easier to assimilate into the American cultural mainstream than have their Muslim counterparts.

An appreciation of Islam is key to understanding Arab and Arab American culture. For a fifth of the world's population, Islam is both a religion and a complete way of life. About 18% of those who follow Islam live in the Arab world. The very name of the religion—Islam—means both submission and peace, for it is in submitting to God's (Allah's) will that human beings gain peace in their lives in this world and in the hereafter.

Islam reveres not only Abraham, who is father of the Arabs as well as of the Jews, but also Moses and Christ. Muhammad, the prophet and messenger of God, was the last of this long line of prophets. Importantly, there is a Judeo-Christian-Islamic tradition, for Islam shares with the other Abrahamic religions their sacred history, the basic ethical teachings contained in the Ten Commandments, and, above all, belief in one God.

For Muslims, or followers of Islam, the Quran (Koran) is the actual word of God. Under the direction of Muhammad, the verses and chapters of the Quran were organized in the order used today. There is only one text of the Quran accepted by all schools of Islamic thought, and there are no other versions.

The Quran is the central sacred reality of Islam. As the direct word of God, the Quran is considered the primary guide for Muslim life. It is the source of all Islamic doctrines and ethics. Both the intellectual aspects of Islam and Islamic law are based in the Quran. The Quran emphasizes the significance of knowledge and encourages Muslims to learn and acquire knowledge of God's laws as well as of the world of nature. It places the gaining of knowledge as the highest religious activity.

Basic to an appreciation of the religion is understanding the Articles of Faith and the Pillars of Islam. The fundamental Articles of Faith are to have faith in God, His angels, His books, His messengers, and the Day of Judgment and God's determination of human destiny.

The five Pillars of Islam are affirmation of the faith (*shahadah*), five daily prayers (*salat*), fasting (*sawm*) from dawn to sunset during the month of Ramadan, making the pilgrimage (*hajj*) to the Holy Kaaba in Mecca at least once in a lifetime, and paying a tax (*zakat*) on one's capital, used for the needs of the community. Ethics lie at the heart of Islamic teachings, and all people are expected to act ethically toward one another at all times.

Islam possesses a religious law that governs the life of Muslims and that they consider to be the embodiment of the will of God. This law, although rooted in the sources of Islamic revelation, is a living law that addresses the needs of Islamic society.

Islamic laws are basically preventative. The faith of the Muslim causes him or her to have respect for the rights of others, and Islamic law is such that it prevents most transgressions.

Nydell (1987) has outlined some basic Islamic values and religious attitudes commonly found among Arabic speaking peoples:

1. A person's dignity, honor, and reputation are of paramount importance.

2. Loyalty to one's family takes precedence over personal needs.
3. It is important to behave at all times in a manner that reflects well on others.
4. Everyone believes in one God and acknowledges His power.
5. Humans cannot control all events; some things depend on God.
6. Piety is one of the most admirable characteristics in a person.

Family

The family is the foundation of Islamic society. The peace and security offered by a stable family is greatly valued and considered essential for spiritual growth. The Arab American family has evolved over time. During the early years of Arab immigration to the United States, many Arab families were not greatly affected by Western values. Newly arrived families cultivated and reinforced values derived from their Arabic tradition and heritage. However, as assimilation and acculturation began to occur, many Arab American families were faced with a choice. On the one hand, there was a strong desire to maintain traditional Arabic family values. On the other hand, there was an awareness of the need to adopt the values of American culture.

Most Arab Americans belong to an extended family system in which members experience loyalty, security, emotional support, and financial assistance (Nydell, 1987). Immediate family members and extended relatives share a closeness that is evident in a high degree of family unity. For example, despite differences they may have with each other, family members will collude with and support one another against an outsider whom they perceive as interfering with family unity. A traditional Arabic expression illustrates this family unity: "It is me and my brother against my cousin; but it is me and my cousin against the outsider."

In many Arab American families men generally are viewed as the head of the household. Older men in the extended family demand the most respect. Grown sons are responsible for their parents and, in the absence of their father, are responsible for their unmarried sisters. This is not to suggest that Arab American women do not play a significant role in family dynamics. Although women may typically adopt a submissive role in public, in the privacy of their homes they may exert a considerable amount of influence, even to the extent of adamantly disagreeing with their husbands on important family matters.

Children are raised in a manner that ensures that they will respect their parents. In Arabic culture, good children show respect for their parents, as well as for all adults, particularly older adults. Recently, however, many Arab American children have been rejecting their cultural traditions. Parents now have to spend more time and effort to exert control and instill traditional discipline in their children. Peer pressure in schools, for example, has begun to compete with parental influence.

Racial-Religious-Ethnic Identification Issues

In the United States, skin color is a primary means of social identification and distinction. Americans of Arab ancestry, however, may trace their origins to countries that do not make skin color distinctions among people. The following classifications, based on racial, religious, and ethnic factors, may be appropriate for identifying Arab Americans: White Christian, White Muslim, Black Christian, and Black Muslim. These four groups are examined here to assist counseling professionals in understanding the influence of race and religion in Arab American culture.

White Christian Arab Americans arrived in this country from Egypt, Iraq, Jordan, Lebanon, Palestine (currently recognized as Israel and the Occupied Territories), and Syria. Members of this racial-religious-ethnic group, despite cultural differences, have found it easier to assimilate into American society. This is primarily because of their racial and religious similarities with the majority American cultural group.

White Muslim Arab Americans in the American population have come from all the Arabic-speaking countries except Eritrea, Ethiopia, Somalia, and Sudan. This group has been subjected to various forms of discrimination and prejudice, primarily because their religious traditions differ significantly from those commonly found in the United States.

Black Christian Arab Americans are a relatively small group of people that may grow in the future. They are from Egypt and parts of northern Africa. Their experience in the United States parallels that of African Americans, who are often confronted with discrimination and prejudice because of the color of their skin.

Black Muslim Arab Americans may be divided into two groups. One group includes individuals whose mother tongue is Arabic or who were born in an Arab country. The second group is composed of African Americans who were originally Christians but who have adopted the Muslim faith. American society, however, often does not distinguish between these two groups. Black Muslim Arab Americans have two disadvantages in American society: they are both Black and Muslim. This generally means that this group has been the least accepted of the four.

If counseling is to be effective with a client of Arab ancestry, it may be necessary to first identify the client's racial-religious-ethnic background. In so doing, a counselor may discover how a client's attitude, values, and behaviors have been shaped by the experience associated with a particular identification.

Arab American Mental Health: The Counselor's Challenge

In American culture, seeking the services of a counseling professional for assistance with problem resolution is a common practice for many groups. However, this is generally not the case with Arab Americans. The first line of psychological defense for Arab Americans is a conference or consultation with a family member about a problem. A man provides guidance for another man, whereas a woman is counseled by another woman. Cross-sex counseling is uncommon. Young men seek guidance from older men, and young women are advised by older women. When the nature of a problem is too sensitive to discuss with an immediate family member, a person looks to a more distant relative. If a family member is unavailable, an Arab American might then talk with a trusted friend.

Generally speaking, Arab Americans do not share personal problems with strangers. A professional counselor will be considered a stranger, outside the Arab American support system. If none of the previously mentioned counseling sources are available, the

Arab American, as a last resort, may decide to seek the services of a professional counselor.

Barriers to Successful Counseling With Arab Americans

Racial and ethnic barriers that have been discussed as problematic in the cross-cultural counseling relationship with culturally different clients seem to be applicable to Arab American clients. Of particular significance is how culture, religion, language, and rapport affect the counseling relationship. As just noted, Arab Americans do not as a rule disclose personal and family matters to strangers. Arabic-speaking people feel more comfortable discussing academic and vocational matters. Some Arab American clients may be reluctant to engage in self-disclosure or experience considerable frustration during the counseling process because of their inability to express themselves fully in English. They may feel verbally handicapped when they are unable to communicate to the counselor exactly what they feel about problems.

As mentioned earlier, the traditional counseling process is an activity foreign to Arabic culture, and therefore may be strange to many Arab Americans. Counselors interested in assisting their clients to self-disclose need to determine the degree of acculturation and assimilation of their client. Failure to make this determination could cause culture-specific barriers, such as language and religion, to be erected between counselor and client.

The most significant impediment to a possible counseling relationship with Americans of Arab ancestry is the hostility that has been fostered in American society through a continuous barrage of negative publicity about and stereotyping of Arabs (Matawi, 1996). This negative stereotyping has been perpetrated in the form of jokes, television programming, cartoons, comic strips, and movies (Stockton, 1994). Counselors need to be sensitive to the negative feelings, often undisplayed, of Arab American clients as a result of the hostility.

Intervention Techniques and Strategies

Professional counselors working with Arab Americans must consider new ways to maximize their chances of therapeutic success with this population. In the counseling literature, rapport has been discussed as a significant factor in the establishment of a positive therapeutic counselor-client relationship. The building of rapport is generally focused on during initial counselor-client interactions. A sensitive counselor committed to bridging cultural differences with Americans of Arab ancestry should consider the following three suggestions to facilitate the development of rapport in the helping relationship:

1. **Counselors should develop knowledge and understanding of the religion and culture of Arab Americans.** This is important so that intelligent differentiations can be made between Christian and Muslim Arab Americans. Counselors should read books and articles and attempt to converse informally with Arab Americans to increase their understanding of Arabic religious and cultural differences. In general, Arab Americans are pleased and excited over opportunities to share information about their culture and religion.

2. **Counselors should be mindful that Arabic-speaking people, as a rule, are not accustomed to, or comfortable with, expressing feelings about personal matters outside the context of the family.** Professional counselors interested in maximizing their effectiveness may want to consider adopting a multimodal or eclectic approach to counseling this population.

3. **Counselors should establish relationships with Arab American clients prior to actually starting the counseling process.** Establishing such a relationship is called *prerapport*. The significant point is for counselors to converse and interact with clients from the Arab American populations in settings outside the traditional counseling office. Consequently, when an Arab American client comes to begin counseling, the amount of time spent on building rapport and trust may be significantly reduced.

Beyond rapport building, there are some other strategies that counselors should consider in their work with Arab Americans. The importance of religion and the family system to Arab Americans cannot be overstated. Counselors familiar with aspects of the Christian and Muslim religions will be welcomed by Arab American clients to initiate a discussion about religion. The Quran indicates that the closer one is to Allah, the easier it is to cope with psychic problems. All counselors need to be aware that Muslim Arab Americans view the Quran together with the sunna, which is the body of Islamic custom and practice based on the words and deeds of the Prophet Muhammad, as providing them with a way of life. These two documents regulate and govern the lives and emotions of Muslim Arab Americans.

One method of intervention the counselor may use to introduce religion into the therapeutic process is to explain to the client in the first session that part of the technique used includes a holistic approach to the resolution of client concerns. This approach focuses not only on the mind and body but also on the spirit. This may provide the counselor with an opportunity to identify the religion of the client and its significance in the client's life.

Another method for maximizing success with Arab American clients is to involve family members in counseling sessions. It is recommended that counselors first meet with the client. The head of the family should be contacted next to discuss the nature of the client's concerns and to share possible solutions. Next, the counselor should meet with family members and the client to discuss the problem jointly.

The Case Study of Hala

The case study presented here illustrates intervention strategies and techniques helpful for Arab Americans.

Hala is a 28-year-old Arab American female. She entered into counseling because it was becoming increasingly difficult for her to cope with stress and anxiety in her life. She indicated that this was caused by her parents rejection of her choice of a marriage partner. Hala's primary complaint was her inability to get over her parents' disapproval of her plans to marry an Arab man who is of the Christian faith. Hala was raised in and continues to follow Islam. Despite the fact that she only saw this young man once a year because he lived and worked in Syria, Hala stated that she loved him dearly and wanted to marry him.

Hala was born in Syria and is currently a permanent resident in the United States and plans to become a naturalized citizen. Her father was born in Syria and her mother in Lebanon. They immigrated to the United States for professional opportunities. She has two older brothers.

Hala's primary language choice is Arabic. This is especially true at social and community Arab-American activities. In the school environment, Hala is comfortable speaking English. She is bilingual but has greater fluency in Arabic. She studied English for 4 years in Syria during high school. Upon arriving in the United States approximately 10 years ago Hala attended English language classes. Her family members converse in Arabic with each other at home and in other situations.

Islam has played a significant role in guiding Hala's life. Her family travels often to Syria to maintain a strong linkage to extended family members. Visiting grandparents and cousins was one of the ways in which Hala's parents were able to reinforce traditional Arabic values and beliefs in her. It is clear that Hala's parents wanted to insure that she grew and developed with the guiding principles of Islam.

Hala has earned an associate degree at a community college. Currently at the university, she is an excellent college student and has a 3.5 grade point average. She plans to complete a bachelor of science degree in business administration. Hala then plans to attend law school. She did not have many friends while at the community college. She indicated that her relationships were restricted to having an occasional cup of tea or coffee with a classmate. Hala is currently employed full time at an international organization. She has always worked since arriving in the United States.

Hala's parents were educated in Lebanon, Syria, and England. Her father earned a master's degree in England, and her mother received a bachelors degree in Lebanon. Her father is employed full time at a local university, and her mother currently does not work outside the home. Her two brothers live in another city.

Hala has had several counseling sessions. Although some progress has been made in reducing the amount of anxiety and stress she is experiencing, Hala still harbors unresolved anxiety related to not finding a marriage partner pleasing to her parents. An excerpt from one of the counseling sessions with her male counselor follows:

Counselor: Good afternoon Hala. How are you doing today?
Hala: Allright, I could be better.
Counselor: What would make it better for you?
Hala: I tried to talk with my parents the other day about my situation. No matter how I expressed myself, they still did not seem to understand the problem I am having.
Counselor: By situation are you referring to your desire to marry Abdulla?

Hala: Yes.

Counselor: It is important to you that your parents really understand that you love Abdulla and do not care that he is a Christian.

Hala: My parents know his parents, and we all are from the same town. I just don't get it. They know he is from a nice family. Abdulla is a medical doctor. I could have a good life with him.

Counselor: Despite the fact your parents have had a social relationship with his family, they still will not give their approval for you to marry Abdulla. And because you do not have their approval, you are not happy.

Hala: Well not exactly. Basically, I am a happy person. But since he will not be in my life, I have begun to spend more time alone. There is no one else that I can foresee having a relationship with who will meet my parent's qualifications.

Counselor: What do you do with yourself when you are alone?

Hala: I work everyday and spend my evenings reading books.

Counselor: What else do you do with your time?

Hala: I am taking two courses at the university. Sometimes I get together with some of my girlfriends, but this does not happen often. My mother and I go to the movies. She is like my best friend. I think she is supportive of me marrying Abdulla. However, it is difficult for the both of us to convince my father.

Counselor: What I now understand is that your mother is supportive and empathetic to your situation even to the point of letting your father know how important Abdulla is to you.

Hala: You are right. I have had many conversations with my mother. She knew from the beginning that I wanted to marry Abdulla. I have always confided in her. She knows just about all my secrets.

Counselor: Your mother has always been there for you when you needed her.

Hala: That is correct. I have even discussed with her in some detail the problem which my father has with Abdulla.

Counselor: What is the problem your father has with Abdulla which has led him to disapprove of your marrying him?

Hala: He stated that Abdulla has different values and beliefs. And since I was raised a Muslim, there is likely to be cultural conflict in the marriage. My father said that marriage is difficult by itself. And to add cultural differences would probably lead to divorce. You know my father has a point. But I believe that love can overcome all obstacles, even cultural differences.

Counselor: You place a greater emphasis on love and your father on values and beliefs. Was there anything else your father shared with you regarding his disapproval?

Hala: Yes. My father was quite direct in his objection. He asked me "If I approved of your marrying Abdulla and children are born, will they be raised Christian or Muslim?" He was quite adamant in saying that his grandchildren will be Muslim not Christian.

Counselor: It is now quite clear to me what your problem is and why your father objects so strongly. You are so deeply in love with Abdulla that beliefs and values and difference in religion are not significant obstacles. On the other hand, your father is so deeply rooted in the Islamic tradition, raised you in the Islamic faith, and the fear that his grandchildren would not be raised Muslim is more than he can bear.

Hala: I think you are right. But what can I do so that he might change his mind?

Counselor: The reality of your situation may be that he may never change his mind. Hala, I want you to know that I am 100% supportive of helping you make the decision which you think is best for you.

Hala: I could just run away and marry Abdulla. However, if I was to do that my father may never talk to me again. I think my mother would always be there if I needed her. Another option I have is to continue trying to convince my father that this marriage would work and that I would do my best to influence Abdulla to be supportive of raising any children as Muslim. The other option I have is to do nothing and hope that time is a healer and my father changes his mind.

Counselor: You have mentioned several different options. Could you share with me the option which you are likely to choose?

Hala: Of course there are advantages and disadvantages to each of the options I mentioned. My heart tells me I should marry Abdulla. If I follow my heart, I take the risk of hurting my father so much he may not speak to me again. Also, if I do not marry Abdulla, I may never be able to find another potential marriage partner who I feel comfortable with.

Counselor: What are your thoughts on the other options?

Hala: Try as I may, it would probably be almost impossible to get my father to change his mind. After all, he lives and breathes the Arabic traditions. So I do not think this is a viable option. I was being optimistic in stating that maybe time will have a favorable impact upon him.

Counselor: Hala, you have just discussed in a general way the different options which you might have and some of the consequences. Are you ready to make a decision?

Hala: No. I was hoping that you would tell me what to do. That's why I entered into counseling. I thought for sure you would direct me in the right direction.

Counselor: Hala, the issue of marriage is a long-time commitment and is one of the most significant decisions which we have to make in life. I cannot tell you what to do. I am keenly aware that you are torn between selecting a marriage partner, and being joyous about that, and being sad about the fact that marriage could isolate you from your father. In addition, I understand that right now you are unhappy being single and approaching 30 years of age. I do not think you should feel compelled to make a decision right now. Maybe you can think about what we have discussed today and let me know at our next counseling session what you have decided.

Hala: That's not a bad idea because I am not ready to make a decision at this moment. I think I want to discuss some of the things we talked about today with my mother and understand what her thoughts might be on my situation.

This counseling session illustrates the challenge of an Arab American Muslim woman in cultural conflict with her parents because of her desire to marry a Christian Arab. The conflict arises because of different cultural values that may impact not only the marriage but any progeny from the union. The client is torn between her love of her parents, and wanting to respect the traditional Arab values she was taught, and her love for a marriage partner. It is obvious the client has been affected by her father's disapproval of the marriage partner.

The client is faced with the existential challenge of making a decision that from her perspective will result in either her parents' unhappiness or her own. The strong bond between the client and her mother provides the client with some family support.

Although Arab Americans do not readily seek counseling outside of the family environment, and generally do not self-disclose personal and family matters, the inability of the client to obtain support from her parents necessitated her reaching out to the counselor. The fact that the counselor was a male is in contrast to Arab Americans' general preference for same-sex helpers. The gender of the counselor, however, appeared not to be an issue for the client. It was critical for the counseling process that the counselor had established rapport with Hala prior to counseling. Significantly, they had previously met at Arab American cultural events on campus. The counselor had established prerapport with Hala. Further, because it had been previously determined that Hala had a degree of acculturation, the counselor was comfortable using traditional counseling techniques.

The goal of the counseling session was to assist Hala toward a more comprehensive understanding of her problem and to direct the client toward resolution. The counselor used a rational direct approach to counseling with her. He did not focus exclusively on her feelings. The counselor felt that if Hala could arrive at a rational and realistic view of her problem, it should be easier for her to make a decision about what she wanted to do with her life.

Toward the end of the counseling session, Hala began to identify options that may help her resolve her problem. The options were only briefly explored, and no resolution was forthcoming. The fact that Hala indicated she wanted to discuss the matter with her mother suggested to the counselor that she needed additional time to make a final decision.

In the next session, the counselor should explore in depth each of the options identified by Hala to enable her to examine the advantages and disadvantages of the options. It is important for the counselor to discuss with Hala in greater detail what the likely ramifications of cultural conflict might be if she married a Christian Arab. Hala stated she planned to discuss the matter with her mother, and this also should be explored in the next session. In addition, the counselor should explore with Hala the impact of her decision on her relationship with her family. The counselor may find it useful to invite Hala to ask her parents to participate in a counseling session. The counselor should make it clear to her that she bears the responsibility for any decision she makes and the action she takes on that decision.

Conclusion

In the emerging era of cultural diversity in American society, Arab Americans are stepping forward to proclaim their cultural heritage and traditions. These Americans of Arab ancestry are a flourishing cultural group whose diversity cannot be denied. They are representative of Arabic-speaking people from throughout the Middle East and northern Africa. Like other immigrant groups before them, Arab Americans are becoming acculturated, in varying degrees, to American lifestyles. In this process they experience problems related to their cultural identity. Arab Americans face the challenge of blending two unique and different worldviews into one homogeneous culture.

Counselors are urged to obtain a comprehensive understanding of the religion and family systems of Arab Americans because they are a significant aspect of Arab American culture and are vital to Arab American psychological well-being. Counselors concerned with bridging cultural barriers may need to rethink their techniques and strategies in order to work with this population effectively. Counselors can play a critical role in ensuring that Arab Americans are not an invisible cultural group.

References

Boland, C. M. (1961). *They all discovered America.* New York: Doubleday.

Hooglund, E. J. (1987). *Crossing the waters.* Washington, DC: Smithsonian Institution Press.

Matawi, A. H. (1996). *Proxemics among male and female Saudi Arabian undergraduate students in Saudi Arabia and the United States.* Unpublished doctoral dissertation, Howard University, Washington, DC.

McCarus, E. (Ed.). (1994). *The development of Arab American identity.* Ann Arbor: University of Michigan Press.

Naff, A. (1994). The early Arab immigrant experience. In E. McCarus (Ed.), *The development of Arab American identity*. Ann Arbor: University of Michigan Press.

Nydell, M. (1987). *Understanding Arabs: A guide for westerners*. Yarmouth, ME: Intercultural Press.

Orfalea, G. (1988). *Before the flames: A quest for the history of Arab Americans*. Austin: University of Texas Press.

Pulcini, T. (1993). Trends in research on Arab Americans. *Journal of American Ethnic History, 12,* 27–60.

Quran [Koran]. A. Yusef, Trans. (1983). *Holy Koran* (Text, translation, and commentary). Beltsville, MD: Amana.

Stockton, R. (1994). Ethnic archetypes and the Arab image. In E. McCarus (Ed.), *The development of Arab American identity*. Ann Arbor: University of Michigan Press.

PART III
CONCLUSION

19

NEW APPROACHES TO DIVERSITY:

Implications for Professional Counselor Training and Research

Courtland C. Lee

T he multicultural realities of American society call for professional counselors who can effectively address the challenges of client diversity. Effective multicultural counseling practice is one of the most significant challenges facing the profession. In order to meet this challenge new directions are needed for the training of culturally responsive professional counselors at both the in-service and preservice levels. In addition, as models and methods related to the practice of multicultural counseling continue to evolve, they must be accompanied by empirical evidence of their validity. The challenge of multicultural counseling practice, therefore, also implies charting some new research directions. This chapter examines implications of cultural diversity for the future training of professional counselors and for multicultural counseling research.

The Nature of Professional Counseling in a Diverse Society

The purpose of professional counseling is to help people meet a wide range of personal, career, and educational challenges. Professional counselors recognize that most people, at some time, may need some assistance in dealing with the developmental issues of childhood, adolescence, and adulthood. In order to provide such assistance, professional counselors receive extensive training and maintain some form of credentialing in order to help empower people to attain maximum potential in their lives.

Although professional counselors may specialize in a variety of areas, such as career counseling, school counseling, mental health counseling, or marriage and family counseling, they must all have a basic understanding of the social and cultural foundations that provide a context for the lives of their clients. Professional counseling, therefore, must be based on an understanding of and appreciation for diverse cultural realities.

Training Implications

In order to engage effectively in multicultural academic, career, and personal-social practice, counselors must participate in an ongoing professional development process. The focus of this process should be the development and upgrading of skills to intervene effectively into the lives of clients from a variety of cultural backgrounds. The ultimate training goal is the emergence of a professional who can be identified as a culturally responsive counselor who uses strategies and techniques that are consistent with the life experiences and cultural values of clients.

The concept of comprehensive multicultural counseling training has been addressed extensively in the literature (Brown & Landrum-Brown, 1995; Carter & Qureshi, 1995; Parker, Valley, & Geary, 1986; Pedersen, 1988; Ponterotto & Casas, 1987; Reynolds, 1995). A major theme that has emerged from the literature is that in order to become culturally responsive as a counselor, one must become more fully aware of his or her own heritage as well as of possible biases that may interfere with helping effectiveness, gain knowledge about the history and culture of diverse groups of people, and develop new skills. In conjunction with these notions Sue, Arredondo, and McDavis (1992) developed a set of landmark multicultural competencies and standards to be used as guidelines for the training of culturally responsive counselors. These competencies and standards form the basis for the evolution of new counselor training paradigms.

In reviewing these competencies and the literature on multicultural counselor training within the context of the ideas on culture and culturally responsive counseling presented in this book, several points need to be underscored about training future counseling professionals:

- **Future training initiatives must go beyond raising awareness and providing knowledge to actual skills development.** How does one actually counsel someone from another culture? For example, what intervention strategies are most effective with diverse client populations? What are some of the indigenous helping sources within a cultural group that have been sought out (in some instances for centuries) to deal with problem resolution and decision making? What cultural dynamics appear to impact optimal mental health and normal development among groups of people? How can these dynamics be exploited positively in a helping relationship? In sum, skills training should center around how to incorporate the cultural dynamics and naturally occurring support systems of diverse groups of people into counseling interventions.
- **An important aspect of multicultural skills development should be an emphasis on experiencing cultural diversity in vivo.** Through practicum and/or internship experiences as well as field trips to diverse communities, counselors should have the opportunity to go out and experience cultural diversity, and the dynamics associated with it, firsthand. There is a limit to how much can be learned about cultural diversity from classes and workshops. Much more can be learned by actually going out and interacting with groups of people. Such experiences have the potential of raising levels of awareness, increasing knowledge, and providing important additions to skill repertoires.
- **Effective multicultural counseling skills can only be developed and used when individuals get beyond a monolithic perspective about people.** Therefore, training efforts must insure that counselors get beyond myths and stereotypes by helping them learn how to discern levels of acculturation and cultural/ethnic/racial identity development among people.

   In order to develop such skills, it is obvious that current multicultural counseling courses and training experiences must be expanded. Additionally, counselor educators must insure that issues of cultural diversity are effectively infused through-out the training curriculum. In addition to formal coursework at the preservice level, comprehensive ongoing professional development experiences related to multicultural counseling are needed for practicing professionals. While providing the opportunity for self-exploration and the development of multicultural knowledge, the bulk of such experiences should be devoted to field-testing of culturally responsive intervention skills for academic, career, and personal-social development.

Research Implications

Research evidence must guide multicultural counseling training and practice. The primary goal of future research should be the empirical validation of the continuously evolving theories and concepts about multicultural counseling and human development. In the past several decades there have been extensive reviews of cross-cultural counseling research (Atkinson, 1983, 1985; Atkinson & Lowe, 1995; Harrison, 1975; Sattler, 1970). From these reviews have emerged ideas that are important in establishing an agenda for future multicultural counseling research:

- **New multicultural counseling process and outcome research must be conducted.** Empirical evidence is needed to support ideas about the effectiveness of indigenous models of helping and culturally responsive counseling interventions in changing client attitudes, values, and behaviors. These investigations must provide answers to fundamental questions such as "Are culturally responsive helping models and methods more effective with American Indian, African American, Asian American, Latino American, or Arab American clients than traditional (i.e., Eurocentric) counseling interventions?" Importantly, evaluation of culturally responsive methodologies should be made an integral part of counseling service delivery in all helping settings.
- **Research is needed on culturally diverse notions of normal human development.** Specific investigations that assess mental health outcomes by attempting to delineate the developmental processes of person-environment interactions among culturally

diverse people need to be conducted. New studies ahould investigate coping styles and mastery skills among diverse groups of people. An empirically validated knowledge base concerning cultural variations on normal psychosocial development is crucial for proactive counseling interventions.

- **Empirical investigation should be continued to produce inventories and scales that assess significant developmental aspects of diverse cultural groups.** A crucial aspect of this process must be studies that produce validity and reliability information for instruments that assess personality factors and behavioral dynamics. As an example, more research on scales that assess the important variable of ethnic identity is needed. Although major strides have been made in such research (Casas, 1984; Cross, Parham, & Helms, 1995; Helms, 1990; Phinney & Chavira, 1992; Ponterotto & Casas, 1991), the widespread usefulness of ethnic identity development assessment tools is questionable due to limited empirical evidence. Until greater empirical data are provided, such instruments will generally remain experimental in nature and of marginal practical use in providing valid and reliable information to enhance multicultural counseling.

- **All research efforts should be structured to investigate intragroup differences among people.** The majority of research evidence concerning the dynamics of counseling people from diverse cultural backgrounds has generally been gathered without consideration for differences in factors such as level of ethnic identity, degree of acculturation, or socioeconomic status. Such evidence lends credence to the concept that cultural groups are monolithic entities with no within-group variability among members. Future counseling research efforts, therefore, should investigate within-group differences among culturally diverse people.

- **Concerted efforts must be undertaken to assess multicultural counseling competencies.** As training models in this discipline become more comprehensive and sophisticated, investigations of their effectiveness in developing awareness, knowledge, and skills must be a part of any multicultural counseling research agenda. Several scales have been developed in recent years to assess the multicultural counseling competencies of both practicing counselors and counselors-in-training (D'Andrea, Daniels, & Heck, 1991; Ponterotto, Rieger, Barrett, & Sparks, 1994; Sodowsky, Taffe, Gutkin, & Wise, 1994), but there is, as yet, limited empirical evidence about their efficacy in assessing the skills development of professional counselors.

Conclusion

As multiculturalism continues moving from theory to practice, a dramatic shift in the focus of professional counseling is needed. Counseling services must be delivered with the beliefs that people from diverse backgrounds are psychologically healthy, undergo normal developmental experiences, and have dynamics and resources indigenous to their culture to deal competently with problem solving and decision making.

A new professional counselor must emerge as the United States prepares to enter a new century, a counselor who has a solid research, knowledge, and skill base with which to meet the challenges of counseling practice with culturally diverse client groups. The development and well-being of Americans from every cultural background demands no less.

References

Atkinson, D. R. (1983). Ethnic similarity in counseling psychology: A review of research. *The Counseling Psychologist, 11*, 79–92.

Atkinson, D. R. (1985). A meta-review of research on cross-cultural counseling and psychotherapy. *Journal of Multicultural Counseling and Development, 13*, 138–153.

Atkinson, D. R., & Lowe, S.M. (1995). The role of ethnicity, cultural knowledge, and conventional techniques in counseling and psychotherapy. In J. G. Ponterotto, J. M. Casas, L. A. Suzuki, & C. M. Alexander (Eds.), *Handbook of multicultural counseling* (pp. 387–414). Thousand Oaks, CA: Sage.

Brown, M. T., & Landrum-Brown, J. (1995). Counselor supervision: Cross-cultural perspectives. In J. G. Ponterotto, J. M. Casas, L. A. Suzuki, & C. M. Alexander (Eds.), *Handbook of multicultural counseling* (pp. 263–286). Thousand Oaks, CA: Sage.

Carter, R. T., & Qureshi, A. (1995). A typology of philosophical assumptions in multicultural counseling and training. In J. G. Ponterotto, J. M. Casas, L. A. Suzuki, & C. M. Alexander (Eds.), *Handbook of multicultural counseling* (pp. 239–262). Thousand Oaks, CA: Sage.

Casas, J. M. (1984). Policy, training, and research in counseling psychology: The racial/ethnic minority perspective. In S. Brown & R. Lent (Eds.), *Handbook of counseling psychology*. New York: Wiley.

Cross, W. E., Parham, T. A., & Helms, J. E. (1995). Nigrescence revisited: Theory and research. In R. L. Jones (Ed.), *Advances in Black psychology* (pp. 1–69). Los Angeles: Cobb & Henry.

D'Andrea, M., Daniels, J., & Heck, R. (1991). Evaluating the impact of multicultural counseling training. *Journal of Counseling and Development, 70*, 143–150.

Harrison, D. K. (1975). Race as a counselor-client variable in counseling and psychotherapy: A review of the research. *The Counseling Psychologist, 5*, 124–133.

Helms, J. E. (1990). *Black and White racial identity: Theory, research, and practice*. Westport, CT: Greenwood Press.

Parham, T. A., & Helms, J. E. (1981). Influence of a Black student's racial identity attitudes on preference for counselor race. *Journal of Counseling Psychology, 28*, 250–257.

Parker, W. M., Valley, M. M., & Geary, C. A. (1986). Acquiring cultural knowledge for counselors in training: A multifaceted approach. *Counselor Education and Supervision, 26*, 61–71.

Pedersen, P. (1988). *Handbook for developing multicultural awareness*. Alexandria, VA: American Association for Counseling and Development.

Phinney, J. S., & Chavira, V. (1992). Ethnic identity and self-esteem: An exploratory longitudinal study. *Journal of Adolescence, 15*, 271–281.

Ponterotto, J. G., & Casas, J. M. (1987). In search of multicultural competence within counselor education. *Journal of Counseling and Development, 65*, 430–434.

Ponterotto, J. G., & Casas, J. M. (1991). *Handbook of racial/ethnic minority counseling research*. Springfield, IL: Charles C Thomas.

Ponterotto, J. G., Rieger, B. P., Barrett, A., & Sparks, R. (1994). Assessing multicultural counseling competence: A review of instrumentation. *Journal of Counseling and Development, 72*, 316–322.

Reynolds, A. L. (1995). Challenges and strategies for teaching multicultural counseling courses. In J. G. Ponterotto, J. M. Casas, L. A. Suzuki, & C. M. Alexander (Eds.), *Handbook of multicultural counseling* (pp. 312–330). Thousand Oaks, CA: Sage.

Sattler, J. M. (1970). Racial "experimenter effects" in experimentation, testing, interviewing, and psychotherapy. *Psychological Bulletin, 73*, 137–160.

Sodowsky, G. R., Taffe, R. C., Gutkin, T. B., & Wise, S. L. (1994). Development of the Multicultural Counseling Inventory: A self-report measure of multicultural competencies. *Journal of Counseling Psychology, 41,* 137–148.

Sue, D. W., Arredondo, P., & McDavis, R. J. (1992). Multicultural counseling competencies and standards: A call to the profession. *Journal of Counseling and Development, 70,* 477–486.

INDEX